UNCOMMON KNOWLEDGE

Exploring Ideas
Through Reading
and Writing

D0972210

ROSE HAWKINS
Community College of Southern Nevada

ROBERT ISAACSON
Allan Hancock College

Houghton Mifflin Company

BOSTON TORONTO GENEVA, ILLINOIS
PALO ALTO PRINCETON, NEW JERSEY

CREDITS

Julia Alvarez, "Dusting," from *Homecoming*. Copyright © 1986 by Julia Alvarez. Published in revised edition by Dutton/New American Library in 1996. Originally published by Grove Press.

Russell Baker, "Summer Beyond Wish," July 4, 1978. Copyright © 1978 by The New York Times Company. Reprinted by permission.

Toni Cade Bambara, "The Lesson," from *Gorilla, My Love*. Copyright © 1960, 1963, 1964, 1965, 1968, 1970, 1971, 1972 by Toni Cade Bambara. Reprinted by permission of Random House, Inc.

Dino Buzzati, "The Falling Girl," from *Restless Nights*. Copyright © 1983 by Dino Buzatti. English language translation copyrighted 1963 by Lawrence Venuti. Published by Arnoldo Mondadori Editore, Milano, Italy and reprinted with permission.

Albert Camus, "The Myth of Sisyphus," from *The Myth of Sisyphus and Other Essays* by Albert Camus, trans., J. O'Brien. Copyright © 1955 by Alfred A. Knopf, Inc. Reprinted by permission of the publisher.

Credits continued on pp. 409–411, which constitute an extension of the copyright page.

Sponsoring Editor: Renee Deljon
Development Editor: Melody Davies
Senior Production/Design Coordinator: Jill Haber
Associate Project Editor: Magdalena Hernandez
Senior Manufacturing Coordinator: Marie Barnes
Marketing Manager: Charles Cavaliere

Printed in the U.S.A.

ISBN: 0-395-70958-X

Library of Congress Catalog Card Number: 95-76948

23456789-QM-99 98 97 96

Contents

CHAPTER THREE

Cultural Knowledge:
What Are My Roots?   **145**

CHAPTER FOUR

Societal Knowledge:
What Do Others Think?   **223**

CHAPTER FIVE

Disturbing Knowledge:
What Do I Think?   311

Preface

Uncommon Knowledge: Exploring Ideas Through Reading and Writing offers a rich mix of challenging stories, poems, and essays from both contemporary and classical writers; extensive journal options to accommodate a wide range of learning styles; and writing assignments that build from concrete to abstract knowledge as demonstrated in James Moffett's Scale of Discourse.

To prepare students for the true rigors of college-level reading and writing, our textbook aims to develop both the students' inner voice and outer voice. Since these private and public voices are symbiotic, the development of one will complement and nourish the other. Practiced in isolation, neither writing unevaluated prose in a private journal nor writing graded academic discourse will accomplish the overall goal of producing confident and capable college readers and writers within the confines of a sixteen-week semester. Our students need specific grammatical and rhetorical skills to meet future academic challenges, as well as the self-confidence that can only be affirmed by the validation of their inner voice, the one they use to speak to themselves and discover meaning.

Uncommon Knowledge acknowledges the benefit of using informal reader-response writing as a means of creating authentic connections between a text and the student through prior knowledge and experience. At the same time, we also recognize our students' need to practice writing a wide range of formal essays since their ability to produce such writing is essential for success in college. In our textbook, writing and reading are thoroughly integrated activities. Personal-response writing is used as a means of enabling students to form genuine connections with what they read. These exploratory activities include a variety of both creative and analytical approaches to accommodate as wide a range of learning styles as possible. We feel that it is imperative that each individual student begins the meaning-making process as comfortably as possible on his or her own terms. We know of no better way to engage students actively in the meaning-making process that culminates in being able to write a formal essay.

ORGANIZATION OF THE TEXT

The text is divided into five thematically arranged chapters, each focusing on a distinct level of knowledge:

1. Personal Knowledge: Who Am I?
2. Family Knowledge: Who Has Shaped Me?
3. Cultural Knowledge: What Are My Roots?
4. Societal Knowledge: What Do Others Think?
5. Disturbing Knowledge: What Do I Think?

The overall organization moves students from the familiar and accessible to the more demanding levels of thinking found toward the end of the book. While some anthologies share a similar thematic arrangement, we have attempted to include a broad selection of readings that challenge a wide range of student abilities. We have included frequently anthologized pieces because they are favorites that work very well, but we have also introduced several that will be new for some instructors. In selecting the readings, our aim was to challenge students to examine their own values and beliefs by exploring the ideas of others. We see this text as an exciting collection of writing and thinking by a diverse group of writers from our past and present world.

Within each chapter, the method employed in mixing the genres is two-fold. First, the readings are grouped in a repeating pattern of story/poem/essay. These selections address the needs of a multicultural audience, while including mainstream works of literature and traditional scholarly discourse. Second, we arranged these clusters according to their cognitive challenge. Thus the first cluster contains a relatively accessible group of readings for the beginning college student while the subsequent clusters offer increasingly challenging reading levels. In the last two clusters of Chapter One, for example, the student is reading texts such as "The Street" by Octavio Paz and "The Allegory of the Cave" by Plato. The rest of the chapters follow this same pattern of cognitive demand.

Obviously, we, as instructors, do not wish our students to remain at their current level of proficiency. Beyond a student's comfort level lies that critical zone in which Vygotsky has determined that maximum learning takes place. According to Vygotsky, the most effective and productive learning occurs when students are acquiring a concept that is slightly more difficult than that which they already know. The overall pattern of these reading clusters in *Uncommon Knowledge: Exploring Ideas Through Reading and Writing* should help instructors guide college students through a range of texts and reading levels toward the reality of traditional college work.

SPECIAL FEATURES

- *Chapter Introductions.* Each chapter contains an overview of the thematic unit to prepare students for the selections that follow.

- *Headnotes/Prereading Questions.* Short introductions are included at the beginning of each reading. Although they do provide some biographical information, especially if it reflects a special interest or a cross-cultural background, their main purpose is to serve as pre-reading exercises by showing how each reading reflects the theme of the chapter. Each of them concludes by asking questions intended to open up students' minds.

- *Reading Logs.* While the reading selections will challenge students with texts that are ever increasing in cognitive difficulty, the use of the reader-response Options for Reading Logs will give students of varying abilities and learning styles a method to approach the more difficult texts. By encouraging students to rely on their personal experience or prior knowledge in the reading logs, they will gain confidence in their reading ability and cultivate a sense of their own identity.

  There are several choices in each of the Options for Reading Logs to provide variety for the analytical as well as for the more creative students. These three options are both generic and text-specific at the same time; these open-ended journal questions allow students to immerse themselves in the reading, writing, and thinking process in a variety of different ways.

  Instructors can use these options as they wish. For example, the double-entry journal exercise could be successfully assigned by the instructor for each reading. Conversely, allowing students to experiment on their own with the various possibilities would allow an instructor to address the different learning styles present in today's classroom.

- *Writing Assignments.* The writing assignments allow students to select, in consultation with the instructor, an appropriate rhetorical response to a text. Following Moffett's Scale of Discourse, the writing assignments range from personal narrative, letter writing, and creative responses to the more formal, thesis-driven options of analysis, evaluation, and argument. These longer essay assignments will permit students to go beyond the private, unevaluated writing in their journal entries and move into the larger arena of public discourse at whatever pace and sequence of tasks the instructor deems appropriate.

- *Glossary.* The Glossary provides definitions of the rhetorical and literary terms used throughout the text.

- *Support for Instructors.*   The Instructor's Resource Manual for *Uncommon Knowledge: Exploring Ideas Through Reading and Writing* offers instructors commentary on Chapters One through Five and teaching suggestions for using the text in the classroom.

ACKNOWLEDGMENTS

We are forever grateful to Dr. Sheridan Blau and the South Coast Writing Project (SCwriP) at the University of California at Santa Barbara, where we learned first-hand that writing teachers should be writers. We also want to thank our students, who were our best teachers. Special thanks go to Melody Davies and the editorial staff at Houghton Mifflin and to the many reviewers who gave us their excellent suggestions:

Carolyn Baker, *San Antonio College, TX*

Sherie Coelho, *Antelope Valley College, CA*

Annette Dambrosio, *Solano Community College, CA*

Connie Eggers, *Western Washington University, WA*

Kathy A. Fitch, *College of DuPage, IL*

Ann H. Judd, *Seward County Community College, KS*

Elisabeth B. Leyson, *Fullerton College, CA*

Jo Alison Lobertini, *East Tennessee State University, TN*

Patricia A. Malinowski, *Finger Lakes Community College, NY*

Faye Parker, *Dyersburg State Community College, TN*

Rita Pollard, *Niagara University, NY*

Jon Wallace, *Graceland College, IA*

Carroll Wilson, *Raritan Valley Community College, NJ*

To the Student

Our hope is that this textbook will offer you an exciting collection of readings and writing assignments that will inspire and challenge you long after the course is over. You will notice that the five chapters of *Uncommon Knowledge* are arranged in a carefully designed sequence beginning with familiar themes from the immediate world around you, and ending with the larger issues of humankind.

Personal Knowledge: Who Am I?

Family Knowledge: Who Has Shaped Me?

Cultural Knowedge: What Are My Roots?

Societal Knowledge: What Do Others Think?

Disturbing Knowledge: What Do I Think?

ABOUT THE READINGS

The stories, poems, and essays we have included have been written by a diverse group of men and women from a wide spectrum of our past and present world. From the very first chapter we have included a broad selection of assignments to prepare you for the rigors of college-level reading, thinking, and writing.

ABOUT THE READING LOGS (JOURNALS)

Keeping a reading log, also known as a journal, is an important process of discovery. It can provide you with the basis for personal knowledge, class discussions, or subsequent papers. You should feel free to modify the following exercises to fit your own needs as a reader. No matter what type of exercise you select, however, you should give it a good chance to work by writing at least one journal page for each entry. As you read this book, you will encounter various versions of the following journal options:

1. **What or Why Questions** (Double-Entry Journal)
   A. Draw a vertical line down the middle of your journal page to create two columns.
   B. In the left column, keep a running list of "what" or "why" questions that occur to you as you are reading. (Aim for three to five questions.)
   C. When you finish your list, move to the top of the left column and answer each question as completely as you can. (If you don't know the answer, make an educated guess.)
   D. End your journal entry with a significant discovery you made about the text: "I discovered that _____."

2. **List of Images or Symbols** (Double-Entry Journal)
   A. Draw a vertical line down the middle of your journal page to create two columns.
   B. In the left column, keep a running list of images from the selection you are reading.
   C. In the right column, speculate on why the author used those images.
   D. End your journal entry by selecting the most powerful image and discussing why it is so effective in terms of the central meaning (theme) of the text.

3. **List of Characters** (Double-Entry Journal)
   A. Draw a vertical line down the middle of your journal page to create two columns.
   B. In the left column, keep a list of characters from the particular selections you are reading.
   C. In the right column, jot down your opinions, observations, and comments about those characters.
   D. End your journal entry by discussing something significant that interests you about one of the characters.

4. **Powerful Lines or Passages** (Double-Entry Journal)
   A. Draw a vertical line down the middle of your journal page to create two columns.
   B. In the left column, copy lines or passages you particularly like in the text.
   C. In the right column, jot down word associations and comments, drawing on those from your personal experience as well as from your reading.

    D.   End your journal entry by selecting one of the lines or phrases and explaining why it held such power or meaning for you.

5. **Personal Reaction**
   A.   Complete one of the following statements by referring to a particular incident in the text.
      a.   "I was struck by _____."
      b.   "I was surprised by _____."
      c.   "I was confused by _____."
   B.   End your journal entry with a detailed explanation of your statement.

6. **Freewriting**
   A.   Freewrite on one or more of the following:
      a.   Memories, dreams, or fantasies connected with the text
      b.   Dialogues between characters
      c.   Doubts, expectations, creative insights
      d.   Reflections on your learning
      e.   A paraphrase or summary of the text
   B.   End your journal entry with a personal discovery about the text.

7. **Concept Map** (Clustering)
   A.   Draw a concept (idea) map, which is a graphic interpretation of the text. Try drawing balloons, clusters, flowcharts, visual symbols, outlines, or diagrams.
   B.   Follow with a story or explanation of your map, including significant words or phrases from the text.
   C.   End your journal entry by stating the theme of the text.

8. **Creative Writing Response**
   A.   Write an original poem in response to the text. Explain why the text triggered this particular creative response from you.
   B.   End your journal entry by stating the theme of the text.

9. **Graphics**
   A.   Create some graphics or draw a picture of your version of the meaning of the text.
   B.   Describe your graphics, using as many specific details as possible.
   C.   End your journal entry by stating the theme of the text.

10. **Parallel Story**
   A.   Drawing on your own experience, tell a story that was triggered by the text.
   B.   Jot down characteristics or events that were similar or different for the two stories.
   C.   End your journal entry by stating the theme of the text.

ABOUT THE WRITING ASSIGNMENTS (PAPERS)

Each reading in this book is followed by writing assignments that are specific to the reading selections. The assignments cover a broad range, from personal topics to the more formal types of writing often required in college classes.

The following writing assignments, designed to help you engage with your readings at a deeper level of meaning, have been modified to fit each selection.

1. **Expanding a Reading Log**

   Do any of your reading logs show promise? Read through them and select one that particularly interests you. Develop it into a more polished piece of writing that explores its subject matter in greater range and depth, using an appropriate form—a poem, a fictional story, a personal narrative, or an essay that examines a central idea.

2. **Recollecting a Memory**

   Do any of the poems, stories, or essays remind you of something from your own past? Compose a narrative or descriptive essay that focuses on a remembered person, place, or event. Throughout your essay, concentrate on using vivid details and descriptions to help recreate your memories.

3. **Exploring a Phase**

   Have you ever been though a distinctive phase lasting several months (or even significantly longer) which you would now like to explore through writing? Think of some specific period characterized by a strong interest or focus that deeply influenced your thoughts and behavior. Explore the phase's beginning, middle, and end: How did that phase begin? In what ways did it influence you? Why did it end?

4. **Interviewing Someone from Your Past**

   Is there some older person, other than a relative, who has had a significant influence on you and your development into the person you are now? Make a list of appropriate questions and interview that individual to discover what made him or her a special influence on your own life. You might want to compose a biography of the person to discover the influences that made him or her so important in your life.

5. **Recounting and Explaining a Dream**

   Have you had a lucid dream or a puzzling recurring dream? Recreate the dream as a story or a poem using concrete details, vivid imagery, and, if possible, dialogue. Also, explore any explanations or reasons you can offer for the dream. What do you feel the dream is trying to tell you? Can you make any generalizations about the function of dreams?

6. **Creating a Dialogue**

   Have you ever wanted to meet the author of a poem, story, or essay and talk with him or her about it? Using one of the reading selections, create a conversation between you and the author. Your conversation might take the form of a question-and-answer interview, an argument representing two opposing points of view, or a freewheeling exploration of the author's ideas and their implications.

7. **Writing a Letter to an Author or a Character**

   Have you ever reacted strongly with curiosity, sympathy, or anger to a character or an event in something you have read? Choose one of the readings and write a personal letter, either to the author or to one of the fictional characters in the reading. Use the traditional letter form, addressing the person directly and giving your reaction to the poem, story, or essay. Use the rich and varied possibilities of the informal letter form to express your own point of view—to complement, criticize, console, or inquire. Use whatever approach is most appropriate to express your reaction to the text.

8. **Using Anecdotes to Illustrate a Point**

   Have you ever discovered an important truth about yourself and who you are? Make a generalization about yourself or some aspect of your life and use several anecdotes to illustrate the truth of your generalization. Your generalization might be some aspect of your personality, such as a lack of self-esteem, an ability to predict the future, a tendency to act without thinking, a quick temper, or a tendency to rely too much on first impressions or on the advice of others. Develop each anecdote fully and be sure each is a good example that supports your generalization.

9. **Writing a Review to Recommend a Poem, Story, or Essay**

   Have you ever had someone ask you what you think of a reading selection? We often rely on the advice of others in selecting reading material. Write a review that clearly recommends or criticizes something you have read. Your evaluation of a poem, story, or essay can be positive, negative, or some interesting mixture of the two. Once you arrive at the evaluation or judgment you want to make, you will need to present several good reasons, supporting each with evidence from the reading to make your judgment convincing.

10. **Interpreting a Text**

    Have you even been asked what a poem, story, or essay means, or have you yourself ever been puzzled by a difficult text? Simply reading a text may not enable us to appreciate its full range of meaning. We often need to re-read, think about, discuss, and write about a poem, story, or essay before we can truly absorb its meaning. Choose one of the readings and explain its meaning in a well-developed essay. Select a complex text that challenges you. Focus your attention on the parts of the text about which you have questions. In your commentary you will need to quote from the text and refer to specific passages to help clear up any difficulties in understanding.

11. **Connecting Effects with Their Causes**

    What have you learned about the causes of change and growth, for either personal or societal issues? Choose one of the readings that illustrates some type of causal development and trace the effects to their causes. Has the author or character or society changed in some significant way? As you trace effects to their causes, are there some discoveries along the way?

Personal Knowledge: Who Am I?

The readings in Chapter One explore the theme of personal knowledge and challenge us to discover who we are. This theme is often the focus of storytellers, poets, and thinkers who write about experiences that mirror events in our own private lives. The reflections of these writers can help us to see who we are and also to learn what we value.

Liliana Heker's "The Stolen Party," for example, asks us to share in the main character's excitement of being invited to a birthday party, unfortunately followed by the pain of her discovery that she is regarded as hired help rather than as an honored guest. Such works can cause us to recall personal moments that marked our own passages from innocence to experience. Other works, such as Plato's "The Allegory of the Cave," reveal the consequences that follow when people live a limited existence without acknowledging their full potential.

The universal message implicit in Chapter One is the notion of Greek philosopher Socrates that the unexamined life is not worth living. Each reading in this chapter illustrates a moment of personal insight or development of the kind that compels each of us to ask the difficult, sometimes painful question: "Who am I?"

The Stolen Party

1982

LILIANA HEKER

 In "The Stolen Party," by Argentinean writer, LILIANA HEKER, Rosaura, the main character, comes to a harsh realization about her place in society. Although Rosaura's mother tries to protect her daughter from getting her hopes up too high, she watches helplessly in the end as the truth dawns on Rosaura. Such stories often help us to discover answers to the important question, "Who am I?"

As you read this story, think about whether you have experienced a moment or incident that, although painful at the time, later helped you to gain personal knowledge. In what ways did your experience increase your understanding of who you are and what you value?

A s soon as she arrived she went straight to the kitchen to see if the monkey was there. It was: what a relief! She wouldn't have liked to admit that her mother had been right. *Monkeys at a birthday?* her mother had sneered. *Get away with you, believing any nonsense you're told!* She was cross, but not because of the monkey, the girl thought; it's just because of the party. 1

"I don't like you going," she told her. "It's a rich people's party." 2

"Rich people go to Heaven too," said the girl, who studied religion at school. 3

"Get away with Heaven," said the mother. "The problem with you, young lady, is that you like to fart higher than your ass." 4

The girl didn't approve of the way her mother spoke. She was barely nine, and one of the best in her class. 5

"I'm going because I've been invited," she said. "And I've been invited because Luciana is my friend. So there." 6

"Ah yes, your friend," her mother grumbled. She paused. "Listen, Rosaura," she said at last. "That one's not your friend. You know what you are to them? The maid's daughter, that's what." 7

3

Rosaura blinked hard: she wasn't going to cry. Then she yelled: "Shut   8
up! You know nothing about being friends!"

Every afternoon she used to go to Luciana's house and they would both   9
finish their homework while Rosaura's mother did the cleaning. They had
their tea in the kitchen and they told each other secrets. Rosaura loved
everything in the big house, and she also loved the people who lived there.

"I'm going because it will be the most lovely party in the whole world,   10
Luciana told me it would. There will be a magician, and he will bring a
monkey and everything."

The mother swung around to take a good look at her child, and pom-   11
pously put her hands on her hips.

"Monkeys at a birthday?" she said. "Get away with you, believing any   12
nonsense you're told!"

Rosaura was deeply offended. She thought it unfair of her mother to   13
accuse other people of being liars simply because they were rich. Rosaura too
wanted to be rich, of course. If one day she managed to live in a beautiful
palace, would her mother stop loving her? She felt very sad. She wanted to
go to that party more than anything else in the world.

"I'll die if I don't go," she whispered, almost without moving her lips.   14

And she wasn't sure whether she had been heard, but on the morning   15
of the party she discovered that her mother had starched her Christmas dress.
And in the afternoon, after washing her hair, her mother rinsed it in apple
vinegar so that it would be all nice and shiny. Before going out, Rosaura
admired herself in the mirror, with her white dress and glossy hair, and
thought she looked terribly pretty.

"How lovely you look today, Rosaura."   16

Rosaura gave her starched skirt a slight toss with her hands and walked   17
into the party with a firm step. She said hello to Luciana and asked about
the monkey. Luciana put on a secretive look and whispered into Rosaura's
ear: "He's in the kitchen. But don't tell anyone, because it's a surprise."

Rosaura wanted to make sure. Carefully she entered the kitchen and   18
there she saw it: deep in thought, inside its cage. It looked so funny that the
girl stood there for a while, watching it, and later, every so often, she would
slip out of the party unseen and go and admire it. Rosaura was the only one
allowed into the kitchen. Señora Ines had said: "You yes, but not the others,
they're much too boisterous, they might break something." Rosaura had
never broken anything. She even managed the jug of orange juice, carrying
it from the kitchen into the dining room. She held it carefully and didn't
spill a single drop. And Señora Ines had said: "Are you sure you can manage
a jug as big as that?" Of course she could manage. She wasn't a butterfingers,

4

like the others. Like the blonde girl with the bow in her hair. As soon as she saw Rosaura, the girl with the bow had said:

"And you? Who are you?"   19

"I'm a friend of Luciana," said Rosaura.   20

"No," said the girl with the bow, "you are not a friend of Luciana   21
because I'm her cousin and I know all her friends. And I don't know you."

"So what," said Rosaura. "I come here every afternoon with my mother   22
and we do our homework together."

"You and your mother do your homework together?" asked the girl,   23
laughing.

"I and Luciana do our homework together," said Rosaura, very seriously.   24

The girl with the bow shrugged her shoulders.   25

"That's not being friends," she said. "Do you go to school together?"   26

"No."   27

"So where do you know her from?" said the girl, getting impatient.   28

Rosaura remembered her mother's words perfectly. She took a deep   29
breath.

"I'm the daughter of the employee," she said.   30

Her mother had said very clearly: "If someone asks, you say you're the   31
daughter of the employee; that's all." She also told her to add: "And proud
of it." But Rosaura thought that never in her life would she dare say something
of the sort.

"What employee?" said the girl with the bow. "Employee in a shop?"   32

"No," said Rosaura angrily. "My mother doesn't sell anything in any   33
shop, so there."

"So how come she's an employee?" said the girl with the bow.   34

Just then Señora Ines arrived saying *sbb sbb,* and asked Rosaura if she   35
wouldn't mind helping serve out the hotdogs, as she knew the house so
much better than the others.

"See?" said Rosaura to the girl with the bow, and when no one was   36
looking she kicked her in the shin.

Apart from the girl with the bow, all the others were delightful. The one   37
she liked best was Luciana, with her golden birthday crown; and then the
boys. Rosaura won the sack race, and nobody managed to catch her when
they played tag. When they split into two teams to play charades, all the boys
wanted her for their side. Rosaura felt she had never been so happy in all her
life.

But the best was still to come. The best came after Luciana blew out the   38
candles. First the cake. Señora Ines had asked her to help pass the cake
around, and Rosaura had enjoyed the task immensely, because everyone called

out to her, shouting "Me, me!" Rosaura remembered a story in which there was a queen who had the power of life or death over her subjects. She had always loved that, having the power of life or death. To Luciana and the boys she gave the largest pieces, and to the girl with the bow she gave a slice so thin one could see through it.

After the cake came the magician, tall and bony, with a fine red cape. A   39
true magician: he could untie handkerchiefs by blowing on them and make a chain with links that had no openings. He could guess what cards were pulled out from a pack, and the monkey was his assistant. He called the monkey "partner." "Let's see here, partner," he would say, "turn over a card." And, "Don't run away, partner: time to work now."

The final trick was wonderful. One of the children had to hold the   40
monkey in his arms and the magician said he would make him disappear.

"What, the boy?" they all shouted.   41

"No, the monkey!" shouted back the magician.   42

Rosaura thought that this was truly the most amusing party in the whole   43
world.

The magician asked a small fat boy to come and help, but the small fat   44
boy got frightened almost at once and dropped the monkey on the floor. The magician picked him up carefully, whispered something in his ear, and the monkey nodded almost as if he understood.

"You mustn't be so unmanly, my friend," the magician said to the fat   45
boy.

"What's unmanly?" said the fat boy.   46

The magician turned around as if to look for spies.   47

"A sissy," said the magician. "Go sit down."   48

Then he stared at all the faces, one by one. Rosaura felt her heart tremble.   49

"You, with the Spanish eyes," said the magician. And everyone saw that   50
he was pointing at her.

She wasn't afraid. Neither holding the monkey, nor when the magician   51
made him vanish; not even when, at the end, the magician flung his red cape over Rosaura's head and uttered a few magic words . . . and the monkey reappeared, chattering happily, in her arms. The children clapped furiously. And before Rosaura returned to her seat, the magician said:

"Thank you very much, my little countess."   52

She was so pleased with the compliment that a while later, when her   53
mother came to fetch her, that was the first thing she told her.

"I helped the magician and he said to me, 'Thank you very much, my   54
little countess.' "

It was strange because up to then Rosaura had thought that she was   55
angry with her mother. All along Rosaura had imagined that she would say

to her "See that the monkey wasn't a lie?" But instead she was so thrilled that she told her mother all about the wonderful magician.

Her mother tapped her on the head and said: "So now we're a countess."   56

But one could see that she was beaming.   57

And now they both stood in the entrance, because a moment ago Señora   58
Ines, smiling, had said: "Please wait here a second."

Her mother suddenly seemed worried.   59

"What is it?" she asked Rosaura.   60

"What is what?" said Rosaura. "It's nothing; she just wants to get the   61
presents for those who are leaving, see?"

She pointed at the fat boy and at a girl with pigtails who were also waiting   62
there, next to their mothers. And she explained about the presents. She knew, because she had been watching those who left before her. When one of the girls was about to leave, Señora Ines would give her a bracelet. When a boy left, Señora Ines gave him a yo-yo. Rosaura preferred the yo-yo because it sparkled, but she didn't mention that to her mother. Her mother might have said: "So why don't you ask for one, you blockhead?" That's what her mother was like. Rosaura didn't feel like explaining that she'd be horribly ashamed to be the odd one out. Instead she said:

"I was the best-behaved at the party."   63

And she said no more because Señora Ines came out into the hall with   64
two bags, one pink and one blue.

First she went up to the fat boy, gave him a yo-yo out of the blue bag,   65
and the fat boy left with his mother. Then she went up to the girl and gave her a bracelet out of the pink bag, and the girl with the pigtails left as well.

Finally she came up to Rosaura and her mother. She had a big smile on   66
her face and Rosaura liked that. Señora Ines looked down at her, then looked up at her mother, and then said something that made Rosaura proud:

"What a marvelous daughter you have, Herminia."   67

For an instant, Rosaura thought that she'd give her two presents: the   68
bracelet and the yo-yo. Señora Ines bent down as if about to look for something. Rosaura also leaned forward, stretching out her arm. But she never completed the movement.

Señora Ines didn't look in the pink bag. Nor did she look in the blue   69
bag. Instead she rummaged in her purse. In her hand appeared two bills.

"You really and truly earned this," she said handing them over. "Thank   70
you for all your help, my pet."

Rosaura felt her arms stiffen, stick close to her body, and then she noticed   71
her mother's hand on her shoulder. Instinctively she pressed herself against her mother's body. That was all. Except her eyes. Rosaura's eyes had a cold, clear look that fixed itself on Señora Ines's face.

Señora Ines, motionless, stood there with her hand outstretched. As if   72
she didn't dare draw it back. As if the slightest change might shatter an
infinitely delicate balance.

◙   ◙   ◙

OPTIONS FOR READING LOGS: "THE STOLEN PARTY"

1. Use the double-entry journal technique (asking "what" or "why" ques-
    tions) to discover meaning in "The Stolen Party." Draw a vertical line
    down the middle of your journal page to create two columns. In the left
    column, keep a running list of "what" or "why" questions that occur
    to you as you are reading. Aim for three to five questions, such as "What
    is the significance of the presents given to each guest at the end of the
    party?" or "Why does Rosaura's mother treat Rosaura so harshly when
    she first hears of the party?" When you finish your list, move to the top
    of the right column and answer your questions as completely as you can.
    Trying to make meaning out of a text requires that you take some risks
    with your answers, so don't be afraid to guess. To demonstrate that you
    have a basic understanding of the story, end your journal entry by jotting
    down its main idea.

2. Examine your personal reaction to "The Stolen Party" by completing
    one of the following statements:

    A. "I was confused by _____ ."
    B. "I was struck by _____ ."
    C. "I was surprised by _____ ."

    Develop your journal entry by adding detailed explanations from your
    own experiences as well as from events in the story. Complete your
    journal entry with a statement of the story's theme.

3. From your own life, tell a parallel story that was triggered by "The Stolen
    Party." Does Rosaura's experience of thinking she was an invited guest
    and later discovering she was "hired help" at the birthday party remind
    you of a painful event in your life? Your story should be connected with
    this chapter's theme of "Personal Knowledge: Who Am I?" Jot down
    elements in your remembered event that were similar to or different from
    Rosaura's situation. Wrap up your journal entry by stating what your
    experience taught you about yourself.

OPTIONS FOR WRITING ASSIGNMENTS: "THE STOLEN PARTY"

1. If "The Stolen Party" reminds you of a painful experience from your own past, expand your reading log entry into a more polished piece of writing. Compose a narrative or descriptive essay that focuses on a remembered person, place, or event. Begin with a thesis statement that names your topic and tells your reader what you learned from your experience. Throughout your essay, concentrate on using vivid details and descriptions to help recreate your own passage from innocence to experience. Above all, make sure you show how your experience in some way ties in with personal knowledge.

2. Write a letter to one of the fictional characters in "The Stolen Party," addressing the character directly and describing your reaction to some event in the story. Use your letter to express your own point of view about how people gain personal knowledge. For example, if you choose to write to Rosaura or her mother, you might empathize with her, console her, or criticize her. Use whatever tone is most appropriate to express your reaction to the story.

3. In "The Stolen Party," Rosaura discovers an important truth about herself and who she is. Write a paper that uses anecdotes (brief stories) to illustrate a generalization about yourself. Begin by making a point about some aspect of your personality and use that point as your thesis statement. You might state, for example, "I am overly critical of people when I first meet them," or "I always allow people to take advantage of me." Then use several anecdotes, fully developed with specific details, to illustrate the truth of your generalization.

4. Write an essay explaining the meaning of some aspect of "The Stolen Party." Focus on parts of the story that you have genuine questions about, such as, "Did Rosaura's mother do enough to protect her daughter from the harsh realities of life?" Decide on one interpretation of the story and list several reasons that back up your interpretation. Review the story for supporting evidence. Your introductory paragraph should end with a thesis statement that makes an arguable point about your particular interpretation of the story. Follow with three or four paragraphs, each beginning with a topic sentence that supports the thesis statement. Throughout your essay you should quote or paraphrase from the story and refer to specific passages to clarify and support your central argument.

Dusting

1984

JULIA ALVAREZ

 JULIA ALVAREZ is a poet and novelist from the Dominican Republic. In her poem "Dusting," the narrator attempts to leave her mark in the world by inscribing her name on the dusty furniture and leaving her fingerprints everywhere. Of course, her mother follows after her like a dutiful mother, wiping away the fingerprints. Through her rebellious actions the daughter reveals that she is in the process of examining her life and her place in the society in which she lives.

As you read the poem, notice how the narrator acknowledges her mother's place in society, yet questions her own personal identity at the same time. Why do children sometimes rebel against the roles set by their parents or guardians?

Each morning I wrote my name   1
on the dusty cabinet, then crossed
the dining table in script, scrawled
in capitals on the backs of chairs,
practising signatures like scales   5
while Mother followed, squirting
linseed from a burping can
into a crumpled-up flannel.

She erased my fingerprints
from the bookshelf and rocker,   10
polished mirrors on the desk
scribbled with my alphabets.
My name was swallowed in the towel
with which she jeweled the table tops.
The grain surfaced in the oak   15

and the pine grew luminous.[1]
But I refused with every mark
to be like her, anonymous.[2]

1. luminous: radiating or reflecting light   2. anonymous: not named or identified

OPTIONS FOR READING LOGS: "DUSTING"

1. Use the double-entry journal technique (asking "what" or "why" questions) to discover meaning in "Dusting." Draw a vertical line down the middle of your journal page to create two columns. In the left column, keep a running list of "what" or "why" questions that occur to you as you are reading. Aim for three to five questions, such as, "Why does the narrator write her name in capital letters?" When you finish your list, move to the top of the right column and answer your questions as completely as you can. Remember that trying to make meaning out of a text requires that you take some risks with your answers, so don't be afraid to guess. To demonstrate that you have a basic understanding of the poem, end your journal entry by jotting down its main idea.

2. Examine your personal reaction to "Dusting" by comparing and contrasting the mother in the poem to the mother in "The Stolen Party." Do you feel their circumstances were similar or different? List their similarities, showing how they are alike in some way. Then list their differences. End your journal entry by explaining whether you think you understand the two mothers' attitudes about their place in society.

3. Create an original poem in response to the text. Begin by copying the two-stanza form of "Dusting." Then cross out the phrases that do not represent your experience and replace words and lines with details from your personal history. Keep substituting until you can no longer recognize Alvarez's poem, and you have created a new, original poem in its place.

OPTIONS FOR WRITING ASSIGNMENTS: "DUSTING"

1. Our parents often serve as role models for us, but sometimes we, like the author of "Dusting," are critical of the choices our parents made in their lives. Such moments of criticism often lead to periods when we question our own values and our goals. Have you been through a distinc-

tive phase in your life—perhaps one that lasted several months or even longer—that you would like to explore through writing? Think of a specific period when you were absorbed by a strong interest or focus that deeply influenced your thoughts and behavior—for example, a time when you rebelled against your family, school, or society. Explore the beginning, middle, and end of that phase. What got you involved? In what ways did others influence you at the time? Why did the period end?

2. Create a conversation between you and the narrator in "Dusting." Your conversation might take the form of a question-and-answer interview, an argument expressing two opposing points of view, or a freewheeling exploration of the ideas and implications of the poem. See if you can gain some insight into your own personal identity through the process of creating a dialogue.

3. Write a formal essay of five or more paragraphs explaining the meaning of "Dusting." Focus on ideas in the poem about which you have genuine questions, such as, "Does the narrator have conflicting emotions about domestic chores like dusting?" End your introductory paragraph with a thesis statement that makes an arguable point about the central theme of the poem—for example, whether the daughter is justified in her refusal to accept her mother's dominance over her. Brainstorm or prewrite to come up with reasons to support your interpretation. In the remaining paragraphs, you will need to quote from the poem and refer to specific words and passages to clarify and support your interpretation.

4. In "Dusting" the narrator changes in a significant way and discovers an important truth about her mother's life and her own life. Try to make connections between causes and effects by thinking about the following questions: Does the poem point to any particular attitude toward women and their roles in our society? What words or phrases hint at this attitude? What might be the cause of the narrator's anger? As you attempt to trace these causes, be alert for hidden discoveries along the way. Focus on the chapter's theme of "Personal Knowledge: Who Am I?"

Beauty: When the Other Dancer Is the Self

1983

ALICE WALKER

 ALICE WALKER was born in Georgia in 1944. Her essays, stories, and poems are often based on recollections of her own childhood. She frequently writes about the suffering of people from all walks of life, in particular about issues confronting African-American women. Walker won the Pulitzer Prize for her novel *The Color Purple* in 1983. In "Beauty: When the Other Dancer Is the Self," she explores a series of incidents in her life that caused her to lose her self-esteem and, ultimately, to regain it when she accepted who she is, both inside and outside.

Where do you think you got your ideas about the meaning of beauty? Have you ever experienced anything in your childhood or adolescence that caused you to be ashamed of your appearance in some way? As you read the story, consider how Walker examines notions of beauty, both real and imagined.

It is a bright summer day in 1947. My father, a fat, funny man with beautiful eyes and a subversive[1] wit, is trying to decide which of his eight children he will take with him to the county fair. My mother, of course, will not go. She is knocked out from getting most of us ready: I hold my neck stiff against the pressure of her knuckles as she hastily completes the braiding and then beribboning of my hair.

My father is the driver for the rich old white lady up the road. Her name is Miss Mey. She owns all the land for miles around, as well as the house in which we live. All I remember about her is that she once offered to pay my mother thirty-five cents for cleaning her house, raking up piles of her magnolia leaves, and washing her family's clothes, and that my mother—she of no money, eight children, and a chronic earache—refused it. But I do not think

---

1. subversive: tending to cause the downfall or ruin

of this in 1947. I am two and a half years old. I want to go everywhere my daddy goes. I am excited at the prospect of riding in a car. Someone has told me fairs are fun. That there is room in the car for only three of us doesn't faze me at all. Whirling happily in my starchy frock, showing off my biscuit-polished patent-leather shoes and lavender socks, tossing my head in a way that makes my ribbons bounce, I stand, hands on hips, before my father. "Take me, Daddy," I say with assurance: "I'm the prettiest!"

Later, it does not surprise me to find myself in Miss Mey's shiny black car, sharing the back seat with the other lucky ones. Does not surprise me that I thoroughly enjoy the fair. At home that night I tell the unlucky ones all I can remember about the merry-go-round, the man who eats live chickens, and the teddy bears, until they say: that's enough, baby Alice. Shut up now, and go to sleep. 3

It is Easter Sunday, 1950. I am dressed in a green, flocked, scalloped-hem dress (handmade by my adoring sister, Ruth) that has its own smooth satin petticoat and tiny hot-pink roses tucked into each scallop. My shoes, new T-strap patent leather, again highly biscuit-polished. I am six years old and have learned one of the longest Easter speeches to be heard that day, totally unlike the speech I said when I was two: "Easter lilies / pure and white / blossom in / the morning light." When I rise to give my speech I do so on a great wave of love and pride and expectation. People in the church stop rustling their new crinolines. They seem to hold their breath. I can tell they admire my dress, but it is my spirit, bordering on sassiness (womanishness), they secretly applaud. 4

"That girl's a little *mess*," they whisper to each other, pleased. 5

Naturally I say my speech without stammer or pause, unlike those who stutter, stammer, or, worst of all, forget. This is before the word "beautiful" exists in people's vocabulary, but "Oh, isn't she the *cutest* thing!" frequently floats my way. "And got so much sense!" they gratefully add . . . for which thoughtful addition I thank them to this day. 6

It was great fun being cute. But then, one day, it ended. 7

I am eight years old and a tomboy. I have a cowboy hat, cowboy boots, checkered shirt and pants, all red. My playmates are my brothers, two and four years older than I. Their colors are black and green, the only difference in the way we are dressed. On Saturday nights we all go to the picture show, even my mother; Westerns are her favorite kind of movie. Back home, "on the ranch," we pretend we are Tom Mix, Hopalong Cassidy, Lash LaRue (we've even named one of our dogs Lash LaRue); we chase each other for 8 hours rustling cattle, being outlaws, delivering damsels from distress. Then my parents decide to buy my brothers guns. These are not "real" guns. They shoot "BBs," copper pellets my brothers say will kill birds. Because I am a girl, I do not get a gun. Instantly I am relegated to the position of Indian. Now there appears a great distance between us. They shoot and shoot at everything with their new guns. I try to keep up with my bow and arrows.

One day while I am standing on top of our makeshift "garage"—pieces   9
of tin nailed across some poles—holding my bow and arrow and looking out toward the fields, I feel an incredible blow in my right eye. I look down just in time to see my brother lower his gun.

Both brothers rush to my side. My eye stings, and I cover it with my   10
hand. "If you tell," they say, "we will get a whipping. You don't want that to happen, do you?" I do not. "Here is a piece of wire," says the older brother, picking it up from the roof; "say you stepped on one end of it and the other flew up and hit you." The pain is beginning to start. "Yes," I say. "Yes, I will say that is what happened." If I do not say this is what happened, I know my brothers will find ways to make me wish I had. But now I will say anything that gets me to my mother.

Confronted by our parents we stick to the lie agreed upon. They place   11
me on a bench on the porch and I close my left eye while they examine the right. There is a tree growing from underneath the porch that climbs past the railing to the roof. It is the last thing my right eye sees. I watch as its trunk, its oranches, and then its leaves are blotted out by the rising blood.

I am in shock. First there is intense fever, which my father tries to break   12
using lily leaves bound around my head. Then there are chills: my mother tries to get me to eat soup. Eventually, I do not know how, my parents learn what has happened. A week after the "accident" they take me to see a doctor. "Why did you wait so long to come?" he asks, looking into my eye and shaking his head. "Eyes are sympathetic," he says. "If one is blind, the other will likely become blind too."

This comment of the doctor's terrifies me. But it is really how I look   13
that bothers me most. Where the BB pellet struck there is glob of whitish scar tissue, a hideous cataract, on my eye. Now when I stare at people—a favorite pastime, up to now—they will stare back. Not at the "cute" little girl, but at her scar. For six years I do not stare at anyone, because I do not raise my head.

Years later, in the throes of a mid-life crisis, I ask my mother and sister whether   14
I changed after the "accident." "No," they say, puzzled. "What do you mean?"

What do I mean?   15

I am eight, and, for the first time, doing poorly in school, where I have   16
been something of a whiz since I was four. We have just moved to the place
where the "accident" occurred. We do not know any of the people around
us because this is a different county. The only time I see the friends I knew
is when we go back to our old church. The new school is the former state
penitentiary. It is a large stone building, cold and drafty, crammed to overflow-
ing with boisterous, ill-disciplined children. On the third floor there is a huge
circular imprint of some partition that has been torn out.

"What used to be here?" I ask a sullen girl next to me on our way past   17
it to lunch.

"The electric chair," says she.   18

At night I have nightmares about the electric chair, and about all the   19
people reputedly "fried" in it. I am afraid of the school, where all the students
seem to be budding criminals.

"What's the matter with your eye?" they ask, critically.   20

When I don't answer (I cannot decide whether it was an "accident" or   21
not), they shove me, insist on a fight.

My brother, the one who created the story about the wire, comes to my   22
rescue. But then brags so much about "protecting" me, I become sick.

After months of torture at the school, my parents decide to send me   23
back to our old community, to my old school. I live with my grandparents
and the teacher they board. But there is no room for Phoebe, my cat. By
the time my grandparents decide there *is* room, and I ask for my cat, she
cannot be found. Miss Yarborough, the boarding teacher, takes me under
her wing, and begins to teach me to play the piano. But soon she marries
an African—a "prince," she says—and is whisked away to his continent.

At my old school there is at least one teacher who loves me. She is the   24
teacher who "knew me before I was born" and bought my first baby clothes.
It is she who makes life bearable. It is her presence that finally helps me turn
on the one child at the school who continually calls me "one-eyed bitch."
One day I simply grab him by his coat and beat him until I am satisfied. It
is my teacher who tells me my mother is ill.

My mother is lying in bed in the middle of the day, something I have never   25
seen. She is in too much pain to speak. She has an abscess in her ear. I stand
looking down on her, knowing that if she dies, I cannot live. She is being
treated with warm oils and hot bricks held against her cheek. Finally a doctor
comes. But I must go back to my grandparents' house. The weeks pass but
I am hardly aware of it. All I know is that my mother might die, my father

is not so jolly, my brothers still have their guns, and I am the one sent away from home.

"You did not change," they say.   26

Did I imagine the anguish of never looking up?   27

I am twelve. When relatives come to visit I hide in my room. My cousin   28
Brenda, just my age, whose father works in the post office and whose mother
is a nurse, comes to find me. "Hello," she says. And then she asks, looking
at my recent school picture, which I did not want taken, and on which the
"glob," as I think of it, is clearly visible. "You still can't see out of that eye?"

"No," I say, and flop back on the bed over my book.   29

That night, as I do almost every night, I abuse my eye. I rant and rave   30
at it, in front of the mirror. I plead with it to clear up before morning. I tell
it I hate and despise it. I do not pray for sight. I pray for beauty.

"You did not change," they say.   31

I am fourteen and baby-sitting for my brother Bill, who lives in Boston. He   32
is my favorite brother and there is a strong bond between us. Understanding
my feelings of shame and ugliness he and his wife take me to a local hospital,
where the "glob" is removed by a doctor named O. Henry. There is still a
small bluish crater where the scar tissue was, but the ugly white stuff is gone.
Almost immediately I become a different person from the girl who does not
raise her head. Or so I think. Now that I've raised my head I win the boyfriend
of my dreams. Now that I've raised my head I have plenty of friends. Now
that I've raised my head classwork comes from my lips as faultlessly as Easter
speeches did, and I leave high school as valedictorian, most popular student,
and *queen,* hardly believing my luck. Ironically, the girl who was voted most
beautiful in our class (and was) was later shot twice through the chest by a
male companion, using a "real" gun, while she was pregnant. But that's
another story in itself. Or is it?

"You did not change," they say.   33

It is now thirty years since the "accident." A beautiful journalist comes to   34
visit and to interview me. She is going to write a cover story for her magazine
that focuses on my latest book. "Decide how you want to look on the cover,"
she says. "Glamorous, or whatever."

Never mind "glamorous," it is the "whatever" that I hear. Suddenly all   35
I can think of is whether I will get enough sleep the night before the photog-
raphy session: if I don't, my eye will be tired and wander, as blind eyes will.

At night in bed with my lover I think up reasons why I should not appear   36
on the cover of a magazine. "My meanest critics will say I've sold out," I
say. "My family will now realize I write scandalous books."

"But what's the real reason you don't want to do this?" he asks.   37

"Because in all probability," I say in a rush, "my eye won't be straight."   38

"It will be straight enough," he says. Then, "Besides, I thought you'd   39
made your peace with that."

And I suddenly remember that I have.   40

I remember: 41

I am talking to my brother Jimmy, asking if he remembers anything   42
unusual about the day I was shot. He does not know I consider that day the
last time my father, with his sweet home remedy of cool lily leaves, chose
me, and that I suffered and raged inside because of this. "Well," he says,
"all I remember is standing by the side of the highway with Daddy, trying
to flag down a car. A white man stopped, but when Daddy said he needed
somebody to take his little girl to the doctor, he drove off."

I remember: 43

I am in the desert for the first time. I fall totally in love with it. I am so   44
overwhelmed by its beauty, I confront for the first time, consciously, the
meaning of the doctor's words years ago: "Eyes are sympathetic. If one is
blind, the other will likely become blind too." I realize I have dashed about
the world madly, looking at that, storing up images against the fading of the
light. *But I might have missed seeing the desert!* The shock of that possibility—
and gratitude for over twenty-five years of sight—sends me literally to my
knees. Poem after poem comes—which is perhaps how poets pray.

ON SIGHT

I am so thankful I have seen
The Desert
And the creatures in the desert
And the desert itself.

The desert has its own moon
Which I have seen
With my own eye.

There is no flag on it.

Trees of the desert have arms
All of which are always up
That is because the moon is up

The sun is up
Also the sky
The stars
Clouds
None with flags.

If there *were* flags, I doubt
the trees would point.
Would you?

But mostly, I remember this: 45

I am twenty-seven, and my baby daughter is almost three. Since her   46
birth, I have worried about her discovery that her mother's eyes are different
from other people's. Will she be embarrassed? I think. What will she say?
Every day she watches a television program called "Big Blue Marble." It
begins with a picture of the earth as it appears from the moon. It is bluish,
a little battered-looking, but full of light, with whitish clouds swirling around
it. Every time I see it I weep with love, as if it is a picture of Grandma's
house. One day when I am putting Rebecca down for her nap, she suddenly
focuses on my eye. Something inside me cringes, gets ready to try to protect
myself. All children are cruel about physical differences, I know from experience, and that they don't always mean to be is another matter. I assume
Rebecca will be the same.

But no-o-o-o. She studies my face intently as we stand, her inside and   47
me outside her crib. She even holds my face maternally between her dimpled
little hands. Then, looking every bit as serious and lawyerlike as her father,
she says, as if it may just possibly have slipped my attention: "Mommy, there's
a *world* in your eye." (As in, "Don't be alarmed, or do anything crazy.")
And then, gently, but with great interest: "Mommy, where did you *get* that
world in your eye?"

For the most part, the pain left then. (So what, if my brothers grew up   48
to buy even more powerful pellet guns for their sons and to carry real guns
themselves. So what, if a young "Morehouse man" once nearly fell off the
steps of Trevos Arnett Library because he thought my eyes were blue.) Crying
and laughing I ran to the bathroom, while Rebecca mumbled and sang herself
off to sleep. Yes indeed, I realized, looking into the mirror. There *was* a world
in my eye. And I saw that it was possible to love it: that in fact, for all it had
taught me of shame and anger and inner vision, I *did* love it. Even to see it
drifting out of orbit in boredom, or rolling up out of fatigue, not to mention
floating back at attention in excitement (bearing witness, a friend has called
it), deeply suitable to my personality, and even characteristic of me.

That night I dream I am dancing to Stevie Wonder's song "Always" (the   49
name of the song is really "As," but I hear it as "Always"). As I dance,
whirling and joyous, happier than I've ever been in my life, another bright-
faced dancer joins me. We dance and kiss each other and hold each other
through the night. The other dancer has obviously come through all right,
as I have done. She is beautiful, whole and free. And she is also me.

▣   ▣   ▣

OPTIONS FOR READING LOGS: "WHEN THE OTHER DANCER IS THE SELF"

1. Use the double-entry journal technique (asking "what" or "why" ques-
    tions) to explore the theme of personal knowledge in "Beauty: When
    the Other Dancer Is the Self." Draw a vertical line down the middle of
    your journal page to create two columns. In the left column, keep a
    running list of "what" or "why" questions that occur to you as you
    are reading. Aim for three to five questions, such as "Why does the
    narrator's mother refuse to take the thirty-five cents from Miss Mey?"
    When you finish your list, move to the top of the right column and
    answer your questions as completely as you can. Remember that trying
    to make meaning out of a text requires that you take some risks with
    your answers, so don't be afraid to guess. To demonstrate that you have
    reached a basic understanding of the story, end your journal entry by
    jotting down its main idea.
2. Copy what you think is the most powerful line or passage in "Beauty:
    When the Other Dancer Is the Self." Using anecdotes and examples
    from your personal experience, explain fully why that particular passage
    held such power or meaning for you.
3. Discover meaning in "Beauty: When the Other Dancer Is the Self" by
    freewriting or jotting down your own personal reflections on one of the
    following:

    A. Your own dreams or fantasies in connection with the story.
    B. Your doubts, expectations, and creative insights that surfaced while
        you read.

    End your journal entry by stating the theme of the story.

OPTIONS FOR WRITING ASSIGNMENTS: "WHEN THE OTHER DANCER IS THE SELF"

1. Expand and develop one of your reading logs for "Beauty: When the Other Dancer Is the Self" into a more polished piece of writing that explores its subject matter in greater range and depth. Begin with a thesis statement that reveals an important discovery you made about yourself. Arrange your story in a clear chronological order, adding enough specific details to make the event come alive for your reader. By the end of your essay, you should have convinced your reader of the significance of your self-discovery.

2. In "Beauty: When the Other Dancer Is the Self," the narrator was influenced greatly both by relatives and by other people. Interview someone from your past who had a significant influence on your own personal development, and then write an essay showing how that person influenced you. Before your interview, make a list of appropriate questions. In your essay you might want to include biographical information that clarifies the characteristics that made the person so important in your life.

3. Write a letter either to the author or to one of the characters in "Beauty: When the Other Dancer Is the Self." Address the person directly, using the letter to express your own point of view. You may choose to praise or criticize the narrator's reaction to her eye injury; or you may wish to empathize with her mother or father. Use whatever tone is most appropriate to express your reaction to the story.

4. We often rely on the advice of others in selecting stories to read, and we are influenced by their evaluations. Write a review of "Beauty: When the Other Dancer Is the Self," making a clear appraisal of the value of the story, especially in challenging us to make personal discoveries about ourselves. Your review can be positive, negative, or an interesting mixture of positive and negative. Once you are clear about the evaluation you want to make, come up with several good reasons, each with supporting evidence from the story, that make your evaluation convincing.

Blackberries

1988

LESLIE NORRIS

 LESLIE NORRIS, a Welsh writer born in 1921, has published many poetry books and short stories. Norris himself has stated that he is used to telling "yarns," and that he was influenced by the strong oral tradition in Wales. In "Blackberries," Norris writes about a young boy who suddenly realizes he is no longer an innocent child. The spontaneous and seemingly harmless act of using his new hat to carry blackberries plunges him into the adult world of his parents and creates a painful awareness of their troubled relationship.

Do you recall a time when you learned some surprising personal knowledge about one of your parents, guardians, or relatives? As you read the story, reflect on the personal knowledge the young boy has gained. What does the child begin to understand at the end of the story when he says he "must learn sometimes to be alone"?

M r. Frensham opened his shop at eight-thirty, but it was past nine 1 when the woman and the child went in. The shop was empty and there were no footmarks on the fresh sawdust shaken onto the floor. The child listened to the melancholy sound of the bell as the door closed behind him and he scuffed his feet in the yellow sawdust. Underneath, the boards were brown and worn, and dark knots stood up in them. He had never been in this shop before. He was going to have his hair cut for the first time in his life, except for the times when his mother had trimmed it gently behind his neck.

Mr. Frensham was sitting in a large chair, reading a newspaper. He could 2 make the chair turn around, and he spun twice about in it before he put down his paper, smiled, and said, "Good morning."

He was an old man, thin, with flat white hair. He wore a white coat. 3

"One gentleman," he said, "to have his locks shorn." 4

He put a board across the two arms of his chair, lifted the child, and sat 5 him on it.

"How are you, my dear? And your father, is he well?" he said to the   6
child's mother.

He took a sheet from a cupboard on the wall and wrapped it about the   7
child's neck, tucking it into his collar. The sheet covered the child completely
and hung almost to the floor. Cautiously the boy moved his hidden feet. He
could see the bumps they made in the cloth. He moved his finger against
the inner surface of the sheet and made a six with it, and then an eight. He
liked those shapes.

"Snip, snip," said Mr. Frensham, "and how much does the gentleman   8
want off? All of it? All his lovely curls? I think not."

"Just an ordinary cut, please, Mr. Frensham," said the child's mother,   9
"not too much off. I, my husband and I, we thought it was time for him to
look like a little boy. His hair grows so quickly."

Mr. Frensham's hands were very cold. His hard fingers turned the boy's   10
head first to one side and then to the other and the boy could hear the
long scissors snapping away behind him, and above his ears. He was quite
frightened, but he liked watching the small tufts of his hair drop lightly on
the sheet which covered him, and then roll an inch or two before they stopped.
Some of the hair fell to the floor and by moving his hand surreptitiously[1] he
could make nearly all of it fall down. The hair fell without a sound. Tilting
his head slightly, he could see the little bunches on the floor, not belonging
to him any more.

"Easy to see who this boy is," Mr. Frensham said to the child's mother.   11
"I won't get redder hair in the shop today. Your father had hair like this
when he was young, very much this color. I've cut your father's hair for fifty
years. He's keeping well, you say? There, I think that's enough. We don't
want him to dislike coming to see me."

He took the sheet off the child and flourished it hard before folding it   12
and putting it on a shelf. He swept the back of the child's neck with a small
brush. Nodding his own old head in admiration, he looked at the child's
hair for flaws in the cutting.

"Very handsome," he said.   13

The child saw his face in a mirror. It looked pale and large, but also   14
much the same as always. When he felt the back of his neck, the new short
hairs stood up sharp against his hand.

"We're off to do some shopping," his mother said to Mr. Frensham as   15
she handed him the money.

They were going to buy the boy a cap, a round cap with a little button   16
on top and a peak over his eyes, like his cousin Harry's cap. The boy wanted

1. surreptitiously: done secretly

the cap very much. He walked seriously beside his mother and he was not impatient even when she met Mrs. Lewis and talked to her, and then took a long time at the fruiterer's buying apples and potatoes.

"This is the smallest size we have," the man in the clothes shop said. "It may be too large for him."   17

"He's just had his hair cut," said his mother. "That should make a difference."   18

The man put the cap on the boy's head and stood back to look. It was a beautiful cap. The badge in front was shaped like a shield and it was red and blue. It was not too big, although the man could put two fingers under it, at the side of the boy's head.   19

"On the other hand, we don't want it too tight," the man said. "We want something he can grow into, something that will last him a long time."   20

"Oh, I hope so," his mother said. "It's expensive enough."   21

The boy carried the cap himself, in a brown paper bag that had "Price, Clothiers, High Street" on it. He could read it all except "Clothiers" and his mother told him that. They put his cap, still in its bag, in a drawer when they got home.   22

His father came home late in the afternoon. The boy heard the firm clap of the closing door and his father's long step down the hall. He leaned against his father's knee while the man ate his dinner. The meal had been keeping warm in the oven and the plate was very hot. A small steam was rising from the potatoes, and the gravy had dried to a thin crust where it was shallow at the side of the plate. The man lifted the dry gravy with his knife and fed it to his son, very carefully lifting it into the boy's mouth, as if he were feeding a small bird. The boy loved this. He loved the hot savor of his father's dinner, the way his father cut away small delicacies for him and fed them to him slowly. He leaned drowsily against his father's leg.   23

Afterwards he put on his cap and stood before his father, certain of the man's approval. The man put his hand on the boy's head and looked at him without smiling.   24

"On Sunday," he said, "we'll go for a walk. Just you and I. We'll be men together."   25

Although it was late in September, the sun was warm and the paths dry. The man and his boy walked beside the disused canal and powdery white dust covered their shoes. The boy thought of the days before he had been born, when the canal had been busy. He thought of the long boats pulled by solid horses, gliding through the water. In his head he listened to the hushed, wet noises they would have made, the soft waves slapping the banks, and green   26 tench[1] looking up as the barges moved above them, their water suddenly darkened. His grandfather had told him about that. But now the channel was filled with mud and tall reeds. Bullrush and watergrass grew in the damp passages. He borrowed his father's walking stick and knocked the heads off a company of seeding dandelions, watching the tiny parachutes carry away their minute dark burdens.

"There they go," he said to himself. "There they go, sailing away to 27
China."

"Come on," said his father, "or we'll never reach Fletcher's Woods." 28

The boy hurried after his father. He had never been to Fletcher's Woods. 29
Once his father had heard a nightingale there. It had been in the summer, long ago, and his father had gone with his friends, to hear the singing bird. They had stood under a tree and listened. Then the moon went down and his father, stumbling home, had fallen into a blackberry bush.

"Will there be blackberries?" he asked. 30

"There should be," his father said. "I'll pick some for you." 31

In Fletcher's Woods there was shade beneath the trees, and sunlight, 32
thrown in yellow patches on to the grass, seemed to grow out of the ground rather than come from the sky. The boy stepped from sunlight to sunlight, in and out of shadow. His father showed him a tangle of bramble,[2] hard with thorns, its leaves just beginning to color into autumn, its long runners dry and brittle on the grass. Clusters of purple fruit hung in the branches. His father reached up and chose a blackberry for him. Its skin was plump and shining, each of its purple globes held a point of reflected light.

"You can eat it," his father said. 33

The boy put the blackberry in his mouth. He rolled it with his tongue, 34
feeling its irregularity,[3] and crushed it against the roof of his mouth. Released juice, sweet and warm as summer, ran down his throat, hard seeds cracked between his teeth. When he laughed his father saw that his mouth was deeply stained. Together they picked and ate the dark berries, until their lips were purple and their hands marked and scratched.

"We should take some for your mother," the man said. 35

He reached with his stick and pulled down high canes where the choicest 36
berries grew, picking them to take home. They had nothing to carry them in, so the boy put his new cap on the grass and they filled its hollow with berries. He held the cap by its edges and they went home.

"It was a stupid thing to do," his mother said, "utterly stupid. What were 37
you thinking of?"

---

1. tench: a freshwater fish   2. bramble: any number of unusually prickly berry-bearing shrubs, such as blackberry and raspberry.   3. irregularity: the state of not having parts the same size or form.

The young man did not answer.   38

"If we had the money, it would be different," his mother said, "Where   39
do you think the money comes from?"

"I know where the money comes from," his father said. "I work hard   40
enough for it."

"His new cap," his mother said. "How am I to get him another?"   41

The cap lay on the table and by standing on tiptoe the boy could see it.   42
Inside it was wet with the sticky juice of blackberries. Small pieces of blackberry
skins were stuck to it. The stains were dark and irregular.

"It will probably dry out all right," his father said.   43

His mother's face was red and distorted, her voice shrill.   44

"If you had anything like a job," she shouted, "and could buy caps by   45
the dozen, then—"

She stopped and shook her head. His father turned away, his mouth   46
hard.

"I do what I can," he said.   47

"That's not much!" his mother said. She was tight with scorn. "You   48
don't do much!"

Appalled, the child watched the quarrel mount and spread. He began   49
to cry quietly, to himself, knowing that it was a different weeping to any he
had experienced before, that he was crying for a different pain. And the child
began to understand that they were different people; his father, his mother,
himself, and that he must learn sometimes to be alone.

◈ ◈ ◈

OPTIONS FOR READING LOGS: "BLACKBERRIES"

1. Use the double-entry journal technique (asking "what" or "why" ques-
    tions) to explore the theme of personal knowledge in "Blackberries."
    Draw a vertical line down the middle of your journal page to create two
    columns. In the left column, keep a running list of "what" or "why"
    questions that occur to you as you are reading. Aim for three to five
    questions, such as "What is the significance of the boy's getting his first
    haircut?" When you finish with your list, move to the top of the right
    column, and answer your questions as completely as you can. Remember
    that trying to make meaning out of a text requires that you take some
    risks with your answers, so don't be afraid to guess. To demonstrate that
    you have reached a basic understanding of the story, end your journal
    entry by jotting down its main idea.

2. Use listing as a way to take a closer look at the characters. Draw a vertical line down the middle of your journal page to create two columns. In the left column, keep a list of characters from the story. In the right column, jot down your opinions, observations, and comments about those characters. Complete your journal entry by discussing some interesting insights you gained about one of the characters.

3. From your own life, tell a parallel story that was triggered by "Blackberries." Does the boy's experience in "Blackberries" remind you of an event in your life? Jot down parts of your remembered event that were similar to or different from those in the story. Wrap up your journal entry by stating what your experience taught you about yourself.

OPTIONS FOR WRITING ASSIGNMENTS: "BLACKBERRIES"

1. Use your imagination to create a completely new ending for "Blackberries." You might want to delete the entire last paragraph of the story and use the parents' quarrel as a starting point for a completely different kind of ending. Experiment with dialogue, allowing all three characters to talk to one another. Following the format of the original story, conclude your new ending with a short paragraph that hints at the theme of personal knowledge.

2. Compare and contrast the discovery of personal knowledge in any one of the three previous readings to the young boy's discovery in "Blackberries." What do the two selections illustrate about the difficulties and rewards of the quest for personal knowledge? In what ways are the two readings alike? In what ways are they different? Begin with two lists, develop them into outlines, and use transitional expressions that signal similarities or differences.

3. At the end of "Blackberries," the boy cries because he has discovered something new about himself and his family. The boy's illusions about his parents have been shattered, and he blames himself for not understanding his parents better. Write a paper making some generalization about one of your tendencies, such as being too self-centered. State your generalization in a thesis sentence in your introductory paragraph. Then, in your supporting paragraphs, use descriptive personal anecdotes to illustrate your thesis statement, taking care to develop each anecdote fully.

4. Write a formal essay of five or more paragraphs explaining the personal knowledge gained by the boy in "Blackberries." Focus on parts of the story about which you have genuine questions, such as, "Why does the

mother react the way she does when she sees the boy's stained cap?" In a thesis statement at the end of your introductory paragraph, write down what you believe the young boy learns. In the following paragraphs, quote from the story and refer to specific passages to clarify and support your central idea.

Theme for English B

1959

LANGSTON HUGHES

 JAMES LANGSTON HUGHES was born in Missouri in 1902 and died in 1967. He was one of our most significant modern American writers, known for his poems, plays, fiction, biographies, and essays. As a young man, Hughes worked as a merchant seaman and had the opportunity to visit Africa. He also lived in Rome and Paris for a time. He constantly examined his Harlem roots and was a major figure during the time when Harlem was a center for African-American writers, musicians, and actors. His greatest contribution to literature was his belief in the universality of human suffering, and his works are filled with realistic portrayals of the lives of African Americans.

In "Theme for English B," the narrator's English instructor challenges him to write the truth about himself. Through this assignment the narrator discovers that "truth" is not such a simple matter to set forth on paper. His attempt compels him to ask some difficult questions about his own identity as well as that of his instructor.

As you read Langston Hughes's poem, think about how the narrator feels about his instructor's perception of him. Do you perceive anger or resentment on the part of the narrator in "Theme for English B," or a desire for mutual acceptance? Was there ever a time in your schooling when your cultural or ethnic identity influenced the way your instructors or classmates treated you? Has your background ever caused misunderstandings between you and others?

The instructor said, 1

> *Go home and write*
> *a page tonight.*
> *And let that page come out of you—*
> *Then, it will be true.* 2

I wonder if it's that simple?
I am twenty-two, colored, born in Winston-Salem.
I went to school there, then Durham, then here
to this college on the hill above Harlem.
I am the only colored student in my class.   3
The steps from the hill lead down into Harlem,
through a park, then I cross St. Nicholas,
Eighth Avenue, Seventh, and I come to the Y,
the Harlem Branch Y, where I take the elevator
up to my room, sit down, and write this page: 4
It's not easy to know what is true for you or me
at twenty-two, my age. But I guess I'm what
I feel and see and hear, Harlem, I hear you:
hear you, hear me—we two—you, me, talk on this page.
(I hear New York, too.) Me—who?   5

Well, I like to eat, sleep, drink, and be in love.
I like to work, read, learn, and understand life.
I like a pipe for a Christmas present,
or records—Bessie, bop, or Bach.
I guess being colored doesn't make me *not* like   6
the same things other folks like who are other races.
So will my page be colored that I write?

Being me, it will not be white.
But it will be
a part of you, instructor.   7
You are white—
yet a part of me, as I am a part of you.
That's American.
Sometimes perhaps you don't want to be a part of me.
Nor do I often want to be a part of you.   8
But we are, that's true!
As I learn from you,
I guess you learn from me—
although you're older—and white—
and somewhat more free.   9

This is my page for English B.

OPTIONS FOR READING LOGS: "THEME FOR ENGLISH B"

1. Use the double-entry journal technique to comment on powerful lines or passages in "Theme for English B." Draw a vertical line down the middle of your journal page to create two columns. In the left column, copy lines or passages that you particularly like or that you feel are somehow important—for example, "will my page be colored that I write?" In the right column, jot down word associations and comments, being sure to include those from your personal experience as well as from your reading. End your journal entry by selecting one line or phrase and explaining why it held such power or meaning for you.

2. Examine your personal reaction to "Theme for English B" by completing one of the statements in the following list.

    A. "I was confused by _____."
    B. "I was struck by _____."
    C. "I was surprised by _____."

    Refer to particular incidents in the poem and explain your reactions. For example, "I was surprised by the narrator's comment to the instructor that he learns from him and vice versa. I thought for some reason that there would be more hostility toward the instructor in the poem and less understanding on the part of the student. In fact, I was surprised by the student's benevolence." Finish your journal entry with a detailed explanation of your statement.

3. Create an original poem that explores your own personal identity. Start your poem with the following lines:

    The instructor said,
    Go home and write
    a page tonight.
    And let that page come out of you—
    Then, it will be true.

    Then, like Hughes, write your own reflections about who you are. Conclude your poem with the line, "This is my page for English B." End your journal entry by stating the theme of your poem.

OPTIONS FOR WRITING ASSIGNMENTS: "THEME FOR ENGLISH B"

1. Does "Theme for English B" remind you of an event from your own experience in school? Compose a narrative or descriptive essay that focuses

on a remembered classroom event in which you learned something important about who you are. Ask yourself what you learned from that event, and use the answer for your thesis statement. Throughout your essay concentrate on using vivid details, dialogue, and anecdotes to describe the event.

2. Write a letter to the narrator in "Theme for English B." Address the narrator directly about your reaction to the story. Express your own reaction to the narrator's attitude toward his own culture and the culture of the rest of the class, including the teacher. Refer to parts of the poem, such as "Sometimes perhaps you don't want to be a part of me. Nor do I often want to be a part of you." You may choose to criticize or empathize with the narrator. Use whatever tone or approach is most appropriate to express your reaction to the poem's theme of self-identity.

3. In "Theme for English B" the narrator thinks about his personal identity in a predominantly white society and some of the tensions and misunderstandings that might result. Prewrite on the following questions: What might be some of the causes of the narrator's attitude toward Harlem? What are some of the causes of his attitude toward white instructors? What are the causes of the narrator's confusion? As you attempt to trace these causes, note any hidden discoveries you make along the way. Then write an essay focusing on the narrator's personal identity and how it was developed.

4. Write an essay comparing and contrasting "Theme for English B" and "Blackberries." What do both readings illustrate about the difficulties and rewards of the quest for self-discovery? In what ways do the two readings reach similar conclusions? In what ways do they differ?

Summer Beyond Wish

1977

RUSSELL BAKER

 RUSSELL BAKER, born in Virginia in 1925, is an American humorist and journalist. He is well known as the author of "Observer," a *New York Times* column. He received a Pulitzer Prize for commentary in 1979 and another in 1983 for his autobiography *Growing Up*. In "Summer Beyond Wish," Baker recalls a "perfect" boyhood summer when all his desires were fulfilled. Of course, since Baker wrote this recollection as a man looking back on his boyhood, his memory is perhaps tainted by his life's experiences. Yet he does manage to capture an innocent time when life was wonderful and he "didn't know anything [else] to wish for."

As you read this essay, think about whether you have experienced a moment or a time in your life when you felt you had everything you wanted. Would you say it is common or uncommon for us to go through phases in our lives when we feel life just can't get any better? Do you think this feeling is universal?

A long time ago I lived in a crossroads village of northern Virginia and during its summer enjoyed innocence and never knew boredom, although nothing of consequence happened there.

Seven houses of varying lack of distinction constituted the community. A dirt road meandered off toward the mountain where a bootleg still supplied whisky to the men of the countryside, and another dirt road ran down to the creek. My cousin Kenneth and I would sit on the bank and fish with earthworms. One day we killed a copperhead which was basking on a rock nearby. That was unusual.

The heat of summer was mellow and produced sweet scents which lay in the air so damp and rich you could almost taste them. Mornings smelled of purple wisteria, afternoons of the wild roses which tumbled over stone fences, and evenings of honeysuckle.

Even by standards of that time it was a primitive place. There was no electricity. Roads were unpaved. In our house there was no plumbing. The routine of summer days was shaped by these deficiencies. Lacking electric lights, one went early to bed and rose while the dew was still in the grass. Kerosene lamps were cleaned and polished in an early-morning hubbub of women, and children were sent to the spring for fresh water.

This afforded a chance to see whether the crayfish population had   5
multiplied. Later, a trip to the outhouse would afford a chance to daydream in the Sears, Roebuck Catalogue, mostly about shotguns and bicycles.

With no electricity, radio was not available for pacifying the young. One   6
or two people did have radios that operated on mail-order batteries about the size of a present-day car battery, but these were not for children, though occasionally you might be invited in to hear "Amos 'n' Andy."

All I remember about "Amos 'n' Andy" at that time is that it was strange   7
hearing voices come out of furniture. Much later I was advised that listening to "Amos 'n' Andy" was racist and was grateful that I hadn't heard much.

In the summer no pleasures were to be had indoors. Everything of delight   8
occurred in the world outside. In the flowers there were hummingbirds to be seen, tiny wings fluttering so fast that the birds seemed to have no wings at all.

In the heat of mid-afternoon the women would draw the blinds, spread   9
blankets on the floor for coolness and nap, while in the fields the cattle herded together in the shade of spreading trees to escape the sun. Afternoons were absolutely still, yet filled with sounds.

Bees buzzed in the clover. Far away over the fields the chug of an ancient   10
steam-powered threshing machine could be faintly heard. Birds rustled under the tin porch of the roof.

Rising dust along the road from the mountains signaled an approaching   11
event. A car was coming. "Car's coming," someone would say. People emerged from houses. The approaching dust was studied. Guesses were hazarded about whom it might contain.

Then—a big moment in the day—the car would cruise past.   12
"Who was it?"   13
"I didn't get a good look."   14
"It looked like Packy Painter to me."   15
"Couldn't have been Packy. Wasn't his car."   16
The stillness resettled itself as gently as the dust, and you could wander   17
past the henhouse and watch a hen settle herself to perform the mystery of laying an egg. For livelier adventure there was the field that contained the bull. There, one could test his courage by seeing how far he dared venture before running back through the fence.

The men drifted back with the falling sun, steaming with heat and fatigue,   18
and washed in tin basins with water hauled in buckets from the spring. I

knew a few of their secrets, such as who kept his whisky hidden in a mason jar behind the lime barrel, and what they were really doing when they excused themselves from the kitchen and stepped out into the orchard and stayed out there laughing too hard.

I also knew what the women felt about it, though not what they thought.   19
Even then I could see that matters between women and men could become very difficult and, sometimes, so difficult that they spoiled the air of summer.

At sunset people sat on the porches. As dusk deepened, the lightning   20
bugs came out to be caught and bottled. As twilight edged into night, a bat swooped across the road. I was not afraid of bats then, although I feared ghosts, which made the approach of bedtime in a room where even the kerosene lamp would quickly be doused seem terrifying.

I was even more afraid of toads and specifically of the toad which lived   21
under the porch steps and which, everyone assured me, would, if touched, give me warts. One night I was allowed to stay up until the stars were in full command of the sky. A woman of great age was dying in the village and it was considered fit to let the children stay abroad into the night. As four of us sat there we saw a shooting star and someone said, "Make a wish."

I did not know what that meant. I didn't know anything to wish for.   22

OPTIONS FOR READING LOGS: "SUMMER BEYOND WISH"

1. Use the double-entry journal technique to clarify thoughts and discover meaning in "Summer Beyond Wish." Draw a vertical line down the middle of your journal page to create two columns. In the left column, keep a running list of "what" or "why" questions that occur to you as you are reading. Aim for three to five questions, such as "Why does the narrator contradict himself by saying he 'never knew boredom, although nothing of consequence happened there.'" When you finish your list, move to the top of the right column and answer your questions as completely as you can. End your journal entry with a significant discovery you made about the essay: "I discovered that . . ."

2. Draw a picture or a timeline of the events in "Summer Beyond Wish." Then, in words, describe your drawing or timeline, using as many specific details as possible. End your journal entry by stating the theme of the essay.

3. From your own personal life, tell a parallel story that was triggered by "Summer Beyond Wish." Does the essay remind you of some event or particular time in your life? Jot down things that were similar to or different from the events in "Summer Beyond Wish." End your journal entry by stating the theme of the essay.

OPTIONS FOR WRITING ASSIGNMENTS: "SUMMER BEYOND WISH"

1. Develop one of your reading logs for "Summer Beyond Wish" into a more polished piece of writing that explores a moment of personal insight or development in greater range and depth, using an appropriate form (a poem, a fictional story, a personal narrative, or an essay that examines a central idea).
2. Create a conversation between you and the narrator of "Summer Beyond Wish" about the discovery of self-knowledge. Your conversation might take the form of a question-and-answer interview, an argument between two opposing points of view, or a freewheeling exploration of the narrator's ideas and their implications.
3. We often rely on the advice of others in selecting essays to read, and we are influenced by their evaluations. Write a review of "Summer Beyond Wish," clearly assessing the value of the essay as an exploration of how the narrator sees himself. Your evaluation can be positive, negative, or an interesting mixture of positive and negative. Once you are clear about the sort of evaluation you want to make, express it clearly in a thesis statement in your opening paragraph. As you work through your essay, come up with several good reasons that make your judgment convincing. Give supporting evidence from "Summer Beyond Wish" for each reason.
4. Write a formal essay of five or more paragraphs explaining the theme of personal knowledge and its importance in "Summer Beyond Wish." Focus on important parts of Baker's essay about which you have genuine questions, such as "Why does the narrator say that 'nothing of consequence happened in northern Virginia' "? End your introductory paragraph with a thesis statement that clearly presents your central idea. In the remaining paragraphs, quote from the text and refer to specific passages to clarify and support your central argument.

The Hand

1924

COLETTE

 SIDONIE GABRIELLE COLETTE was born in 1873 and died in 1954. Known by her last name only, Colette was a French writer who was well known for her insight into human psychology and her use of vivid sensory images. Many of her writings, like "The Hand," explore feminist issues. She herself was married three times and was known to have had numerous love affairs. The young bride in "The Hand" examines her thoughts about being newly married and comes to a startling discovery about her real feelings toward marriage and its duties.

Is it true that when we first meet people we tend to overlook their weaknesses, but that we become more critical as we get to know them better? Do you think some people who claim to be "in love" are actually in love with the idea of love? As you read this story, ask yourself whether the young woman's changing perceptions of her husband seem reasonable or extreme on her road to self-discovery.

He had fallen asleep on his young wife's shoulder, and she proudly 1 bore the weight of the man's head, blond, ruddy-complexioned, eyes closed. He had slipped his big arm under the small of her slim, adolescent back, and his strong hand lay on the sheet next to the young woman's right elbow. She smiled to see the man's hand emerging there, all by itself and far away from its owner. Then she let her eyes wander over the half-lit room. A veiled conch shed a light across the bed the color of periwinkle.

"Too happy to sleep," she thought. 2

Too excited also, and often surprised by her new state. It had been only 3 two weeks since she had begun to live the scandalous life of a newlywed who tastes the joys of living with someone unknown and with whom she is in love. To meet a handsome, blond young man, recently widowed, good at tennis and rowing, to marry him a month later: her conjugal[1] adventure had

---

1. conjugal: pertaining to marriage

been little more than a kidnapping. So that whenever she lay awake beside her husband, like tonight, she still kept her eyes closed for a long time, then opened them again in order to savor, with astonishment, the blue of the brand-new curtains, instead of the apricot-pink through which the first light of day filtered into the room where she had slept as a little girl.

A quiver ran through the sleeping body lying next to her, and she tight-   4
ened her left arm around her husband's neck with the charming authority exercised by weak creatures. He did not wake up.

"His eyelashes are so long," she said to herself.   5

To herself she also praised his mouth, full and likable, his skin the color   6
of pink brick, and even his forehead, neither noble nor broad, but still smooth and unwrinkled.

Her husband's right hand, lying beside her, quivered in turn, and beneath   7
the curve of her back she felt the right arm, on which her whole weight was resting, come to life.

"I'm so heavy . . . I wish I could get up and turn the light off. But   8
he's sleeping so well . . ."

The arm twisted again, feebly, and she arched her back to make herself   9
lighter.

"It's as if I were lying on some animal," she thought.   10

She turned her head a little on the pillow and looked at the hand lying   11
there next to her.

"It's so big! It really is bigger than my whole head."   12

The light, flowing out from under the edge of a parasol of bluish crystal,   13
spilled up against the hand, and made every contour of the skin apparent, exaggerating the powerful knuckles and the veins engorged by the pressure on the arm. A few red hairs, at the base of the fingers, all curved in the same direction, like ears of wheat in the wind, and the flat nails, whose ridges the nail buffer had not smoothed out, gleamed, coated with pink varnish.

"I'll tell him not to varnish his nails," thought the young wife. "Varnish   14
and pink polish don't go with a hand so . . . a hand that's so . . ."

An electric jolt ran through the hand and spared the young woman from   15
having to find the right adjective. The thumb stiffened itself out, horribly long and spatulate,[2] and pressed tightly against the index finger, so that the hand suddenly took on a vile, apelike appearance.

"Oh!" whispered the young woman, as though faced with something   16
slightly indecent.

The sound of a passing car pierced the silence with a shrillness that   17
seemed luminous. The sleeping man did not wake, but the hand, offended,

2. spatulate: shaped like a spatula; broad or rounded

reared back and tensed up in the shape of a crab and waited, ready for battle. The screeching sound died down and the hand, relaxing gradually, lowered its claws, and became a pliant beast, awkwardly bent, shaken by faint jerks which resembled some sort of agony. The flat, cruel nail of the overlong thumb glistened. A curve in the little finger, which the young woman had never noticed, appeared, and the wallowing hand revealed its fleshy palm like a red belly.

"And I've kissed that hand! . . . How horrible! Haven't I ever looked   18
at it?"

The hand, disturbed by a bad dream, appeared to respond to this startling   19
discovery, this disgust. It regrouped its forces, opened wide, and splayed its tendons, lumps, and red fur like battle dress, then slowly drawing itself in again, grabbed a fistful of the sheet, dug into it with its curved fingers, and squeezed, squeezed with the methodical pleasure of a strangler.

"Oh!" cried the young woman.   20

The hand disappeared and a moment later the big arm, relieved of its   21
burden, became a protective belt, a warm bulwark against all the terrors of night. But the next morning, when it was time for breakfast in bed—hot chocolate and toast—she saw the hand again, with its red hair and red skin, and the ghastly thumb curving out over the handle of a knife.

"Do you want this slice, darling? I'll butter it for you."   22

She shuddered and felt her skin crawl on the back of her arms and down   23
her back.

"Oh, no . . . no . . ."   24

Then she concealed her fear, bravely subdued herself, and, beginning   25
her life of duplicity, of resignation, and of a lowly, delicate diplomacy, she leaned over and humbly kissed the monstrous hand.

OPTIONS FOR READING LOGS: "THE HAND"

1. Use the double-entry journal technique (asking "what" or "why" questions) to discover meaning in "The Hand." Draw a vertical line down the middle of your journal page to create two columns. In the left column, keep a running list of "what" or "why" questions that occur to you as you are reading. Aim for three to five questions, such as "What is the significance of the use of animal imagery in the story?" When you finish your list, move to the top of the right column and answer your questions as completely as you can. To demonstrate that you have a basic under-

standing of the text, end your journal entry by jotting down the main idea of the story.

2. Examine your personal reaction to "The Hand" by completing one of the following statements:

    A.   "I was confused by _____ ."

    B.   "I was struck by _____ ."

    C.   "I was surprised by _____ ."

Refer to particular incidents in the story and explain your reactions. For example, "I was confused by the narrator's quick shift from happiness to disgust." Develop your journal entry by adding detailed explanations from your own experience as well as from the story. Finish the entry with a statement of the story's theme.

3. From your personal life, tell some parallel story that was triggered by "The Hand," even though it may not have been as dramatic. Does the essay remind you of an event or a particular time in your life? Jot down things that were similar to or different from the narrator's reactions in "The Hand." Wrap up your journal entry by stating what your experience taught you about yourself.

OPTIONS FOR WRITING ASSIGNMENTS: "THE HAND"

1. The situation in which the narrator in "The Hand" finds herself seems like a bad dream. Does this story remind you of a puzzling but recurring dream? If so, recreate the dream as a story or a poem, using concrete details, vivid imagery, and, if possible, dialogue. Also explore any explanations you might have for the dream. What might the dream be trying to tell you? End with a generalization about the function of your dream and how it helped you to make a discovery about yourself. If you are not a dreamer, use your imagination to create a story with the elements of a dream.

2. Review your journal entries to see if you can make any connections between this story and any of the earlier readings in this book. Notice whether any similarities or differences are evident between "The Hand" and one of the other stories, poems, or essays. For example, looking at themes, you might see marked similarities between "Dusting" by Julia Alvarez and "The Hand" by Colette. You could combine and expand your journal entries into a more polished piece of writing that explores its subject matter (for example, the role of women) in greater range and

depth. A comparison and contrast essay might be an appropriate mode for this purpose. Begin with a list (two lists for comparison and contrast), develop it into an outline, and use transitional expressions that signal similarities or differences.

3. Write a letter to the narrator in "The Hand." Address the person directly, giving your reaction to the story. You may choose to empathize with the wife or to praise or criticize her submissive attitude.

4. Write a formal essay of five or more paragraphs explaining the meaning of "The Hand." Focus your attention on parts of the story about which you have genuine questions, such as "Is the narrator's feeling of disgust toward the hand normal or abnormal?" End your introductory paragraph with a thesis statement that makes an arguable point about the central meaning of the story. For example, you may wish to take a stand on whether the wife's acceptance of her marital situation is a positive or a negative act. Brainstorm or prewrite to come up with several reasons to support your interpretation. Consider beginning each paragraph in the body of your essay with a topic sentence that states the main idea of that particular paragraph. Throughout your essay, quote from the story and refer to specific passages to clarify and support your central argument. Your concluding paragraph should attempt to wrap up all the ideas and to restate your thesis.

Birches

1916

ROBERT FROST

 ROBERT FROST was born in San Francisco in 1874, and he died in 1963. He is one of the most highly acclaimed twentieth-century American poets and was a four-time winner of the Pulitzer Prize. Often known as the "nature poet," Frost wrote his poems with a simplicity of language that often hides their ambiguity and complexity. In "Birches," he recalls the memory of being a "swinger of birches" during boyhood, and he illustrates a moment of personal insight in which he sees his childhood play as an analogy for life.

In what types of games or activities did you participate as a child? Do you think those games and activities allowed you to practice some of the roles you now fulfill as an adult? Is it true that such childhood games prepare you for "the game of life"? As you read this poem, consider how Frost's childhood game of swinging on trees served as an analogy for life and helped him to discover who he was and what he valued.

When I see birches bend to left and right   1
Across the lines of straighter darker trees,
I like to think some boy's been swinging them.
But swinging doesn't bend them down to stay.
Ice-storms do that. Often you must have seen them   2
Loaded with ice a sunny winter morning
After a rain. They click upon themselves
As the breeze rises, and turn many-colored
As the stir cracks and crazes their enamel.
Soon the sun's warmth makes them shed crystal shells   3
Shattering and avalanching on the snow-crust—
Such heaps of broken glass to sweep away
You'd think the inner dome of heaven had fallen.

They are dragged to the withered bracken by the load,
And they seem not to break; though once they are bowed   4
So low for long, they never right themselves:
You may see their trunks arching in the woods
Years afterwards, trailing their leaves on the ground
Like girls on hands and knees that throw their hair
Before them over their heads to dry in the sun.   5
But I was going to say when Truth broke in
With all her matter-of-fact about the ice-storm
I should prefer to have some boy bend them
As he went out and in to fetch the cows—
Some boy too far from town to learn baseball,   6
Whose only play was what he found himself,
Summer or winter, and could play alone.
One by one he subdued his father's trees
By riding them down over and over again
Until he took the stiffness out of them,   7
And not one but hung limp, not one was left
For him to conquer. He learned all there was
To learn about not launching out too soon
And so not carrying the tree away
Clear to the ground. He always kept his poise[1]   8
To the top branches, climbing carefully
With the same pains you use to fill a cup
Up to the brim, and even above the brim.
Then he flung outward, feet first, with a swish,
Kicking his way down through the air to the ground.   9
So was I once myself a swinger of birches.
And so I dream of going back to be.
It's when I'm weary of considerations,
And life is too much like a pathless wood
Where your face burns and tickles with the cobwebs   10
Broken across it, and one eye is weeping
From a twig's having lashed across it open.
I'd like to get away from earth awhile
And then come back to it and begin over.
May no fate willfully misunderstand me   11
And half grant what I wish and snatch me away
Not to return. Earth's the right place for love:

---

1. poise: state of balance or equilibrium

I don't know where it's likely to go better.
I'd like to go by climbing a birch tree,
And climb black branches up a snow-white trunk   12
Toward heaven, till the tree could bear no more,
But dipped its top and set me down again.
That would be good both going and coming back.
One could do worse than be a swinger of birches.

◆   ◆   ◆

OPTIONS FOR READING LOGS: "BIRCHES"

1. Use the double-entry journal technique (asking "what" or "why" questions) to discover meaning in "Birches." Draw a vertical line down the middle of your journal page to create two columns. In the left column, keep a running list of "what" or "why" questions that occur to you as you are reading. Aim for three to five questions, such as "Why would the narrator prefer to have 'some boy' bend the birches rather than have them bent by ice storms, which are a part of nature?" When you finish your list, move to the top of the right column and answer your questions as completely as you can. To demonstrate that you have a basic understanding of the poem, end your journal entry by jotting down its central idea.

2. Paraphrase the poem by writing it again in your own words. Work your way through the poem, line by line or section by section, explaining the literal meaning of the poem. Along the way, if you notice any symbolic meaning, jot down those ideas, too. Complete your journal entry by stating the theme of the poem.

3. Use your imagination to create some graphics, perhaps by drawing a picture of your version of Frost's birch tree. Your picture should be both literal and symbolic. After you complete your drawing, use words or phrases to label the main parts of the tree, just as you would a diagram. Finally, wrap up your journal entry by writing a paragraph that explains the poem, using as many specific details or images as possible. State the central theme of the poem in your last sentence.

OPTIONS FOR WRITING ASSIGNMENTS: "BIRCHES"

1. Does "Birches" remind you of an event from your own past? Compose a narrative or descriptive essay that focuses on a remembered event from

your life. Write a thesis statement that points out the significance of that event in your life. Throughout your essay, concentrate on using vivid details and descriptions to help recreate your memory. (As an example, you might remember how you passed an entire summer building a tree house and spending a lot of time there with your friends. Your thesis statement might be expressed like this: "That endless summer we spent in our own special tree house taught me an important lesson about friendship.")

2. Create a conversation between you and the narrator of "Birches." Your conversation might take the form of a question-and-answer interview or an argument presenting two opposing points of view. For example, you might ask, "Could one 'do worse than be a swinger of birches'?" or "Is this a poem about a simple childhood memory or does it have a deeper meaning about life and death?" Begin the dialogue with your question. Then start a new paragraph with the narrator's answer. Again, begin a new paragraph for your response to the narrator's answer, and so on, creating a conversation as you move back and forth on the page.

3. We often rely on the advice of others in selecting poems to read, and we also are influenced by their evaluations. Write a review of "Birches," making a clear recommendation as to either the positive or negative value of the poem. Write your evaluation or judgment as a thesis statement. Then come up with several good reasons to make your judgment convincing, each with supporting evidence from the poem.

4. Write a well-developed essay explaining the meaning of "Birches." Focus your attention on parts of the poem about which you have genuine questions, such as, "Why does the narrator contradict himself in the poem?" Begin your essay with an arguable thesis statement, for example, "In 'Birches,' adolescent play represents an important phase in the narrator's life." You will need to quote from the poem and refer to specific passages to clarify and support your central argument.

The Brown Wasps

1971

LOREN EISELEY

 LOREN EISELEY, born in Nebraska in 1907 and died in 1977, was an American anthropologist. Many of his works focus on science and human behavior. In his essay, "The Brown Wasps," Eiseley discovers a hidden part of himself by closely observing the behavior of some confused pigeons and a lost field mouse. He goes on to associate these two incidents with his own deeply personal longing to see a tree he and his father planted many years ago, thousands of miles away. Exploring his own personal knowledge of who he is and his own unique place in the world, Eiseley narrates several personal anecdotes and uses them to evoke thoughtful, even mysterious, generalizations about their significance.

As you read this essay, think about Eiseley's assertion that "the world" changes but we do not. What place do you think of when you hear the word home? *Is it a nearby place or somewhere far away?*

There is a corner in the waiting room of one of the great Eastern stations where women never sit. It is always in the shadow and overhung by rows of lockers. It is, however, always frequented—not so much by genuine travelers as by the dying. It is here that a certain element of the abandoned poor seeks a refuge out of the weather, clinging for a few hours longer to the city that has fathered them. In a precisely similar manner I have seen, on a sunny day in midwinter, a few old brown wasps creep slowly over an abandoned wasp nest in a thicket. Numbed and forgetful and frost-blackened, the hum of the spring hive still resounded faintly in their sodden tissues. Then the temperature would fall and they would drop away into the white oblivion of the snow. Here in the station it is in no way different save that the city is busy in its snows. But the old ones cling to their seats as though these were symbolic and could not be given up. Now and then they sleep, their gray old heads resting with painful awkwardness on the backs of the benches.

Also they are not at rest. For an hour they may sleep in the gasping 2
exhaustion of the ill-nourished and aged who have to walk in the night. Then
a policeman comes by on his round and nudges them upright.

"You can't sleep here," he growls. 3

A strange ritual then begins. An old man is difficult to waken. After a 4
muttered conversation the policeman presses a coin into his hand and passes
fiercely along the benches prodding and gesturing toward the door. In his
wake, like birds rising and settling behind the passage of a farmer through a
cornfield, the men totter up, move a few paces and subside once more upon
the benches.

One man, after a slight, apologetic lurch, does not move at all. Tubercu- 5
larly thin, he sleeps on steadily. The policeman does not look back. To him,
too, this has become a ritual. He will not have to notice it again officially
for another hour.

Once in a while one of the sleepers will not awake. Like the brown wasps, 6
he will have had his wish to die in the great droning center of the hive rather
than in some lonely room. It is not so bad here with the shuffle of footsteps
and the knowledge that there are others who share the bad luck of the world.
There are also the whistles and the sounds of everyone, everyone in the
world, starting on journeys. Amidst so many journeys somebody is bound
to come out all right. Somebody.

Maybe it was on a like thought that the brown wasps fell away from the 7
old paper nest in the thicket. You hold till the last, even if it is only to a
public seat in a railroad station. You want your place in the hive more than
you want a room or a place where the aged can be eased gently out of the
way. It is the place that matters, the place at the heart of things. It is life that
you want, that bruises your gray old head with the hard chairs; a man has a
right to his place.

But sometimes the place is lost in the years behind us. Or sometimes it 8
is a thing of air, a kind of vaporous distortion above a heap of rubble. We
cling to a time and place because without them man is lost, not only man
but life. This is why the voices, real or unreal, which speak from the floating
trumpets at spiritualist seances are so unnerving. They are voices out of
nowhere whose only reality lies in their ability to stir the memory of a living
person with some fragment of the past. Before the medium's cabinet both
the dead and the living revolve endlessly about an episode, a place, an event
that has already been engulfed by time.

This feeling runs deep in life; it brings stray cats running over endless 9
miles, and birds homing from the ends of the earth. It is as though all living
creatures, and particularly the more intelligent, can survive only by fixing or
transforming a bit of time into space or by securing a bit of space with its

objects immortalized and made permanent in time. For example, I once saw, on a flower pot in my own living room, the efforts of a field mouse to build a remembered field. I have lived to see this episode repeated in a thousand guises, and since I have spent a large portion of my life in the shade of a nonexistent tree, I think I am entitled to speak for the field mouse.

One day as I cut across the field which at that time extended on one   10 side of our suburban shopping center, I found a giant slug feeding from a runnel of pink ice cream in an abandoned Dixie cup. I could see his eyes telescope and protrude in a kind of dim, uncertain ecstasy as his dark body bunched and elongated in the curve of the cup. Then, as I stood there at the edge of the concrete, contemplating the slug, I began to realize it was like standing on a shore where a different type of life creeps up and fumbles tentatively among the rocks and sea wrack. It knows its place and will only creep so far until something changes. Little by little as I stood there I began to see more of this shore that surrounds the place of man. I looked with sudden care and attention at things I had been running over thoughtlessly for years. I even waded out a short way into the grass and the wild-rose thickets to see more. A huge black-belted bee went droning by and there were some indistinct scurryings in the underbrush.

Then I came to a sign which informed me that this field was to be the   11 site of a new Wanamaker suburban store. Thousands of obscure lives were about to perish, the spores of puffballs would go smoking off to new fields, and the bodies of little white-footed mice would be crunched under the inexorable wheels of the bulldozers. Life disappears or modifies its appearances so fast that everything takes on an aspect of illusion—a momentary fizzing and boiling with smoke rings, like pouring dissident chemicals into a retort. Here man was advancing, but in a few years his plaster and bricks would be disappearing once more into the insatiable maw of the clover. Being of an archaeological cast of mind, I thought of this fact with an obscure sense of satisfaction and waded back through the rose thickets to the concrete parking lot. As I did so, a mouse scurried ahead of me, frightened of my steps if not of that ominous Wanamaker sign. I saw him vanish in the general direction of my apartment house, his little body quivering with fear in the great open sun on the blazing concrete. Blinded and confused, he was running straight away from his field. In another week scores would follow him.

I forgot the episode then and went home to the quiet of my living room.   12 It was not until a week later, letting myself into the apartment, that I realized I had a visitor. I am fond of plants and had several ferns standing on the floor in pots to avoid the noon glare by the south window.

As I snapped on the light and glanced carelessly around the room, I saw   13 a little heap of earth on the carpet and a scrabble of pebbles that had been kicked merrily over the edge of one of the flower pots. To my astonishment I discovered a full-fledged burrow delving downward among the fern roots. I waited silently. The creature who had made the burrow did not appear. I remembered the wild field then, and the flight of the mice. No house mouse, no *Mus domesticus,* had kicked up this little heap of earth or sought refuge under a fern root in a flower pot. I thought of the desperate little creature I had seen fleeing from the wild-rose thicket. Through intricacies of pipes and attics, he, or one of his fellows, had climbed to this high green solitary room. I could visualize what had occurred. He had an image in his head, a world of seed pods and quiet, of green sheltering leaves in the dim light among the weed stems. It was the only world he knew and it was gone.

Somehow in his flight he had found his way to this room with drawn   14
shades where no one would come till nightfall. And here he had smelled green leaves and run quickly up the flower pot to dabble his paws in common earth. He had even struggled half the afternoon to carry his burrow deeper and had failed. I examined the hole, but no whiskered twitching face appeared. He was gone. I gathered up the earth and refilled the burrow. I did not expect to find traces of him again.

Yet for three nights thereafter I came home to the darkened room and   15
my ferns to find the dirt kicked gaily about the rug and the burrow reopened, though I was never able to catch the field mouse within it. I dropped a little food about the mouth of the burrow, but it was never touched. I looked under beds or sat reading with one ear cocked for rustlings in the ferns. It was all in vain; I never saw him. Probably he ended in a trap in some other tenant's room.

But before he disappeared I had come to look hopefully for his evening   16
burrow. About my ferns there had begun to linger the insubstantial vapor of an autumn field, the distilled essence, as it were, of a mouse brain in exile from its home. It was a small dream, like our dreams, carried a long and weary journey along pipes and through spider webs, past holes over which loomed the shadows of waiting cats, and finally, desperately, into this room where he had played in the shuttered daylight for an hour among the green ferns on the floor. Every day these invisible dreams pass us on the street, or rise from beneath our feet, or look out upon us from beneath a bush.

Some years ago the old elevated railway in Philadelphia was torn down   17
and replaced by a subway system. This ancient El with its barnlike stations containing nut-vending machines and scattered food scraps had, for generations, been the favorite feeding ground of flocks of pigeons, generally one flock to a station along the route of the El. Hundreds of pigeons were dependent upon the system. They flapped in and out of its stanchions and steel work or gathered in watchful little audiences about the feet of anyone

who rattled the peanut-vending machines. They even watched people who jingled change in their hands, and prospected for food under the feet of the crowds who gathered between trains. Probably very few among the waiting people who tossed a crumb to an eager pigeon realized that this El was like a food-bearing river, and that the life which haunted its banks was dependent upon the running of the trains with their human freight.

I saw the river stop.   18

The time came when the underground tubes were ready; the traffic was   19
transferred to a realm unreachable by pigeons. It was like a great river subsiding suddenly into desert sands. For a day, for two days, pigeons continued to circle over the El or stand close to the red vending machines. They were patient birds, and surely this great river which had flowed through the lives of unnumbered generations was merely suffering from some momentary drought.

They listened for the familiar vibrations that had always heralded an   20
approaching train: they flapped hopefully about the head of an occasional workman walking along the steel runways. They passed from one empty station to another, all the while growing hungrier. Finally they flew away.

I thought I had seen the last of them about the El, but there was a revival   21
and it provided a curious instance of the memory of living things for a way of life or a locality that has long been cherished. Some weeks after the El was abandoned workmen began to tear it down. I went to work every morning by one particular station, and the time came when the demolition crews reached this spot. Acetylene torches showered passersby with sparks, pneumatic drills hammered at the base of the structure, and a blind man who, like the pigeons, had clung with his cup to a stairway leading to the change booth, was forced to give up his place.

It was then, strangely, momentarily, one morning that I witnessed the   22
return of a little band of the familiar pigeons. I even recognized one or two members of the flock that had lived around this particular station before they were dispersed into the streets. They flew bravely in and out among the sparks and the hammers and the shouting workmen. They had returned—and they had returned because the hubbub of the wreckers had convinced them that the river was about to flow once more. For several hours they flapped in and out through the empty windows, nodding their heads and watching the fall of girders with attentive little eyes. By the following morning the station was reduced to some burned-off stanchions in the street. My bird friends had gone. It was plain, however, that they retained a memory for an insubstantial structure now compounded of air and time. Even the blind man clung to it. Someone had provided him with a chair, and he sat at the same

corner staring sightlessly at an invisible stairway where, so far as he was concerned, the crowds were still ascending to the trains.

I have said my life has been passed in the shade of a nonexistent tree, so   23
that such sights do not offend me. Prematurely I am one of the brown wasps and I often sit with them in the great droning hive of the station, dreaming sometimes of a certain tree. It was planted sixty years ago by a boy with a bucket and a toy spade in a little Nebraska town. That boy was myself. It was a cottonwood sapling and the boy remembered it because of some words spoken by his father and because everyone died or moved away who was supposed to wait and grow old under its shade. The boy was passed from hand to hand, but the tree for some intangible reason had taken root in his mind. It was under its branches that he sheltered; it was from this tree that his memories, which are my memories, led away into the world.

After sixty years the mood of the brown wasps grows heavier upon one.   24
During a long inward struggle I thought it would do me good to go and look upon that actual tree. I found a rational excuse in which to clothe this madness. I purchased a ticket and at the end of two thousand miles I walked another mile to an address that was still the same. The house had not been altered.

I came close to the white picket fence and reluctantly, with great effort,   25
looked down the long vista of the yard. There was nothing there to see. For sixty years that cottonwood had been growing in my mind. Season by season its seeds had been floating farther on the hot prairie winds. We had planted it lovingly there, my father and I, because he had a great hunger for soil and live things growing, and because none of these things had long been ours to protect. We had planted the little sapling and watered it faithfully, and I remembered that I had run out with my small bucket to drench its roots the day we moved away. And all the years since it had been growing in my mind, a huge tree that somehow stood for my father and the love I bore him. I took a grasp on the picket fence and forced myself to look again.

A boy with the hard bird eye of youth pedaled a tricycle slowly up beside   26
me.

"What'cha lookin' at?" he asked curiously.   27

"A tree," I said.   28

"What for?" he said.   29

"It isn't there," I said, to myself mostly, and began to walk away at a   30
pace just slow enough not to seem to be running.

"What isn't there?" the boy asked. I didn't answer. It was obvious I was   31
attached by a thread to a thing that had never been there, or certainly not for long. Something that had to be held in the air, or sustained in the mind,

because it was part of my orientation in the universe and I could not survive without it. There was more than an animal's attachment to a place. There was something else, the attachment of the spirit to a grouping of events in time; it was part of our morality.

So I had come home at last, driven by a memory in the brain as surely   32
as the field mouse who had delved long ago into my flower pot or the pigeons flying forever amidst the rattle of nut-vending machines. These, the burrow under the greenery in my living room and the red-bellied bowls of peanuts now hovering in midair in the minds of pigeons, were all part of an elusive world that existed nowhere and yet everywhere. I looked once at the real world about me while the persistent boy pedaled at my heels.

It was without meaning, though my feet took a remembered path. In   33
sixty years the house and street had rotted out of my mind. But the tree, the tree that no longer was, that had perished in its first season, bloomed on in my individual mind, unblemished as my father's words. "We'll plant a tree here, son, and we're not going to move any more. And when you're an old, old man you can sit under it and think how we planted it here, you and me, together."

I began to outpace the boy on the tricycle.   34

"Do you live here, Mister?" he shouted after me suspiciously. I took a   35
firm grasp on airy nothing—to be precise, on the bole of a great tree. "I do," I said. I spoke for myself, one field mouse, and several pigeons. We were all out of touch but somehow permanent. It was the world that had changed.

OPTIONS FOR READING LOGS: "THE BROWN WASPS"

1. Use the double-entry journal technique (asking " what" or "why" questions) to discover meaning in "The Brown Wasps." Draw a vertical line down the middle of your journal page to create two columns. In the left column, keep a running list of "what" or "why" questions that occur to you as you are reading. Aim for three to five questions, such as "What is the point of the mouse anecdote?" or "Why are we . . . all out of touch but somehow permanent?" When you finish your list, move to the top of the right column and answer your questions as completely as you can. To demonstrate that you have a basic understanding of the essay, end your journal entry by jotting down its main idea.

2. Tell your own personal story that was triggered by the text. Do Eiseley's anecdotes about the wasps, the field mouse, the pigeons, and his own journey home cause you to reflect on some aspect of your own experience? In what ways is your own story similar to or different from Eiseley's? Wrap up your journal entry by clarifying what you learned from reading "The Brown Wasps."

3. Draw a concept (idea) map that explores the meaning of "The Brown Wasps." As you recall vivid details and experiences from Eiseley's essay (for example, the tired old men sitting in the train station, the confused mouse in the flowerpot, and Eiseley's own compulsive trip into his past), draw balloons, clusters, flow charts, timelines, outlines, or diagrams to represent these details and their interconnections. After you complete your concept map, write a brief journal entry that explains your map. End with a statement of the central theme of "The Brown Wasps."

OPTIONS FOR WRITING ASSIGNMENTS: "THE BROWN WASPS"

1. Develop one of your reading logs for "The Brown Wasps" into a more polished piece of writing that explores a moment of personal insight or development in greater range and depth, using an appropriate form (a poem, a fictional story, a personal narrative, or an essay that examines a central idea).

2. Does anything in "The Brown Wasps" remind you of something from your own past? As a child, did you ever have an experience that stayed in your mind for many years until you finally grew to understand its significance? Compose a narrative or descriptive essay that focuses on a remembered event from your life. Write a thesis statement pointing out the significance of that event in your life. Throughout your essay, concentrate on using vivid details to describe the event.

3. As Eiseley does in "The Brown Wasps," recall a time and place in your own past when you discovered something important that lead you to a better understanding of who you are. Begin with a generalization about yourself. For example, "My basic values were formed in my middle school years when we lived in a small town in Kansas." Use several anecdotes—as Eiseley does with the pigeons, the field mouse, and the tree—to illustrate the truth of your generalization. Develop each anecdote fully and be sure that each serves as a good example for supporting your thesis statement.

4. Were you initially puzzled by Eiseley's message in "The Brown Wasps"? It is, indeed, a complex and ultimately very personal expression of the

value of the past in our minds, our reaction to the ever-changing world we all inhabit, and our search for truth and permanence in an unpredictable world. Prewrite to come up with several reasons to support your interpretation. Then write a formal essay of five or more paragraphs explaining the meaning of "The Brown Wasps." End your introductory paragraph with a thesis statement that makes an arguable point about the central meaning of the essay. Consider beginning each paragraph in the body of your essay with a topic sentence that states the main idea of that particular paragraph. Throughout your essay, quote from the essay and refer to specific passages to clarify and support your central argument. Your concluding paragraph should attempt to wrap up all the ideas and to restate your thesis.

The Grave

1944

KATHERINE ANNE PORTER

 KATHERINE ANNE PORTER, a short-story writer and novelist, was born in Texas in 1890 and died in 1980. She was famous for her short fiction. Although she had no formal education, she received wide acclaim as a writer, and her short-story collection won the Pulitzer Prize for fiction in 1966.

In "The Grave," Porter narrates the experience of a young girl, Miranda, who makes some special discoveries about herself while hunting with her brother. Exploring an empty graveyard and shooting a pregnant rabbit seem to teach her more about life than she realizes at the time. At one point, her brother says, "Listen now. Now you listen to me, and don't ever forget. Don't you ever tell a living soul that you saw this. Don't tell a soul. Don't tell Dad because I'll get into trouble. He'll say I'm leading you into things you ought not to do." He swears her to secrecy.

Our childhood experiences are often huge unconscious reservoirs of unexamined life that can profoundly shape who we are and what we become. Can you recall an early childhood experience that suddenly resurfaced in your mind years later "without warning"? Why do you think some incidents lie so deeply buried, only to come rushing forward at the hint of a long-forgotten fragrance or a particular sound or sight?

The grandfather, dead for more than thirty years, had been twice   1 disturbed in his long repose by the constancy and possessiveness of his widow. She removed his bones first to Louisiana and then to Texas as if she had set out to find her own burial place, knowing well she would never return to the places she had left. In Texas she set up a small cemetery in a corner of her first farm, and as the family connection grew, and oddments[1] of relations came over from Kentucky to settle, it contained at last about twenty graves. After the grandmother's death, part of her land

---

1. oddments: odd articles; bits; remnants

was to be sold for the benefit of certain of her children, and the cemetery happened to lie in the part set aside for sale. It was necessary to take up the bodies and bury them again in the family plot in the big new public cemetery, where the grandmother had been buried. At last her husband was to lie beside her for eternity, as she had planned.

The family cemetery had been a pleasant small neglected garden of   2
tangled rose bushes and ragged cedar trees and cypress, the simple flat stones rising out of uncropped sweet-smelling wild grass. The graves were lying open and empty one burning day when Miranda and her brother Paul, who often went together to hunt rabbits and doves, propped their twenty-two Winchester rifles carefully against the rail fence, climbed over, and explored among the graves. She was nine years old and he was twelve.

They peered into the pits all shaped alike with such purposeful accuracy,   3
and looking at each other with pleased adventurous eyes, they said in solemn tones: "These were graves!" trying by words to shape a special, suitable emotion in their minds, but they felt nothing except an agreeable thrill of wonder: they were seeing a new sight, doing something they had not done before. In them both there was also a small disappointment at the entire commonplaceness of the actual spectacle. Even if it had once contained a coffin for years upon years, when the coffin was gone a grave was just a hole in the ground. Miranda leaped into the pit that had held her grandfather's bones. Scratching around aimlessly and pleasurably as any young animal, she scooped up a lump of earth and weighed it in her palm. It had a pleasantly sweet, corrupt smell, being mixed with cedar needles and small leaves, and as the crumbs fell apart, she saw a silver dove no larger than a hazel nut, with spread wings and a neat fan-shaped tail. The breast had a deep round hollow in it. Turning it up to the fierce sunlight, she saw that the inside of the hollow was cut in little whorls.[2] She scrambled out, over the pile of loose earth that had fallen back into one end of the grave, calling to Paul that she had found something, he must guess what . . . His head appeared smiling over the rim of another grave. He waved a closed hand at her. "I've got something too!" They ran to compare treasures, making a game of it, so many guesses each, all wrong, and a final showdown with opened palms. Paul had found a thin wide gold ring carved with intricate flowers and leaves. Miranda was smitten at sight of the ring and wished to have it. Paul seemed more impressed by the dove. They made a trade, with some little bickering. After he had got the dove in his hand, Paul said, "Don't you know what this is? This is a screw head for a *coffin!* . . . I'll bet nobody else in the world has one like this!"

2. whorls: circular arrangements of like parts

Miranda glanced at it without covetousness. She had the gold ring on   4
her thumb; it fitted perfectly. "Maybe we ought to go now," she said, "maybe
one of the niggers'll see us and tell somebody." They knew the land had
been sold, the cemetery was no longer theirs, and they felt like trespassers.
They climbed back over the fence, slung their rifles loosely under their arms—
they had been shooting at targets with various kinds of firearms since they
were seven years old—and set out to look for the rabbits and doves or
whatever small game might happen along. On these expeditions Miranda
always followed at Paul's heels along the path, obeying instructions about
handling her gun when going through fences; learning how to stand it up
properly so it would not slip and fire unexpectedly; how to wait her time for
a shot and not just bang away in the air without looking, spoiling shots for
Paul, who really could hit things if given a chance. Now and then, in her
excitement at seeing birds whizz up suddenly before her face, or a rabbit
leap across her very toes, she lost her head, and almost without sighting she
flung her rifle up and pulled the trigger. She hardly ever hit any sort of mark.
She had no proper sense of hunting at all. Her brother would be often
completely disgusted with her. "You don't care whether you get your bird
or not," he said. "That's no way to hunt." Miranda could not understand
his indignation. She had seen him smash his hat and yell with fury when
he had missed his aim. "What I like about shooting," said Miranda, with
exasperating inconsequence, "is pulling the trigger and hearing the noise."

"Then by golly," said Paul, "whyn't you go back to the range and shoot   5
at bulls-eyes?"

"I'd just as soon," said Miranda, "only like this, we walk around more."   6

"Well, you just stay behind and stop spoiling my shots," said Paul, who,   7
when he made a kill, wanted to be certain he had made it. Miranda, who
alone brought down a bird once in twenty rounds, always claimed as her
own any game they got when they fired at the same moment. It was tiresome
and unfair and her brother was sick of it.

"Now, the first dove we see, or the first rabbit, is mine," he told her.   8
"And the next will be yours. Remember that and don't get smarty."

"What about snakes?" asked Miranda idly. "Can I have the first snake?"   9

Waving her thumb gently and watching her gold ring glitter, Miranda   10
lost interest in shooting. She was wearing her summer roughing outfit: dark
blue overalls, a light blue shirt, a hired-man's straw hat, and thick brown
sandals. Her brother had the same outfit except his was a sober hickorynut
color. Ordinarily Miranda preferred her overalls to any other dress, though
it was making rather a scandal in the countryside, for the year was 1903, and
in the back country the law of female decorum had teeth in it. Her father

had been criticized for letting his girls dress like boys and go careening around astride barebacked horses. Big sister Maria, the really independent and fearless one, in spite of her rather affected ways, rode at a dead run with only a rope knotted around her horse's nose. It was said the motherless family was running down, with the grandmother no longer there to hold it together. It was known that she had discriminated against her son Harry in her will, and that he was in straits about money. Some of his old neighbors reflected with vicious satisfaction that now he would probably not be so stiffnecked, nor have any more high-stepping horses either. Miranda knew this, though she could not say how. She had met along the road old women of the kind who smoked corn-cob pipes, who had treated her grandmother with most sincere respect. They slanted their gummy old eyes side-ways at the granddaughter and said, "Ain't you ashamed of yoself, Missy? It's against the Scriptures to dress like that. Whut yo Pappy thinkin about?" Miranda, with her powerful social sense, which was like a fine set of antennae radiating from every pore of her skin, would feel ashamed because she knew well it was rude and ill-bred to shock anybody, even bad-tempered old crones, though she had faith in her father's judgment and was perfectly comfortable in the clothes. Her father said, "They're just what you need, and they'll save your dresses for school. . . ." This sounded quite simple and natural to her. She had been brought up in rigorous economy. Wastefulness was vulgar. It was also a sin. These were truths; she had heard them repeated many times and never once disputed.

Now the ring, shining with the serene purity of fine gold on her rather grubby thumb, turned her feelings against her overalls and sockless feet, toes sticking through the thick brown leather straps. She wanted to go back to the farmhouse, take a good cold bath, dust herself with plenty of Maria's violet talcum powder—provided Maria was not present to object, of course—put on the thinnest, most becoming dress she owned, with a big sash, and sit in a wicker chair under the trees. . . . These things were not all she wanted, of course; she had vague stirrings of desire for luxury and a grand way of living which could not take precise form in her imagination but were founded on family legend of past wealth and leisure. These immediate comforts were what she could have, and she wanted them at once. She lagged rather far behind Paul, and once she thought of just turning back without a word and going home. She stopped, thinking that Paul would never do that to her, and so she would have to tell him. When a rabbit leaped, she let Paul have it without dispute. He killed it with one shot.

When she came up with him, he was already kneeling, examining the wound, the rabbit trailing from his hands. "Right through the head," he said complacently, as if he had aimed for it. He took out his sharp, competent bowie knife and started to skin the body. He did it very cleanly and quickly. Uncle Jimbilly knew how to prepare the skins so that Miranda always had fur coats for her dolls, for though she never cared much for her dolls she liked seeing them in fur coats. The children knelt facing each other over the dead animal. Miranda watched admiringly while her brother stripped the skin away as if he were taking off a glove. The flayed flesh emerged dark scarlet, sleek, firm: Miranda with thumb and finger felt the long fine muscles with the silvery flat strips binding them to the joints. Brother lifted the oddly bloated belly. "Look," he said, in a low amazed voice. "It was going to have young ones."

Very carefully he slit the thin flesh from the center ribs to the flanks, and a scarlet bag appeared. He slit again and pulled the bag open, and there lay a bundle of tiny rabbits, each wrapped in a thin scarlet veil. The brother pulled these off and there they were, dark gray, their sleek wet down lying in minute even ripples, like a baby's head just washed, their unbelievably small delicate ears folded close, their little blind faces almost featureless. 13

Miranda said, "Oh, I want to *see*," under her breath. She looked and looked—excited but not frightened, for she was accustomed to the sight of animals killed in hunting—filled with pity and astonishment and a kind of shocked delight in the wonderful little creatures for their own sakes, they were so pretty. She touched one of them ever so carefully, "Ah, there's blood running over them," she said and began to tremble without knowing why. Yet she wanted most deeply to see and to know. Having seen, she felt at once as if she had known all along. The very memory of her former ignorance faded, she had always known just this. No one had ever told her anything outright, she had been rather unobservant of the animal life around her because she was so accustomed to animals. They seemed simply disorderly and unaccountably rude in their habits, but altogether natural and not very interesting. Her brother had spoken as if he had known about everything all along. He may have seen all this before. He had never said a word to her, but she knew now a part at least of what he knew. She understood a little of the secret, formless intuitions in her own mind and body, which had been clearing up, taking form, so gradually and so steadily she had not realized that she was learning what she had to know. Paul said cautiously, as if he were talking about something forbidden: "They were just about to be born." His voice dropped on the last word. "I know," said Miranda, "like kittens. I know, like babies." She was quietly and terribly agitated, standing again with her rifle under her arm, looking down at the bloody heap. "I don't want the skin," she said. "I won't have it." Paul buried the young rabbits again in their mother's body, wrapped the skin around her, carried her to a clump of sage bushes, and hid her away. He came out again at once and said 14 to Miranda, with an eager friendliness, a confidential tone quite unusual in him, as if he were taking her into an important secret on equal terms: "Listen now. Now you listen to me, and don't ever forget. Don't you ever tell a living soul that you saw this. Don't tell a soul. Don't tell Dad because I'll get into trouble. He'll say I'm leading you into things you ought not to do. He's always saying that. So now don't you go and forget and blab out sometime the way you're always doing. . . . Now, that's secret. Don't you tell."

Miranda never told, she did not even wish to tell anybody. She thought about   15
the whole worrisome affair with confused unhappiness for a few days. Then it sank quietly into her mind and was heaped over by accumulated thousands of impressions, for nearly twenty years. One day she was picking her path among the puddles and crushed refuse of a market street in a strange city of a strange country, when without warning, plain and clear in its true colors as if she looked through a frame upon a scene that had not stirred nor changed since the moment it happened, the episode of that far-off day leaped from its burial place before her mind's eye. She was so reasonlessly horrified she halted suddenly staring, the scene before her eyes dimmed for the vision back of them. An Indian vendor had held up before her a tray of dyed sugar sweets, in the shapes of all kinds of small creatures: birds, baby chicks, baby rabbits, lambs, baby pigs. They were in gay colors and smelled of vanilla, maybe. . . . It was a very hot day and the smell in the market, with its piles of raw flesh and wilting flowers, was like the mingled sweetness and corruption she had smelled that other day in the empty cemetery at home: the day she had remembered always until now vaguely as the time she and her brother had found treasure in the opened graves. Instantly upon this thought the dreadful vision faded, and she saw clearly her brother, whose childhood face she had forgotten, standing again in the blazing sunshine, again twelve years old, a pleased sober smile in his eyes, turning the silver dove over and over in his hands.

OPTIONS FOR READING LOGS: "THE GRAVE"

1. Use your creative imagination to draft a completely new ending for "The Grave." Try to stay focused on the theme of personal knowledge, but experiment freely with dialogue, allowing the characters to converse with one another.

2. Writers often use images or symbols to represent an idea or concept and to give a deeper, more important value or interpretation than is at first apparent. Use the double-entry technique to clarify the meaning of some of the powerful images or symbols in Porter's short story, "The Grave." Draw a vertical line down the middle of your journal page and, in the left column, copy a list of all the images or symbols you identify in the story, such as the ring Miranda's brother discovers in the old grave. Then, in the right column, jot down possible interpretations, personal associations, or explanatory comments. End your journal entry with a brief statement about a significant discovery you made by examining "The Grave" closely.

3. Your immediate, personal reaction to a story often begins a process that will lead you to an important insight. For example, readers of "The Grave" are often struck by the two children's discovery of treasures in the old family grave, or they are surprised by Paul's strong reaction to seeing the dead pregnant rabbit and his insistence on keeping it a secret. Complete one of the following statements by referring to a particular incident in "The Grave":

   A. "I was confused by _____."
   B. "I was struck by _____."
   C. "I was surprised by _____."

   After completing one of the statements, continue your journal entry with a detailed explanation of your personal reaction and explain how it provides some insight into the theme of "The Grave."

4. Use clustering to draw a concept (idea) map that explores the meaning of "The Grave." Recall vivid details and experiences from Porter's short story (the old, abandoned family graves, the silver dove-shaped screwhead, the pregnant rabbit, and Miranda's sudden memory twenty years later). Draw balloons, clusters, flowcharts, symbols, timelines, outlines, or diagrams to examine the story. When you have created your concept map, write a brief entry that explains your map. Conclude by stating the central theme of "The Grave."

OPTIONS FOR WRITING ASSIGNMENTS: "THE GRAVE"

1. Does anything in "The Grave" remind you of something you learned about yourself by recalling something from your own past? As a child, did you ever have an experience that you did not fully comprehend at

the time but understood at some later time? Compose a narrative or descriptive essay that focuses on a remembered person, place, or event. Express your main point in a clear thesis statement at the end of your opening paragraph. Throughout your essay, concentrate on using vivid details, dialogue, and descriptions to help recreate your memories.

2. Did you react strongly with curiosity, sympathy, or anger to what Miranda learns about herself in "The Grave"? Write a letter, either to the author or to one of the characters in the story, addressing the person directly and giving your reaction to Miranda's personal knowledge. Use the rich and varied possibilities of the informal letter form to express your own point of view—to complement, criticize, console, or inquire. Use whatever tone is most appropriate to express your reaction to the text.

3. We often rely on the advice of others in selecting things to read and evaluating their worth. What did you think of "The Grave" as a story about who we are? Would you recommend the story to a friend? Write a critical review giving a clear appraisal of the value of "The Grave" as a story of self-discovery. In your introductory paragraph, include a thesis statement that makes your judgment clear to your reader. Your evaluation can be positive, negative, or some interesting mixture of positive and negative. Once you are clear on the sort of evaluation or judgment you want to make, you need to state some good reasons in the remaining paragraphs, supporting each with evidence that makes your judgment convincing.

The Street

OCTAVIO PAZ

 Born in 1914, OCTAVIO PAZ is a Mexican poet, essayist, and literary critic. In 1990 he won the Nobel Prize for literature. His curious poem, "The Street," has the quality of a lucid dream—a dream in which all the details are clearly recalled. The narrator of the poem seems to be trapped in a maze of darkened streets from which there is no escape, and the man before him and the man behind him are identified only as "nobody." The narrator is on a journey, but the journey only leads "forever to the street / where nobody waits for, nobody follows me." In recounting this dreamlike experience, the poet seems to be attempting to communicate a condition, a situation life has imposed on the speaker of the poem. The journey to find oneself is constantly thwarted by the fear of being a mere "nobody."

As you read "The Street," ask yourself what personal knowledge the speaker of the poem is revealing. Would you characterize it as nightmarish, humorous, baffling, despairing, or ironic?

A long silent street. 1
I walk in blackness and I stumble and fall
and rise, and I walk blind, my feet
stepping on silent stones and dry leaves.
Someone behind me also stepping on stones, leaves: 5
if I slow down, he slows;
if I run, he runs. I turn: nobody.
Everything dark and doorless.
Turning and turning among these corners
which lead forever to the street 10
where nobody waits for, nobody follows me,

where I pursue a man who stumbles,
and rises and says when he sees me: nobody.

◈ ◈ ◈

OPTIONS FOR READING LOGS: "THE STREET"

1. Use the double-entry journal technique to clarify the meaning of some of the powerful lines in "The Street." Draw a vertical line down the middle of your journal page and use the left column to copy phrases or lines that you particularly like or are even puzzled by, such as "Everything dark and doorless . . ." or "I walk blind . . ." Then, in the right column, jot down possible interpretations, personal associations, or explanatory comments. To demonstrate that you have reached a basic understanding of the poem, end your journal entry by stating its central idea.

2. Write a creative response by coming up with an original poem of your own. If you have trouble getting started, copy the first line of the poem, "A long silent street," as your own first line. Allow your own poem to grow in any way you wish: for example, you could develop it as a dream, a private memory, or an invented story. Use rhymes if you wish, but consider experimenting with free verse, as illustrated by "The Street." If ending your poem becomes a problem, try steering it toward the last line of Paz's poem: "and rises and says when he sees me: nobody." Then begin again, this time substituting words or phrases until every line in your poem is original. When you finish, briefly explain why "The Street" triggered this particular creative response.

3. Tell your own personal story that "The Street" helped you to recall. What is the message of Paz's mysterious poem: human loneliness, private frustrations, pointless fears, a loss of personal identity? Does the theme of the poem cause you to reflect on some dream or experience you have had? In what ways is your own experience similar to or different from the one Paz describes? End your entry by clarifying what you learned from reading "The Street."

OPTIONS FOR WRITING ASSIGNMENTS: "THE STREET"

1. Develop your reading log entry on "The Street" into a more polished piece of writing that explores its subject matter in greater range and

depth, using an appropriate form—a poem, a fictional story, a personal narrative, or an essay that examines a central idea.

2. "The Street" could be seen as having some of the characteristics of a dream: it has clear, vivid imagery, yet it seems unreal and mysterious, possibly containing a hidden meaning. Have you ever had a puzzling recurring dream or a dream in which you were asleep but you actually knew you were dreaming? If so, capture your dream as a story or poem using concrete details, vivid imagery, and, if possible, dialogue. Also, explore the value of the dream in defining who you are and what you value. Can you make any generalizations about yourself from the dream?

3. What personal knowledge do you think the poet wants readers to gain from this strange poem? If you could meet with Octavio Paz, the author of "The Street," to ask questions and give your ideas and interpretations, what would you say to him? How do you think he would respond? Create a conversation between you and Octavio Paz in the form of a question-and-answer interview, an argument between two opposing points of view, or a freewheeling exploration of his ideas about personal identity and how we discover who we are.

4. If you were asked what "The Street" means and how it teaches us to know ourselves better, what would you say? Simply reading a text is often not enough to appreciate its full range of meaning. We often need to reread, think about, discuss, and write about a poem before we fully appreciate its meaning. Explain the meaning of "The Street" in a formal essay of five or more paragraphs. Focus your attention on parts of the poem about which you have genuine questions. Is the poem about a fear of death, unnamed fears, or human isolation? End your introductory paragraph with a thesis statement that makes an arguable point about the central meaning of the poem. In the remaining paragraphs, focus on the parts of the poem that support your thesis statement. Consider beginning each paragraph in the body of your essay with a topic sentence that states the main idea of that particular paragraph. Throughout your essay, quote from the poem and refer to specific passages to clarify and support your central argument. Your concluding paragraph should attempt to wrap up all the ideas and to restate your thesis.

The Allegory of the Cave

380 B.C.

PLATO

 A student of the ancient Greek philosopher Socrates, PLATO was one of the most important thinkers of the ancient world, and critics regard him as a master of the dialogue form. Plato's "The Allegory of the Cave" takes the form of a dialogue between Socrates and one of his students. Socrates announces that he wants to demonstrate "how far our nature is enlightened or unenlightened." He does this by describing a strange, imaginary underground world inhabited by men who have never been above the ground and by showing how their perception of reality would differ from that of normal people. In doing so, Socrates raises many disturbing, universal human issues about the power of ignorance, education, and truth. The men in the caves live unexamined lives, and because they live in a shadow world of illusions, they fail not only to see the world as it is but also to know themselves as they really are.

As you read "The Allegory of the Cave," think about why most of the men in the cave might want to stay there. Why would they feel threatened by the few who venture out of the cave and learn the truth? Do the ones who return to the cave have an obligation to teach their comrades the truth?

And now, I said, let me show in a figure how far our nature is enlight- 1
ened or unenlightened:—Behold! human beings living in an underground den, which has a mouth open towards the light and reaching all along the den; here they have been from their childhood, and have their legs and necks chained so that they cannot move, and can only see before them, being prevented by the chains from turning round their heads. Above and behind them a fire is blazing at a distance, and between the fire and the prisoners there is a raised way; and you will see, if you look, a low wall built along the way, like the screen which marionette players have in front of them, over which they show the puppets.

I see.   2

And do you see, I said, men passing along the wall carrying all sorts of   3
vessels, and statues and figures of animals made of wood and stone and
various materials, which appear over the wall? Some of them are talking,
others silent.

You have shown me a strange image, and they are strange prisoners.   4

Like ourselves, I replied; and they see only their own shadows, or the   5
shadows of one another, which the fire throws on the opposite wall of the
cave?

True, he said; how could they see anything but the shadows if they were   6
never allowed to move their heads?

And of the objects which are being carried in like manner they would   7
only see the shadows?

Yes, he said.   8

And if they were able to converse with one another, would they not   9
suppose that they were naming what was actually before them?

Very true.   10

And suppose further that the prison had an echo which came from the   11
other side, would they not be sure to fancy when one of the passers-by spoke
that the voice which they heard came from the passing shadow?

No question, he replied.   12

To them, I said, the truth would be literally nothing but the shadows of   13
the images.

That is certain.   14

And now look again, and see what will naturally follow if the prisoners   15
are released and disabused of their error. At first, when any of them is liberated
and compelled suddenly to stand up and turn his neck round and walk and
look towards the light, he will suffer sharp pains; the glare will distress him,
and he will be unable to see the realities of which in his former state he had
seen the shadows; and then conceive some one saying to him, that what he
saw before was an illusion, but that now, when he is approaching nearer to
being and his eye is turned towards more real existence, he has a clearer
vision—what will be his reply? And you may further imagine that his instructor
is pointing to the objects as they pass and requiring him to name them,—will
he not be perplexed? Will he not fancy that the shadows which he formerly
saw are truer than the objects which are now shown to him?

Far truer.   16

And if he is compelled to look straight at the light, will he not have a   17
pain in his eyes which will make him turn away to take refuge in the objects
of vision which he can see, and which he will conceive to be in reality clearer
than the things which are now being shown to him?

True, he said.   18

And suppose once more, that he is reluctantly dragged up a steep and   19
rugged ascent, and held fast until he is forced into the presence of the sun
himself, is he not likely to be pained and irritated? When he approaches the
light his eyes will be dazzled, and he will not be able to see anything at all
of what are now called realities.

Not all in a moment, he said.   20

He will require to grow accustomed to the sight of the upper world.   21
And first he will see the shadows best, next the reflections of men and other
objects in the water, and then the objects themselves; then he will gaze upon
the light of the moon and the stars and the spangled heaven; and he will see
the sky and the stars by night better than the sun or the light of the sun by
day?

Certainly.   22

Last of all he will be able to see the sun, and not mere reflections of him   23
in the water, but he will see him in his own proper place, and not in another,
and he will contemplate him as he is.

Certainly.   24

He will then proceed to argue that this is he who gives the season and   25
the years, and is the guardian of all that is in the visible world, and in a certain
way the cause of all things which he and his fellows have been accustomed
to behold?

Clearly, he said, he would first see the sun and then reason about him.   26

And when he remembered his old habitation, and the wisdom of the   27
den and his fellow prisoners, do you not suppose that he would felicitate[1]
himself on the change, and pity them?

Certainly, he would.   28

And if they were in the habit of conferring honors among themselves   29
on those who were quickest to observe the passing shadows and to remark
which of them went before, and which followed after, and which were together; and who were therefore best able to draw conclusions as to the future,
do you think that he would care for such honors and glories, or envy the
possessors of them? Would he not say with Homer,

> Better to be the poor servant of a poor master,

and to endure anything, rather than think as they do and live after their
manner?

Yes, he said, I think that he would rather suffer anything than entertain   30
these false notions and live in this miserable manner.

---

1. felicitate: to compliment upon a happy event; congratulate

Imagine once more, I said, such an one coming suddenly out of the sun   31
to be replaced in his old situation; would he not be certain to have his eyes
full of darkness?

To be sure, he said.   32

And if there were a contest, and he had to compete in measuring the   33
shadows with the prisoners who had never moved out of the den, while his
sight was still weak, and before his eyes had become steady (and the time
which would be needed to acquire this new habit of sight might be very
considerable), would he not be ridiculous? Men would say of him that up
he went and down he came without his eyes; and that it was better not even
to think of ascending; and if any one tried to loose another and lead him up
to the light, let them only catch the offender, and they would put him to
death.

No question, he said.   34

This entire allegory, I said, you may now append, dear Glaucon, to the   35
previous argument; the prison house is the world of sight, the light of the
fire is the sun, and you will not misapprehend me if you interpret the journey
upwards to be the ascent of the soul into the intellectual world according to
my poor belief, which, at your desire, I have expressed—whether rightly or
wrongly God knows. But, whether true or false, my opinion is that in the
world of knowledge the idea of good appears last of all, and is seen only with
an effort; and, when seen, is also inferred to be the universal author of all
things beautiful and right, parent of light and of the lord of light in this
visible world, and the immediate source of reason and truth in the intellectual;
and that this is the power upon which he who would act rationally either in
public or private life must have his eye fixed.

I agree, he said, as far as I am able to understand you.   36

Moreover, I said, you must not wonder that those who attain to this   37
beatific[2] vision are unwilling to descend to human affairs; for their souls are
ever hastening into the upper world where they desire to dwell; which desire
of theirs is very natural, if our allegory may be trusted.

Yes, very natural.   38

And is there anything surprising in one who passes from divine contempla-   39
tions to the evil state of man, misbehaving himself in a ridiculous manner;
if, while his eyes are blinking and before he has become accustomed to the
surrounding darkness, he is compelled to fight in courts of law, or in other
places, about the images or the shadows of images of justice, and is endeav-
oring to meet the conceptions of those who have never yet seen absolute
justice?

---

2. beatific: bestowing bliss, blessings, happiness

Anything but surprising, he replied.   40

Anyone who has common sense will remember that the bewilderments   41
of the eyes are of two kinds, and arise from two causes, either from coming
out of the light or from going into the light, which is true of the mind's eye,
quite as much as of the bodily eye; and he who remembers this when he sees
anyone whose vision is perplexed and weak, will not be too ready to laugh;
he will first ask whether that soul of man has come out of the brighter life,
and is unable to see because unaccustomed to the dark, or having turned
from darkness to the day is dazzled by excess of light. And he will count the
one happy in his condition and state of being, and he will pity the other; or,
if he have a mind to laugh at the soul which comes from below into the
light, there will be more reason in this than in the laugh which greets him
who returns from above out of the light into the den.

That, he said, is a very just distinction.   42

◼ ◼ ◼

OPTIONS FOR READING LOGS: "THE ALLEGORY OF THE CAVE"

1. Writers often use images or symbols to represent an idea or concept and
   to provide a deeper, more important value or interpretation than is at
   first apparent. Use the double-entry journal technique to clarify the
   meaning of some of the powerful images or symbols in Plato's "The
   Allegory of the Cave." Draw a vertical line down the middle of your
   journal page and, in the left column, copy a list of all the images or
   symbols you identify in the story, such as the men with their heads
   chained to look one way in the darkness or the sun shining outside
   the cave. Then, in the right column, jot down possible interpretations,
   personal associations, or explanatory comments. End your journal entry
   with a brief statement about a significant discovery you made about "The
   Allegory of the Cave."
2. Draw a picture or map that represents Plato's "The Allegory of the
   Cave." Create a detailed graphic representation that clearly illustrates all
   the components of Plato's cave and the ways they work together to form
   what happens in the cave. After you have finished your picture or map,
   write a description of the dynamics of the cave, clearly stating the main
   point Plato is trying to illustrate in "The Allegory of the Cave."
3. From your own experience, tell a story that you feel was enhanced or
   clarified by "The Allegory of the Cave." Have you ever felt like the poor

souls chained in the cave, unable to see things as they really are? Do you know anyone who is in a "cave," unable to see the truth about a situation? Or do you know anyone who has recently left the darkness of a "cave," such as an abusive family, a gang, or drug or alcohol abuse? Think about your own discovery of truth, or someone else's, and tell that story. End your story by explaining what you learned from reading Plato's "The Allegory of the Cave."

OPTIONS FOR WRITING ASSIGNMENTS: "THE ALLEGORY OF THE CAVE"

1. Does anything in "The Allegory of the Cave" remind you of something from your own past? Has reading "The Allegory of the Cave" shed light on your own quest for personal knowledge or helped you discover who you are? Compose a narrative or descriptive essay that focuses on a remembered person, place, or event. Throughout your essay, concentrate on using vivid details and descriptions to help recreate your memories.

2. Plato's "The Allegory of the Cave" explores the dynamics of unenlightened and enlightened individuals. Have you ever been through a distinctive phase that lasted several months, or even longer, when you felt as though you were "in the cave" and denied the truth about a relationship, a family situation, or some other personal experience? Explore the phase's beginning, middle, and end: How did it start? How did you act and feel? How did you finally discover the truth? Why and how did the phase end? What personal knowledge did you gain about yourself and your situation?

3. What personal knowledge do you think Socrates wanted us to gain in "The Allegory of the Cave"? If you could meet with the philosopher and ask him questions, hear his answers, and give him your ideas and interpretations, how do you think he would respond? Create a conversation between you and Socrates about the ideas in "The Allegory of the Cave." Your conversation might take the form of a question-and-answer interview, an argument presenting two opposing points of view, or a freewheeling exploration of the philosopher's ideas and their implications.

4. If you were asked about the meaning of "The Allegory of the Cave" and how it relates to knowing the truth about ourselves and who we are, what would you say? In a formal essay of five or more paragraphs, explain the role of personal knowledge in "The Allegory of the Cave." End your introductory paragraph with a thesis statement that makes an arguable point about the central meaning of the text. In the remaining

paragraphs, focus on parts of the text that support your thesis statement. Consider beginning each paragraph in the body of your essay with a topic sentence that states the main idea of that particular paragraph. In those paragraphs, quote from "The Allegory of the Cave" and refer to specific passages to clarify and support your central argument. In your concluding paragraph, attempt to wrap up all your ideas and restate your thesis.

Family Knowledge: Who Has Shaped Me?

The readings in Chapter Two explore the theme of family knowledge and help us to become more aware of the immediate forces that shape us as individuals. These glimpses of family relationships reveal the importance of community among human beings, despite our varied cultures and backgrounds. Each of us learns about that sense of community primarily through family lessons. In recent years sociologists have documented the loss of the family unit, giving blame to a number of factors: high divorce rates, increases in single-parent families, the high rate of teenage pregnancies, changing definitions of the family, and the fast pace of our lifestyles in this highly technological world. Some experts say it is far easier to witness family solidarity among recent immigrants to the United States, but that, too, changes, as the next generation of children assimilates and adopts new ways of surviving. Nevertheless, in spite of its changing definition, the family is alive and well today.

Each reading in this chapter focuses on the theme of the family and the shaping forces of the family unit. In "Winter Sundays" by Robert Hayden, for example, the narrator reassesses his relationship with his father and senses that he failed to appreciate his father as much as he should have. In Jerome Weidman's short story, "My Father Sits in the Dark," the narrator discovers the enduring mystery of a large part of his father's life. The final selection, Joan Didion's essay "On Going Home" explores the guilt and complexity of family relationships and compares family dynamics to a "guerilla" war that no one fully understands. Ultimately, the message in these readings is that however varied our attitudes and values, the family—in all its emerging configurations—remains central to our total human experience.

How would you define *family*? Do you think your definition differs from the definition your parents or grandparents would have given when they were your age? What are some of the forces that contribute to the ever-changing definition of *family*?

Ball Game

1987

CLAUDIA MADISON

 In "Ball Game" the narrator questions her family's reminiscences about happy times, for she now filters them through the realization that they had only "pretended to be happy." In this story she describes an afternoon during which her family played a game of baseball and found true happiness, even if only for a short time.

Do you feel there are certain behaviors or activities that constitute a "happy" family life? What are they? How do early childhood experiences in keeping the peace within the family affect the way we approach family situations as adults? Did you ever pretend to be happy during a family gathering, only to feel angry at yourself later for being dishonest?

I must be cautious about speaking of happy times in my family. I was older than I should have been when I realized that the occasions we five children reminisce about were not happy times for us at all. Rather, on outings, picnics, and holidays we had pretended to be happy. If one of the children got cranky or our father lost his temper, Mother would say "Can't you please just *try* to be happy." Tears might be already puddling in the creases by her mouth. Our father would be too far gone in his bad mood to try, and some of the children were too young to understand what was expected of them, but the rest of us would fix brittle smiles and interested expressions on our faces. Early on I recognized these expressions on my brother's face. I thought he was a phony until I was much older and realized I had arranged my own face just as carefully as he had his.

But the day I want to talk about was happy, I think, without our having to try hard to make it so.

It was a Saturday. Father's restless nature never allowed him to spend a weekend day at home without having a rage about something, but he worked overtime that day. This was a boon to him, whose chronic complaint was that his greedy children were making him flat broke. It was a boon to the rest of us, too, because we were never really comfortable with him around.

Jack was the baby then, and, as I recall, he'd slept dry through the night   4
for the first time. It was a small thing, but enough to cheer our mother who
was depressed most of the time and overwhelmed by how much her children
needed.

Mother expected relatives for Sunday dinner next day, so she and I got   5
the house ready, stowing away all the baby and toddler toys, dusting, and
scrubbing. It wasn't often that we cleaned so thoroughly, though Mother
always said she liked nothing better than to sit in a nice clean house. I asked
her once why we didn't just clean it up every Saturday, since she liked it so
much. She didn't answer but gave me a characteristic look, like she'd never
seen me before in her life and hadn't the slightest notion of what I was talking
about.

The two little girls played in the yard. Jack stayed in his pen, and I moved   6
it from room to room and talked to him while I worked. After lunch Mother
made a molded salad for next day, and I cleaned spots off all the drinking
glasses.

Nothing went wrong, no fighting or accidents, to upset Mother. By mid-   7
afternoon, she was sitting in the orderly house as she liked to do, and the
little children were taking naps. She told me I could go outside and play.

My brother was already out in the vacant lot next to our yard. The lot   8
was the neighborhood playground, pounded bare of weeds and grass by
much bicycle riding, running, and scuffing. It was my favorite place.

There were no other neighborhood kids out that Saturday. I batted   9
fielding practice for my brother—high fly balls and grounders. This was my
only athletic talent. I could not hit a ball pitched to me to save my soul, and
I was not very good at catching or throwing.

I mindlessly hit balls until the shadow of the phone pole in front of the   10
lot was just beginning to swing around and lengthen. Mother came out of
the house with a book like she was going to sit in what she called "the arbor,"
a spindly construction of chicken wire and morning glory vines. Instead, she
came out the back gate and stood beside me with her hands on her hips for
at least a full minute. I didn't know what she wanted. Her blue eyes looked
clear, for a change *not* like she was about to cry.

My brother's old glove was lying by my feet. He always brought his bat,   11
his two gloves, our old ball for practice, and, should a real game develop,
our new ball, bought just the month before and the cover not yet resewn.

Mother put her book down and picked up the old glove. She fitted it   12
to her hand, gave it a punch, and took it off and moved the strap over one
notch. She put it on again and trotted to the back of the field, motioning
for my brother to move over away from her some. He was so befuddled by
Mother being out in the field that he wasn't watching what he was doing

and threw the ball right past me. I was pretty dumbfounded too and just let the ball go by. I had to go out to the street for it, and when I got back, Mother was in a crouch like an infielder, her housedress brushing the dirt where it dipped down between her legs.

At first I was afraid of hurting her and hit easy grounders and high- 13
lob fly balls right to her. But she moved pretty well, so I let rip and hit the balls all over the field like always. They took turns catching and kept track of points: three for line drives (which I hardly ever hit), two for flies, one for grounders.

I don't believe I'd ever heard my brother laugh when either of my parents 14
was around, but he did that day, at something—I didn't hear what—Mother said to him. The younger children finished their naps and one-by-one came out to the backyard. They lined up along the chain-link fence and cheered when the ball was caught. Jack clapped and laughed when the others did.

We were all a little drunk on Mother's good humor. And if that wasn't 15
enough, our father came home from work and stripped off his outside shirt and went out to the field, too. Mother and my brother started their game over so he could play, and we didn't count line drives which he couldn't catch without a glove.

I don't know how long the game lasted. It was long enough, as a look 16
back at the younger kids in the yard showed me, for Jack to have piddled his pants and then sat in the dirt so the back of his shorts was muddy. I figured there would be heck to pay for that, but in the meantime I thwocked that baseball out to my parents like my life depended on it.

OPTIONS FOR READING LOGS: "BALL GAME"

1. Use the double-entry journal technique to discover meaning in "Ball Game." After drawing a vertical line down the middle of your journal page, use the left column to keep a running list of "what" or "why" questions that occur to you as you are reading. Aim for three to five questions, such as, "What is the significance of the thorough house-cleaning in preparation for the Sunday dinner?" When you finish your list, answer your questions as completely as you can in the right column. (Remember that such interpretation will require you to take educated guesses.) To demonstrate that you have reached a basic understanding of the text, end your journal entry by jotting down the main idea of this story about a family's afternoon game.

2. Copy the most powerful line or passage in "Ball Game." Using anecdotes and examples from your own experience, explain fully why that particular passage held such power or meaning for you.

3. Did the narrator's description of that perfect time when the whole family was "a little drunk on Mother's good humor" trigger a memory of a similar event in your childhood? Tell a parallel story from your personal life, connecting the story with the theme of "Family Knowledge: Who Has Shaped Me?"

OPTIONS FOR WRITING ASSIGNMENTS: "BALL GAME"

1. Expand and develop one of your reading logs for "Ball Game" into a more polished piece of writing that explores its subject matter in greater range and depth. Begin with a thesis statement that reveals an important discovery you made about your own family—your biological family, adoptive family, or extended family. Arrange your story in a clear chronological order, adding enough specific details to make the event come alive for your reader. By the end of your essay, you should have convinced your reader of the significance of your discovery.

2. Create a dialogue between you and the narrator of "Ball Game," focusing on family gatherings or happy times in a family. Your dialogue might take the form of a question-and-answer interview, a casual conversation, an argument, or a freewheeling exploration of the narrator's ideas and their implications.

3. In "Ball Game" the narrator thinks about the elements that make up a happy family life. You might think about the following questions and connect effects with their causes in this story. What are some of the causes of happiness within a family? What are some of the causes of strain? What are the causes of the mother's tension? As you trace effects to their causes, see if you encounter some hidden discoveries along the way. Focus on the theme of "Family Knowledge: Who Has Shaped Me?"

4. Write a formal essay of five or more paragraphs explaining the meaning of "Ball Game." Focus your attention on parts of the story about which you have genuine questions, such as "What is significant about the narrator's statement that her brother had never laughed in the presence of their parents?" End your introductory paragraph with a thesis statement that makes your central idea clear. For example, you may wish to take a stand on whether or not this story accurately depicts the true meaning of happiness in a typical family. Brainstorm or prewrite to come up with

reasons to support your interpretation. In your essay, you will need to quote from "Ball Game" and refer to specific passages to clarify and support your central argument.

Those Winter Sundays

1962

ROBERT HAYDEN

 ROBERT HAYDEN was an African-American poet who made his living by teaching at Fisk University and the University of Michigan, among others. His parents were poor and uneducated, but they always encouraged their son, who showed an interest in writing when he was quite young. Hayden is known for his narrative poems and strong character studies. In "Those Winter Sundays," he reflects on his childhood to express his complex past and present feelings toward his father.

In Hayden's poem, the narrator reveals conflicting emotions toward his father. On one hand, the father made many sacrifices for his son; on the other hand, he may have been responsible for the "chronic angers of that house." How do our own parents serve as role models for us if we become parents ourselves? Do you feel that most people appreciate their parents' sacrifices more after they become adults themselves? Is a sense of guilt a basic part of a parent-child relationship?

Sundays too my father got up early 1
and put his clothes on in the blueblack cold,
then with cracked hands that ached
from labor in the weekday weather made
banked fires blaze. No one ever thanked him. 2

I'd wake and hear the cold splintering, breaking.
When the rooms were warm, he'd call,
and slowly I would rise and dress,
fearing the chronic angers of that house,

Speaking indifferently to him, 3
who had driven out the cold
and polished my good shoes as well.

What did I know, what did I know
of love's austere[1] and lonely offices?

1. austere: severe in manner or appearance; strict; forbidding

OPTIONS FOR READING LOGS:
"THOSE WINTER SUNDAYS"

1. Using the double-entry journal technique, draw a vertical line down the middle of your journal page, creating two columns. In the left column, keep a running list of "what" or "why" questions that occur to you as you read "Those Winter Sundays." Aim for three to five questions such as, "What is the significance of 'blue-black cold'?" or "What exactly does 'speaking indifferently' mean?" When you finish your list, move to the top of the right column and answer your questions as completely as you can. (Remember that such interpretation will require you to take educated guesses.) To demonstrate that you have reached a basic understanding of the text, end your journal entry by jotting down the main idea of "Those Winter Sundays."

2. Paraphrase the poem by writing its meaning in your own words. Work your way through the entire poem, thoroughly explaining and clarifying all its details and images and explaining it line by line and stanza by stanza. End your paraphrase by stating the theme of "Those Winter Sundays."

3. Tell your own story of a typical Sunday you experienced as a child. Perhaps your Sundays were far from being wintry or were days of rest for everyone in your family. In what ways were your experiences similar to or different from the Sundays Hayden describes? End your journal entry by stating or implying the overall mood of your family on a typical Sunday.

OPTIONS FOR WRITING ASSIGNMENTS:
"THOSE WINTER SUNDAYS"

1. What do we learn about families from "Those Winter Sundays"? Explain the meaning of the poem in a formal essay of five or more paragraphs. Reread, think about, and discuss the poem fully before you begin your

essay. In an introductory paragraph state the poem's main idea clearly. In your supporting paragraphs focus on parts of the poem about which you have questions and on words or phrases that help clarify the main idea. Treat the poem in all its complexity: What might the "chronic angers" be? Why did no one ever thank the father? What kind of family does the poem portray? In your commentary, you should quote from the poem, referring to specific passages to back up your ideas.

2. Did you identify with the narrator's feelings in "Those Winter Sundays"? What do you think his feelings are about his father? Is he full of guilt or is he happy with their relationship? Using the letter form and addressing the narrator directly, write a personal letter giving your reaction to the message of the poem, especially as it pertains to the relationship between the father and the son.

3. What do you think of "Those Winter Sundays" as a poem about family relationships? Would you recommend it to a friend? In a formal essay of five or more paragraphs, write a review that clearly assesses the value of "Those Winter Sundays" as a poem of discovery about parent-child relationships. Your evaluation can be positive, negative, or a mixture of the two, but it should be stated as a thesis in your introductory paragraph. For example, your judgment might be that the poem accurately addresses the way children take the care and nurturing of their parents for granted. State that in your first paragraph. In each supporting paragraph, provide evidence from the poem that makes your judgment convincing.

4. If you were asked what "Those Winter Sundays" means and how it relates to knowing the truth about our families and how we are shaped, what would you say? Reread, think about, and discuss the poem with others to explore its meaning fully. Write a formal essay of five or more paragraphs, explaining the role of family relationships in "Those Winter Sundays." In your introductory paragraph, express your main idea in a clear thesis statement. In your supporting paragraphs, explore those parts of the poem that caused you to have questions or that clarify your main idea. In your commentary you will need to quote from the text and to refer to specific words or passages.

I Stand Here Ironing

1961

TILLIE OLSEN

 TILLIE OLSEN was born in Omaha, Nebraska, in 1912. To escape persecution, her family had fled from Czarist Russia. Olsen grew up in poverty in the United States and was forced to quit school during the eleventh grade so she could earn a living. Although we have all had to face changing definitions of what *family* means, none of us can deny that we are profoundly affected by the circumstances of our upbringing. "I Stand Here Ironing" reads like an autobiography, and it is important to note that in real life Olsen's first husband deserted her and left her with a child. She later remarried and became a political activist and writer. "I Stand Here Ironing" takes place in the 1930s, a society in which adequate child care was largely unavailable for single, working mothers. In this story, the mother did her best, but she found little time to be a nurturing parent to her first child.

How did you feel about the demands made on your parents or guardians during your own upbringing? Did those demands influence your present attitude toward family life? How do parents manage to find a proper balance between work time and "quality time" with their children today? How do parents and children compensate for the time they spend apart?

I stand here ironing, and what you asked me moves tormented back and forth with the iron. 1

"I wish you would manage the time to come in and talk with me about your daughter. I'm sure you can help me understand her. She's a youngster who needs help and whom I'm deeply interested in helping." 2

"Who needs help." . . . Even if I came, what good would it do? You think because I am her mother I have a key, or that in some way you could use me as a key? She has lived for nineteen years. There is all that life that has happened outside of me, beyond me. 3

And when is there time to remember, to sift, to weigh, to estimate, to total? I will start and there will be an interruption and I will have to gather 4 it all together again. Or I will become engulfed with all I did or did not do, with what should have been and what cannot be helped.

She was a beautiful baby. The first and only one of our five that was beauti-   5
ful at birth. You do not guess how new and uneasy her tenancy in her now-loveliness. You did not know her all those years she was thought homely, or see her poring over her baby pictures, making me tell her over and over how beautiful she had been—and would be, I would tell her—and was now, to the seeing eye. But the seeing eyes were few or nonexistent. Including mine.

I nursed her. They feel that's important nowadays. I nursed all the chil-   6
dren, but with her, with all the fierce rigidity of first motherhood, I did like the books then said. Though her cries battered me to trembling and my breasts ached with swollenness, I waited till the clock decreed.

Why do I put that first? I do not even know if it matters, or if it explains   7
anything.

She was a beautiful baby. She blew shining bubbles of sound. She loved   8
motion, loved light, loved color and music and textures. She would lie on the floor in her blue overalls patting the surface so hard in ecstasy her hands and feet would blur. She was a miracle to me, but when she was eight months old I had to leave her daytimes with the woman downstairs to whom she was no miracle at all, for I worked or looked for work and for Emily's father, who "could no longer endure" (he wrote in his good-bye note) "sharing want with us."

I was nineteen. It was the pre-relief, pre-WPA world of the depression.   9
I would start running as soon as I got off the streetcar, running up the stairs, the place smelling sour, and awake or asleep to startle awake, when she saw me she would break into a clogged weeping that could not be comforted, a weeping I can hear yet.

After a while I found a job hashing[1] at night so I could be with her days,   10
and it was better. But it came to where I had to bring her to his family and leave her.

It took a long time to raise the money for her fare back. Then she got   11
chicken pox and I had to wait longer. When she finally came, I hardly knew her, walking quick and nervous like her father, looking like her father, thin, and dressed in a shoddy red that yellowed her skin and glared at the pockmarks. All the baby loveliness gone.

She was two. Old enough for nursery school they said, and I did not   12
know then what I know now—the fatigue of the long day, and the lacerations[2] of group life in the kinds of nurseries that are only parking places for children.

---

1. hashing: to cook at a restaurant (slang)   2. lacerations: rough, jagged tears or wounds

Except that it would have made no difference if I had known. It was the   13
only place there was. It was the only way we could be together, the only way
I could hold a job.

And even without knowing, I knew. I knew the teacher that was evil   14
because all these years it has curdled into my memory, the little boy hunched
in the corner, her rasp, "why aren't you outside, because Alvin hits you?
that's no reason, go out, scaredy." I knew Emily hated it even if she did not
clutch and implore "don't go Mommy" like the other children, mornings.

She always had a reason why we should stay home. Momma, you look   15
sick. Momma, I feel sick. Momma, the teachers aren't there today, they're
sick. Momma, we can't go, there was a fire there last night. Momma, it's a
holiday today, no school, they told me.

But never a direct protest, never rebellion. I think of our others in their   16
three-four-year-oldness—the explosions, the tempers, the denunciations,
the demands—and I feel suddenly ill. I put the iron down. What in me
demanded that goodness in her? And what was the cost, the cost to her of
such goodness?

The old man living in the back once said in his gentle way: "You should   17
smile at Emily more when you look at her." What *was* in my face when I
looked at her? I loved her. There were all the acts of love.

It was only with the others I remembered what he said, and it was the   18
face of joy, and not of care or tightness or worry I turned to them—too late
for Emily. She does not smile easily, let alone almost always as her brothers
and sisters do. Her face is closed and somber, but when she wants, how fluid.
You must have seen it in her pantomimes, you spoke of her rare gift for
comedy on the stage that rouses laughter out of the audience so dear they
applaud and applaud and do not want to let her go.

Where does it come from, that comedy? There was none of it in her   19
when she came back to me that second time, after I had had to send her
away again. She had a new daddy now to learn to love, and I think perhaps
it was a better time.

Except when we left her alone nights, telling ourselves she was old   20
enough.

"Can't you go some other time, Mommy, like tomorrow?" she would   21
ask. "Will it be just a little while you'll be gone? Do you promise?"

The time we came back, the front door open, the clock on the floor in   22
the hall. She rigid awake. "It wasn't just a little while. I didn't cry. Three
times I called you, just three times, and then I ran downstairs to open the
door so you could come faster. The clock talked loud. I threw it away, it
scared me what it talked."

She said the clock talked loud again that night I went to the hospital to   23
have Susan. She was delirious with the fever that comes from red measles,

but she was fully conscious all the week I was gone and the week after we were home when she could not come near the new baby or me.

She did not get well. She stayed skeleton thin, not wanting to eat, and   24
night after night she had nightmares. She would call for me, and I would rouse from exhaustion to sleepily call back: "You're all right, darling, go to sleep, it's just a dream," and if she still called, in a sterner voice, "now go to sleep, Emily, there's nothing to hurt you." Twice, only twice, when I had to get up for Susan anyhow, I went in to sit with her.

Now when it is too late (as if she would let me hold and comfort her   25
like I do the others) I get up and go to her at once at her moan or restless stirring. "Are you awake, Emily? Can I get you something?" And the answer is always the same: "No, I'm all right, go back to sleep, Mother."

They persuaded me at the clinic to send her away to a convalescent   26
home in the country where "she can have the kind of food and care you can't manage for her, and you'll be free to concentrate on the new baby." They still send children to that place. I see pictures on the society page of sleek young women planning affairs to raise money for it, or dancing at the affairs, or decorating Easter eggs or filling Christmas stockings for the children.

They never have a picture of the children so I do not know if the girls   27
still wear those gigantic red bows and the ravaged looks on the every other Sunday when parents can come to visit "unless otherwise notified"—as we were notified the first six weeks.

Oh it is a handsome place, green lawns and tall trees and fluted flower   28
beds. High up on the balconies of each cottage the children stand, the girls in their red bows and white dresses, the boys in white suits and giant red ties. The parents stand below shrieking up to be heard and the children shriek down to be heard, and between them the invisible wall: "Not to Be Contaminated by Parental Germs or Physical Affection."

There was a tiny girl who always stood hand in hand with Emily. Her   29
parents never came. One visit she was gone. "They moved her to Rose Cottage," Emily shouted in explanation. "They don't like you to love any-body here."

She wrote once a week, the labored writing of a seven-year-old. "I am   30
fine. How is the baby. If I write my leter nicly I will have a star. Love." There never was a star. We wrote every other day, letters she could never hold or keep but only hear read—once. "We simply do not have room for children to keep any personal possessions," they patiently explained when we pieced one Sunday's shrieking together to plead how much it would mean to Emily, who loved so to keep things, to be allowed to keep her letters and cards.

Each visit she looked frailer. "She isn't eating," they told us.   31

(They had runny eggs for breakfast or mush with lumps, Emily said later,   32
I'd hold it in my mouth and not swallow. Nothing ever tasted good, just
when they had chicken.)

It took us eight months to get her released home, and only the fact that   33
she gained back so little of her seven lost pounds convinced the social worker.

I used to try to hold and love her after she came back, but her body   34
would stay stiff, and after a while she'd push away. She ate little. Food sickened
her, and I think much of life too. Oh she had physical lightness and bright-
ness, twinkling by on skates, bouncing like a ball up and down up and down
over the jump rope, skimming over the hill: but these were momentary.

She fretted about her appearance, thin and dark and foreign-looking at   35
a time when every little girl was supposed to look or thought she should
look a chubby blonde replica of Shirley Temple. The doorbell sometimes
rang for her, but no one seemed to come and play in the house or be a best
friend. Maybe because we moved so much.

There was a boy she loved painfully through two school semesters.   36
Months later she told me how she had taken pennies from my purse to buy
him candy. "Licorice was his favorite and I brought him some every day, but
he still liked Jennifer better'n me. Why, Mommy?" The kind of question for
which there is no answer.

School was a worry to her. She was not glib[3] or quick in a world where   37
glibness and quickness were easily confused with ability to learn. To her
overworked and exasperated teachers she was an overconscientious "slow
learner" who kept trying to catch up and was absent entirely too often.

I let her be absent, though sometimes the illness was imaginary. How   38
different from my now-strictness about attendance with the others. I wasn't
working. We had a new baby, I was home anyhow. Sometimes, after Susan
grew old enough, I would keep her home from school, too, to have them
all together.

Mostly Emily had asthma, and her breathing, harsh and labored, would   39
fill the house with a curiously tranquil sound. I would bring the two old
dresser mirrors and her boxes of collections to her bed. She would select
beads and single earrings, bottle tops and shells, dried flowers and pebbles,
old postcards and scraps, all sorts of oddments; then she and Susan would
play Kingdom, setting up landscapes and furniture, peopling them with action.

Those were the only times of peaceful companionship between her and   40
Susan. I have edged away from it, that poisonous feeling between them, that

---

3. glib: readily fluent, often thoughtlessly, superficially, or insincerely so

terrible balancing of hurts and needs I had to do between the two, and did so badly, those earlier years.

Oh there are conflicts between the others too, each one human, needing, demanding, hurting, taking—but only between Emily and Susan, no, Emily toward Susan that corroding resentment. It seems so obvious on the surface, yet it is not obvious. Susan, the second child, Susan, golden- and curly-haired and chubby, quick and articulate and assured, everything in appearance and manner Emily was not; Susan, not able to resist Emily's precious things, losing or sometimes clumsily breaking them; Susan telling jokes and riddles to company for applause while Emily sat silent (to say to me later: that was *my* riddle, Mother, I told it to Susan); Susan, who for all the five years' difference in age was just a year behind Emily in developing physically.   41

I am glad for that slow physical development that widened the difference between her and her contemporaries, though she suffered over it. She was too vulnerable for that terrible world of youthful competition, of preening and parading, of constant measuring of yourself against every other, of envy, "If I had the copper hair," "If I had that skin. . . ." She tormented herself enough about not looking like the others, there was enough of the unsureness, the having to be conscious of words before you speak, the constant caring— what are they thinking of me? without having it all magnified by the merciless physical drives.   42

Ronnie is calling. He is wet and I change him. It is rare there is such a cry now. That time of motherhood is almost behind me when the ear is not one's own but must always be racked and listening for the child cry, the child call. We sit for a while and I hold him, looking out over the city spread in charcoal with its soft aisles of light. *"Shoogily,"* he breathes and curls closer. I carry him back to bed, asleep. *Shoogily.* A funny word, a family word, inherited from Emily, invented by her to say: *comfort.*   43

In this and other ways she leaves her seal, I say aloud. And startle at my saying it. What do I mean? What did I start to gather together, to try and make coherent? I was at the terrible, growing years. War years. I do not remember them well. I was working, there were four smaller ones now, there was not time for her. She had to help be a mother, and housekeeper, and shopper. She had to set her seal. Mornings of crisis and near hysteria trying to get lunches packed, hair combed, coats and shoes found, everyone to school or Child Care on time, the baby ready for transportation. And always the paper scribbled on by a smaller one, the book looked at by Susan then mislaid, the homework not done. Running out to that huge school where she was one, she was lost, she was a drop; suffering over the unpreparedness, stammering and unsure in her classes.   44

There was so little time left at night after the kids were bedded down.   45
She would struggle over books, always eating (it was in those years she
developed her enormous appetite that is legendary in our family) and I would
be ironing, or preparing food for the next day, or writing V-mail to Bill, or
tending the baby. Sometimes, to make me laugh, or out of her despair, she
would imitate happenings or types at school.

I think I said once: "Why don't you do something like this in the school   46
amateur show?" One morning she phoned me at work, hardly understandable
through the weeping: "Mother, I did it. I won, I won; they gave me first
prize; they clapped and clapped and wouldn't let me go."

Now suddenly she was Somebody, and as imprisoned in her difference   47
as she had been in anonymity.

She began to be asked to perform at other high schools, even in colleges,   48
then at city and statewide affairs. The first one we went to, I only recognized
her that first moment when thin, shy, she almost drowned herself into the
curtains. Then: Was this Emily? The control, the command, the convulsing
and deadly clowning, the spell, then the roaring, stamping audience, unwilling
to let this rare and precious laughter out of their lives.

Afterwards: You ought to do something about her with a gift like that—   49
but without money or knowing how, what does one do? We have left it all
to her, and the gift has as often eddied inside, clogged and clotted, as been
used and growing.

She is coming. She runs up the stairs two at a time with her light graceful   50
step, and I know she is happy tonight. Whatever it was that occasioned your
call did not happen today.

"Aren't you ever going to finish the ironing, Mother? Whistler painted   51
his mother in a rocker. I'd have to paint mine standing over an ironing
board." This is one of her communicative nights and she tells me everything
and nothing as she fixes herself a plate of food out of the icebox.

She is so lovely. Why did you want me to come in at all? Why were you   52
concerned? She will find her way.

She starts up the stairs to bed. "Don't get me up with the rest in the   53
morning." "But I thought you were having midterms." "Oh, those," she
comes back in, kisses me, and says quite lightly, "in a couple of years when
we'll all be atom-dead they won't matter a bit."

She has said it before. She *believes* it. But because I have been dredging[4]   54
the past, and all that compounds a human being is so heavy and meaningful
in me, I cannot endure it tonight.

4. dredging: to discover or reveal

I will never total it all. I will never come in to say: She was a child seldom   55
smiled at. Her father left me before she was a year old. I had to work her
first six years when there was work, or I sent her home and to his relatives.
There were years she had care she hated. She was dark and thin and foreign-
looking in a world where the prestige went to blondeness and curly hair and
dimples, she was slow where glibness was prized. She was a child of anxious,
not proud, love. We were poor and could not afford for her the soil of easy
growth. I was a young mother, I was a distracted mother. There were other
children pushing up, demanding. Her younger sister seemed all that she was
not. There were years she did not want me to touch her. She kept too much
in herself, her life was such she had to keep too much in herself. My wisdom
came too late. She has much to her and probably little will come of it. She
is a child of her age, of depression, of war, of fear.

Let her be. So all that is in her will not bloom—but in how many does   56
it? There is still enough left to live by. Only help her to know—help make
it so there is cause for her to know—that she is more than this dress on the
ironing board, helpless before the iron.

◉   ◉   ◉

OPTIONS FOR READING LOGS: "I STAND HERE IRONING"

1. Use the double-entry journal technique to discover meaning in "I Stand
    Here Ironing." In the left column of your journal page, list three to five
    "what" or "why" questions that occur to you as you are reading, such
    as, "Who is the 'you' that the mother addresses in the story?" When
    you finish your list, move to the top of the right column and answer
    your questions as completely as you can. (Remember that such interpreta-
    tion will require you to take educated guesses.) To demonstrate that you
    have a basic understanding of the text, end your journal entry by jotting
    down the main idea of "I Stand Here Ironing."

2. The narrator's first-person monologue is so direct and honest, it is almost
    painful at times. Copy the most poignant line or passage in "I Stand
    Here Ironing." Then, using personal anecdotes and examples, explain
    fully why that particular passage held such power or meaning for you.

3. Does Emily's early start in life remind you of your own upbringing or
    is it vastly different from your experience? Tell a parallel story from your
    personal life that was triggered by "I Stand Here Ironing." Your story

should be connected with the theme of "Family Knowledge: Who Has Shaped Me?"

OPTIONS FOR WRITING ASSIGNMENTS: "I STAND HERE IRONING"

1. Write a letter to the narrator in "I Stand Here Ironing." Address her directly, using the letter to express your own point of view about the type of mother she felt she was. As examples, you may choose to be sympathetic toward her, to be angry with her, or to praise her. Use whatever tone is most appropriate to express your reaction to the story.

2. What do you think of "I Stand Here Ironing" as a story about family lessons? Is it a good sociological study? Write a critical review giving a clear appraisal of "I Stand Here Ironing" as a story of discovery about parent-child lessons. Your evaluation can be positive, negative, or a mixture of the two, but it should be stated as a thesis in your introductory paragraph. Each of the following paragraphs should contain supporting evidence that makes your judgment convincing.

3. In "I Stand Here Ironing," the narrator explains how much she loved her daughter, Emily, in spite of the circumstances of poverty. Yet she seems to harbor some guilt about her role as Emily's mother. What might be the causes of the mother's feelings? As you trace effects to their causes, watch for hidden discoveries along the way. Focus on the theme of "Family Knowledge: Who Has Shaped Me?"

4. Does "I Stand Here Ironing" remind you of your own family relationships? The mother in the story says, "My wisdom came too late," a lament that perhaps is familiar to all parents. Compose a narrative or descriptive essay that focuses on an incident from your past that taught you something about parent-child relationships. In your introductory paragraph write a thesis statement that points out the significance of that incident in your life. Be sure the other paragraphs contain anecdotes and specific details that support your thesis statement.

A Family Supper

1990

KAZUO ISHIGURO

 KAZUO ISHIGURO was born in Nagasaki, Japan; however, he moved to England with his parents at the age of six and was brought up there. He attended the University of Kent and later studied fiction writing at the University of East Anglia. An award-winning writer, he is probably best known for his novel *The Remains of the Day,* which was made into a movie. His story "A Family Supper" deals with the complexities of family life, especially the conflict between generations. The son's and daughter's values and goals, in terms of work, family, and other important issues, differ from those of their father. It almost seems that the children have adopted another culture that, with its own set of values and goals, strongly rejects the father's way of life. In fact, both children are, to some extent, more influenced by American culture, and the father tells the son, "It must feel strange for you, being back in Japan."

As you read "A Family Supper," think about generational conflicts that frequently create differences between parents and their children. Based on your own experience, how do you feel the two generations deal with their differences? Are such conflicts an unavoidable stage in an individual's growth? Do many children eventually return to the values of their parents and accept them?

Fugu is a fish caught off the Pacific shores of Japan. The fish has held a special significance for me ever since my mother died after eating one. The poison resides in the sex glands of the fish, inside two fragile bags. These bags must be removed with caution when preparing the fish, for any clumsiness will result in the poison leaking into the veins. Regrettably, it is not easy to tell whether or not this operation has been carried out successfully. The proof is, as it were, in the eating. 1

Fugu poisoning is hideously painful and almost always fatal. If the fish has been eaten during the evening, the victim is usually overtaken by pain 2 during his sleep. He rolls about in agony for a few hours and is dead by morning. The fish became extremely popular in Japan after the war. Until stricter regulations were imposed, it was all the rage to perform the hazardous gutting operation in one's own kitchen, then to invite neighbors and friends round for the feast.

At the time of my mother's death, I was living in California. My relation-ship with my parents had become somewhat strained around that period and consequently I did not learn of the circumstances of her death until I re-turned to Tokyo two years later. Apparently, my mother had always refused to eat fugu, but on this particular occasion she had made an exception, having been invited by an old school friend whom she was anxious not to offend. It was my father who supplied me with the details as we drove from the airport to his house in the Kamakura district. When we finally arrived, it was nearing the end of a sunny autumn day.

"Did you eat on the plane?" my father asked. We were sitting on the tatami floor of his tearoom.

"They gave me a light snack."

"You must be hungry. We'll eat as soon as Kikuko arrives."

My father was a formidable-looking man with a large stony jaw and furious black eyebrows. I think now, in retrospect, that he much resembled Chou En-lai, although he would not have cherished such a comparison, being particularly proud of the pure samurai blood that ran in the family. His general presence was not one that encouraged relaxed conversation; neither were things helped much by his odd way of stating each remark as if it were the concluding one. In fact, as I sat opposite him that afternoon, a boyhood memory came back to me of the time he had struck me several times around the head for "chattering like an old woman." Inevitably, our conversation since my arrival at the airport had been punctuated by long pauses.

"I'm sorry to hear about the firm," I said when neither of us had spoken for some time. He nodded gravely.

"In fact, the story didn't end there," he said. "After the firm's collapse, Watanabe killed himself. He didn't wish to live with the disgrace."

"I see."

"We were partners for seventeen years. A man of principle and honor. I respected him very much."

"Will you go into business again?" I asked.

"I am . . . in retirement. I'm too old to involve myself in new ventures now. Business these days has become so different. Dealing with foreigners. Doing things their way. I don't understand how we've come to this. Neither did Watanabe." He sighed. "A fine man. A man of principle."

The tearoom looked out over the garden. From where I sat I could make   14
out the ancient well that as a child I had believed to be haunted. It was just
visible now through the thick foliage. The sun had sunk low and much of
the garden had fallen into shadow.

"I'm glad in any case that you've decided to come back," my father said.   15
"More than a short visit, I hope."

"I'm not sure what my plans will be."   16

"I, for one, am prepared to forget the past. Your mother, too, was always   17
ready to welcome you back—upset as she was by your behavior."

"I appreciate your sympathy. As I say, I'm not sure what my plans are."   18

"I've come to believe now that there were no evil intentions in your   19
mind," my father continued. "You were swayed by certain . . . influences.
Like so many others."

"Perhaps we should forget it, as you suggest."   20

"As you will. More tea?"   21

Just then a girl's voice came echoing through the house.   22

"At last." My father rose to his feet. "Kikuko has arrived."   23

Despite our difference in years, my sister and I had always been close.   24
Seeing me again seemed to make her excessively excited, and for a while she
did nothing but giggle nervously. But she calmed down somewhat when my
father started to question her about Osaka and her university. She answered
him with short, formal replies. She in turn asked me a few questions, but
she seemed inhibited by the fear that her question might lead to awkward
topics. After a while, the conversation had become even sparser than prior
to Kikuko's arrival. Then my father stood up, saying: "I must attend to the
supper. Please excuse me for being burdened by such matters. Kikuko will
look after you."

My sister relaxed quite visibly once he had left the room. Within a few   25
minutes, she was chatting freely about her friends in Osaka and about her
classes at university. Then quite suddenly she decided we should walk in the
garden and went striding out onto the veranda. We put on some straw sandals
that had been left along the veranda rail and stepped out into the garden.
The light in the garden had grown very dim.

"I've been dying for a smoke for the last half hour," she said, lighting   26
a cigarette.

"Then why didn't you smoke?"   27

She made a furtive gesture back toward the house, then grinned mischie-   28
vously.

"Oh, I see," I said.   29

"Guess what? I've got a boyfriend now."   30

"Oh, yes?"   31

"Except I'm wondering what to do. I haven't made up my mind yet."   32

"Quite understandable."   33

"You see, he's making plans to go to America. He wants me to go with   34
him as soon as I finish studying."

"I see. And you want to go to America?"   35

"If we go, we're going to hitchhike." Kikuko waved a thumb in front of   36
my face. "People say it's dangerous, but I've done it in Osaka and it's fine."

"I see. So what is it you're unsure about?"   37

We were following a narrow path that wound through the shrubs and   38
finished by the old well. As we walked, Kikuko persisted in taking unnecessarily
theatrical puffs on her cigarette.

"Well, I've got lots of friends now in Osaka. I like it there. I'm not sure   39
I want to leave them all behind just yet. And Suichi . . . I like him, but I'm
not sure I want to spend so much time with him. Do you understand?"

"Oh, perfectly."   40

She grinned again, then skipped on ahead of me until she had reached   41
the well. "Do you remember," she said as I came walking up to her, "how
you used to say this well was haunted?"

"Yes, I remember."   42

We both peered over the side.   43

"Mother always told me it was the old woman from the vegetable store   44
you'd seen that night," she said. "But I never believed her and never came
out here alone."

"Mother used to tell me that too. She even told me once the old woman   45
had confessed to being the ghost. Apparently, she'd been taking a shortcut
through our garden. I imagine she had some trouble clambering over these
walls."

Kikuko gave a giggle. She then turned her back to the well, casting her   46
gaze about the garden.

"Mother never really blamed you, you know," she said, in a new voice.   47
I remained silent. "She always used to say to me how it was their fault, hers
and Father's, for not bringing you up correctly. She used to tell me how
much more careful they'd been with me, and that's why I was so good."
She looked up and the mischievous grin had returned to her face. "Poor
Mother," she said.

"Yes. Poor Mother."   48

"Are you going back to California?"   49

"I don't know. I'll have to see."   50

"What happened to . . . to her? To Vicki?"   51

"That's all finished with," I said. "There's nothing much left for me   52
now in California."

"Do you think I ought to go there?"   53

"Why not? I don't know. You'll probably like it." I glanced toward the   54
house. "Perhaps we'd better go in soon. Father might need a hand with the
supper."

But my sister was once more peering down into the well. "I can't see   55
any ghosts," she said. Her voice echoed a little.

"Is Father very upset about his firm collapsing?"   56

"Don't know. You never can tell with Father." Then suddenly she   57
straightened up and turned to me. "Did he tell you about old Watanabe?
What he did?"

"I heard he committed suicide."   58

"Well, that wasn't all. He took his whole family with him. His wife and   59
his two little girls."

"Oh, yes?"   60

"Those two beautiful little girls. He turned on the gas while they were   61
all asleep. Then he cut his stomach with a meat knife."

"Yes, Father was just telling me how Watanabe was a man of principle."   62

"Sick." My sister turned back to the well.   63

"Careful. You'll fall right in."   64

"I can't see any ghost," she said. "You were lying to me all that   65
time."

"But I never said it lived down the well."   66

"Where is it then?"   67

We both looked around at the trees and shrubs. The daylight had almost   68
gone. Eventually I pointed to a small clearing some ten yards away.

"Just there I saw it. Just there."   69

We stared at the spot.   70

"What did it look like?"   71

"I couldn't see very well. It was dark."   72

"But you must have seen something."   73

"It was an old woman. She was just standing there, watching me."   74

We kept staring at the spot as if mesmerized.   75

"She was wearing a white kimono," I said. "Some of her hair came   76
undone. It was blowing around a little."

Kikuko pushed her elbow against my arm. "Oh, be quiet. You're trying   77
to frighten me all over again." She trod on the remains of her cigarette, then
for a brief moment stood regarding it with a perplexed expression. She kicked
some pine needles over it, then once more displayed her grin. "Let's see if
supper's ready," she said.

We found my father in the kitchen. He gave us a quick glance, then   78
carried on with what he was doing.

"Father's become quite a chef since he's had to manage on his own," 79
Kikuko said with a laugh.

He turned and looked at my sister coldly. "Hardly a skill I'm proud of," 80
he said. "Kikuko, come here and help."

For some moments my sister did not move. Then she stepped forward 81
and took an apron hanging from a drawer.

"Just these vegetables need cooking now," he said to her. "The rest just 82
needs watching." Then he looked up and regarded me strangely for some
seconds. "I expect you want to look around the house," he said eventually.
He put down the chopsticks he had been holding. "It's a long time since
you've seen it."

As we left the kitchen I glanced toward Kikuko, but her back was turned. 83

"She's a good girl," my father said. 84

I followed my father from room to room. I had forgotten how large the 85
house was. A panel would slide open and another room would appear. But
the rooms were all startlingly empty. In one of the rooms the lights did not
come on, and we stared at the stark walls and tatami in the pale light that
came from the windows.

"This house is too large for a man to live in alone," my father said. "I 86
don't have much use for most of these rooms now."

But eventually my father opened the door to a room packed full of books 87
and papers. There were flowers in vases and pictures on the walls. Then I
noticed something on a low table in the corner of the room. I came nearer
and saw it was a plastic model of a battleship, the kind constructed by
children. It had been placed on some newspaper; scattered around it were
assorted pieces of gray plastic.

My father gave a laugh. He came up to the table and picked up the 88
model.

"Since the firm folded," he said, "I have a little more time on my hands." 89
He laughed again, rather strangely. For a moment his face looked almost
gentle. "A little more time."

"That seems odd," I said. "You were always so busy." 90

"Too busy, perhaps." He looked at me with a small smile. "Perhaps I 91
should have been a more attentive father."

I laughed. He went on contemplating his battleship. Then he looked 92
up. "I hadn't meant to tell you this, but perhaps it's best that I do. It's my
belief that your mother's death was no accident. She had many worries. And
some disappointments."

We both gazed at the plastic battleship. 93

"Surely," I said eventually, "my mother didn't expect me to live here 94
forever."

"Obviously you don't see. You don't see how it is for some parents. Not only must they lose their children, they must lose them to things they don't understand." He spun the battleship in his fingers. "These little gunboats here could have been better glued, don't you think?"

"Perhaps. I think it looks fine."

"During the war I spent some time on a ship rather like this. But my ambition was always the air force. I figured it like this: If your ship was struck by the enemy, all you could do was struggle in the water hoping for a lifeline. But in an airplane—well, there was always the final weapon." He put the model back onto the table. "I don't suppose you believe in war."

"Not particularly."

He cast an eye around the room. "Supper should be ready by now," he said. "You must be hungry."

Supper was waiting in a dimly lit room next to the kitchen. The only source of light was a big lantern that hung over the table, casting the rest of the room in shadow. We bowed to each other before starting the meal.

There was little conversation. When I made some polite comment about the food, Kikuko giggled a little. Her earlier nervousness seemed to have returned to her. My father did not speak for several minutes. Finally he said:

"It must feel strange for you, being back in Japan."

"Yes, it is a little strange."

"Already, perhaps, you regret leaving America."

"A little. Not so much. I didn't leave behind much. Just some empty rooms."

"I see."

I glanced across the table. My father's face looked stony and forbidding in the half-light. We ate on in silence.

Then my eye caught something at the back of the room. At first I continued eating, then my hands became still. The others noticed and looked at me. I went on gazing into the darkness past my father's shoulder.

"Who is that? In that photograph there?"

"Which photograph?" My father turned slightly, trying to follow my gaze.

"The lowest one. The old woman in the white kimono."

My father put down his chopsticks. He looked first at the photograph, then at me.

"Your mother." His voice had become very hard. "Can't you recognize your own mother?"

"My mother. You see, it's dark. I can't see it very well."

No one spoke for a few seconds, then Kikuko rose to her feet. She took the photograph down from the wall, came back to the table, and gave it to me.

"She looks a lot older," I said.   116

"It was taken shortly before her death," said my father.   117

"It was the dark. I couldn't see very well."   118

I looked up and noticed my father holding out a hand. I gave him the   119
photograph. He looked at it intently, then held it toward Kikuko. Obediently,
my sister rose to her feet once more and returned the picture to the wall.

There was a large pot left unopened at the center of the table. When   120
Kikuko had seated herself again, my father reached forward and lifted the
lid. A cloud of steam rose up and curled toward the lantern. He pushed the
pot a little toward me.

"You must be hungry," he said. One side of his face had fallen into   121
shadow.

"Thank you." I reached forward with my chopsticks. The steam was   122
almost scalding. "What is it?"

"Fish."   123

"It smells very good."   124

In the soup were strips of fish that had curled almost into balls. I picked   125
one out and brought it to my bowl.

"Help yourself. There's plenty."   126

"Thank you." I took a little more, then pushed the pot toward my father.   127
I watched him take several pieces to his bowl. Then we both watched as
Kikuko served herself.

My father bowed slightly. "You must be hungry," he said again. He took   128
some fish to his mouth and started to eat. Then I, too, chose a piece and
put it in my mouth. It felt soft, quite fleshy against my tongue.

The three of us ate in silence. Several minutes went by. My father lifted   129
the lid and once more steam rose up. We all reached forward and helped
ourselves.

"Here," I said to my father, "you have this last piece."   130

"Thank you."   131

When we had finished the meal, my father stretched out his arms and   132
yawned with an air of satisfaction. "Kikuko," he said, "prepare a pot of tea,
please."

My sister looked at him, then left the room without comment. My father   133
stood up.

"Let's retire to the other room. It's rather warm in here."   134

I got to my feet and followed him into the tearoom. The large sliding   135
windows had been left open, bringing in a breeze from the garden. For a
while we sat in silence.

"Father," I said, finally.   136

"Yes?"   137

"Kikuko tells me Watanabe-san took his whole family with him."   138

My father lowered his eyes and nodded. For some moments he seemed   139
deep in thought. "Watanabe was very devoted to his work," he said at last.
"The collapse of the firm was a great blow to him. I fear it must have
weakened his judgment."

"You think what he did . . . it was a mistake?"   140

"Why, of course. Do you see it otherwise?"   141

"No, no. Of course not."   142

"There are other things besides work," my father said.   143

"Yes."   144

We fell silent again. The sound of locusts came in from the garden. I   145
looked out into the darkness. The well was no longer visible.

"What do you think you will do now?" my father asked. "Will you stay   146
in Japan for a while?"

"To be honest, I hadn't thought that far ahead."   147

"If you wish to stay here, I mean here in this house, you would be very   148
welcome. That is, if you don't mind living with an old man."

"Thank you. I'll have to think about it."   149

I gazed out once more into the darkness.   150

"But of course," said my father, "this house is so dreary now. You'll no   151
doubt return to America before long."

"Perhaps. I don't know yet."   152

"No doubt you will."   153

For some time my father seemed to be studying the back of his hands.   154
Then he looked up and sighed.

"Kikuko is due to complete her studies next spring," he said. "Perhaps   155
she will want to come home then. She's a good girl."

"Perhaps she will."   156

"Things will improve then."   157

"Yes, I'm sure they will."   158

We fell silent once more, waiting for Kikuko to bring the tea.   159

❖   ❖   ❖

OPTIONS FOR READING LOGS: "A FAMILY SUPPER"

1. Writers often use images or symbols to represent an idea or concept and
    thus provide a deeper, more important message than the one that is
    initially apparent. Use the double-entry journal technique to explore the
    meaning of some of the more powerful images or symbols in "A Family
    Supper." For example, some questions in the left column might be,

"What is the significance of how the narrator's mother died?" "What may have caused the son to move to America?" "Why doesn't the son recognize his own mother in the photograph?" Use the right column to explore possible answers to each question. To demonstrate that you have reached a basic understanding of the story, end your journal entry by jotting down the main idea of "A Family Supper."

2. An analysis of the main characters in a short story can help isolate its central idea. Draw a vertical line down the middle of your journal page to create two columns. In the left column, list the son, the daughter, the father, the mother, and the ghost. In the right column, jot down your opinions, observations, and comments about each of those characters. Complete your journal entry by discussing some interesting insights you gained about one or more of the characters.

3. Examine your personal reaction to "A Family Supper" by completing one of the following statements:

   A. "I was struck by _____ ."
   B. "I was confused by _____ ."
   C. "I was surprised by _____ ."

   Refer to particular incidents in the story and explain your reactions. For example, "I was struck by what is not said during the father-son conversation more so than by what is actually said. Their conversation, which is 'punctuated by long pauses,' tells a lot about their relationship," or "I was confused by the death of Watanabe; why did he murder his whole family?" Finish your journal entry with a detailed explanation of your statement.

OPTIONS FOR WRITING ASSIGNMENTS: "A FAMILY SUPPER"

1. Review your journal entries to see if you can make any connections between this story and any of the earlier readings in this text. Notice whether any similarities or differences are evident between "A Family Supper" and one of the other stories, poems, or essays. You could combine and expand your journal entries into a more polished piece of writing that explores its subject matter (for example, family conflicts and generation gaps) in greater range and depth. A comparison-and-contrast essay might be an appropriate mode for this purpose. Begin with a list (two lists for comparison and contrast), develop it into an outline, and use transitional expressions that signal similarities or differences.

2. Does "A Family Supper" remind you of an event from your own family life? Compose a narrative or descriptive essay that focuses on some remembered event from your past. Write a thesis statement that points out the significance of that event in your life; then, throughout your essay, concentrate on using vivid details and descriptions to help recreate your memory. For example, you might recall a time during your adolescence when your parents either divorced or came close to divorcing each other. Your thesis statement might be phrased like this: "That stormy sixteenth year of my life introduced me to my own strengths, which I had never even glimpsed before."

3. How would you characterize Kikuko, the sister? Since not much is explained about her, the reader is left to make inferences about what she is like and what made her that way. In "A Family Supper," Kikuko was probably influenced greatly by tradition and her family. Interview someone from your own extended family and write an essay showing how that person has significantly influenced your personal development. Before your interview, draw up a list of appropriate questions. Come up with a thesis sentence that presents some generalization about the person, and write five or more paragraphs to support that idea. In your essay you might want to include biographical information that clarifies the influences (either positive or negative) that have made this person an important part of your life.

4. Write a formal essay of five or more paragraphs, exploring the theme of family knowledge and its importance in "A Family Supper." Focus on important parts of the story about which you have genuine questions, such as "Do the father and son ultimately reconcile their differences?" or "What options are open to the son? Should he stay with his father in Japan?" In your introductory paragraph, include a thesis statement that expresses your main idea clearly. For example, "Ishiguro's 'A Family Supper' is an exploration of a family torn apart by generational differences." In your supporting paragraphs, use quotes from the text and refer to specific passages to clarify and support your thesis statement.

My Papa's Waltz

1948

THEODORE ROETHKE

 THEODORE ROETHKE was an American poet who was born in Saginaw, Michigan. Although he occasionally suffered from a nervous condition and called himself a "mad" poet, he also suffered bouts of alcoholism. He was considered a brilliant teacher, having taught at several colleges and universities, including the University of Washington. Those who attended his readings described him as a heavyset man who prepared for his performances by pacing back and forth on the stage like an athlete warming up for an event.

In "My Papa's Waltz" the speaker recalls a vivid childhood experience of being waltzed around the kitchen by his father while his frowning mother watched. Some readers see this poem as a warm memory of a childhood romp with a happy, though boisterous father. Others see a darker, more complex father figure, one who is potentially threatening, violent, and out of control.

Happy times in our younger lives can sometimes have a darker side that was hidden from us as children. Can you recall such an experience from your own past? Or do you recall some playful time in your childhood that represents a moment of closeness or community with a family member and somehow sticks in your mind after the passage of some years? What in the poem connects in some way—good, bad, or both—with memorable family experiences of your own?

The whiskey on your breath   1
Could make a small boy dizzy;
But I hung on like death:
Such waltzing was not easy.

We romped until the pans   2
Slid from the kitchen shelf;
My mother's countenance
Could not unfrown itself.

The hand that held my wrist
Was battered on one knuckle;   3
At every step you missed
My right ear scraped a buckle.

You beat time on my head
With a palm caked hard by dirt,
Then waltzed me off to bed   4
Still clinging to your shirt.

OPTIONS FOR READING LOGS: "MY PAPA'S WALTZ"

1. Use the double-entry journal technique to discover meaning in "My Papa's Waltz." For example, a "why" question in the left column might be, "Why is the dance named a 'waltz' rather than a dance or a romp?" or "Why does the poet mention the smell of whiskey on his father's breath?" Use the right column to explore possible answers to each of your questions. To demonstrate that you have a basic understanding of the poem, end your journal entry by jotting down the main idea of "My Papa's Waltz."

2. Students and critics of "My Papa's Waltz" usually have strong emotional reactions to this poem and often differ in their interpretations of it. Some see it in a positive light, whereas others see it quite negatively. Use the double-entry journal technique to clarify the meaning of some of the poem's powerful images and symbols, both positive and negative. Draw a vertical line down the middle of your journal page. Use the left column to list all of the positive images or symbols—such as "romped"; use the right column to list all the negative images—for example, "hung on like death." End your journal entry with a brief interpretation of the poem.

3. Reconstruct Roethke's "My Papa's Waltz" by drawing a picture of the characters and of the entire scene that the poem creates, particularly the kitchen. Add some close-up details, like the pots and pans and the look on the mother's face. After you complete your drawing, write a detailed description of the "waltz" as you imagined it, clearly stating the main idea of the poem.

OPTIONS FOR WRITING ASSIGNMENTS: "MY PAPA'S WALTZ"

1. What family knowledge are we meant to gain from "My Papa's Waltz"? Would you like to talk with Theodore Roethke, the author of the poem, and ask him questions, hear his answers, and discuss your ideas? Create a dialogue between you and Roethke about the ideas in "My Papa's Waltz." Begin by asking him how he felt about the incident as a child and if his feelings changed as he grew older. Your conversation might take the form of a question-and-answer interview, an argument, or an open-ended discussion of the author's ideas and their implications in terms of how people are shaped by their early experiences with family members.

2. Write a personal letter to one of the characters depicted in "My Papa's Waltz." Address the person directly, using the letter to express your own point of view about his or her family situation. You could, for example, choose to empathize with the boy in the poem, explaining that you understand what he went through and telling why you understand his experience. Use whatever tone is most appropriate to express your reaction to the poem.

3. Review your journal entries to see if you can make any connections between this poem and any of the earlier readings in the book. Notice whether any similarities or differences are evident between "My Papa's Waltz" and one of the other stories, poems, or essays. For example, you might see significant connections between the theme of "My Papa's Waltz" and the theme of "Those Winter Sundays" by Robert Hayden. You could combine and expand two of your journal entries into a more polished piece of writing that explores its subject matter (for example, father-son relationships) in greater range and depth. A comparison-and-contrast essay might be an appropriate mode for this purpose. Begin with a list (two lists for comparison and contrast), develop it into an outline, and use transitional expressions that signal similarities or differences.

4. In "My Papa's Waltz" the narrator writes about a childhood event, yet he describes it from an adult's perspective. How does this reveal his feelings about his father? Write a formal essay of five or more paragraphs, explaining the meaning of "My Papa's Waltz." Focus your attention on anything you have genuine questions about, such as, "Is this poem about fear or is it about love?" or "Is it about abuse or about harmless roughhousing." This is a complex issue, but take a stand and begin with a thesis statement that makes an arguable point about your particular interpretation of the poem. Brainstorm to come up with reasons to back up your interpretation, and review the poem for words or phrases that support your central argument.

From
Hunger of Memory

1981

RICHARD RODRIGUEZ

 RICHARD RODRIGUEZ, a Mexican-American writer, addresses the complexities of growing up bilingual in the United States. He attended Stanford and Columbia Universities and eventually received his doctorate in English literature from the University of California at Berkeley. He has chosen to focus his career, however, on writing rather than on college teaching. In this excerpt from *Hunger of Memory,* Rodriguez compares the way he felt about speaking English while growing up with the way he felt about speaking Spanish.

As a child, Rodriguez was often troubled by his parents' halting English. Indeed children often feel more pain than adults do at seeing themselves or their families as "different." Rodriguez claims that as an adult he was "embarrassed by childhood fears." He states, "I felt that I had somehow committed a sin of betrayal by learning English. . . . I felt I had betrayed my immediate family."

Do you think most adults look back later and are ashamed of their childhood feelings, especially regarding their own parents? Were you ever overly self-conscious about who you were and about the impression your family members were making on other people? Why do you think children are so much more sensitive than adults about such issues?

I grew up victim to a disabling confusion. As I grew fluent in English, I no longer could speak Spanish with confidence. I continued to understand spoken Spanish. And in high school, I learned how to read and write Spanish. But for many years I could not pronounce it. A powerful guilt blocked my spoken words; an essential glue was missing whenever I'd try to connect words to form sentences. I would be unable to break a barrier of sound, to speak freely. I would speak, or try to speak, Spanish, and I would manage to utter halting, hiccuping sounds that betrayed my unease.

1

106

When relatives and Spanish-speaking friends of my parents came to the   2
house, my brother and sisters seemed reticent[1] to use Spanish, but at least
they managed to say a few necessary words before being excused. I never
managed so gracefully. I was cursed with guilt. Each time I'd hear myself
addressed in Spanish, I would be unable to respond with any success. I'd
know the words I wanted to say, but I couldn't manage to say them. I would
try to speak, but everything I said seemed to me horribly anglicized.[2] My
mouth would not form the words right. My jaw would tremble. After a
phrase or two, I'd cough up a warm, silvery sound. And stop.

It surprised my listeners to hear me. They'd lower their heads, better to   3
grasp what I was trying to say. They would repeat their questions in gentle,
affectionate voices. But by then I would answer in English. No, no, they
would say, we want you to speak to us in Spanish. ("*. . . en español.*") But
I couldn't do it. *Pocho* then they called me. Sometimes playfully, teasingly,
using the tender diminutive[3]—*mi pochito*. Sometimes not so playfully, mock-
ingly, *Pocho*. (A Spanish dictionary defines that word as an adjective meaning
"colorless" or "bland." But I heard it as a noun, naming the Mexican-
American who, in becoming an American, forgets his native society.)
"*¡Pocho!*" the lady in the Mexican food store muttered, shaking her head. I
looked up to the counter where red and green peppers were strung like
Christmas tree lights and saw the frowning face of the stranger. My mother
laughed somewhere behind me. (She said that her children didn't want to
practice "our Spanish" after they started going to school.) My mother's
smiling voice made me suspect that the lady who faced me was not really
angry at me. But, searching her face, I couldn't find the hint of a smile.

Embarrassed, my parents would regularly need to explain their children's   4
inability to speak flowing Spanish during those years. My mother met the
wrath of her brother, her only brother, when he came up from Mexico one
summer with his family. He saw his nieces and nephews for the very first
time. After listening to me, he looked away and said what a disgrace it was
that I couldn't speak Spanish, "*su proprio idioma.*" He made that remark to
my mother; I noticed, however, that he stared at my father.

I clearly remember one other visitor from those years. A long-time friend   5
of my father from San Francisco would come to stay with us for several days
in late August. He took great interest in me after he realized that I couldn't
answer his questions in Spanish. He would grab me as I started to leave the
kitchen. He would ask me something. Usually he wouldn't bother to wait
for my mumbled response. Knowingly, he'd murmur: "*¿Ay Pocho, Pocho,*

1. reticent: restrained   2. anglicized: made English in form and character   3. diminutive: pertaining
to a form denoting smallness

adónde vas?" And he would press his thumbs into the upper part of my arms, making me squirm with currents of pain. Dumbly, I'd stand there, waiting for his wife to notice us, for her to call him off with a benign smile. I'd giggle, hoping to deflate the tension between us, pretending that I hadn't seen the glittering scorn in his glance.

I remember that man now, but seek no revenge in this telling. I recount   6 such incidents only because they suggest the fierce power Spanish had for many people I met at home; the way Spanish was associated with closeness. Most of those people who called me a *pocho* could have spoken English to me. But they would not. They seemed to think that Spanish was the only language we could use, that Spanish alone permitted our close association. (Such persons are vulnerable always to the ghetto merchant and the politician who have learned the value of speaking their clients' family language to gain immediate trust.) For my part, I felt that I had somehow committed a sin of betrayal by learning English. But betrayal against whom? Not against visitors to the house exactly. No, I felt that I had betrayed my immediate family. I *knew* that my parents had encouraged me to learn English. I *knew* that I had turned to English only with angry reluctance. But once I spoke English with ease, I came to *feel* guilty. (This guilt defied logic.) I felt that I had shattered the intimate bond that had once held the family close. This original sin against my family told whenever anyone addressed me in Spanish and I responded, confounded.

But even during those years of guilt, I was coming to sense certain   7 consoling truths about language and intimacy. I remember playing with a friend in the backyard one day, when my grandmother appeared at the window. Her face was stern with suspicion when she saw the boy (the *gringo*) I was with. In Spanish she called out to me, sounding the whistle of her ancient breath. My companion looked up and watched her intently as she lowered the window and moved, still visible, behind the light curtain, watching us both. He wanted to know what she had said. I started to tell him, to say—to translate her Spanish words into English. The problem was, however, that though I knew how to translate exactly *what* she had told me, I realized that any translation would distort the deepest meaning of her message: It had been directed only to me. This message of intimacy could never be translated because it was not *in* the words she had used but passed *through* them. So any translation would have seemed wrong; her words would have been stripped of an essential meaning. Finally, I decided not to tell my friend anything. I told him that I didn't hear all she had said.

This insight unfolded in time. Making more and more friends outside   8 my house, I began to distinguish intimate voices speaking through *English*. I'd listen at times to a close friend's confidential tone or secretive whisper.

Even more remarkable were those instances when, for no special reason apparently, I'd become conscious of the fact that my companion was speaking only to me. I'd marvel just hearing his voice. It was a stunning event: to be able to break through his words, to be able to hear this voice of the other, to realize that it was directed only to me. After such moments of intimacy outside the house, I began to trust hearing intimacy conveyed through my family's English. Voices at home at last punctured sad confusion. I'd hear myself addressed as an intimate at home once again. Such moments were never as raucous with sound as past times had been when we had had "private" Spanish to use. (Our English-sounding house was never to be as noisy as our Spanish-speaking house had been.) Intimate moments were usually soft moments of sound. My mother was in the dining room while I did my homework nearby. And she looked over at me. Smiled. Said something—her words said nothing very important. But her voice sounded to tell me *(We are together)* I was her son.

(Richard!)   9

Intimacy thus continued at home; intimacy was not stilled by English.   10
It is true that I would never forget the great change of my life, the diminished occasions of intimacy. But there would also be times when I sensed the deepest truth about language and intimacy: *Intimacy is not created by a particular language; it is created by intimates.* The great change in my life was not linguistic but social. If, after becoming a successful student, I no longer heard intimate voices as often as I had earlier, it was not because I spoke English rather than Spanish. It was because I used public language for most of the day. I moved easily at last, a citizen in a crowded city of words.

·   ·   ·

This boy became a man. In private now, alone, I brood over language and   11
intimacy—the great themes of my past. In public I expect most of the faces I meet to be the faces of strangers. (How do you do?) If meetings are quick and impersonal, they have been efficiently managed. I rush past the sounds of voices attending only to the words addressed to me. Voices seem planed to an even surface of sound, soundless. A business associate speaks in a deep baritone, but I pass through the timbre to attend to his words. The crazy man who sells me a newspaper every night mumbles something crazy, but I have time only to pretend that I have heard him say hello. Accented versions of English make little impression on me. In the rush-hour crowd a Japanese tourist asks me a question, and I inch past his accent to concentrate on what he is saying. The Eastern European immigrant in a neighborhood delicatessen speaks to me through a marinade of sounds, but I respond to his words. I

note for only a second the Texas accent of the telephone operator or the Mississippi accent of the man who lives in the apartment below me.

My city seems silent until some ghetto black teenagers board the bus I   12
am on. Because I do not take their presence for granted, I listen to the sounds of their voices. Of all the accented versions of English I hear in a day, I hear theirs most intently. They are *the* sounds of the outsider. They annoy me for being loud—so self-sufficient and unconcerned by my presence. Yet for the same reason they seem to me glamorous. (A romantic gesture against public acceptance.) Listening to their shouted laughter, I realize my own quiet. Their voices enclose my isolation. I feel envious, envious of their brazen intimacy.

I warn myself away from such envy, however. I remember the black   13
political activists who have argued in favor of using black English in schools. (Their argument varies only slightly from that made by foreign-language bilingualists.) I have heard "radical" linguists make the point that black English is a complex and intricate version of English. And I do not doubt it. But neither do I think that black English should be a language of public instruction. What makes black English inappropriate in classrooms is not something *in* the language. It is rather what lower-class speakers make of it. Just as Spanish would have been a dangerous language for me to have used at the start of my education, so black English would be a dangerous language to use in the schooling of teenagers for whom it reenforces feelings of public separateness.

This seems to me an obvious point. But one that needs to be made. In   14
recent years there have been attempts to make the language of the alien public language. "Bilingual education, two ways to understand . . . ," television and radio commercials glibly announce. Proponents of bilingual education are careful to say that they want students to acquire good schooling. Their argument goes something like this: Children permitted to use their family language in school will not be so alienated and will be better able to match the progress of English-speaking children in the crucial first months of instruction. (Increasingly confident of their abilities, such children will be more inclined to apply themselves to their studies in the future.) But then the bilingualists claim another, very different goal. They say that children who use their family language in school will retain a sense of their individuality—their ethnic heritage and cultural ties. Supporters of bilingual education thus want it both ways. They propose bilingual schooling as a way of helping students acquire the skills of the classroom crucial for public success. But they likewise insist that bilingual instruction will give students a sense of their identity apart from the public.

Behind this screen there gleams an astonishing promise: One can be-   15
come a public person while still remaining a private person. At the very same
time one can be both! There need be no tension between the self in the
crowd and the self apart from the crowd! Who would not want to believe
such an idea? Who can be surprised that the scheme has won the support of
many middle-class Americans? If the barrio or ghetto child can retain his
separateness even while being publicly educated, then it is almost possible to
believe that there is no private cost to be paid for public success. Such is the
consolation offered by any of the current bilingual schemes. Consider, for
example, the bilingual voters' ballot. In some American cities one can cast a
ballot printed in several languages. Such a document implies that a person
can exercise that most public of rights—the right to vote—while still keeping
apart, unassimilated[4] from public life.

It is not enough to say that these schemes are foolish and certainly   16
doomed. Middle-class supporters of public bilingualism toy with the confusion of those Americans who cannot speak standard English as well as they
can. Bilingual enthusiasts, moreover, sin against intimacy. An Hispanic-Ameri-
can writer tells me, "I will never give up my family language; I would as
soon give up my soul." Thus he holds to his chest a skein[5] of words, as
though it were the source of his family ties. He credits to language what he
should credit to family members. A convenient mistake. For as long as he
holds on to words, he can ignore how much else has changed in his life.

It has happened before. In earlier decades, persons newly successful and   17
ambitious for social mobility similarly seized upon certain "family words."
Working-class men attempting political power took to calling one another
"brother." By so doing they escaped oppressive public isolation and were
able to unite with many others like themselves. But they paid a price for this
union. It was a public union they forged. The word they coined to address
one another could never be the sound *(brother)* exchanged by two in intimate
greeting. In the union hall the word "brother" became a vague metaphor;
with repetition a weak echo of the intimate sound. Context forced the change.
Context could not be overruled. Context will always guard the realm of the
intimate from public misuse.

Today nonwhite Americans call "brother" to strangers. And white femi-   18
nists refer to their mass union of "sisters." And white middle-class teenagers
continue to prove the importance of context as they try to ignore it. They
seize upon the idioms of the black ghetto. But their attempts to appropriate

---

4. unassimilated: not brought into conformity with the customs and attitudes of a dominant cultural group
or national culture   5. skein: a series of similar or interrelated things

such expressions invariably changes the words. As it becomes a public expression, the ghetto idiom loses its sound—its message of public separateness and strident intimacy. It becomes with public repetition a series of words, increasingly lifeless.

The mystery remains: intimate utterance. The communication of intimacy passes through the word to enliven its sound. But it cannot be held by the word. Cannot be clutched or ever quoted. It is too fluid. It depends not on word but on person.   19

My grandmother!   20

She stood among my other relations mocking me when I no longer spoke Spanish. *"Pocho,"* she said. But then it made no difference. (She'd laugh.) Our relationship continued. Language was never its source. She was a woman in her eighties during the first decade of my life. A mysterious woman to me, my only living grandparent. A woman of Mexico. The woman in long black dresses that reached down to her shoes. My one relative who spoke no word of English. She had no interest in *gringo* society. She remained completely aloof from the public. Protected by her daughters. Protected even by me when we went to Safeway together and I acted as her translator. Eccentric woman. Soft. Hard.   21

When my family visited my aunt's house in San Francisco, my grandmother searched for me among my many cousins. She'd chase them away. Pinching her granddaughters, she'd warn them all away from me. Then she'd take me to her room, where she had prepared for my coming. There would be a chair next to the bed. A dusty jellied candy nearby. And a copy of *Life en Español* for me to examine. "There," she'd say. I'd sit there content. A boy of eight. *Pocho.* Her favorite. I'd sift through the pictures of earthquake-destroyed Latin American cities and blond-wigged Mexican movie stars. And all the while I'd listen to the sound of my grandmother's voice. She'd pace round the room, searching through closets and drawers, telling me stories of her life. Her past. They were stories so familiar to me that I couldn't remember the first time I'd heard them. I'd look up sometimes to listen. Other times she'd look over at me. But she never seemed to expect a response. Sometimes I'd smile or nod. (I understood exactly what she was saying.) But it never seemed to matter to her one way or another. It was enough I was there. The words she spoke were almost irrelevant to that fact—the sounds she made. Content.   22

The mystery remained: intimate utterance.   23

OPTIONS FOR READING LOGS: "FROM *HUNGER OF MEMORY*"

1. Use the double-entry journal technique to comment on powerful lines or passages in the excerpt from *Hunger of Memory*. Draw a vertical line down the middle of your journal page to create two columns. In the left column, copy lines or passages that you particularly like or that you feel are important somehow—for example, "Intimate moments were usually soft moments of sound." In the right column, jot down word associations, interpretations, and comments, including those from your personal experience as well as from your reading. End your journal entry by selecting one of the lines or phrases and explaining why it held such power or meaning for you.

2. Examine your personal reaction to this excerpt from *Hunger of Memory* by completing one of the following statements:

   A. "I was confused by _____."
   B. "I was struck by _____."
   C. "I was surprised by _____."

   Refer to particular incidents in the story and explain your reactions. For example, your statement might say something like "I was surprised that Rodriguez opposes bilingual education, saying, 'It is not enough to say that these schemes are foolish and certainly doomed.' " Finish your journal entry with a detailed explanation of your statement.

3. Examine your personal reaction to the excerpt from *Hunger of Memory* by comparing and contrasting Rodriguez's feelings about his family's background with those of any of the previous writers in this text. What other writers have explored conflicting feeling or attitudes toward their own families? Have any of them expressed a sense of betrayal or guilt? Begin by listing their similarities and showing how they are alike in some way. Then make a list of their differences. End your journal entry by explaining whether you think you understand and empathize with the writers' attitudes about their families.

OPTIONS FOR WRITING ASSIGNMENTS: "FROM *HUNGER OF MEMORY*"

1. Does this excerpt from *Hunger of Memory* remind you of an event from your own family's experiences with language or appearance? Children's slang, haircuts, and clothing can all be symbols of their attempt to define

themselves as being different from the inhabitants of their parents' world. Compose a narrative or descriptive essay that focuses on a remembered event connected with your family, whether it was in the home, in school, or in a public place. Throughout your essay, concentrate on using vivid details and descriptions to help recreate your memory and make your feelings clear.

2. Compare and contrast the discovery of family knowledge in this essay with a similar discovery in any of the previous readings in this book. What do they illustrate about the difficulties and rewards of the powerful and sometimes limiting influence of the family? In what ways, for example, are Rodriguez's essay and Ishiguro's short story "A Family Supper" alike? In what ways are they different? Begin with two lists, develop them into an outline, and use transitional expressions that signal similarities or differences.

3. Our parents often serve as role models for us, but sometimes we are critical of the way they act or speak, especially if they seem vastly different from the accepted norm. Such moments of criticism often mark the beginning of phases in which we question our personal values or feel guilty or ambivalent about our ancestry. Have you experienced a specific period in your life when some strong interest or focus deeply influenced your thoughts and behavior—for example, a time when you rebelled against your family or had conflicting thoughts about them? If you would like to examine that phase through writing, begin with a thesis statement that expresses your main point. Write a formal essay of five or more paragraphs exploring the beginning, middle, and end of that phase. In what ways did other people influence you? How and why did the phase end?

4. Write a formal essay of five or more paragraphs, explaining the meaning of some aspect of the excerpt from *Hunger of Memory*. Focus your attention on parts of the story about which you have genuine questions, such as, "When Rodriguez describes himself as a 'listening child,' is that a positive or a negative statement?" or "What is the significance of his description of sitting with his grandmother, listening to her tell stories? Why does he save that anecdote for the end of his essay?" Begin with a thesis statement that makes an arguable point about your particular interpretation of the story. Brainstorm to come up with reasons to support your interpretation, and review the story for supporting evidence. In your essay, you may want to quote or paraphrase from the story and refer to specific passages to clarify and support your central argument.

Love, Your Only Mother

1987

DAVID MICHAEL KAPLAN

 In "Love, Your Only Mother," DAVID MICHAEL KAPLAN, a contemporary American short-story writer, tells the strange story of a daughter whose only connection with her mother is the mysterious postcards the mother sends her. The mother seems to wander aimlessly from one obscure small town to another, all over the United States, and Kaplan explores how these post-cards have a comforting and yet also profoundly disturbing effect on the daughter, who will awaken and "sit bolt upright," afraid that her lost mother has returned home.

In a family, the influences and interrelationships between members can be clear and ambiguous at the same time. Have you ever had a complex, difficult relationship with a brother, sister, parent, or other relative? How did it make you feel? Do you have strong memories of someone in your family who has moved away or is no longer close to you? As you read this story, reflect on its connections to your own sense of family and family life.

I received another postcard from you today, Mother, and I see by the blurred postmark that you're in Manning, North Dakota now and that you've dated the card 1961. In your last card you were in Nebraska, and it was 1962; you've lost some time, I see. I was a little girl, nine years old, in 1961. You'd left my father and me only two years before. Four months after leaving, you sent me—always me, never him—your first postcard, of a turnpike in the Midwest, postmarked Enid, Oklahoma. You called me "My little angel" and said that the sunflowers by the side of the road were tall and very pretty. You signed it, as you always have, "Your only mother." My father thought, of course, that you were in Enid, and he called the police there. But we quickly learned that postmarks meant nothing: you were never where you had been, had already passed through in the wanderings only you understand.

A postcard from my mother, I tell my husband, and he grunts.   2

Well, at least you know she's still alive, he says.   3

Yes.   4

This postcard shows a wheat field bending in the wind. The colors are   5
badly printed: the wheat's too red, the sky too blue—except for where it
touches the wheat, there becoming aquamarine, as if sky and field could
somehow combine to form water. There's a farmhouse in the distance.
People must live there, and for a moment I imagine you do, and I could
walk through the red wheat field, knock on the door, and find you. It's a
game I've always played, imagining you were hiding somewhere in the postcards you've sent. Your scrawled message, as always, is brief: "The beetles
are so much larger this year. I know you must be enjoying them. Love, your
only mother."

What craziness is it this time? my husband asks. I don't reply.   6

Instead, I think about your message, measure it against others. In the   7
last postcard seven months ago, you said you'd left something for me in a
safety deposit box in Ferndale. The postmark was Nebraska, and there's no
Ferndale in Nebraska. In the card before that, you said you were making me
a birthday cake that you'd send. Even though I've vowed I'd never do it
again, I try to understand what you are telling me.

"Your only mother." I've mulled that signature over and over, won-   8
dering what you meant. Are you worried I'd forget *you,* my only mother? In
favor of some other? My father, you know, never divorced you. It wouldn't
be fair to her, he told me, since she might come back.

Yes, I said.   9

Or maybe you mean singularity: out of all the mothers I might have had,   10
I have you. You exist for me alone. Distances, you imply, mean nothing. You
might come back.

And it's true: somehow, you've always found me. When I was a child,   11
the postcards came to the house, of course; but later, when I went to college,
and then to the first of several apartments, and finally to this house of my
own, with husband and daughter of my own, they still kept coming. How
you did this I don't know, but you did. You pursued me, and no matter how
far away, you always found me. In your way, I guess, you've been faithful.

I put this postcard in a box with all the others you've sent over the   12
years—postcards from Sioux City, Jackson Falls, Horseshoe Bend, Truckee,
Elm City, Spivey. Then I pull out the same atlas I've had since a child and
look up Manning, North Dakota, and yes, there you are, between Dickinson
and Killdeer, a blip on the red highway line.

She's in Manning, North Dakota, I tell my husband, just as I used to   13
tell my friends, as if that were explanation enough for your absence. I'd point
out where you were in the atlas, and they'd nod.

But in all those postcards, Mother, I imagined you: you were down   14
among the trees in the mountain panorama, or just out of frame on that
street in downtown Tupelo, or already through the door to The World's
Greatest Reptile Farm. And I was there, too, hoping to find you and say to
you, Come back, come back, there's only one street, one door, we didn't
mean it, we didn't know, whatever was wrong will be different.

Several times I decided you were dead, even wished you were dead, but   15
then another postcard would come, with another message to ponder. And
I've always read them, even when my husband said not to, even if they've
driven me to tears or rage or a blankness when I've no longer cared if you
were dead or anyone were dead, including myself. I've been faithful, too,
you see. I've always looked up where you were in the atlas, and put your
postcards in the box. Sixty-three postcards, four hundred–odd lines of scrawl:
our life together.

Why are you standing there like that? my daughter asks me.   16

I must have been away somewhere, I say. But I'm back.   17

Yes.   18

You see, Mother, I always come back. That's the distance that sepa-   19
rates us.

But on summer evenings, when the windows are open to the dusk, I   20
sometimes smell cities . . . wheat fields . . . oceans—strange smells from
far away—all the places you've been to that I never will. I smell them as if
they weren't pictures on a postcard, but real, as close as my outstretched
hand. And sometimes in the middle of the night, I'll sit bolt upright, my
husband instantly awake and frightened, asking, What is it? What is it? And
I'll say, She's here, she's here, and I am terrified that you are. And he'll say,
No, no, she's not, she'll never come back, and he'll hold me until my terror
passes. She's not here, he says gently, stroking my hair, she's not—except
you are, my strange and only mother: like a buoy in a fog, your voice, dear
Mother, seems to come from everywhere.

OPTIONS FOR READING LOGS:
"LOVE, YOUR ONLY MOTHER"

1. Examine your personal reaction to "Love Your Only Mother" by completing one of the following statements:

   A.   "I was confused by _____ ."

B. "I was struck by _____ ."

C. "I was surprised by _____ ."

For example, "I was surprised by the narrator's terror at the end of the story. Why wouldn't she want her mother to return?" Develop your journal entry by adding detailed explanations of events in the story or making observations based on your own family experiences. End your journal entry with a statement of the story's theme.

2. Use clustering to draw a concept (idea) map that explores the meaning of "Love, Your Only Mother." Recall vivid details and experiences from Kaplan's short story (the mother's signature, the places the mother moved, the husband's comments) and try brainstorming by drawing visual symbols, making diagrams, creating word lists. Once you have sketched in these items, examine their relationships to one another. Draw lines or use arrows to make connections between the items, creating a concept map. Finish your exploration with a brief entry explaining what you have done and a concluding statement of the central theme of "Love, Your Only Mother."

3. Examine your personal reaction to "Love, Your Only Mother" by comparing and contrasting the daughter's feelings about her mother with those expressed by the narrator in Roethke's poem "My Papa's Waltz." What do these two readings illustrate about our relationships with and feelings for our parents? Begin your journal entry by making a list of their similarities, showing how the two readings are alike in some way. Then list their differences. Finish your entry by explaining whether you think you understand or empathize with the narrators' attitudes about their parents.

OPTIONS FOR WRITING ASSIGNMENTS: "LOVE, YOUR ONLY MOTHER"

1. Does anything in "Love, Your Only Mother" remind you of an experience with a family member who, although absent, nonetheless exercised a powerful influence? Compose a narrative or descriptive essay that explores such an experience with a family member. State your main point in a clear thesis statement in your opening paragraph. Throughout your essay, concentrate on using vivid details, dialogue, and descriptions to help recreate your memories.

2. Write a personal letter to the daughter or the mother in "Love, Your Only Mother." Use the traditional letter form, addressing the character

directly and expressing your reaction to the narrator's story. For example, you may choose to praise the daughter for her loyalty to her absent mother or to warn her about ways her mother's influence could affect the daughter's marriage. Your approach should be one appropriate in terms of the story's theme of family relationships and their lasting influences.

3. In some ways "Love, Your Only Mother" is an incomplete story that causes the reader to imagine an eventual encounter between the mother and the daughter. How and where might this encounter take place? What would they say to each other? Would it be emotionally explosive or a deep disappointment? Take the story beyond its present conclusion, continuing with the daughter's voice as narrator and adding another scene in which the mother and daughter actually meet. Create the conversation they would have. As you write this next scene, try to bring this strange, long-distance relationship to some sort of closure and provide the reader with a sense of the meaning of the story.

4. What did you think of "Love, Your Only Mother" as a story about who we are and why? Would you recommend it to a friend? Write a critical review that clearly assesses the value of "Love, Your Only Mother" as a story of a mother-daughter relationship. Do you feel that it is an eccentric story with almost supernatural implications? Do you think its theme touches on something universal in all parent-child relationships? Do you have another assessment you would share with a friend? In your introductory paragraph, make your judgment clear to your reader in your thesis statement. Your evaluation can be positive, negative, or some interesting mixture of both. After you decide what sort of evaluation or judgment you want to make, offer good reasons for it in your supporting paragraphs, adding supporting evidence that makes your judgment convincing.

After Making Love We Hear Footsteps

1980

GALWAY KINNELL

 GALWAY KINNELL is an important contemporary American poet. He has published five volumes of poems and has won a Pulitzer Prize, among other literary awards. In "After Making Love We Hear Footsteps," he humorously explores the deep mysteries of sex, procreation, and family unity. Kinnell's gentle, personal poem meditates on the deep, intuitive unity and knowledge in his own family. Even though the poem narrates a humorous, even embarrassing, intimate event, it nonetheless can be seen as offering a powerful and affirmative portrait of married love and family unity.

Was there ever a time in your life when you became aware of the power of family ties and how they shape our individual lives? Have other members of your immediate or extended family ever revealed an unconditional loyalty or affection that you had not expected? As you read the poem, think about a time when your own family ties were tested or revealed in an unexpected way.

For I can snore like a bullhorn   1
or play loud music
or sit up talking with any reasonably sober Irishman
and Fergus will only sink deeper
into his dreamless sleep, which goes by all in one flash,   5
but let there be that heavy breathing
or a stifled come-cry anywhere in the house
and he will wrench himself awake
and make for it on the run—as now, we lie together,
after making love, quiet, touching along the length of our bodies,   10
familiar touch of the long-married,
and he appears—in his baseball pajamas, it happens,
the neck opening so small
he has to screw them on, which one day may make him wonder

about the mental capacity of baseball players—   15
and says, "Are you loving and snuggling? May I join?"
He flops down between us and hugs us and snuggles himself to sleep,
his face gleaming with satisfaction at being this very child.

In the half darkness we look at each other
and smile   20
and touch arms across his little, startlingly muscled body—
this one whom habit of memory propels to the ground of his making,
sleeper only the mortal sounds can sing awake,
this blessing love gives again into our arms.

OPTIONS FOR READING LOGS: "AFTER MAKING LOVE WE HEAR FOOTSTEPS"

1. Use the double-entry journal technique to comment on powerful lines
    or passages in "After Making Love We Hear Footsteps." Draw a vertical
    line down the middle of your journal page to create two columns. In
    the left column, copy lines or phrases that you particularly like or that
    you feel are important—for example, "his face gleaming with satisfaction
    at being this very child." In the right column, jot down word associations,
    interpretations, and comments, including those from your personal expe-
    rience as well as from your reading. End your journal entry by selecting
    the most significant of the lines or phrases and explaining why it held
    such power or meaning for you.

2. Examine your personal reaction to "After Making Love We Hear Foot-
    steps" by completing one of the following statements:

    A. "I was confused by _____ ."
    B. "I was struck by _____ ."
    C. "I was surprised by _____ ."

    For example, "I was confused by the line, 'sleeper only the mortal sounds
    can sing awake.' " Develop your journal entry by adding detailed explana-
    tions for pertinent images, symbols, and lines in the poem. Conclude
    your entry with a statement of the poem's theme.

3. Create an original poem in response to the text. For example, you might
    want to write a poem that celebrates or commemorates a trip, meal, or
    other special occasion when your own family felt close and harmonious.

Then write an explanation of why you think "After Making Love We Hear Footsteps" triggered this particular creative response from you. End your journal entry by stating the theme of "After Making Love We Hear Footsteps."

OPTIONS FOR WRITING ASSIGNMENTS: "AFTER MAKING LOVE WE HEAR FOOTSTEPS"

1. In "After Making Love We Hear Footsteps," the poet discovers an important truth about his family. Write a paper that uses anecdotes (brief stories) to illustrate a point about yourself. Begin by making a generalization about some aspect of your family, using that generalization as your thesis statement. For example, your statement might be "Members of my family try to protect one another," or "Being raised as an only child has helped to give me independence and self-confidence." Use several anecdotes with specific details to illustrate the truth of your generalization. Develop your anecdotes fully and be sure each serves as a good example that supports your generalization.

2. Create a conversation in which you and the speaker of the poem in "After Making Love We Hear Footsteps" discuss his view of his son. Your conversation might take the form of a question-and-answer interview, an argument between two opposing points of view, or a freewheeling exploration of his ideas and their implications for others. For example, you might want to argue that the poem is sentimental in its premise that a child would be so magically drawn in such a way ". . . to the ground of its making." What questions would you want to ask the narrtor?

3. What do you think of "After Making Love We Hear Footsteps" as a poem about family relationships? Would you recommend it to a friend? State your opinions in a critical review that makes a clear judgment of the value of "After Making Love We Hear Footsteps," as a poem exploring the mysterious origins of parent-child relationships. Your evaluation can be positive, negative, or a mixture of the two, but your judgment should be stated as a thesis in your introductory paragraph. For example, you might feel that the poem represents a positive and thoughtful portrait of a close and caring family. Write a formal essay of five or more paragraphs. Each supporting paragraph should contain evidence from the poem that makes your judgment convincing.

4. In "After Making Love We Hear Footsteps," the narrator discovers an important truth about family life, in particular about his relationship with his son. Try to make connections between causes and effects by thinking

about the following questions: Do sons have a special relationship with their fathers and do daughters have a similar special tie with their mothers? Or is the reverse true? Analyze your own relationship with one of your parents, exploring the causes that have created that unique relationship. As you attempted to trace these causes, did you encounter some hidden discoveries along the way? Come up with a thesis statement that expresses your main point. Express your ideas in a formal essay of five or more paragraphs.

The Kitchen

1951

ALFRED KAZIN

 ALFRED KAZIN, an American essayist and literary critic, is a well-known figure in New York intellectual circles. In addition to his focus on American literature, Kazin has also produced a considerable amount of autobiographical writing, such as his trilogy *A Walker in the City, Starting Out in the Thirties,* and *New York Jew.* The following excerpt, "The Kitchen," is from *A Walker in the City.* In this very detailed and descriptive selection, Kazin affirms the powerful influence of his mother and her kitchen, and the lasting power of those memories in his life.

Does Kazin's mother compare or contrast with a parent, other relative, or caregiver in your own family life? What was the dominant attitude towards the work ethic in your upbringing? As you read "The Kitchen," think of a family member in your own life who shaped you and your own attitudes and values.

In Brownsville tenements the kitchen is always the largest room and the 1 center of the household. As a child I felt that we lived in a kitchen to which four other rooms were annexed. My mother, a "home" dressmaker, had her workshop in the kitchen. . . . Our apartment was always full of women in their housedresses sitting around the kitchen table waiting for a fitting. My little bedroom next to the kitchen was the fitting room. The sewing machine, an old nut-brown Singer with golden scrolls painted along the black arm and engraved along the two tiers of little drawers massed with needles and thread on each side of the treadle, stood next to the window and the great coal-black stove which up to my last year in college was our main source of heat. By December the two outer bedrooms were closed off, and used to chill bottles of milk and cream, cold borscht and jellied calves' feet.

The kitchen held our lives together. My mother worked in it all day long, 2 we ate in it almost all meals except the Passover *seder,* I did my homework and first writing at the kitchen table, and in winter I often had a bed made up for me on three kitchen chairs near the stove. On the wall just over the table hung a long horizontal mirror that sloped to a ship's prow at each end and was lined in cherry wood. It took up the whole wall, and drew every object in the kitchen to itself. The walls were a fiercely stippled whitewash, so often rewhitened by my father in slack seasons that the paint looked as if it had been squeezed and cracked into the walls. A large electric bulb hung down the center of the kitchen at the end of a chain that had been hooked into the ceiling; the old gas ring and key still jutted out of the wall like antlers. In the corner next to the toilet was the sink at which we washed, and the square tub in which my mother did our clothes. Above it, tacked to the shelf on which were pleasantly ranged square, blue-bordered white sugar and spice jars, hung calendars from the Public National Bank on Pitkin Avenue and the Minsker Progressive Branch of the Workman's Circle; receipts for the payment of insurance premiums, and household bills on a spindle; two little boxes engraved with Hebrew letters. One of these was for the poor, the other to buy back the Land of Israel. . . .

The kitchen gave a special character to our lives; my mother's character. 3 All my memories of that kitchen are dominated by the nearness of my mother sitting all day long at her sewing machine, by the clacking of the treadle against the linoleum floor, by the patient twist of her right shoulder as she automatically pushed at the wheel with one hand or lifted the foot to free the needle where it had got stuck in a thick piece of material. The kitchen was her life. Year by year, as I began to take in her fantastic capacity for labor and her anxious zeal, I realized it was ourselves she kept stitched together. I can never remember a time when she was not working. She worked because the law of her life was work, work and anxiety; she worked because she would have found life meaningless without work. . . . When I awoke in the morning she was already at her machine, or in the great morning crowd of housewives at the grocery getting fresh rolls for breakfast. When I returned from school she was at her machine, or conferring over *McCall's* with some neighborhood woman who had come in pointing hopefully to an illustration—"Mrs. Kazin! Mrs. Kazin! Make me a dress like it shows here in the picture!" When my father came home from work she had somehow mysteriously interrupted herself to make supper for us, and the dishes cleared and washed, was back at her machine. When I went to bed at night, often she was still there, pounding away at the treadle, hunched over the wheel, her hands steering a piece of gauze under the needle with a finesse that always contrasted sharply with her swollen hands and broken nails. . . .

The kitchen was the great machine that set our lives running; it whirred 4 down a little only on Saturdays and holy days. From my mother's kitchen I gained my first picture of life as a white, overheated, starkly lit workshop redolent with Jewish cooking, crowded with women in housedresses, strewn with fashion magazines, patterns, dress material, spools of thread—and at whose center, so lashed to her machine that bolts of energy seemed to dance out of her hands and feet as she worked, my mother stamped the treadle hard against the floor, hard, hard, and silently, grimly at war, beat out the first rhythm of the world for me. . . .

At night the kitchen contracted around the blaze of light on the cloth,   5
the patterns, the ironing board where the iron had burned a black border around the tear in the muslin cover; the finished dresses looked so frilly as they jostled on their wire hangers after all the work my mother had put into them. And then I would get that strangely ominous smell of tension from the dress fabrics and the burn in the cover of the ironing board—as if each piece of cloth and paper crushed with light under the naked bulb might suddenly go up in flames. Whenever I pass some small tailoring shop still lit up at night and see the owner hunched over his steam press; whenever in some poorer neighborhood of the city I see through a window some small crowded kitchen naked under the harsh light glittering in the ceiling, I still smell that fiery breath, that warning of imminent fire. I was always holding my breath. What I must have felt most about ourselves, I see now, was that we ourselves were like kindling—that all the hard-pressed pieces of ourselves and all the hard-used objects in that kitchen were like so many slivers of wood that might go up in flames if we came too near the white-blazing filaments in that naked bulb. Our tension itself was fire, we ourselves were forever burning—to live, to get down the foreboding in our souls, to make good.

OPTIONS FOR READING LOGS: "THE KITCHEN"

1. Use the double-entry journal technique to discover meaning in Kazin's "The Kitchen." Draw a vertical line down the middle of your journal page to create two columns. In the left column, keep a running list of three to five "what" or "why" questions that occur to you as you are reading, such as, "What does he mean by 'that warning of imminent fire'?" or "Why does the mother feel life would be meaningless without work?" When you finish your list, move to the top of the right column and answer your questions as completely as you can. (Remember that such interpretation will require you to take educated guesses.) To demon-

strate that you have a basic understanding of the text, end your journal entry by jotting down the main idea of "The Kitchen."

2. Copy the most powerful line or passage in "The Kitchen." One powerful sentence is the last one: "Our tension itself was fire, we ourselves were forever burning—to live, to get down the foreboding in our souls, to make good." Does it make you think of some aspect of your own family memories or feelings? Perhaps another will appeal more directly to you. Using anecdotes and examples from your own personal experience, explain fully why the particular passage you choose holds such power or meaning for you.

3. Kazin's essay reveals much about his own mother, her enormous energy and her dynamic capacity for managing both family and work. Who was the strong person in your family—the one who kept the family "stitched together"? Narrate a brief anecdote about that person, using any ideas from "The Kitchen" that made you recall this family member. Jot down any characteristics or events that were similar to or different from Kazin's experience. End your journal entry by stating the theme of "The Kitchen."

OPTIONS FOR WRITING ASSIGNMENTS: "THE KITCHEN"

1. As Kazin does in "The Kitchen," write a descriptive essay that portrays an important family member. If appropriate, you might choose, as Kazin does, to emphasize a place that is closely associated with the person. Concentrate on using vivid details and descriptions to breathe life into this family member for your reader. Before you begin writing, reread Kazin's essay to see how he uses details to create the environment in which he often saw his mother: "At night the kitchen contracted around the blaze of light on the cloth, the patterns, the ironing board where the iron had burned a black border around the tear in the muslin cover." Make your main point clear in a thesis statement in your first paragraph.

2. Although Kazin's essay uses very little dialogue, the reader still gets a keen impression of the mother and her values and personality. What do you think of her as she is portrayed in the essay? Create a conversation between you and Kazin's mother. Your conversation might take the form of a question-and-answer interview, an argument representing two opposing points of view, or an exploration of the mother's role in the Kazin family and its implications for them as a group.

3. Write an essay based on a family photograph. Kazin's essay "The Kitchen" reminds us of the powerful influence our families have on us and of the lasting impact they can have on our lives. His prose is often very visual, almost photographic in its careful attention to details and imagery. Kazin virtually creates a picture of his mother as he talks about her strong faith in the work ethic: "When I went to bed at night, often she was still there, pounding away at the treadle, hunched over the wheel, her hands steering a piece of gauze under the needle with a finesse that always contrasted with her swollen hands and broken nails." Locate a memorable family photograph, study it for its revealing details, and explore your own memories and feelings. Then, based on what you see in the photo, write your own essay. Include the overall impression the photo made on you and the anecdotes you remembered while looking at it.

4. If you were asked what "The Kitchen" means and how it teaches us to understand our family relationships better, what would you say? In a formal essay of five or more paragraphs, explain the meaning of Kazin's memory of his mother and her kitchen. Is she a "supermother" who can handle family and work and all the pressures those two responsibilities entail? Is she happy or merely a driven, compulsive workaholic? What exactly does Kazin mean when he says, "What I . . . felt most about ourselves, I see now, was that we ourselves were like kindling—that all the hard-pressed pieces of ourselves and all the hard-used objects in that kitchen were like so many slivers of wood that might go up in flames"? In your introductory paragraph, express Kazin's main idea in a thesis statement. In your supporting paragraphs, focus on the parts of "The Kitchen" that help you clarify your main idea. In your commentary you will need to quote from the essay and refer to specific passages.

My Father Sits in the Dark

1934

JEROME WEIDMAN

 JEROME WEIDMAN, a New York writer, has written novels, plays, and musicals in addition to short stories. In "My Father Sits in the Dark," Weidman explores the relationship of a father and his son. The son is unable to understand his father and is frustrated by the lack of communication between them. This problem creates a serious family problem for him, one that only insight and understanding can resolve. Sometimes our relationships with our parents are faulty not because of actual differences but because of simple misunderstandings. Learning to see things from the other person's perspective often reopens the channels of communication.

Have you ever had a serious conflict or misunderstanding with a close family member? As you read the story, reflect on your various relationships with family members or relatives. Can you recall having some problem that, when it was resolved, actually led to feelings of greater sympathy and understanding between you and a family member? Does Weidman's story of a father and a son shed any light on that relationship?

My father has a peculiar habit. He is fond of sitting in the dark, alone. Sometimes I come home very late. The house is dark. I let myself in quietly because I do not want to disturb my mother. She is a light sleeper. I tiptoe into my room and undress in the dark. I go to the kitchen for a drink of water. My bare feet make no noise. I step into the room and almost trip over my father. He is sitting in a kitchen chair, in his pajamas, smoking his pipe. 1

"Hello, Pop," I say. 2

"Hello, son." 3

"Why don't you go to bed, Pa?" 4

"I will," he says. 5

But he remains there. Long after I am asleep I feel sure that he is still sitting there, smoking. 6

Many times I am reading in my room. I hear my mother get the house   7
ready for the night. I hear my kid brother go to bed. I hear my sister come
in. I hear her do things with jars and combs until she, too, is quiet. I know
she has gone to sleep. In a little while I hear my mother say good night to
my father. I continue to read. Soon I become thirsty. (I drink a lot of water.)
I go to the kitchen for a drink. Again I almost stumble across my father.
Many times it startles me. I forget about him. And there he is—smoking,
sitting, thinking.

"Why don't you go to bed, Pop?"   8

"I will, son."   9

But he doesn't. He just sits there and smokes and thinks. It worries me. 10
I can't understand it. What can he be thinking about? Once I asked him.

"What are you thinking about, Pa?"   11

"Nothing," he said.   12

Once I left him there and went to bed. I awoke several hours later.   13
I was thirsty. I went to the kitchen. There he was. His pipe was out. But
he sat there, staring into a corner of the kitchen. After a moment I became accustomed to the darkness. I took my drink. He still sat and stared.
His eyes did not blink. I thought he was not even aware of me. I was
afraid.

"Why don't you go to bed, Pop?"   14

"I will, son," he said. "Don't wait up for me."   15

"But," I said, "you've been sitting here for hours. What's wrong? What 16
are you thinking about?"

"Nothing, son," he said. "Nothing. It's just restful. That's all."   17

The way he said it was convincing. He did not seem worried. His voice   18
was even and pleasant. It always is. But I could not understand it. How could
it be restful to sit alone in an uncomfortable chair far into the night, in
darkness?

What can it be?   19

I review all the possibilities. It can't be money. I know that. We haven't 20
much, but when he is worried about money he makes no secret of it. It can't
be his health. He is not reticent about that either. It can't be the health of
anyone in the family. We are a bit short on money, but we are long on health.
(Knock wood, my mother would say.) What can it be? I am afraid I do not
know. But that does not stop me from worrying.

Maybe he is thinking of his brothers in the old country. Or of his   21
mother and two step-mothers. Or of his father. But they are all dead.
And he would not brood about them like that. I say brood, but it is not
really true. He does not brood. He does not even seem to be thinking.
He looks too peaceful, too, well not contented, just too peaceful, to be

brooding. Perhaps it is as he says. Perhaps it is restful. But it does not seem possible. It worries me.

If I only knew what he thinks about. If I only knew that he thinks at all. 22 I might not be able to help him. He might not even need help. It may be as he says. It may be restful. But at least I would not worry about it.

Why does he just sit there, in the dark? Is his mind failing? No, it can't 23 be. He is only fifty-three. And he is just as keen-witted as ever. In fact, he is the same in every respect. He still likes beet soup. He still reads the second section of the *Times* first. He still wears wing collars. He still believes that Debs could have saved the country and that T.R. was a tool of the moneyed interests. He is the same in every way. He does not even look older than he did five years ago. Everybody remarks about that. Well-preserved, they say. But he sits in the dark, alone, smoking, staring straight ahead of him, unblinking, into the small hours of the night.

If it is as he says, if it is restful, I will let it go at that. But suppose it is 24 not. Suppose it is something I cannot fathom. Perhaps he needs help. Why doesn't he speak? Why doesn't he frown or laugh or cry? Why doesn't he do something? Why does he just sit there?

Finally I become angry. Maybe it is just my unsatisfied curiosity. Maybe 25 I *am* a bit worried. Anyway, I become angry.

"Is something wrong, Pop?" 26

"Nothing, son. Nothing at all." 27

But this time I am determined not to be put off. I am angry. 28

"Then why do you sit here all alone, thinking, till late?" 29

"It's restful, son. I like it." 30

I am getting nowhere. Tomorrow he will be sitting there again. I will 31 be puzzled. I will be worried. I will not stop now. I am angry.

"Well, what do you *think* about, Pa? Why do you just sit here? What's 32 worrying you? What do you think about?"

"Nothing's worrying me, son. I'm all right. It's just restful. That's all. 33 Go to bed, son."

My anger has left me. But the feeling of worry is still there. I must get 34 an answer. It seems so silly. Why doesn't he tell me? I have a funny feeling that unless I get an answer I will go crazy. I am insistent.

"But what do you *think* about, Pa? What is it?" 35

"Nothing, son. Just things in general. Nothing special. Just things." 36

I can get no answer. 37

It is very late. The street is quiet and the house is dark. I climb the steps 38 softly, skipping the ones that creak. I let myself in with my key and tiptoe into my room. I remove my clothes and remember that I am thirsty. In my bare feet I walk to the kitchen. Before I reach it I know he is there.

I can see the deeper darkness of his hunched shape. He is sitting in the   39
same chair, his elbows on his knees, his cold pipe in his teeth, his unblinking
eyes staring straight ahead. He does not seem to know I am there. He did
not hear me come in. I stand quietly in the doorway and watch him.

Everything is quiet, but the night is full of little sounds. As I stand there   40
motionless I begin to notice them. The ticking of the alarm clock on the
icebox. The low hum of an automobile passing many blocks away. The swish
of papers moved along the street by the breeze. A whispering rise and fall of
sound, like low breathing. It is strangely pleasant.

The dryness in my throat reminds me. I step briskly into the kitchen.   41

"Hello, Pop," I say.   42

"Hello, son," he says. His voice is low and dreamlike. He does not   43
change his position or shift his gaze.

I cannot find the faucet. The dim shadow of light that comes through   44
the window from the street lamp only makes the room seem darker. I reach
for the short chain in the center of the room. I snap on the light.

He straightens up with a jerk, as though he has been struck. "What's   45
the matter, Pop?" I ask.

"Nothing," he says. "I don't like the light."   46

"What's the matter with the light?" I say. "What's wrong?"   47

"Nothing," he says. "I don't like the light."   48

I snap the light off. I drink my water slowly. I must take it easy, I say to   49
myself. I must get to the bottom of this.

"Why don't you go to bed? Why do you sit here so late in the dark?"   50

"It's nice," he says. "I can't get used to lights. We didn't have lights   51
when I was a boy in Europe."

My heart skips a beat and I catch my breath happily. I begin to think   52
I understand. I remember the stories of his boyhood in Austria. I see the
wide-beamed *kretchma,* with my grandfather behind the bar. It is late, the
customers are gone, and he is dozing. I see the bed of glowing coals, the
last of the roaring fire. The room is already dark, and grower darker. I see a
small boy, crouched on a pile of twigs at one side of the huge fireplace, his
starry gaze fixed on the dull remains of the dead flames. The boy is my father.

I remember the pleasure of those few moments while I stood quietly in   53
the doorway watching him.

"You mean there's nothing wrong? You just sit in the dark because you   54
like it, Pop?" I find it hard to keep my voice from rising in a happy shout.

"Sure," he says. "I can't think with the light on."   55

I set my glass down and turn to go back to my room. "Good night,   56
Pop," I say.

"Good night," he says.   57

Then I remember. I turn back. "What do you think about, Pop?" I ask.   58

His voice seems to come from far away. It is quiet and even again.   59
"Nothing," he says softly. "Nothing special."

❖   ❖   ❖

OPTIONS FOR READING LOGS: "MY FATHER SITS IN THE DARK"

1. Discover meaning in Weidman's "My Father Sits in the Dark" by dividing your journal page into two vertical columns. In the left column, keep a running list of three to five "what" or "why" questions, such as, "Why is the father reluctant to tell his secret to his son?" or "Exactly what is it that makes the son grow so angry at his father?" After you finish your list of questions, go back to the first one and answer it as completely as possible in the right column. (Remember that such interpretation will require you to take educated guesses.) To demonstrate that you have a basic understanding of the text, end your journal entry by jotting down the main idea of "My Father Sits in the Dark."

2. Examine your personal reaction to "My Father Sits in the Dark" by completing one of the following statements:

    A. "I was confused by _____ ."
    B. "I was struck by _____ ."
    C. "I was surprised by _____ ."

    You might say, for example, "I was surprised by the fact that the son was so upset by his father's actions." Develop your journal entry by adding detailed explanations of important parts of the story. Wrap it up with a statement of the story's theme.

3. Drawing on your personal life, tell a parallel story that was triggered by "My Father Sits in the Dark." Does the son's experience remind you of a time when you experienced some difficulty understanding or getting along with a member of your own family? Use dialogue and descriptive details to recreate that experience for your reader. End your journal entry by stating how both "My Father Sits in the Dark" and your parallel story share a common theme.

OPTIONS FOR WRITING ASSIGNMENTS: "MY FATHER SITS IN THE DARK"

1. As Weidman does in "My Father Sits in the Dark," write a narrative essay exploring a memorable family experience with one of your parents, siblings, or relatives. Like Weidman, you might want to explore some misunderstanding and the way you eventually resolved the problem. What specific personal insight or insights did the experience give you about being in a family? Make your main idea clear in a thesis statement in your first paragraph. Throughout your essay, concentrate on using vivid details, dialogue, and descriptions to help recreate the experience for your reader.

2. Write a letter to the father or the son in "My Father Sits in the Dark," telling him what the story taught you about family relations. Do all family members have large sections of their lives closed off from one another, as the father has in the story? Is this need for privacy an essential part of who we are? Do these private places tend to foster conflicts and misunderstandings? Using the letter form, address the person directly and express your answers to these questions and your reaction to the story. Your letter should reflect your real point of view—you can praise, criticize, empathize, console, or inquire.

3. Toward the end of "My Father Sits in the Dark," the son finds it hard to keep his voice "from rising in a happy shout" because he has finally realized the simple explanation for his father's apparently strange behavior. This discovery no doubt has a lasting influence on the son's relationship with his father. Write a formal essay that makes a generalization about a similar discovery that influenced your relationship with one of your own family members—perhaps a long-kept secret, an inexplicable jealousy, or a serious misunderstanding. Use five or more paragraphs, including a thesis statement in your introductory paragraph to state your generalization about the experience. The main body of your essay should present several vivid, well-described personal anecdotes to illustrate your thesis. Develop each anecdote fully, and be sure that each is a good example that supports your generalization.

4. Write a formal essay of five or more paragraphs, explaining the knowledge the son gained about his father and his father's childhood in "My Father Sits in the Dark." Focus on parts of the story about which you have genuine questions, such as, "Why does the son react the way he does when he cannot understand his father's behavior?" In a thesis statement at the end of your introductory paragraph, write your interpretation of what the son learns. In your essay's supporting paragraphs, quote from the story and refer to specific passages to clarify and support your central idea.

Now That I Am Forever with Child

1963

AUDRE LORDE

 AUDRE LORDE is an African-American poet who was born in Harlem, a part of New York City. Her parents had emigrated to the United States from the West Indies. Lorde attended Hunter College and Columbia University, where she trained to be a librarian. She has been a college teacher of English in New York City for most of her career. She also taught at the John Jay College of Criminal Justice, where New York City police are trained. She knew she was going to be a poet at the age of twelve, and she has devoted her poetry to exploring African myths and history, as well as personal, political, and sexual themes. Her poem "Now That I Am Forever with Child" shows us a mother speaking to her child, reflecting on the always extraordinary experience of bearing and raising a child and watching the child grow up and away.

A parent's relationship with a child is dominated by nurturing and raising this new person. However, no matter how concerned, caring, or controlling the parent is, the time comes when children must begin to assume control over their own lives and parents must allow them to discover things for themselves. Some parents find it easy to let go of their children, even feeling a sense of relief felt when they begin to negotiate the world successfully on their own. Others find it more difficult.

Can you recall a time when you began to feel that you wanted to break away from the care and security of your family? Can you look back and distinguish the various "selves" you as a child passed through before arriving at who you are today? What role did your parents or parent play in the evolution of who you are today?

How the days went   1
while you were blooming within me
I remember each upon each—
the swelling changed planes of my body

and how you first fluttered, then jumped   2
and I thought it was my heart.

How the days wound down
and the turning of winter
I recall, with you growing heavy
against the wind. I thought   3
now her hands
are formed, and her hair
has started to curl
now her teeth are done
now she sneezes.   4
Then the seed opened
I bore you one morning just before spring
My head rang like a fiery piston
my legs were towers between which
A new world was passing.   5

Since then
I can only distinguish
one thread between running hours
You, flowing through selves
toward You.   6

◈   ◈   ◈

OPTIONS FOR READING LOGS: "NOW THAT I AM FOREVER WITH CHILD"

1. Use the double-entry journal technique to clarify the meaning of some of the powerful lines in "Now That I Am Forever with Child." For example, why would Lorde use the phrase "my head rang like a fiery piston" to describe childbirth? End your journal entry with a brief statement about a significant discovery you made about the poem as a whole during this process.

2. Freewrite on the title of the poem, "Now That I Am Forever with Child." What do you think Lorde means? Why did she choose that particular title? Can the title be understood in more than one way? How does it help you read and understand the poem? Would the poem have a different meaning if the poet had published it without a title? What title would you give the poem if it you had written it? Try finishing the

title as if it were an incomplete sentence: Now that I am forever with child . . .

3. Tell some personal story that reading "Now That I Am Forever with Child" helps you to recall. How does the poem cause you to reflect on a long-term relationship with a parent or a child of your own? Is it a positive experience or one that seems troubling? End your entry by clarifying what you learned about family relationships from reading "Now That I Am Forever with Child."

OPTIONS FOR WRITING ASSIGNMENTS: "NOW THAT I AM FOREVER WITH CHILD"

1. Develop one of your reading logs for "Now That I Am Forever with Child" into a more polished piece of writing that explores a complex familial relationship in greater range and depth, using an appropriate form, such as a poem, a fictional story, a personal narrative, or an essay that examines a central idea.

2. What do you think the child in "Now That I Am Forever with Child" would say about the relationship between him or her and the mother? Create a conversation between the grown child and the mother. In your dialogue, allow each person to express his or her own point of view. For example, do you think the mother is expressing regret or happiness as she sees her child developing into an ever-changing, unique individual as she is "flowing through selves / toward You"? Why does the mother use the plural form *selves* in describing her growing child? Is that perspective unique to a parent, or would the grown child also see himself or herself as having passed through many selves?

3. In a creative response to "Now That I Am Forever with Child," write an original poem of your own. If you have trouble getting started, try beginning with the two lines of the poem, "How the days went / while you . . .". You could focus your poem on a child—a younger brother or cousin, for example—or on a parent. Allow your own poem to develop in any way you wish. For example, you may explore a happy parent-child relationship or a troubled one. You may use rhymes, but you could also try your hand at free verse, as used in Audre Lorde's poem. After you have written your poem, briefly explain why "Now That I Am Forever with Child" triggered this particular creative response from you.

4. If you were asked what "Now That I Am Forever with Child" means and how it teaches us to understand our family relationships better, what would you say? If your reaction to that question is to read the poem

again, you are not alone. After the first reading of a text, we often fail to appreciate its full range of meaning. Full appreciation of a poem may follow only when we reread, think about, discuss, and write about it. Expand your appreciation by writing a formal essay of five or more paragraphs, explaining the meaning of "Now That I Am Forever with Child." How has watching her child grow and develop affected the mother? What does she mean when she describes her child as "one thread within running hours"? In a thesis statement, write down the poem's main idea. In your supporting paragraphs, focus on the parts of the poem that need interpreting and that help you clarify your main idea. Your commentary should include quotes from the poem. Refer to specific passages that support your ideas.

On Going Home

1968

JOAN DIDION

 JOAN DIDION, a contemporary journalist, essayist, and novelist, grew up in California's Sacramento Valley and attended the University of California at Berkeley. After working as an editor and writer in New York, she moved to southern California near Los Angeles. Her themes and topics often focus on California, as they do in her best-known collection of nonfiction, *Slouching Towards Bethlehem*. In this collection, Didion focuses on the unique characteristics of California, such as the mysterious influence of its Santa Ana winds, its wealthy neighborhoods, and its film industry. The following essay, "On Going Home," is from that collection and describes Didion's return home to visit her family near Sacramento.

Have you ever left home to establish your own life elsewhere? Was it a difficult or easy experience? When you return to your family's house, do you feel relieved to be home again, or do you feel ill at ease and constricted in what you can say and do? As you read "On Going Home," think about your family home and all the thoughts and emotions you experience as you walk through its doors.

I am home for my daughter's first birthday. By "home" I do not mean the house in Los Angeles where my husband and I and the baby live, but the place where my family is, in the Central Valley of California. It is a vital although troublesome distinction. My husband likes my family but is uneasy in their house, because once there I fall into their ways, which are difficult, oblique,[1] deliberately inarticulate, not my husband's ways. We live in dusty houses ("D-U-S-T," he once wrote with his finger on surfaces all over the house, but no one noticed it) filled with mementos quite without value to him (what could the Canton dessert plates mean to him? how could

---

1. oblique: indirectly stated or expressed

he have known about the assay scales,[2] why should he care if he did know?),
and we appear to talk exclusively about people we know who have been
committed to mental hospitals, about people we know who have been
booked on drunk-driving charges, and about property, particularly about
property, land, price per acre and C-2 zoning and assessments and freeway
access. My brother does not understand my husband's inability to perceive
the advantage in the rather common real-estate transaction known as "sale-
leaseback," and my husband in turn does not understand why so many of
the people he hears about in my father's house have recently been committed
to mental hospitals or booked on drunk-driving charges. Nor does he understand that when we talk about sale-leasebacks and right-of-way condemna-
tions we are talking in code about the things we like best, the yellow fields
and the cottonwoods and the rivers rising and falling and the mountain roads
closing when the heavy snow comes in. We miss each other's points, have
another drink and regard the fire. My brother refers to my husband, in his
presence, as "Joan's husband." Marriage is the classic betrayal.

Or perhaps it is not any more. Sometimes I think that those of us who   2
are now in our thirties were born into the last generation to carry the burden
of "home," to find in family life the source of all tension and drama. I had
by all objective accounts a "normal" and a "happy" family situation, and yet
I was almost thirty years old before I could talk to my family on the telephone without crying after I had hung up. We did not fight. Nothing was
wrong. And yet some nameless anxiety colored the emotional charges between
me and the place that I came from. The question of whether or not you
could go home again was a very real part of the sentimental and largely
literary baggage with which we left home in the fifties; I suspect that it is
irrelevant to the children born of the fragmentation after World War II. A
few weeks ago in a San Francisco bar I saw a pretty young girl on crystal
take off her clothes and dance for the cash prize in an "amateur-topless"
contest. There was no particular sense of moment about this, none of the
effect of romantic degradation, of "dark journey," for which my generation
strived so assiduously.[3] What sense could that girl possibly make of, say, _Long
Day's Journey into Night?_ Who is beside the point?

That I am trapped in this particular irrelevancy is never more apparent   3
to me than when I am home. Paralyzed by the neurotic lassitude[4] engendered
by meeting one's past at every turn, around every corner, inside every cupboard, I go aimlessly from room to room. I decide to meet it head-on and
clean out a drawer, and I spread the contents on the bed. A bathing suit I

2. assay scales: scales used to weigh precious ores like gold or silver   3. assiduously: constantly   4. lassitude: weariness of body or mind from strain

wore the summer I was seventeen. A letter of rejection from *The Nation,* an aerial photograph of the site for a shopping center my father did not build in 1954. Three teacups hand-painted with cabbage roses and signed "E.M.," my grandmother's initials. There is no final solution for letters of rejection from *The Nation* and teacups hand-painted in 1900. Nor is there any answer to snapshots of one's grandfather as a young man on skis, surveying around Donner Pass in the year 1910. I smooth out the snapshot and look into his face, and do and do not see my own. I close the drawer, and have another cup of coffee with my mother. We get along very well, veterans of a guerrilla war we never understood.

Days pass. I see no one. I come to dread my husband's evening call, not only because he is full of news of what by now seems to me our remote life in Los Angeles, people he has seen, letters which require attention, but because he asks what I have been doing, suggests uneasily that I get out, drive to San Francisco or Berkeley. Instead I drive across the river to a family graveyard. It has been vandalized since my last visit and the monuments are broken, overturned in the dry grass. Because I once saw a rattlesnake in the grass I stay in the car and listen to a country-and-Western station. Later I drive with my father to a ranch he has in the foothills. The man who runs his cattle on it asks us to the roundup, a week from Sunday, and although I know that I will be in Los Angeles I say, in the oblique way my family talks, that I will come. Once home I mention the broken monuments in the graveyard. My mother shrugs.   4

I go to visit my great-aunts. A few of them think now that I am my cousin, or their daughter who died young. We recall an anecdote about a relative last seen in 1948, and they ask if I still like living in New York City. I have lived in Los Angeles for three years, but I say that I do. The baby is offered a horehound drop[5] and I am slipped a dollar bill "to buy a treat." Questions trail off, answers are abandoned, the baby plays with the dust motes in a shaft of afternoon sun.   5

It is time for the baby's birthday party: a white cake, strawberry-marsh-mallow ice cream, a bottle of champagne saved from another party. In the evening, after she has gone to sleep, I kneel beside the crib and touch her face, where it is pressed against the slats, with mine. She is an open and trusting child, unprepared for and unaccustomed to the ambushes of family life, and perhaps it is just as well that I can offer her little of that life. I would like to give her more. I would like to promise her that she will grow up with a sense of her cousins and of rivers and of her great-grandmother's teacups, would like to pledge her a picnic on a river with fried chicken and her hair   6

---

5. horehound drop: a lozenge flavored with horehound extract

uncombed, would like to give her *home* for her birthday, but we live differently now and I can promise her nothing like that. I give her a xylophone and a sundress from Madeira, and promise to tell her a funny story.

OPTIONS FOR READING LOGS: "ON GOING HOME"

1. Copy the most powerful line or passage in "On Going Home." Consider, for example, Didion's sentence: "Marriage is the classic betrayal." What exactly does she mean by that? Who is being betrayed, and why? Does this or some other powerful line or passage in this essay make you think of some of your own family memories or the feelings you have about them? Using anecdotes and examples from your personal experience explain fully why the particular passage you choose holds such power or meaning for you.

2. Examine your personal reaction to "On Going Home" by completing one of the following statements:

   A. "I was confused by _____."
   B. "I was struck by _____."
   C. "I was surprised by _____."

   For instance, "I was confused by the idea that she and her mother are 'veterans of a guerrilla war we never understood.' " Develop your journal entry by adding detailed explanations of important parts of the essay. End the entry with a statement of the essay's theme.

3. Drawing on your personal life, tell a story parallel to "On Going Home." Does Didion's experience of returning home remind you of your returning to a place where you once lived with your family? Briefly tell the story of that experience, using dialogue and descriptive details to recreate it for the reader. Conclude your entry by stating how both "On Going Home" and your own story share a common theme.

OPTIONS FOR WRITING ASSIGNMENTS: "ON GOING HOME"

1. Does Didion's experience in "On Going Home" remind you of the way you behave when you are with your family? Do your family members have unique habits, ways of communicating, and traditions that another

family might not understand? Write a narrative essay, focusing on some experience you have had with your own family members, such as their dining habits, a place you have visited with them, or some private family tradition. In your essay, illustrate some unique quality of your family and its behavior. Concentrate on using vivid details and descriptions to help recreate your experience.

2. Write a letter to Joan Didion, the author of "On Going Home." Address her directly and express your own reaction to her essay. You may choose to clarify what you think is her main point in the essay or to criticize her notion of the dangers of "family." Use whatever tone is most appropriate to express your reaction to the story's theme of family relationships and influences.

3. What did you think of "On Going Home" as a story about a particular family? Would you recommend Didion's essay to a friend? Write a critical review that makes a clear judgment, recommending or not recommending "On Going Home" as a statement on the world a family creates. Do you feel that Didion's family situation is unique or does it touch on something universal in all families? Write a formal essay of five or more paragraphs. In your introductory paragraph, make your judgment clear to your reader in your thesis statement. Your evaluation can be positive, negative, or some interesting mixture of both. Once you are clear on what sort of evaluation or judgment you want to make, you will need to come up with good reasons in your supporting paragraphs, each with supporting evidence that makes your judgment convincing.

4. Explain the meaning of "On Going Home" in a formal essay of five or more paragraphs. What does Didion mean when she says, "Marriage is the classic betrayal," or that she and her mother are "veterans of a guerilla war we never understood." In your introductory paragraph, clearly state Didion's main idea—what "On Going Home" means and what it teaches us about the idea of "family." In your supporting paragraphs, focus on any parts of her essay that caused you to have questions and that helped you clarify your main idea. In your commentary you may need to quote from the essay and refer to specific passages to help your reader understand what you mean.

CHAPTER THREE

Cultural Knowledge: What Are My Roots?

Culture is a general term loosely used to describe the values, arts, spiritual beliefs, and collective skills of a given people at a given time. Everyone has a culture, or even parts of several cultures, whether it is acknowledged or not. Our culture is manifested in conscious and unconscious habits of mind, dress codes, and values from the immediate world we have inhabited since birth. Cultural boundaries, such as those between various ethnic and economic groups, sometimes separate us from one another and cause us to focus on our differences, which can create lasting misunderstandings and even open conflict.

Today the world seems headed toward a vast "monoculture" in which, for better or worse, all individual cultures will eventually merge into a single amorphous global culture. Travelers to the most isolated parts of remote countries, expecting to find the inhabitants clothed in unique and colorful traditional dress, find instead that tee shirts, jeans, tennis shoes, and baseball caps like those purchased at U.S. shopping malls are the clothing of choice. The truth is that a culture, once established, is not forever fixed and unchanging but is dynamic, rising and falling through time. A culture may even merge with others, to be rebuilt into something new and unexpected.

Whatever the case, attempts to explain culture and its effects often seem contradictory by their very nature. Siv Cedering's "Family Album" brings up joy as well as the grief of discovering one's roots. Likewise, Clyde Kluckhohn, in "Customs," points out several instances of cultural differences among human beings, but then counters by asserting that we are "very much alike." The other selections in this chapter, such as Inés Hernández's "Para Teresa," N. Scott Momaday's "The Last of the Kiowas," and Cathy Song's "Lost Sister" all testify to the undeniable significance of our cultural heritage.

Despite the ramifications of living in a global village, many people still actively seek to preserve their own culture's unique characteristics and to maintain the values and traditions they have inherited from the past. In our own country, which to some extent has always been a complex patchwork of many interacting cultures, Native Americans and descendants of people from Asia, Africa, Europe, and other regions have struggled to preserve their uniqueness and cultures. As you read the following selections, think about your own roots. Can you define your cultural background? What values and traditions have you inherited from it? Are they valuable and worth preserving for your own children or others to enjoy, or should they be discarded and forgotten?

Family Album

1978

SIV CEDERING

 "Family Album" portrays the narrator's relatives and family through detailed descriptions of family photographs, each accompanied by a story that characterizes that family member. In the final paragraph the narrator attempts to sum up her cultural inheritance, showing the heavy impact her roots had on the person she has become.

Is it understandable that individuals are so strongly influenced by family pictures and the stories that accompany them? What role, if any, do family albums play in your family? How has your cultural background and history shaped your personality and way of thinking?

This is their wedding picture. Pappa wears a tuxedo, and Mamma is wearing a white satin dress. She is smiling at the white lilies. This is the house Pappa built for Mamma, when they were engaged. Then this house, then that; they were always making blueprints together.

Mamma came from Lapland. She was quite poor and dreamed of pretty dresses. Her mother died when Mamma was small. Pappa met her when he came to Lapland as a conscientious objector. He preached in her church. There he is with his banjo.

Pappa was quite poor too; everyone was in those days. He told me he didn't have any shoes that fit him, one spring, and he had to wear his father's big shoes. Pappa said he was so ashamed that he walked in the ditch, all the way to school.

Pappa was one of eleven children, but only five of them grew up. The others died of tuberculosis or diphtheria. Three died in a six-week period, and Pappa says death was accepted then, just like changes in the weather and a bad crop of potatoes. His parents were religious. I remember Grandfather Anton rocking in the rocker and riding on the reaper, and I remember Grandmother Maria, though I was just two when she died. The funeral was like a party: birch saplings decorated the yard, relatives came from all around, and my sister and I wore new white dresses. Listen to the names of her eleven children:

Anna Viktoria, Karl Sigurd, Johan Martin, Hulda Maria, Signe Sofia, Bror Hilding, Judit Friedeborg, Brynhild Elisabet, John Rudolf, Tore Adils, and Clary Torborg.

We called the eldest Tora. She was fat and never got married. Tore was the youngest son. I remember sitting next to him, outside by the flagpole, eating blood pancakes after a slaughter, and calf-dance—a dish made from the first milk a cow gives after it has calved. Tore recently left his wife and took a new one. He once told me that when he was a boy, he used to ski out in the dark afternoons of the North and stand still, watching the sky and feeling himself get smaller and smaller. This is Uncle Rudolf in his uniform, and this is Torborg, Pappa's youngest sister. Her fiancé had tried to make love to her once before they were married, and—Mamma told me—Torborg tore the engagement ring off her finger, threw it on the floor of the large farmhouse kitchen, and hollered, loud enough for everyone to hear: "What does that whoremonger think I am?" He was the son of a big-city mayor and well educated, but you can bet he married a virgin. Don't they look good in this picture? Three of their five children are doctors. They say that Torborg got her temper from Great-grandfather. When he got drunk he cussed and brought the horse into the kitchen. This is the Kell people from the Kell farm. I am told I have the Kell eyes. Everyone on this side of the family hears ghosts and dreams prophecies. To us it isn't supernatural; it is natural.

Mamma's oldest brother Karl went to America when he was eighteen. There he is chopping down a redwood tree, and there he is working in a gold mine. He married a woman named Viviann, and she visited us in Sweden. Let me tell you, the village had never seen anyone like her. Not only had she been divorced, but she had bobbed hair, wore makeup, and dresses with padded shoulders, matching shoes, and purses. Vanity of all vanities was quoted from the Bible. So of course everyone knew the marriage wouldn't last—besides, they didn't have any children. Uncle Karl is now old and fat, the darling and benefactor of a Swedish Old Folks Home in Canada. Silver mines help him. This is Mamma's second brother. He had to have a leg amputated. I used to think about that leg, all alone in heaven. This is Aunt Edith. She once gave me a silver spoon that had my name written on it. And this is Aunt Elsa who has a large birthmark on her face. I used to wonder what mark I had to prove that I was born.

Mamma's father was a Communist. He came to Lapland to build the large power plant that supplies most of Sweden's electricity. He told me, once, that he ate snake when he was young and worked on the railroad. His

5

6

7

8

wife Emma was a beauty and a lady, and when the household money permitted, she washed her face with heavy cream and her hair with beer or egg whites. My hair? Both grandmothers had hair long enough to sit on.

I am talking about my inheritance—the family jewelry that I wear in my hair, so to speak, the birthmark that stays on my face forever. I am motherless in Lapland, brought down to size by the vastness of the sky. I rock in the rocker of old age and ride the reaper, while some part of me has already preceded me to heaven. I change one husband for another, and toss my ring, furiously moral at any indignation. I am a pacifist, I am a Communist, I am a preacher coddling my father's language and abandoning my mother tongue forever. I eat blood pancakes, calf-dance, snake, and I bring the horse into the kitchen. I build new houses, dream of new dresses, bury my parents and my children. I hear ghosts, see the future and know what will happen. If I step on a crack and break my mother's back, I can say the shoes were too large for my feet, for I know, I know: these are the fairy tales that grieve us. And save us.

OPTIONS FOR READING LOGS: "FAMILY ALBUM"

1. Using the double-entry journal technique, you can discover meaning in "Family Album." In the left column of your journal page, draw up a list of "what" or "why" questions that occur to you as you read this selection. Aim for three to five questions, such as "Why does the narrator say she is 'motherless in Lapland, brought down to size by the vastness of the sky'?" When you finish your list, answer your questions as completely as you can in the right column. (Remember that such interpretation will require you to take educated guesses.) To demonstrate that you have a basic understanding of "Family Album," end your journal entry by jotting down the main idea of the story.

2. Copy the most powerful line or passage in "Family Album." Using anecdotes and examples from your personal experience, explain fully why that particular line or passage held such power or meaning for you.

3. Create some drawings, such as a cartoon or caricature of one of the family members described in "Family Album." Describe what you create, using as many specific details as possible. End your journal entry by stating the main idea the author was trying to express in "Family Album."

OPTIONS FOR WRITING ASSIGNMENTS: "FAMILY ALBUM"

1. Do the descriptions in "Family Album" remind you of members of your own immediate or extended family? Explain why you see some or no resemblance. Then compose a descriptive essay of five or more paragraphs, focusing on a particularly memorable relative. Your thesis statement should give an overall impression of that person. Throughout your essay, concentrate on using vivid details and descriptions to help make your family member come alive for your reader.

2. In "Family Album," the narrator was influenced greatly by the sum total of her relatives' various personalities. If possible, interview someone from your extended family and write an essay showing how that person had such a significant influence on your own personal development. Prepare for your interview by making a list of appropriate questions. In your essay you might want to include biographical information that clarifies the influences that have made this person so important in your life. If you cannot interview a family member, interview a friend or a classmate who claims to have been influenced by a relative. Write a narrative essay that tells your friend's or classmate's story.

3. In "Family Album," the narrator discovers an important truth about her cultural background. Write a paper that uses anecdotes (brief stories) to illustrate a particular family trait. Begin by making a generalization showing how that trait shows up in your personality. Use that generalization as your thesis statement, as, for example, "When I start talking, I feel very excited and interrupt a lot." In the body of your essay, include several anecdotes. Develop your anecdotes fully and be sure each serves as a good example that supports your generalization.

4. Write an essay explaining the cultural knowledge gained by the narrator in "Family Album." Focus your attention on parts of the story that cause you to have genuine questions, such as "Why does the narrator describe her family stories as 'the fairy tales that grieve us. And save us'?" In a thesis statement at the end of your introductory paragraph, clearly state what you believe the narrator learns. In the remaining paragraphs, you will need to quote from "Family Album" and refer to specific passages to clarify and support your thesis statement.

Sonrisas

1986

PAT MORA

 "Sonrisas" reveals a narrator caught between two contrasting worlds: the formal culture of the academic world and the familiar culture of the narrator's Mexican heritage.

Have you ever felt pulled in two different directions by two different cultures, sometimes feeling in tune with one aspect of your personality and character, and at other times leaning in another direction? Do you think this cultural conflict is common?

I live in a doorway   1
between two rooms, I hear
quiet clicks, cups of black
coffee, *click, click* like facts
  budgets, tenure, curriculum,   5
from careful women in crisp beige
suits, quick beige smiles
that seldom sneak into their eyes.

I peek
in the other room señoras   10
in faded dresses stir sweet
milk coffee, laughter whirls
with steam from fresh *tamales*
  sh, sh, mucho ruido,
they scold one another,   15
press their lips, trap smiles
in their dark, Mexican eyes.

OPTIONS FOR READING LOGS: "SONRISAS"

1. Use the double-entry journal technique to comment on powerful lines or passages in "Sonrisas." In the left column, copy the lines or passages you particularly like or that you feel are somehow important, such as "quick beige smiles." Then use the right column to jot down word associations and ideas from your personal experience as well as from your reading. Your commentary in the right column could lead to further questions, which you should also attempt to answer. End your journal entry by selecting the most significant line or phrase and explaining why it held such power or meaning for you.

2. Examine your personal reaction to "Sonrisas" by comparing and contrasting the two different rooms described in the poem. Before providing your detailed commentary, list the differences between the two worlds on either side of the doorway. End your journal entry by stating the central idea of the poem.

3. Create an original poem that explores your own cultural identity. Start your poem with the following lines:

    > I live in a doorway,
    > between two _____ (*fill in the blank*)

Then, roughly following the pattern of "Sonrisas," add lines that character- 20
ize the different worlds you sometimes inhabit. End your poem, as Mora
did, with a description of the eyes of the inhabitants of one of the worlds.

OPTIONS FOR WRITING ASSIGNMENTS: "SONRISAS"

1. Since we often dream about rooms, the poem "Sonrisas" could be seen as having some of the characteristics of a dream. The images are vivid and clear, yet they also seem unreal and mysterious, possibly containing a hidden or symbolic meaning. Have you ever had a strange dream or a puzzling recurring dream? Recreate the dream as a story or poem using concrete details, vivid imagery, and, if possible, dialogue. Also, explore the value of the dream in defining your cultural values. What do you feel the dream is trying to tell you about who you are? What can you learn about yourself from analyzing the dream? Can you make any generalizations about yourself from the dream?

2. Does "Sonrisas" remind you of an event from your own past that is somehow connected to your cultural identity? Compose a narrative or descriptive essay that focuses on this remembered event and write a thesis

statement that points out the significance of that event in your life. Throughout your essay, concentrate on using vivid details and descriptions to help recreate your memory. As an example, you might remember how you as a child participated with your family in some traditional celebration without knowing its full significance. An example of a thesis statement might be, "Little did I know that our joyful celebration was actually in honor of our ancestors who had died."

3. In "Sonrisas" the narrator seems to be on the boundary between two worlds. The poem might bring up the following questions: "Why are the 'careful women' so cold compared with the señoras from the 'other room'?" "In which room does the speaker feel most comfortable?" "What are some of the causes of the narrator's attitude?" "What are the causes of the narrator's mixed emotions?" As you trace effects to their causes, watch for hidden discoveries along the way. Focus on the theme of "Cultural Knowledge: What Are My Roots?"

4. Write a formal essay of five paragraphs or more explaining the meaning of "Sonrisas" in terms of cultural knowledge. Focus on parts of the poem about which you have genuine questions, such as "Why has the narrator taken up residence in the doorway?" In your essay you should begin with an arguable thesis statement, for example, "In 'Sonrisas' the narrator needs to be more accepting of both worlds." Use quotes from the poem and refer to specific passages to clarify and support your central argument.

Customs

1949

CLYDE KLUCKHOHN

 CLYDE KLUCKHOHN, born in Iowa in 1905, was a noted authority on the study of cultural values and personality. He had a lifelong interest in the Navaho people and their language, publishing numerous works on the Navahos and other anthropological topics. Kluckhohn was a professor of anthropology at Harvard University at the time of his death in 1960. His essay "Customs" shows how our cultural backgrounds influence our behavior.

Think about the ways in which you react to people and events. Try to trace your reactions to your background. Does any aspect of your behavior have specific cultural roots?

Why do the Chinese dislike milk and milk products? Why would the Japanese die willingly in a Banzai[1] charge that seemed senseless to Americans? Why do some nations trace descent through the father, others through the mother, still others through both parents? Not because different peoples have different instincts, not because they were destined by God or Fate to different habits, not because the weather is different in China and Japan and the United States. Sometimes shrewd common sense has an answer that is close to that of the anthropologist: "because they were brought up that way." By "culture" anthropology means the total life way of a people, the social legacy the individual acquires from his group. Or culture can be regarded as that part of the environment that is the creation of man.

This technical term has a wider meaning than the "culture" of history and literature. A humble cooking pot is as much a cultural product as is a Beethoven sonata. In ordinary speech a man of culture is a man who can speak languages other than his own, who is familiar with history, literature, philosophy, or the fine arts. In some cliques[2] that definition is still narrower.

1. Banzai: a Japanese patriotic cry or joyous shout   2. cliques: a small, exclusive group of people

The cultured person is one who can talk about James Joyce, Scarlatti, and Picasso. To the anthropologist, however, to be human is to be cultured. There is culture in general, and then there are the specific cultures such as Russian, American, British, Hottentot, Inca. The general abstract notion serves to remind us that we cannot explain acts solely in terms of the biological properties of the people concerned, their individual past experience, and the immediate situation. The past experience of other men in the form of culture enters into almost every event. Each specific culture constitutes a kind of blueprint for all of life's activities.

One of the interesting things about human beings is that they try to understand themselves and their own behavior. While this has been particularly true of Europeans in recent times, there is no group which has not developed a scheme or schemes to explain man's actions. To the insistent human query "why?" the most exciting illumination anthropology has to offer is that of the concept of culture. Its explanatory importance is comparable to categories such as evolution in biology, gravity in physics, disease in medicine. A good deal of human behavior can be understood, and indeed predicted, if we know a people's design for living. Many acts are neither accidental nor due to personal peculiarities nor caused by supernatural forces nor simply mysterious. Even those of us who pride ourselves on our individualism follow most of the time a pattern not of our own making. We brush our teeth on arising. We put on pants—not a loincloth or a grass skirt. We eat three meals a day—not four or five or two. We sleep in a bed—not in a hammock or on a sheep pelt. I do not have to know the individual and his life history to be able to predict these and countless other regularities, including many in the thinking process of all Americans who are not incarcerated[3] in jails or hospitals for the insane.

To the American woman a system of plural wives seems "instinctively" abhorrent.[4] She cannot understand how any woman can fail to be jealous and uncomfortable if she must share her husband with other women. She feels it "unnatural" to accept such a situation. On the other hand, a Koryak woman of Siberia, for example, would find it hard to understand how a woman could be so selfish and so undesirous of feminine companionship in the home as to wish to restrict her husband to one mate.

Some years ago I met in New York City a young man who did not speak a word of English and was obviously bewildered by American ways. By "blood" he was as American as you or I, for his parents had gone from Indiana to China as missionaries. Orphaned in infancy, he was reared by a Chinese family in a remote village. All who met him found him more Chinese

3. incarcerated: imprisoned or confined   4. abhorrent: causing repugnance or aversion

than American. The facts of his blue eyes and light hair were less impressive than a Chinese style of gait, Chinese arm and hand movements, Chinese facial expression, and Chinese modes of thought. The biological heritage was American, but the cultural training had been Chinese. He returned to China.

Another example of another kind: I once knew a trader's wife in Arizona   6
who took a somewhat devilish interest in producing a cultural reaction. Guests who came her way were often served delicious sandwiches filled with a meat that seemed to be neither chicken nor tuna fish yet was reminiscent of both. To queries she gave no reply until each had eaten his fill. She then explained that what they had eaten was not chicken, not tuna fish, but the rich, white flesh of freshly killed rattlesnakes. The response was instantaneous—vomiting, often violent vomiting. A biological process is caught in a cultural web.

A highly intelligent teacher with long and successful experience in the   7
public schools of Chicago was finishing her first year in an Indian school. When asked how her Navaho pupils compared in intelligence with Chicago youngsters, she replied, "Well, I just don't know. Sometimes the Indians seem just as bright. At other times they just act like dumb animals. The other night we had a dance in the high school. I saw a boy who is one of the best students in my English class standing off by himself. So I took him over to a pretty girl and told them to dance. But they just stood there with their heads down. They wouldn't even say anything." I inquired if she knew whether or not they were members of the same clan. "What difference would that make?"

"How would you feel about getting into bed with your brother?" The   8
teacher walked off in a huff, but, actually, the two cases were quite comparable in principle. To the Indian the type of bodily contact involved in our social dancing has a directly sexual connotation.[5] The incest taboos between members of the same clan are as severe as between true brothers and sisters. The shame of the Indians at the suggestion that a clan brother and sister should dance and the indignation of the white teacher at the idea that she should share a bed with an adult brother represent equally nonrational responses, culturally standardized unreason.

All this does not mean that there is no such thing as raw human nature.   9
The very fact that certain of the same institutions are found in all known societies indicates that at bottom all human beings are very much alike. The files of the Cross-Cultural Survey at Yale University are organized according to categories such as "marriage ceremonies," "life crisis rites," "incest taboos." At least seventy-five of these categories are represented in every single

5. connotation: an act or instance signifying or suggesting certain meanings

one of the hundreds of cultures analyzed. This is hardly surprising. The members of all human groups have about the same biological equipment. All men undergo the same poignant[6] life experiences such as birth, helplessness, illness, old age, and death. The biological potentialities[7] of the species are the blocks with which cultures are built. Some patterns of every culture crystallize around focuses provided by the inevitables of biology, the difference between the sexes, the presence of persons of different ages, the varying physical strength and skill of individuals. The facts of nature also limit culture forms. No culture provides patterns for jumping over trees or for eating iron ore.

6. poignant: affecting or involving the emotions   7. potentialities: the states or qualities of being possible

OPTIONS FOR READING LOGS: "CUSTOMS"

1. Using the double-entry journal technique, draw a vertical line down the middle of your journal page to create two columns. In the left column, keep a running list of "what" or "why" questions that occur to you as you are reading "Customs." Aim for three to five questions, such as "Why does Kluckhohn give us two definitions of the word *culture* in his essay?" When you finish, go back and answer your questions as completely as you can in the right column. If those answers lead to other questions, jot them down and attempt to answer them, too. To demonstrate that you have reached a basic understanding of "Customs," end your journal entry by jotting down its main idea.

2. Does "Customs" remind you of some custom you follow that differs from culture to culture? Explain how you acquired your beliefs regarding this custom.

3. Examine your personal reaction to "Customs" by completing one of the following statements:

    A. "I was confused by _____."
    B. "I was struck by _____."
    C. "I was surprised by _____."

    Develop your journal entry by adding detailed explanations from your own experiences as well as from events in the essay. Finish your journal entry with a statement of the central idea of "Customs."

OPTIONS FOR WRITING ASSIGNMENTS: "CUSTOMS"

1. Expand and develop one of your reading logs for "Customs" into a more polished piece of writing that explores its subject matter in greater range and depth. Begin with a thesis statement that reveals an important discovery you made about your cultural identity, even a discovery that may not have been an earthshaking event. Arrange your story in a clear chronological order, adding enough specific details to make the event come alive for your reader. By the end of your essay, you should have convinced your reader of the cultural significance of your self-discovery.

2. Our own customs often serve as general guides, but sometimes they make us critical of the customs and beliefs of cultures that are foreign to us. Such moments of criticism cause us to go through phases in which we question our own personal values and our goals. Have you experienced some strong reaction to the customs of a different culture that you could explore through writing? Write a formal essay of five or more paragraphs about an event that caused you to have a strong or negative reaction, for example, discovering that a delicacy you had just eaten was the flesh of an animal you were not accustomed to eating. Examine closely the beginning, middle, and end of your response. What affected you the most? In what ways were you influenced by your cultural upbringing? How important is the preservation and continuation of cultural activities in our multicultural society?

3. Write a formal essay of five or more paragraphs explaining the meaning of "Customs." Focus your attention on ideas in the essay that you have genuine questions about, such as, "How do cultural differences reflect a contrast in values?" End your introductory paragraph with a thesis statement that makes an arguable point about the central theme of the essay. Brainstorm or prewrite to come up with ideas that support your thesis statement. In the body of your essay, you will need to quote from "Customs" and refer to specific words and passages to clarify and support your argument.

4. In "Customs," Kluckhohn points out several interesting cultural differences between various groups. Interview someone to discover how his or her life has been uniquely enriched by cultural influences passed on by family members. How has that person's attitudes, religion, foods, or societal roles been determined by deeply felt inherited cultural standards? Before your interview, make a list of appropriate questions. Write an essay showing how that person's cultural background has played an important role in his or her life. In your essay you might want to include biographical information that shows any profound influences.

The Lesson

1972

TONI CADE BAMBARA

 TONI CADE BAMBARA, an African-American author, was born in 1939 in
New York City. She was educated in New York and Paris, and she has published short stories, screenplays, and a novel. Her stories often draw on her
New York City background for their settings and characters. As a result of her
diverse background and interests, she calls herself a Pan-Africanist-socialist-
feminist. In the story, "The Lesson," Sylvia, the street-smart narrator, unwill-
ingly learns an important lesson about herself and her place in American
society.

*Have you ever had an experience that taught you something impor-
tant about your place in society? Was that experience a positive or
negative one? Did it tend to set you apart from others or did it make
you feel comfortable with your place in society?*

Back in the days when everyone was old and stupid or young and   1
foolish and me and Sugar were the only ones just right, this lady
moved on our block with nappy hair and proper speech and no
makeup. And quite naturally we laughed at her, laughed the way we did at
the junk man who went about his business like he was some big-time president and his sorry-ass horse his secretary. And we kinda hated her too, hated
the way we did the winos who cluttered up our parks and pissed on our
handball walls and stank up our hallways and stairs so you couldn't halfway
play hide-and-seek without a goddamn gas mask. Miss Moore was her name.
The only woman on the block with no first name. And she was black as hell,
cept for her feet, which were fish-white and spooky. And she was always
planning these boring-ass things for us to do, us being my cousin, mostly,
who lived on the block cause we all moved North the same time and to the
same apartment then spread out gradual to breathe. And our parents would
yank our heads into some kinda shape and crisp up our clothes so we'd be
presentable for travel with Miss Moore, who always looked like she was going

to church, though she never did. Which is just one of the things the grownups talked about when they talked behind her back like a dog. But when she came calling with some sachet she'd sewed up or some gingerbread she'd made or some book, why then they'd all be too embarrassed to turn her down and we'd get handed over all spruced up. She'd been to college and said it was only right that she should take responsibility for the young ones' education, and she not even related by marriage or blood. So they'd go for it. Specially Aunt Gretchen. She was the main gofer in the family. You got some ole dumb shit foolishness you want somebody to go for, you send for Aunt Gretchen. She been screwed into the go-along for so long, it's a blood-deep natural thing with her. Which is how she got saddled with me and Sugar and Junior in the first place while our mothers were in a la-de-da apartment up the block having a good ole time.

So this one day Miss Moore rounds us all up at the mailbox and it's puredee hot and she's knockin herself out about arithmetic. And school suppose to let up in summer I heard, but she don't never let up. And the starch in my pinafore scratching the shit outta me and I'm really hating this nappy-head bitch and her goddamn college degree. I'd much rather go to the pool or to the show where it's cool. So me and Sugar leaning on the mailbox being surly, which is a Miss Moore word. And Flyboy checking out what everybody brought for lunch. And Fat Butt already wasting his peanut-butter-and-jelly sandwich like the pig he is. And Junebug punchin on Q.T.'s arm for potato chips. And Rosie Giraffe shifting from one hip to the other waiting for somebody to step on her foot or ask her if she from Georgia so she can kick ass, preferably Mercedes'. And Miss Moore asking us do we know what money is, like we a bunch of retards. I mean real money, she say, like it's only poker chips or monopoly papers we lay on the grocer. So right away I'm tired of this and say so. And would much rather snatch Sugar and go to the Sunset and terrorize the West Indian kids and take their hair ribbons and their money too. And Miss Moore files that remark away for next week's lesson on brotherhood, I can tell. And finally I say we oughta get to the subway cause it's cooler and besides we might meet some cute boys. Sugar done swiped her mama's lipstick, so we ready.

So we heading down the street and she's boring us silly about what things cost and what our parents make and how much goes for rent and how money ain't divided up right in this country. And then she gets to the part about we all poor and live in the slums, which I don't feature. And I'm ready to speak on that, but she steps out in the street and hails two cabs just like that. Then she hustles half the crew in with her and hands me a five-dollar bill and tells me to calculate 10 percent tip for the driver. And we're off. Me and Sugar and Junebug and Flyboy hangin out the window and hollering to everybody, putting lipstick on each other cause Flyboy a faggot anyway, and making farts with our sweaty armpits. But I'm mostly trying to figure how to spend this money. But they all fascinated with the meter ticking and Junebug starts laying bets to how much it'll read when Flyboy can't hold his breath no more. Then Sugar lays bets as to how much it'll be when we get there. So I'm stuck. Don't nobody want to go for my plan, which is to jump out at the next light and run off to the first bar-b-que we can find. Then the driver tells us to get the hell out cause we there already. And the meter reads eighty-five cents. And I'm stalling to figure out the tip and Sugar say give him a dime. And I decide he don't need it as bad as I do, so later for him. But then he tries to take off with Junebug's foot still in the door so we talk about his mama something ferocious. Then we check out that we on Fifth Avenue and everybody dressed up in stockings. One lady in a fur coat, hot as it is. White folks crazy.

"This is the place," Miss Moore say, presenting it to us in the voice she 4
uses at the museum. "Let's look in the windows before we go in."

"Can we steal?" Sugar asks very serious like she's getting the ground 5
rules squared away before she plays. "I beg your pardon," say Miss Moore, and we fall out. So she leads us around the windows of the toy store and me and Sugar screamin, "This is mine, that's mine, I gotta have that, that was made for me, I was born for that," till Big Butt drowns us out.

"Hey, I'm goin to buy that there." 6

"That there? You don't even know what it is, stupid." 7

"I do so," he say punchin on Rosie Giraffe. "It's a microscope." 8

"Whatcha gonna do with a microscope, fool?" 9

"Look at things." 10

"Like what, Ronald?" ask Miss Moore. And Big Butt ain't got the first 11
notion. So here go Miss Moore gabbing about the thousands of bacteria in a drop of water and the somethinorother in a speck of blood and the million and one living things in the air around us is invisible to the naked eye. And what she say that for? Junebug go to town on that "naked" and we rolling. Then Miss Moore ask what it cost. So we all jam into the window smudgin it up and the price tag say $300. So then she ask how long'd take for Big Butt and Junebug to save up their allowances. "Too long," I say. "Yeh," adds Sugar, "outgrown it by that time." And Miss Moore say no, you never outgrow learning instruments. "Why, even medical students and interns and," blah, blah, blah. And we ready to choke Big Butt for bringing it up in the first damn place.

"This here costs four hundred eighty dollars," say Rosie Giraffe. So we 12
pile up all over her to see what she pointin out. My eyes tell me it's a chunk of glass cracked with something heavy, and different-color inks dripped into the splits, then the whole thing put into a oven or something. But for $480 it don't make sense.

"That's a paperweight made of semi-precious stones fused together   13
under tremendous pressure," she explains slowly, and her hands doing the
mining and all the factory work.

"So what's a paperweight?" asks Rosie Giraffe.   14

"To weigh paper with, dumbbell," say Flyboy, the wise man from the   15
East.

"Not exactly," say Miss Moore, which is what she say when you warm   16
or way off too. "It's to weigh paper down so it won't scatter and make your
desk untidy." So right away me and Sugar curtsy to each other and then to
Mercedes who is more the tidy type.

"We don't keep paper on top of the desk in my class," say Junebug,   17
figuring Miss Moore crazy or lyin one.

"At home, then," she say. "Don't you have a calendar and a pencil case   18
and a blotter and a letter-opener on your desk at home where you do your
homework?" And she know damn well what our homes look like cause she
nosys around in them every chance she gets.

"I don't even have a desk," say Junebug. "Do we?"   19

"No. And I don't get no homework neither," says Big Butt.   20

"And I don't even have a home," say Flyboy like he do at school to   21
keep the white folks off his back and sorry for him. Send this poor kid to
camp posters, is his specialty.

"I do," says Mercedes. "I have a box of stationery on my desk and a   22
picture of my cat. My godmother bought the stationery and the desk. There's
a big rose on each sheet and the envelopes smell like roses."

"Who wants to know about your smelly-ass stationery," say Rosie Giraffe   23
fore I can get my two cents in.

"It's important to have a work area all your own so that . . ."   24

"Will you look at this sailboat, please," say Flyboy, cuttin her off and   25
pointin to the thing like it was his. So once again we tumble all over each
other to gaze at this magnificent thing in the toy store which is just big
enough to maybe sail two kittens across the pond if you strap them to the
posts tight. We all start reciting the price tag like we in assembly. "Hand-
crafted sailboat of fiberglass at one thousand one hundred ninety-five
dollars."

"Unbelievable," I hear myself say and am really stunned. I read it again   26
for myself just in case the group recitation put me in a trance. Same thing.
For some reason this pisses me off. We look at Miss Moore and she lookin
at us, waiting for I dunno what.

"Who'd pay all that when you can buy a sailboat set for a quarter at   27
Pop's, a tube of glue for a dime, and a ball of string for eight cents? It must
have a motor and a whole lot else besides," I say. "My sailboat cost me about
fifty cents."

"But will it take water?" say Mercedes with her smart ass. 28

"Took mine to Alley Pond Park once," say Flyboy. "String broke. Lost 29
it. Pity."

"Sailed mine in Central Park and it keeled over and sank. Had to ask 30
my father for another dollar."

"And you got the strap," laugh Big Butt. "The jerk didn't even have a 31
string on it. My old man wailed on his behind."

Little Q.T. was staring hard at the sailboat and you could see he wanted 32
it bad. But he too little and somebody'd just take it from him. So what the
hell. "This boat for kids, Miss Moore?"

"Parents silly to buy something like that just to get all broke up," say 33
Rosie Giraffe.

"That much money it should last forever," I figure. 34

"My father'd buy it for me if I wanted it." 35

"Your father, my ass," say Rosie Giraffe getting a chance to finally push 36
Mercedes.

"Must be rich people shop here," say Q.T. 37

"You are a very bright boy," say Flyboy. "What was your first clue?" 38
And he rap him on the head with the back of his knuckles, since Q.T. the
only one he could get away with. Though Q.T. liable to come up behind
you years later and get his licks in when you half expect it.

"What I want to know is," I says to Miss Moore though I never talk to 39
her, I wouldn't give the bitch that satisfaction, "is how much a real boat
costs? I figure a thousand'd get you a yacht any day."

"Why don't you check that out," she says, "and report back to the 40
group?" Which really pains my ass. If you gonna mess up a perfectly good
swim day least you could do is have some answers. "Let's go in," she say
like she got something up her sleeve. Only she don't lead the way. So me
and Sugar turn the corner to where the entrance is, but when we get there
I kinda hang back. Not that I'm scared, what's there to be afraid of, just a
toy store. But I feel funny, shame. But what I got to be shamed about? Got
as much right to go in as anybody. But somehow I can't seem to get hold
of the door, so I step away for Sugar to lead. But she hangs back too. And
I look at her and she looks at me and this is ridiculous. I mean, damn, I
have never ever been shy about doing nothing or going nowhere. But then
Mercedes steps up and then Rosie Giraffe and Big Butt crowd in behind and
shove, and next thing we all stuffed into the doorway with only Mercedes
squeezing past us, smoothing out her jumper and walking right down the
aisle. Then the rest of us tumble in like a glued-together jigsaw done all
wrong. And people lookin at us. And it's like the time me and Sugar crashed
into the Catholic church on a dare. But once we got in there and everything
so hushed and holy and the candles and the bowin and the handkerchiefs on

all the drooping heads, I just couldn't go through with the plan. Which was for me to run up to the altar and do a tap dance while Sugar played the nose flute and messed around in the holy water. And Sugar kept givin me the elbow. Then later teased me so bad I tied her up in the shower and turned it on and locked her in. And she'd be there till this day if Aunt Gretchen hadn't finally figured I was lyin about the boarder takin a shower.

Same thing in the store. We all walkin on tiptoe and hardly touchin the   41
games and puzzles and things. And I watched Miss Moore who is steady watchin us like she waitin for a sign. Like Mama Drewery watches the sky and sniffs the air and takes note of just how much slant is in the bird forma- tion. Then me and Sugar bump smack into each other, so busy gazing at the toys, 'specially the sailboat. But we don't laugh and go into our fat-lady bump-stomach routine. We just stare at that price tag. Then Sugar run a finger over the whole boat. And I'm jealous and want to hit her. Maybe not her, but I sure want to punch somebody in the mouth.

"Whatcha bring us here for, Miss Moore?"   42

"You sound angry, Sylvia. Are you mad about something?" Givin me   43
one of them grins like she tellin a grown-up joke that never turns out to be funny. And she's lookin very closely at me like maybe she plannin to do my portrait from memory. I'm mad, but I won't give her that satisfaction. So I slouch around the store bein very bored and say, "Let's go."

Me and Sugar at the back of the train watchin the tracks whizzin by large   44
then small then gettin gobbled up in the dark. I'm thinkin about this tricky toy I saw in the store. A clown that somersaults on a bar then does chin-ups just cause you yank lightly at his leg. Cost $35. I could see me askin my mother for a $35 birthday clown. "You wanna who that costs what?" she'd say, cocking her head to the side to get a better view of the hole in my head. Thirty-five dollars and the whole household could go visit Granddaddy Nelson in the country. Thirty-five dollars would pay for the rent and the piano bill too. Who are these people that spend that much for performing clowns and $1000 for toy sailboats? What kinda work they do and how they live and how come we ain't in on it? Where we are is who we are, Miss Moore always pointin out. But it don't necessarily have to be that way, she always adds then waits for somebody to say that poor people have to wake up and demand their share of the pie and don't none of us know what kind of pie she talkin about in the first damn place. But she ain't so smart cause I still got her four dollars from the taxi and she sure ain't gettin it. Messin up my day with this shit. Sugar nudges me in my pocket and winks.

Miss Moore lines us up in front of the mailbox where we started from,   45
seem like years ago, and I got a headache for thinkin so hard. And we lean all over each other so we can hold up under the draggy-ass lecture she always

finishes us off with at the end before we thank her for borin us to tears. But she just looks at us like she readin tea leaves. Finally she say, " Well, what do you think of F.A.O. Schwartz?"

Rosie Giraffe mumbles, "White folks crazy."   46

"I'd like to go there again when I get my birthday money," says Mercedes,   47
and we shove her out the pack so she has to lean on the mailbox by herself.

"I'd like a shower. Tiring day," say Flyboy.   48

Then Sugar surprises me by sayin, "You know, Miss Moore, I don't think   49
all of us here put together eat in a year what that sailboat costs." And Miss
Moore lights up like somebody goosed her. "And?" she say, urging Sugar
on. Only I'm standin on her foot so she don't continue.

"Imagine for a minute what kind of society it is in which some people   50
can spend on a toy what it would cost to feed a family of six or seven. What
do you think?"

"I think," say Sugar pushing me off her feet like she never done   51
before, cause I whip her ass in a minute, "that this is not much of a
democracy if you ask me. Equal chance to pursue happiness means an
equal crack at the dough, don't it?" Miss Moore is besides herself and I
am disgusted with Sugar's treachery. So I stand on her foot one more
time to see if she'll shove me. She shuts up, and Miss Moore looks at
me, sorrowfully I'm thinkin. And somethin weird is goin on, I can feel
it in my chest.

"Anybody else learn anything today?" lookin dead at me. I walk away   52
and Sugar has to run to catch up and don't even seem to notice when I
shrug her arm off my shoulder.

"Well, we got four dollars anyway," she says.   53

"Uh hunh."   54

"We could go to Hascombs and get half a chocolate layer and then go   55
to the Sunset and still have plenty money for potato chips and ice cream
sodas."

"Uh hunh."   56

"Race you to Hascombs," she say.   57

We start down the block and she gets ahead which is O.K. by me cause   58
I'm going to the West End and then over to the Drive to think this day
through. She can run if she want to and even run faster. But ain't nobody
gonna beat me at nuthin.

OPTIONS FOR READING LOGS: "THE LESSON"

1. Use the double-entry journal technique (asking "what" or "why" questions) to discover meaning in "The Lesson." As an example, in the left column you might ask, "Why does the narrator feel compelled to use language in the opening paragraph that some readers might find offensive?" Try to come up with three to five questions that will somehow unlock the meaning of the story. Your answers in the right column will require you to speculate or take educated guesses. To demonstrate that you have a basic understanding of "The Lesson," end your journal entry by jotting down its central idea.

2. At the end of "The Lesson," the main character, Sylvia, seems a bit angry about being shown a whole new world. Rewrite the end of the story, giving it a new and altogether different ending. Use dialogue, if you wish, to make your story plausible.

3. From your own life, tell a parallel story that was triggered by reading "The Lesson." Your story should be connected with the theme of "Cultural Knowledge: What Are My Roots?" Does Sylvia's experience of visiting the toy store with the other kids and Miss Moore remind you of a similar learning experience in your life? Jot down some events or feelings that were similar or different. Wrap up your journal entry by stating what your experience taught you about your own cultural background.

OPTIONS FOR WRITING ASSIGNMENTS: "THE LESSON"

1. If "The Lesson" brings to mind an experience from your own past, expand your reading log entry into a more polished piece of writing. Compose a narrative or descriptive essay focusing on an important event that helped you to see your own cultural roots more clearly. End your introductory paragraph with a thesis statement that names your topic and tells your reader what you learned from your experience. In the rest of your paragraphs, concentrate on using vivid details and descriptions to help bring your experience to life.

2. Write a letter to Sylvia to help her "think this day through." Address her directly, expressing your understanding of what the "lesson" actually was. Use the letter to state your personal point of view to Sylvia. For example, you could encourage Sylvia to think better of Miss Moore, empathize with Sylvia for the anger she feels in the toy store, or criticize Sylvia for her lack of consideration of others. Use whatever tone—critical,

sincere, sad, angry, or another—that seems most appropriate for expressing your reaction to the story.

3. In "The Lesson," Sylvia discovers an important truth about her relationship to the society in which she lives, especially as symbolized by F.A.O. Schwartz. Write an essay using anecdotes (brief stories) to illustrate a similar experience of your own. At the end of your introductory paragraph, make a generalization about some aspect of your own cultural background or roots, using that generalization as your thesis statement. For example, "My small-town southern background made me feel naive and vulnerable when I moved to a large metropolitan area," or "Being raised as a traditional Hmong in California has given me a unique perspective on American culture." In the remaining paragraphs in your essay, include several anecdotes with enough specific details to illustrate the truth of your generalization. Develop your anecdotes fully and be sure each is a good example that supports your thesis statement.

4. Write a formal essay of five or more paragraphs explaining the overall meaning of "The Lesson" as an example of cultural knowledge. Focus on important events in the story that caused you to have genuine questions, such as, "Why does Sylvia seem to feel betrayed when her friend Sugar answers Miss Moore's question at the end of the day?" End your introductory paragraph with a thesis statement that makes an arguable point about your particular interpretation of the story. In the following paragraphs, include some evidence to support your interpretations. To do this, you will need to quote or paraphrase from the story and refer to specific passages that clarify and support your central argument.

Homage to My Hips

1991

LUCILLE CLIFTON

 LUCILLE CLIFTON, born in 1936, is an African-American poet who grew up in New York and went to Howard University. A Pulitzer Prize nominee, she was thirty-three years old when her first book of poems, *Good Times,* was published. At the time she had six children, all under the age of ten. Her poems are simple but heavily influenced by African-American spirituals and the blues. In her poem "Homage to My Hips" the narrator celebrates her hips with wit and energy. Throughout the poem, she adds more reasons to see her hips as a positive, rather than an embarrassing, feature. The narrator asks us to see her hips as "free," "magical," and "mighty." With incantation and humor, this brief poem asserts with great power the narrator's contentment with exactly who and what she is, both individually and culturally.

As you read the poem, notice how the narrator works hard to make others see her oversized hips not as a source of low self-esteem and embarrassment but as a wondrous feature others might desire and envy. Do you think most people are comfortable with the way they look? What influences shape our self-image? Can you think of any legacies (like Clifton's "hips") from your own genetic background?

these hips are big hips.   1
they need space to
move around in.
they don't fit into little
petty places. these hips   5
are free hips.
they don't like to be held back.
these hips have never been enslaved,
they go where they want to go
they do what they want to do.   10

168

these hips are mighty hips.
these hips are magic hips.
i have known them
to put a spell on a man and
spin him like a top!

15

OPTIONS FOR READING LOGS:
"HOMAGE TO MY HIPS"

1. Drawing a vertical line down the middle of your journal page, create two columns and use the double-entry journal technique to comment on powerful lines or passages in "Homage to My Hips." In the left column, copy lines or passages that you particularly like or that you feel are somehow important, like "These hips are magic hips." Find three or four other lines or passages that are particularly memorable. In the right column, jot down word associations and comments, including those from your personal experience as well as from your reading, to clarify the quotations. End your journal entry by selecting one of the key lines or phrases and explaining why it held such power or meaning for you.

2. Tell a parallel story that "Homage to My Hips" triggered from your own life. For example, if Clifton's praise of her large hips reminded you of some similar feelings, jot down the details that were similar or different. Wrap up your journal entry by stating what your experience taught you about yourself and your unique place in our culture.

3. Create an original poem in response to the text. Focus on some unique feature of yourself, connecting it with your own cultural roots. Start with Clifton's poem, but make it your own by changing the word *hips* to some unique aspect of your own life and culture that you wish to celebrate. Then continue to replace Clifton's words and lines with your own details. After your repeated substitutions, Clifton's poem will be unrecognizable and a new original poem about you and some unique feature of your life or culture will be in its place.

OPTIONS FOR WRITING ASSIGNMENTS:
"HOMAGE TO MY HIPS"

1. The author of "Homage to My Hips" offers a very positive self-portrait. Have you ever been through a phase your life (lasting several months or

even longer) in which you felt proud or ashamed of your own background or cultural values? Explore this period of your life through writing. Think of a specific positive or negative period in your life when you had a strong preoccupation with some aspect of your own background, roots, or culture. Perhaps, for example, at one time you rebelled against the values of your community or family, or maybe you found great reinforcement and strength in those important cultural institutions. Write your thesis statement at the end of your introductory paragraph. In the following paragraphs explore the beginning, middle, and end of that phase. Think about the following questions to get you started: What started the phase? What did you learn that was important? Why did the phase end? What replaced it?

2. Create a conversation between you and the narrator of "Homage to My Hips." Your conversation might take the form of a question-and-answer interview, an argument between two opposing points of view, or an open-ended discussion of the ideas and implications of her poem. See if you gain any insight into your own roots and culture through the process of creating this dialogue.

3. In "Homage to My Hips" the speaker celebrates a positive attitude about who and what she is. Try to make connections between causes and effects by thinking about the following questions: What is the typical attitude of our culture to the human body? Does our culture demand perfection of us? If we are not physically perfect, how does this fact affect our feelings about ourselves? Do such demanding and exacting cultural attitudes harm us or help us? Why does our culture care so much about physical appearance? Where did it begin? As you attempt to trace these causes, refer frequently to "Homage to My Hips" as a point of reference and example of these attitudes.

4. We often rely on the advice of others in selecting texts to read, and we are influenced by their evaluations. Write a critical review of "Homage to My Hips," perhaps focusing on the poem as a personal reaction against our culture's expectations and demands for physical "perfection." Your evaluation of the poem might be positive, negative, or some interesting mixture of the two. Once you know what sort of evaluation or judgment you want to make, write it clearly as a thesis statement in your opening paragraph. As you work through your essay, come up with several good reasons, each with supporting evidence from the essay, that make your judgment convincing.

The Bath

19—

KAREN TEI YAMASHITA

 KAREN TEI YAMASHITA is a contemporary writer of poetry, stories, and plays. Her essay on what most people see as an ordinary, everyday occurrence, taking a bath, accentuates the profoundly different Japanese perspective on that activity. Yamashita's exploration of the Japanese approach to bathing offers us a unique insight into another culture's assumptions and traditions.

As you read Yamashita's essay, think about similarities and differences between the customs she describes and your own culture's approach to bathing. Did you ever experience bathing in the way she describes it? If not, do you think you would prefer the Japanese approach to your own?

I

In their house they have often said that mother has a special fascination for the bath. Father pointed this out many years ago. Perhaps it was only in answer to mother's suggestion that father might take a bath more frequently. Remembering, father seemed to take baths once a week on Saturday nights. Father bragged of his once a week bath but only in relation to mother's nightly affair. Over the years, it seems mother has taken to early morning baths as well, so father's comments on mother and the bath continue with an added flourish. He seems to believe that certain of mother's habits have come together to conspire against him by beginning all at once in the morning.

Mother is not one to deny such things. She laughs at herself in an embarrassed manner, pressing her lips together and looking around at the floor. Father's banter is an old and recurring one, and mother is not without her usual reply. She defends herself on two accounts, saying that a hot bath is the most relaxing thing. Her other retort is a more defensive stance on the necessity to be clean. "You perspire, and isn't it nice to have a clean

171

body? You feel so much better." "After all," she will finally say, "the bath is my only luxury."

These are statements typical of mother. They suggest perhaps a certain simplicity. This is not to say mother is simple-minded. Not at all. Rather it is to suggest a sensibility that respects necessities for what they are, a practical sense that finds contentment, sometimes even luxury, in the simple duties to necessity. Mother is simple in that she does not carry around anything in excess be it pretension, desire, or fashionable decoration. As father says, "She is what she is." Mother's simplicity is finally honest. It is clean and naked in a hot bath tub.

It has been sometimes suggested that the bath is a return to the womb, to a fetal state. Mother freely admits that this must be a part of its pleasure. Nakedness is not something mother is shy about. Birth and bodies, it is all very natural and beautiful. However they have had some difficulty extracting from mother explanations as to processes, action, causes in the matter of birth and naked bodies. It is all very much a mystery. Mother's standard answer in these cases is, "What do you have that others haven't got?" That has somehow had to suffice for everything, that which is natural and that, mysterious.

Speaking of the bath, one has in mind the bathroom in the old house where they first lived as a family. It seems that this bathroom was painted all over in pink enamel. The built-in wood drawers and the large wood medicine cabinet behind the mirror: these too were painted in pink enamel. But the amazing thing was the tub itself, an old curving tub standing on four legs like a huge white iron pig in the middle of peeling linoleum.

In those days, the three of them, mother and the twins, took baths in this tub together. Mother would squat at the front of the tub adjusting cold and hot water while her two naked daughters stood leaning into her shoulders, splashing and floating rubber toys and bars of ivory soap. Mother would take a wash cloth and soap and scrub herself and the two children, rinse, and send them out before the *aka* or tub scum could gather much. Mother did this generally and quickly in a way they called *ikagen*. *Ikagen* is "just so" or "to suit your taste" or "just enough." *Ikagen* is a word mother used to describe what her mother had said about how much salt or *shōyu* to use in this or that recipe. If it was *ikagen*, it was an amount of common sense or taste. *Ikagen* is descriptive of a general approach mother maintains toward household duties, secretarial filing, letter writing, reading, and washing children.

But if mother washed *ikagen*, shampooing was sometimes a different matter. Not that the general style was not *ikagen*, a quick scrubbing on four sides of the scalp, it was that every once in a while, she would bring to bath three eggs. The eggs were cold out of the refrigerator. The twins leaned against the white curve of the old tub as she cracked the cold shells gently on the tops of wet heads. She let the yellow lump fall and the cool slime ooze, dribbling down the backs of ears and over the forehead around eyebrows, tongues reaching for taste. Then, *īkagen,* mother massaged the scalp, scrambling yellow eggs and black hair. She said, "When I was little, my mother always washed my hair with an egg. It gets it clean and shiny."

After a time, the twins took baths together without mother. And without   8
mother's *īkagen* technique, they were free to develop an entire and gradually complicated ritual surrounding bathtime. It probably began with two tiny bodies at opposite ends of that steaming pink enamel bathroom scudding about with protruding stomachs and ramming into each other, laughing hysterically.

"My pompom's bigger! Yes it is."   9

"Lookit your belly button. It's all itchy."   10

"Don' touchit!"   11

Later applying the fruits of elementary school education, mother would   12
find them performing the entire sequence of "You Do the Hokey-Pokey" from "You put your left foot in" to the final "whole self." In those days, baths were apt to be rather lukewarm. But after mother had them draw their own water for the bath, their ritual accommodated by creating a system of fore and aft as in "two men in a tub—." That is, one sat up front weathering the hot water and adding the cold and yelling at appropriate intervals, "Row! Row left!" while the other twin in the aft paddled, stirring up the incoming hot or cold. Sometimes they were able to coordinate several rounds of "Row Row Your Boat," changing directions at new verses. By the end of these songs, they were in a virtual whirlpool, water spilling over the sides of the tub, warping the linoleum.

The bubble bath was a new challenge to bathtime, calling for exceptionally   13
delicate rowing technique in order to get the water stirred with the greatest and deepest amount of bubbles. They sat fore and aft in a white tub of white bubbles hardly daring to move or breathe. These were almost silent baths. They moved slowly, whispering like cloud people, listening to the soft snapping fizzle of dying bubbles. These were often lengthy bathtimes waiting silently for the bubbles to pass before getting to the business of washing the body, which was by now quite a minor portion of the main preoccupation of bathtime fantasy.

Emerging finally flushed, with wrinkled skinny bodies, the twins watched   14
the grey *aka* accumulate in a wide scummy ring, and the water finally disap-

pearing in a tiny rushing whirl, the old tub sending up a long sucking noise beyond the dark rusting drain, its navel.

Now they came often to watch mother at her bath alone. They would usually find her lying deep in the tub, her head and shoulders propped up in a curve against the slope of the tub, a square wash cloth floating over her soft mound of stomach and hair. She would say, "Come in and close the door. It's cold air." 15

They leaned over the edge of the tub, talking. "Mommy you have a scar on your tummy? So isn't that where when I was a baby I came out of?" 16

"No, that's when I had my appendix taken out." 17

"See, I told you." 18

Watching mother was never much entertainment. She never used much soap but scrubbed her skin generally. It was in the usual manner of *ikagen*, the soaking horizontally being the thing. 19

It was quite a different thing to watch father's weekly productions which were extravagant in soap and water and flourish. He sat at the edge of the tub with a bar of soap, rubbing it into a thick white lather all over his body. He seemed to be very hairy. And then there was his bad leg and the wound in his right hip; a scarred hole, it seemed as big as one's small hand. 20

"Daddy you hurt your leg in the war?" 21

"No, I was a bad boy and fell off a fence." 22

"Oh." 23

The best part of his bath was to watch him plunge a hairy lather man into the deep white water, all the grey foam rising in waves, splashing about with water up to his chin. And when he rose, the water surged beneath him, and the tub echoed the din and squeak of his body and flat feet beating and rubbing against iron, and there was that wonderful and unbeatable amount of grey *aka*. It never occurred to them then, but the reason why father washed with the soap bar always melting it to half its size was probably because the washcloth somehow remained draped between his legs throughout the bath. 24

It was perhaps grandmother who had an ultimate flair for bathtime ritual, and when she came to visit, they followed her around the house watching to see what she would do next. It was not simply the bath, it was everything that led up to and continued after. Grandmother was a proud and somewhat stern woman, but they were able to talk with her through her broken English. She said so herself, "I bery broken Engurish." 25

She was a plump woman, fat at the middle, and she had long grey hair braided up in a longish bun at the back. They came to her like two young pages volunteering for buttons and zippers, but mostly they were fascinated with her heavy under-armor, a stiff thick pink corset with metal catches and a crisscross of lacing up the middle. The twins, each taking an end of lace, 26 tugged and unhooked step by step, attached to grandmother by corset strings that slowly stretched across the room.

Grandmother always went to bathe with a long strip of cotton cloth, a 27
tenugui for washing decorated by Japanese writing and design. In the tub, the thin cloth adhered to the fat folds of her old body, Japanese characters and woven ends trailing off in the clear hot water. Around her stomach, they saw the tight crisscross and wrinkles embedded by the confining corset swell and disappear.

She would begin by washing her face, working down over the entire 28
surface of her body to her toes and using the cloth *tenugui* in a variety of ways, expressing a versatility remarkable in a thing so simple. The *tenugui* grasped at both ends across her back scoured every inch of skin in a seesaw fashion. The *tenugui* could bunch up in a soft round sponge with a smooth woven surface. She rubbed in circular motions over and under the loose layers of freckled flesh and sagging breasts. Finally, the *tenugui* squeezed within a breath of being dry served to soak up and even dry her entire body. Now she stood outside the tub steamy and damp, mopping the perspiration at her forehead. Grandmother and her *tenugui* in the tub seemed simply self-sufficient.

After came creaming the face and brushing and braiding her long grey 29
hair. Then they would join her in pajamas on the large double bed for a session in group exercises. These were motions that ranged from rolling the head in circles and hunching up the shoulders to bicycling upside-down while lying in bed. These things the three did simultaneously while grandmother expounded on their obvious virtues, "The bery good for regs. Now you do. Old be much bettah."

It was not until many years later in Japan that they were to see such as 30
grandmother's *tenugui*. In fact, it would be many years before they should again see an aging body naked at bath. It was not that one missed seeing grandmother in her bathing but that in rediscovering the bath in Japan, there was a vibrant sense of an old intimacy that seemed to radiate through the steam and crouching jostle at the public bath. It was great aunt Yae on mother's side who first introduced one of the twins to the public bath, the *sentō*.

II

She came in February to Kyoto, cold with a barren sense of an old winter. 31
She had just become twenty-one and had been studying Japanese in Tokyo since the fall. She had never been so far from home before.

Great aunt Yae and her husband Chihiro lived retired in an old house,   32
a small house of old polished wood and deteriorating paper and mats, a house
perhaps over one or two hundred years old with the wear and darkness of
time passing, passing through the war when Chihiro had been an officer in
the Imperial Army, passing with the birth of children now married and gone,
passing through the bitterness of war and the poverty after.

But of this past, she knew little, and it seemed then that she had passed   33
into an old folktale beginning, *"Mukashi mukashi,"* long long ago there lived
an old man and old woman in a little house at the bottom of a hill. They
were poor. They lived alone. They had no children. Everyday the old man
went out to chop wood to sell, carrying his heavy bundle on his back, trudging
through the snow. This is the simple beginning of a recurring story; it seemed
to convey the sad gracious charm of an old couple whose lives are simple
and resigned.

Her old uncle was hard of hearing, and Yae was continually yelling into   34
his ear, repeating words her niece had said or reminding him of various details
he had forgotten. Yae, on the other hand, was rather blind; squinting behind
thick wire spectacles, she read newspapers and letters two and three inches
from her nose. Sometimes her niece found her washing dishes, inspecting
bowls and cups a few inches from her face, shifting her spectacles and poking
at cracks and spots.

Yae said that she and *ojisan* could not live without each other. She said,   35
laughing, that they were sometimes like characters in a cartoon. One day she
had heard rain on the roof above and announced to her husband that it was
raining. Chihiro looked up from his newspapers and said, "That can't be. I
don't hear anything. . . . Look, no rain today. *Omae,* you're wrong."

Yae went to the door and slid it aside. Looking out she saw nothing and   36
came back to confirm that it was not raining after all.

Yae disappeared into the kitchen, but the old man's curiosity drew him   37
to the door. Looking out he saw the falling rain and called his wife to the
door, tugging at her hand and pushing it into the rain. They stood at the
door looking out to the garden and the pouring rain, laughing.

At the door, Yae put her niece in a pair of her old wooden *geta*. They   38
were so worn down at the outer toe side that she was forced to walk awkwardly,
imitating Yae's pigeon-toed trot. Yae handed her a small plastic basin in which
she had placed a folded *tenugui* along with soap, shampoo and combs. They
stepped out. A light snow was falling, disappearing into the gravel about
their *geta*. Nodding over her basin to curious neighbors, Yae led her to the
sentō.

There she saw the layers of *kimono* fall away and Yae's thin aged body   39
plump and wrinkled at the stomach. Yae stood naked slightly stooped in

those thick wire spectacles, scrutinizing her belongings and folding everything into a small pile.

They enter the bathroom gripping their plastic basins, swimming through the warm steam that billows as the glass door slides aside. Rows of squatting women and children wash before running faucets. Yae leads her between the rows and echoing commotion of spilling water. Women flushed and dripping emerge from the deep pools. Others meditate silently, squatting low in the great tubs, hot water caressing their hunching shoulders; black wisps of fallen hair cling pasted to cheek and neck. Finding two free places, Yae goes off to steep herself in the hot tub. 40

Women of every age and shape scrub their bodies with the *tenugui*, busy at wash, vigorous and skillful in their movements. Women kneel and squat, never sitting on the tile, filling their basins and sending cascades of water over an area almost confined to their bodies. All stretching and standing returns to a compact crouch before the faucet or in the tub. 41

Under the bright shiny lights of the bath, their skin is a beautiful clear white, smooth rich flesh, full at the thighs and hips and small and round at the breasts. She watches a woman with her back turned, following the curving back to the nape of the neck and the fullness of the shoulders sloping forward over breasts and skin, shaking. Turning to draw the *tenugui* over her own back, she blushes to see her own shoulder. 42

The woman next to her kneels with her baby. She washes the baby gently. Leaning forward, the child rests in the curve of her two arms, its head supported in her hands. Her breasts hang swollen with milk. The baby's stubby arms and legs flap and kick. 43

Yae is now at her place, squatting and scrubbing vigorously. She and other elderly women kneel and squat easily without strain, without the brittle quality that would seem to signify age. Old women small and folded scrub their skin, rich lustre lost to a worn toughness, thin loose folds now useless, once fat and swollen. 44

A young woman rises from the water, her steaming flushing body waddles forward full and round with child. 45

Yae crouches behind her niece and offers to wash her back. She scrubs with a vigor the girl has not felt since her mother had done so. Finally spreading the damp *tenugui* over a well-polished back, Yae sends hot water in a smooth stream that, penetrating the cloth, clings. Yae peels the *tenugui* carefully up from the bottom edge to the shoulders; old skin falls away. 46

She turns to wash Yae's back. She is embarrassed, not being able to wash Yae in the same way. Yae turns squinting and laughing, saying that it does not matter, taking the *tenugui* from her niece and turning to continue her own washing. Yae is brusque in a way that does not care to indulge in matters 47 that cannot change or sentimentality that forfeits honesty or pride. She is brusque but with a wry humor that cannot make one take offense but to know a sparse quality that is honest.

There are children in the bath. There is a beautiful girl child, her feet   48
paddling across the wet tile from the tub to her mother and then to another woman who must be her grandmother. One follows her small protruding stomach and thin shoulders and dark eyes.

Before arriving in Kyoto to see Yae and Chihiro, she had been to Ise,   49
alone, carrying a small blue backpack with all the necessities needed for a month and a half of travel. The days on the Ise peninsula were cold and crisp and the sky a deep blue. She found herself traveling in silence, listening to the noises and conversations of her surroundings, attempting to remain an observer unnoticed, another Japanese youth fading into the background and comfort of nondescription. In her attempt to melt into scenic obscurity, she found herself a sensitive observer as to whether or not others were indeed aware of her and what they might have to say about it. She wanted to be alone and an observer and yet felt constantly the paranoia of her situation: acting the part of a traveling Japanese student and yet beset by an anxious desire to know if she had succeeded in her disguise and angry at any evidence of failure. So she came on pilgrimage alone to the great Shinto shrines of Ise, walking in silence through the ancient woods of *hinoki* cedar, pausing as others to wash in the clear waters of the Isuzu.

Leaving the shrines, she found a small Buddhist temple that had opened   50
recently its rooms for traveling youth. She was the only one to stop there that evening.

Two small children, a boy and a girl, beautiful with dark eyes, leaned   51
into her window. They scuttled around by the back way and stood shyly, leaning against the edge of the door. Slowly their voices began to ease into her room, filling silent travels with a warmth she had forgotten. They watched her unpack with curiosity, standing or sitting, leaning elbows and faces against the low table.

"Are you really from America? Really?"   52
"No, you don't look like one."   53
"No, it's a lie. Really?"   54
"Teach us English, please. My other sister learns English in school."   55
"Hurry, teach us English!"   56
"Say something."   57
Then as if some other curiosity had aroused their attention, the two   58
children were drawn away. She heard them running with excited voices.

She sat a long time in the doorway like a cat warming herself under the   59
last rays of evening sun. Below her balcony, a young pregnant woman was

hanging clothes to dry, sliding the damp pieces along a bamboo pole, reaching to expose her full blooming bag. The woman was the proprietress of the hostel. She said the two children were not her own but a neighbor's. She scolded the children gently for bothering her guest.

But when the woman left, they came again, this time with a friend and more aggressively, stepping inside the room to examine any recent changes.   60

"Are you really from America? Really?"   61

"Speak English! Hurry hurry. Teach us English. Hurry!"   62

The young woman's voice called from a distance. Only the girl child stayed lingering at the door. The child had been munching from a small bag of potato chips. "These are potato chips," the child informed her and leaving her with the small bag, ran off calling after the others.   63

She sat in the doorway a while longer, eating the remaining chips, and the cold air and shadows came slowly. Distant in America, grandmother was dying. Mother had written, "Granma wakes every morning and says, '*Mada ikite iru no.*'" (Still living.)   64

The proprietress slid open the paper door passing through from the hallway. Her face shone clean like a wet peach. The warmth of the bath seemed to radiate from her body and the wetness of her hair. Her stomach was round like a balloon, the weight of a child beneath her knitted dress. She said, "You may take your bath now."   65

Naked, Yae trots toward the steaming glass doors and steps out. A billow of steam follows her, and so does she.   66

❖   ❖   ❖

OPTIONS FOR READING LOGS: "THE BATH"

1. Use the double-entry journal technique (asking "what" or "why" questions) to explore the theme of cultural uniqueness in "The Bath." Draw a vertical line down the middle of your journal page to create two columns; use the left column to keep a running list of three to five "what" or "why" questions that are puzzling, yet answerable, such as, "Why does the father consider his wife's changing bath habits 'conspire against him'?" Then, after you write all your questions, answer them as completely as you can in the right column. (Remember that such interpretation will require you to make educated guesses.) To demonstrate that you have a basic understanding of "The Bath," end your journal entry by explaining its central idea.

2. From your personal life, tell a parallel story that was triggered by reading "The Bath." Does the essay remind you of some aspect of your own life and culture? Jot down similarities to or differences from the family relationships described in "The Bath." How does this memory tie in with cultural knowledge? End your journal entry by stating the theme of "The Bath."
3. Discover meaning in "The Bath" by jotting down your own personal reflections on one of the following:

    a. Your own dreams or fantasies in connection with the essay.
    b. Your doubts, expectations, or creative insights that surfaced while reading. Allow your writing to flow freely from one idea or question to another. Give yourself license to discover fresh insights through this open format. End your journal entry by stating the theme of the essay.

OPTIONS FOR WRITING ASSIGNMENTS: "THE BATH"

1. Expand and develop one of your reading logs for "The Bath" into a more polished piece of writing that explores its subject matter in greater range and depth. Begin with a thesis statement that reveals an important discovery you made about your own culture and its assumptions about the act of bathing or some other unique activity that you find fascinating, such as your culture's dining habits, dress codes, or family structure. Arrange your story in a clear chronological order, adding enough specific details to clarify your experience and to make it informative for your reader. By the end of your essay, you should have convinced your reader of the cultural uniqueness of the activity you have discussed.
2. Write a letter to Karen Tei Yamashita, the author of "The Bath." Addressing her directly in the letter, express your own point of view about what she has taught you about the Japanese tradition of bathing. Do you find it strange, fascinating, or even enviable? Use whatever tone (formal or informal, sincere or sarcastic, serious or humorous) that is most appropriate to express your reaction to her essay.
3. Compare and contrast the role of bathing in your own culture and in the Japanese culture, as revealed in "The Bath." What does each approach tell you about the two cultures and what they value? Begin by discussing several key points that the author raises in "The Bath." Then explore

their parallels in your own culture. In your opinion, does one tradition make more sense than the other?

4. We often rely on the advice of others in selecting essays to read, and we also are influenced by their evaluations. Write a critical review of "The Bath," making a clear recommendation on whether a friend should or should not read it. Write your evaluation or judgment as a thesis statement. Then create several additional paragraphs to make your judgment convincing, each with supporting evidence from the text itself.

Girlhood Among Ghosts

1976

MAXINE HONG KINGSTON

 MAXINE HONG KINGSTON is the daughter of a Chinese couple who immigrated to America in the 1930s. "Girlhood Among Ghosts" is an excerpt from *The Woman Warrior: Memories of a Girlhood Among Ghosts*. At the beginning of this selection the narrator discovers that her mother cut the narrator's tongue when she was a baby so she "would not be tongue-tied." Still, because of her shame at speaking a different language, the narrator spent years of schooling in silence.

Do you recall any stories that you heard as a child and that had a drastic influence on you, especially during your childhood? Do you think those stories are largely true? Or are they mostly exaggerations of the truth?

Long ago in China, knot-makers tied string into buttons and frogs, and rope into bell pulls. There was one knot so complicated that it blinded the knot-maker. Finally an emperor outlawed this cruel knot, and the nobles could not order it anymore. If I had lived in China, I would have been an outlaw knot-maker.

Maybe that's why my mother cut my tongue. She pushed my tongue up and sliced the frenum.[1] Or maybe she snipped it with a pair of nail scissors. I don't remember her doing it, only her telling me about it, but all during childhood I felt sorry for the baby whose mother waited with scissors or knife in hand for it to cry—and then, when its mouth was wide open like a baby bird's, cut. The Chinese say "a ready tongue is an evil."

I used to curl up my tongue in front of the mirror and tauten[2] my frenum into a white line, itself as thin as a razor blade. I saw no scars in my mouth. I thought perhaps I had had two frena, and she had cut one. I made other

1. frenum: a fold of membrane, as on the underside of the tongue, that checks or restrains motion
2. tauten: to make tightly drawn

182

children open their mouths so I could compare theirs to mine. I saw perfect pink membranes stretching into precise edges that looked easy enough to cut. Sometimes I felt very proud that my mother committed such a powerful act upon me. At other times I was terrified—the first thing my mother did when she saw me was to cut my tongue.

"Why did you do that to me, Mother?"   4

"I told you."   5

"Tell me again."   6

"I cut it so that you would not be tongue-tied. Your tongue would be   7
able to move in any language. You'll be able to speak languages that are completely different from one another. You'll be able to pronounce anything. Your frenum looked too tight to do those things, so I cut it."

"But isn't 'a ready tongue an evil'?"   8

"Things are different in this ghost country."   9

"Did it hurt me? Did I cry and bleed?"   10

"I don't remember. Probably."   11

She didn't cut the other children's. When I asked cousins and other   12
Chinese children whether their mothers had cut their tongues loose, they said, "What?"

"Why didn't you cut my brothers' and sisters' tongues?"   13

"They didn't need it."   14

"Why not? Were theirs longer than mine?"   15

"Why don't you quit blabbering and get to work?"   16

If my mother was not lying she should have cut more, scraped away the   17
rest of the frenum skin, because I have a terrible time talking. Or she should not have cut at all, tampering with my speech. When I went to kindergarten and had to speak English for the first time, I became silent. A dumbness—a shame—still cracks my voice in two, even when I want to say "hello" casually, or ask an easy question in front of the check-out counter, or ask directions of a bus driver. I stand frozen, or I hold up the line with the complete, grammatical sentence that comes squeaking out at impossible length. "What did you say?" says the cab driver, or "Speak up," so I have to perform again, only weaker the second time. A telephone call makes my throat bleed and takes up that day's courage. It spoils my day with self-disgust when I hear my broken voice come skittering out into the open. It makes people wince to hear it. I'm getting better, though. Recently I asked the postman for special-issue stamps; I've waited since childhood for postmen to give me some of their own accord. I am making progress, a little every day.

My silence was thickest—total—during the three years that I covered my   18
school paintings with black paint. I painted layers of black over houses and flowers and suns, and when I drew on the blackboard, I put a layer of chalk

on top. I was making a stage curtain, and it was the moment before the curtain parted or rose. The teachers called my parents to school, and I saw they had been saving my pictures, curling and cracking, all alike and black. The teachers pointed to the pictures and looked serious, talked seriously too, but my parents did not understand English. ("The parents and teachers of criminals were executed," said my father.) My parents took the pictures home. I spread them out (so black and full of possibilities) and pretended the curtains were swinging open, flying up, one after another, sunlight underneath, mighty operas.

During the first silent year I spoke to no one at school, did not ask before   19
going to the lavatory, and flunked kindergarten. My sister also said nothing for three years, silent in the playground and silent at lunch. There were other quiet Chinese girls not of our family, but most of them got over it sooner than we did. I enjoyed the silence. At first it did not occur to me I was supposed to talk or to pass kindergarten. I talked at home and to one or two of the Chinese kids in class. I made motions and even made some jokes. I drank out of a toy saucer when the water spilled out of the cup, and everybody laughed, pointing at me, so I did it some more. I didn't know that Americans don't drink out of saucers.

I liked the Negro students (Black Ghosts) best because they laughed the   20
loudest and talked to me as if I were a daring talker too. One of the Negro girls had her mother coil braids over her ears Shanghai-style like mine; we were Shanghai twins except that she was covered with black like my paintings. Two Negro kids enrolled in Chinese school, and the teachers gave them Chinese names. Some Negro kids walked me to school and home, protecting me from the Japanese kids, who hit me and chased me and stuck gum in my ears. The Japanese kids were noisy and tough. They appeared one day in kindergarten, released from concentration camp, which was a tic-tac-toe mark, like barbed wire, on the map.

It was when I found out I had to talk that school became a misery, that   21
the silence became a misery. I did not speak and felt bad each time that I did not speak. I read aloud in first grade, though, and heard the barest whisper with little squeaks come out of my throat. "Louder," said the teacher, who scared the voice away again. The other Chinese girls did not talk either, so I knew the silence had to do with being a Chinese girl.

Reading out loud was easier than speaking because we did not have to   22
make up what to say, but I stopped often, and the teacher would think I'd gone quiet again. I could not understand "I." The Chinese "I" has seven strokes, intricacies. How could the American "I," assuredly wearing a hat like the Chinese, have only three strokes, the middle so straight? Was it out of politeness that this writer left off strokes the way a Chinese has to write

her own name small and crooked? No, it was not politeness; "I" is a capital and "you" is lower-case. I stared at that middle line and waited so long for its black center to resolve into tight strokes and dots that I forgot to pronounce it. The other troublesome word was "here," no strong consonant to hang on to, and so flat, when "here" is two mountainous ideographs.[3] The teacher, who had already told me every day how to read "I" and "here," put me in the low corner under the stairs again, where the noisy boys usually sat.

When my second grade class did a play, the whole class went to the auditorium except the Chinese girls. The teacher, lovely and Hawaiian, should have understood about us, but instead left us behind in the classroom. Our voices were too soft or nonexistent, and our parents never signed the permission slips anyway. They never signed anything unnecessary. We opened the door a crack and peeked out, but closed it again quickly. One of us (not me) won every spelling bee, though.

I remember telling the Hawaiian teacher, "We Chinese can't sing 'land where our fathers died.' " She argued with me about politics, while I meant because of curses. But how can I have that memory when I couldn't talk? My mother says that we, like the ghosts, have no memories.

After American school, we picked up our cigar boxes, in which we had arranged books, brushes, and an inkbox neatly, and went to Chinese school, from 5:00 to 7:30 P.M. There we chanted together, voices rising and falling, loud and soft, some boys shouting, everybody reading together, reciting together and not alone with one voice. When we had a memorization test, the teacher let each of us come to his desk and say the lesson to him privately, while the rest of the class practiced copying or tracing. Most of the teachers were men. The boys who were so well behaved in the American school played tricks on them and talked back to them. The girls were not mute. They screamed and yelled during recess, when there were no rules; they had fist-fights. Nobody was afraid of children hurting themselves or of children hurting school property. The glass doors to the red and green balconies with the gold joy symbols were left wide open so that we could run out and climb the fire escapes. We played capture-the-flag in the auditorium, where Sun Yat-sen and Chiang Kai-shek's pictures hung at the back of the stage, the Chinese flag on their left and the American flag on their right. We climbed the teak ceremonial chairs and made flying leaps off the stage. One flag headquarters was behind the glass door and the other on stage right. Our feet drummed on the hollow stage. During recess the teachers locked themselves up in their office with the shelves of books, copybooks, inks from China. They drank tea and warmed their hands at a stove. There was no play

23

24

25

---

3. ideographs: a written symbol that represents an idea or object directly

supervision. At recess we had the school to ourselves, and also we could roam as far as we could go—downtown, Chinatown stores, home—as long as we returned before the bell rang.

At exactly 7:30 the teacher again picked up the brass bell that sat on his   26
desk and swung it over our heads, while we charged down the stairs, our cheering magnified in the stairwell. Nobody had to line up.

Not all of the children who were silent at American school found voice   27
at Chinese school. One new teacher said each of us had to get up and recite in front of the class, who was to listen. My sister and I had memorized the lesson perfectly. We said it to each other at home, one chanting, one listening. The teacher called on my sister to recite first. It was the first time a teacher had called on the second-born to go first. My sister was scared. She glanced at me and looked away; I looked down at my desk. I hoped that she could do it because if she could, then I would have to. She opened her mouth and a voice came out that wasn't a whisper, but it wasn't a proper voice either. I hoped that she would not cry, fear breaking up her voice like twigs underfoot. She sounded as if she were trying to sing though weeping and strangling. She did not pause or stop to end the embarrassment. She kept going until she said the last word, and then she sat down. When it was my turn, the same voice came out, a crippled animal running on broken legs. You could hear splinters in my voice, bones rubbing jagged against one another. I was loud, though. I was glad I didn't whisper. There was one little girl who whispered.

◈   ◈   ◈

OPTIONS FOR READING LOGS: "GIRLHOOD AMONG GHOSTS"

1. Use the double-entry journal technique to discover meaning in "Girl-hood Among Ghosts." Draw a vertical line down the middle of your journal page to create two columns. In the left column, keep a running list of three to five "what" or "why" questions that occur to you as you are reading, such as "Why does the narrator think she 'would have been an outlaw knot-maker' herself?" When you are finished with your list, move to the top of the right column and answer your questions as completely as you can. (Critical thinking requires that you take uninhibited guesses and risks to figure out the meaning of a text. Even wild guesses often lead to important discoveries.) To demonstrate a basic

understanding of the text, end your journal entry by jotting down the central idea of "Girlhood Among Ghosts."

2. Use clustering to draw a concept (idea) map that explores the meaning of "Girlhood Among Ghosts." Recalling vivid details and experiences from the story, draw balloons, clusters, flowcharts, visual symbols, outlines, or diagrams to examine the relationship of one idea to another. When you have created your concept map, examine it closely and write a brief entry that explains your graphic depiction. Conclude with a statement of the central theme of the story.

3. Writers often use images or symbols in poems and stories to represent an idea or concept and to impart a deeper, more important value or interpretation than is at first apparent. Use the double-entry technique to clarify the meaning of some of the powerful images or symbols in "Girlhood Among Ghosts." Draw a vertical line down the middle of your journal page and, in the left column, copy a list of all the images or symbols you identify in the story, such as the cutting of the narrator's tongue. Use the right column to jot down possible interpretations, personal associative memories, or explanatory comments. End your journal entry with a significant discovery you made about "Girlhood Among Ghosts."

OPTIONS FOR WRITING ASSIGNMENTS: "GIRLHOOD AMONG GHOSTS"

1. Does "Girlhood Among Ghosts" remind you of an event from your own experience or an experience you saw a close friend go through in school? Compose a narrative or descriptive essay focusing on the remembered classroom event. Throughout your essay, concentrate on using vivid details and descriptions to help recreate your memory.

2. In "Girlhood Among Ghosts," the narrator was influenced greatly by her mother. Write a four-paragraph cause-and-effect essay explaining who taught you lessons about your culture. To organize your essay, you might want to begin with an introductory paragraph that ends with a thesis statement. One of the paragraphs in the body of your essay should focus on the causes. Include autobiographical information that explains the cultural influences in your life. The other paragraph in the body of your essay should explain the effects. Your essay should end with a concluding paragraph that restates the main idea.

3. Do you react strongly with curiosity, sympathy, or anger to what the narrator learns about herself in "Girlhood Among Ghosts"? Write a

letter to Maxine Hong Kingston, the author, addressing her directly and relating your reaction to the lessons of her culture. Use the rich and varied possibilities of the informal letter form to express your own point of view—to compliment, criticize, console, or inquire. Use whatever tone or approach is most appropriate to express your reaction to the text.

4. At the end of "Girlhood Among Ghosts," the narrator seems proud that she did not whisper when called upon to recite. Yet she describes her voice as "a crippled animal running on broken legs." Do you see this as a positive experience for her or a negative one? Write an essay that argues your point. Take a stand and use it as your thesis statement in your introductory paragraph. In the remaining paragraphs, support your central idea with descriptive personal anecdotes and references to the story.

Para Teresa[1]

1977

INÉS HERNÁNDEZ

 INÉS HERNÁNDEZ, who was born in Texas, is part Nez Percé Indian and part Hispanic. She has taught English and Chicano Studies at the University of Texas in Austin. Her poem "Para Teresa" is about a confrontation between two Chicana schoolgirls concerning their identity.

As you read this poem, think about classmates you had during elementary school or high school who chose to set themselves apart by their outward behavior as well as by their appearance. Perhaps you were one of them, or maybe you were more of a conformist. Did you feel more comfortable fitting in with the crowd? How do you account for your individual choices concerning actions, behavior, and dress?

A tí-Teresa Compean   1
Te dedico las palabras estás
que explotan de mi corazón[2]

That day during lunch hour
at Alamo which-had-to-be-its-name   5
Elementary
my dear raza
That day in the bathroom
Door guarded
Myself cornered   10
I was accused by you, Teresa
Tú y las demás de tus amigas
Pachucas todas
Eran Uds. cinco.[3]

1. For Teresa. [Author's note]   2. To you, Teresa Compean, I dedicate these words that explode from my heart. [Author's note]   3. You and the rest of your friends, all Pachucas, there were five of you. [Author's note]

189

Me gritaban que porque me creía tan grande[4]   15
What was I trying to do, you growled
Show you up?
Make the teachers like me, pet me,
Tell me what a credit to my people I was?
I was playing right into their hands, you challenged   20
And you would have none of it.
I was to stop.

I was to be like you
I was to play your game of deadly defiance
Arrogance, refusal to submit.   25
The game in which the winner takes nothing
Asks for nothing
Never lets his weaknesses show.

But I didn't understand.
My fear salted with confusion   30
Charged me to explain to you
I did nothing *for the teachers.*
I studied for my parents and for my grandparents
Who cut out honor roll lists
Whenever their nietos'[5] names appeared   35
For my shy mother who mastered her terror
to demand her place in mother's clubs
For my carpenter-father who helped me patiently with my math.
For my abuelos que me regalaron lápices en la Navidad[6]
And for myself.   40

Porque reconocí en aquel entonces
una verdad tremenda
que me hizo a mi un rebelde
Aunque tú no te habías dadocuenta[7]
We were not inferior   45
You and I, y las demás de tus amigas
Y los demás de nuestra gente[8]
I knew it the way I know I was alive

---

4. You were screaming at me, asking me why I thought I was so hot. [Author's note]   5. Grandchildren's.
[Author's note]   6. Grandparents who gave me gifts of pencils at Christmas. [Author's note]   7. Because
I recognized a great truth then that made me a rebel, even though you didn't realize it. [Author's note]
8. And the rest of your friends / And the rest of our people. [Author's note]

We were good, honorable, brave
Genuine, loyal, strong   50

And smart.
Mine was a deadly game of defiance, also.
My contest was to prove
beyond any doubt
that we were not only equal but superior to them.   55
That was why I studied.
If I could do it, we all could.

You let me go then,
Your friends unblocked the way
I who-did-not-know-how-to-fight   60
was not made to engage with you-who-grew-up-fighting
Tu y yo, Teresa[9]
We went in different directions
Pero fuimos juntas.[10]

In sixth grade we did not understand   65
Uds. with the teased, dyed-black-but-reddening hair,
Full petticoats, red lipsticks
and sweaters with the sleeves
pushed up
Y yo conformándome con lo que deseaba mi mamá[11]   70
Certainly never allowed to dye, to tease, to paint myself
I did not accept your way of anger,
Your judgements
You did not accept mine.

But now in 1975, when I am twenty-eight   75
Teresa Compean
I remember you.
Y sabes—
Te comprendo,
Es más, te respeto.   80
Y, si me permites,
Te nombro—"hermana."[12]

9. You and I. [Author's note]   10. But we were together. [Author's note]   11. And I conforming to
my mother's wishes. [Author's note]   12. And do you know what, I understand you. Even more, I respect
you. And, if you permit me, I name you my sister. [Author's note]

OPTIONS FOR READING LOGS: "PARA TERESA"

1. Use the double-entry journal technique to clarify thoughts and discover meaning in "Para Teresa." In the left column of your journal page, maintain a running list of "what" or "why" questions that occur to you as you are reading. Aim for three to five questions, such as, "Why is the poem partly in Spanish and partly in English?" Finish your list, then answer your questions as completely as you can in the right column. End your journal entry with a significant discovery you made about the poem.

2. Does anything in "Para Teresa" remind you of something you have learned about your own cultural identity? As a child, did you ever have an experience (either positive or negative) or a confrontation with someone from a culture different from your own? Write about that experience, using vivid details and describing the full range of emotions involved.

3. Paraphrase "Para Teresa" by writing down its meaning in your own words. Work your way through the poem, line by line or section by section. Complete your journal entry by stating the theme of the poem.

OPTIONS FOR WRITING ASSIGNMENTS: "PARA TERESA"

1. Develop one of your reading logs for "Para Teresa" into a more polished piece of writing that explores a moment of personal insight or development in greater range and depth, using an appropriate form (a poem, a fictional story, a personal narrative, or an essay that examines a central idea).

2. Create a dialogue between you and the narrator of "Para Teresa" about cultural knowledge. Your conversation might take the form of a question-and-answer interview, an argument between two opposing points of view, or an open-ended exploration of her ideas and their implications.

3. In terms of your own cultural identity as well as the cultural background of your classmates, were you more of a conformist or a nonconformist during your elementary or secondary school days? Why? At the beginning of your essay, state whether you were one or the other, and use several anecdotes that support your statement.

4. Write a formal essay of five paragraphs or more explaining the meaning of "Para Teresa." Direct your attention to parts of the poem that you have genuine questions about, such as, "Why does the narrator call Teresa a 'sister' at the end of the poem?" End your introductory paragraph with an arguable thesis statement, for example, "Calling Teresa a 'sister' is an

act that pays high tribute to her." In the other paragraphs, use quotes from the poem and refer to specific passages to clarify and support your central argument.

The Last of the Kiowas

1967

N. SCOTT MOMADAY

Born in Lawton, Oklahoma in 1934, N. SCOTT MOMADAY is a member of the Kiowa tribe. He grew up on a reservation and later received a Ph.D. from Stanford University. Momaday has written many award-winning poems, essays, and novels that portray Native American cultures and the experience of his people. His first novel, *The House Made of Dawn,* won the Pulitzer Prize. It is about the modern Native American who is caught between white society and the tribal community. In "The Last of the Kiowas" Momaday returns to Rainy Mountain to visit his grandmother's grave, but his visit is much more than that. It is a pilgrimage. During his visit he reminisces about the history of the Kiowa Indians and the lessons he learned from his grandmother.

As you read Momaday's essay, which is an excerpt from his autobiogra-phy, The Way to Rainy Mountain, *think about your own roots. Can each individual claim his or her roots within a specific culture? Which culture do you identify with most strongly? Who took the responsibility for teaching you about that culture?*

single knoll rises out of the plain in Oklahoma, north and west of   1
the Wichita Range. For my people, the Kiowas, it is an old landmark,
and they gave it the name Rainy Mountain. The hardest weather in
the world is there. Winter brings blizzards, hot tornadic winds arise in the
spring, and in summer the prairie is an anvil's edge. The grass turns brittle
and brown, and it cracks beneath your feet. There are green belts along the
rivers and creeks, linear groves of hickory and pecan, willow and witch hazel.
At a distance in July or August the steaming foliage seems almost to writhe
in fire. Great green and yellow grasshoppers are everywhere in the tall grass,
popping up like corn to sting the flesh, and tortoises crawl about on the red
earth, going nowhere in the plenty of time. Loneliness is an aspect of the
land. All things in the plain are isolate; there is no confusion of objects in

the eye, but *one* hill or *one* tree or *one* man. To look upon that landscape in the early morning, with the sun at your back, is to lose the sense of proportion. Your imagination comes to life, and this, you think, is where Creation was begun.

I returned to Rainy Mountain in July. My grandmother had died in the spring, and I wanted to be at her grave. She had lived to be very old and at last infirm. Her only living daughter was with her when she died, and I was told that in death her face was that of a child. 2

I like to think of her as a child. When she was born, the Kiowas were living the last great moment of their history. For more than a hundred years they had controlled the open range from the Smoky Hill River to the Red, from the headwaters of the Canadian to the fork of the Arkansas and Cimarron. In alliance with the Comanches, they had ruled the whole of the southern Plains. War was their sacred business, and they were among the finest horsemen the world has ever known. But warfare for the Kiowas was preeminently a matter of disposition rather than of survival, and they never understood the grim, unrelenting advance of the U.S. Cavalry. When at last, divided and ill-provisioned, they were driven onto the Staked Plains in the cold rains of autumn, they fell into panic. In Palo Duro Canyon they abandoned their crucial stores to pillage and had nothing then but their lives. In order to save themselves, they surrendered to the soldiers at Fort Sill and were imprisoned in the old stone corral that now stands as a military museum. My grandmother was spared the humiliation of those high gray walls by eight or ten years, but she must have known from birth the affliction of defeat, the dark brooding of old warriors. 3

Her name was Aho, and she belonged to the last culture to evolve in North America. Her forebears came down from the high country in western Montana nearly three centuries ago. They were a mountain people, a mysterious tribe of hunters whose language has never been positively classified in any major group. In the late seventeenth century they began a long migration to the south and east. It was a journey toward the dawn, and it led to a golden age. Along the way the Kiowas were befriended by the Crows, who gave them the culture and religion of the Plains. They acquired horses, and their ancient nomadic spirit was suddenly free of the ground. They acquired Tai-me, the sacred Sun Dance doll, from that moment the object and symbol of their worship, and so shared in the divinity of the sun. Not least, they acquired the sense of destiny, therefore courage and pride. When they entered upon the southern Plains they had been transformed. No longer were they slaves to the simple necessity of survival; they were a lordly and dangerous society of fighters and thieves, hunters and priests of the sun. According to their origin myth, they entered the world through a hollow log. From one 4 point of view, their migration was the fruit of an old prophecy, for indeed they emerged from a sunless world.

Although my grandmother lived out her long life in the shadow of Rainy   5
Mountain, the immense landscape of the continental interior lay like memory in her blood. She could tell of the Crows, whom she had never seen, and of the Black Hills, where she had never been. I wanted to see in reality what she had seen more perfectly in the mind's eye, and traveled fifteen hundred miles to begin my pilgrimage.

Yellowstone, it seemed to me, was the top of the world, a region of deep   6
lakes and dark timber, canyons and waterfalls. But, beautiful as it is, one might have the sense of confinement there. The skyline in all directions is close at hand, the high wall of the woods and deep cleavages of shade. There is a perfect freedom in the mountains, but it belongs to the eagle and the elk, the badger and the bear. The Kiowas reckoned their stature by the distance they could see, and they were bent and blind in the wilderness.

Descending eastward, the highland meadows are a stairway to the plain.   7
In July the inland slope of the Rockies is luxuriant with flax and buckwheat, stonecrop and larkspur. The earth unfolds and the limit of the land recedes. Clusters of trees, and animals grazing far in the distance, cause the vision to reach away and wonder to build upon the mind. The sun follows a longer course in the day, and the sky is immense beyond all comparison. The great billowing clouds that sail upon it are shadows that move upon the grain like water, dividing light. Farther down, in the land of the Crows and Blackfeet, the plain is yellow. Sweet clover takes hold of the hills and bends upon itself to cover and seal the soil. There the Kiowas paused on their way; they had come to the place where they must change their lives. The sun is at home on the plains. Precisely there does it have the certain character of a god. When the Kiowas came to the land of the Crows, they could see the dark lees of the hills at dawn across the Bighorn River, the profusion of light on the grain shelves, the oldest deity ranging after the solstices. Not yet would they veer southward to the caldron of the land that lay below; they must wean their blood from the northern winter and hold the mountains a while longer in their view. They bore Tai-me in procession to the east.

A dark mist lay over the Black Hills, and the land was like iron. At the   8
top of a ridge I caught sight of Devil's Tower upthrust against the gray sky as if in the birth of time the core of the earth had broken through its crust and the motion of the world was begun. There are things in nature that engender an awful quiet in the heart of man; Devil's Tower is one of them. Two centuries ago, because they could not do otherwise, the Kiowas made a legend at the base of the rock. My grandmother said:

Eight children were there at play, seven sisters and their brother. Suddenly the boy was struck dumb; he trembled and began to run upon his hands and feet. His fingers became claws, and his body was covered with fur. Directly there was a bear where the boy had been. The sisters were terrified; they ran, and the bear after them. They came to the stump of a great tree, and the tree spoke to them. It bade them climb upon it, and as they did so it began to rise into the air. The bear came to kill them, but they were just beyond its reach. It reared against the tree and scored the bark all around with its claws. The seven sisters were borne into the sky, and they became the stars of the Big Dipper.

From that moment, and so long as the legend lives, the Kiowas have kinsmen 9 in the night sky. Whatever they were in the mountains, they could be no more. However tenuous their well-being, however much they had suffered and would suffer again, they had found a way out of the wilderness.

My grandmother had a reverence for the sun, a holy regard that now is 10 all but gone out of mankind. There was a wariness in her, and an ancient awe. She was a Christian in her later years, but she had come a long way about, and she never forgot her birthright. As a child she had been to the Sun Dances; she had taken part in those annual rites, and by them she had learned the restoration of her people in the presence of Tai-me. She was about seven when the last Kiowa Sun Dance was held in 1887 on the Washita River above Rainy Mountain Creek. The buffalo were gone. In order to consummate the ancient sacrifice—to impale the head of a buffalo bull upon the medicine tree—a delegation of old men journeyed into Texas, there to beg and barter for an animal from the Goodnight herd. She was ten when the Kiowas came together for the last time as a living Sun Dance culture. They could find no buffalo; they had to hang an old hide from the sacred tree. Before the dance could begin, a company of soldiers rode out from Fort Sill under orders to disperse the tribe. Forbidden without cause the essential act of their faith, having seen the wild herds slaughtered and left to rot upon the ground, the Kiowas backed away forever from the medicine tree. That was July 20, 1890, at the great bend of the Washita. My grandmother was there. Without bitterness, and for as long as she lived, she bore a vision of deicide.

Now that I can have her only in memory, I see my grandmother in the 11 several postures that were peculiar to her: standing at the wood stove on a winter morning and turning meat in a great iron skillet; sitting at the south window, bent above her beadwork, and afterwards, when her vision failed, looking down for a long time into the fold of her hands; going out upon a cane, very slowly as she did when the weight of age came upon her; praying. I remember her most often at prayer. She made long, rambling prayers out of suffering and hope, having seen many things. I was never sure that I had the right to hear, so exclusive were they of all mere custom and company. The last time I saw her she prayed standing by the side of her bed at night, naked to the waist, the light of a kerosene lamp moving upon her dark skin. Her long, black hair, always drawn and braided in the day, lay upon her shoulders and against her breasts like a shawl. I do not speak Kiowa, and I never understood her prayers, but there was something inherently sad in the sound, some merest hesitation upon the syllables of sorrow. She began in a high and descending pitch, exhausting her breath to silence; then again and again—and always the same intensity of effort, of something that is, and is not, like urgency in the human voice. Transported so in the dancing light among the shadows of her room, she seemed beyond the reach of time. But that was illusion; I think I knew then that I should not see her again.

Houses are like sentinels in the plain, old keepers of the weather watch.   12
There, in a very little while, wood takes on the appearance of great age. All colors wear soon away in the wind and rain, and then the wood is burned gray and the grain appears and the nails turn red with rust. The windowpanes are black and opaque; you imagine there is nothing within, and indeed there are many ghosts, bones given up to the land. They stand here and there against the sky, and you approach them for a longer time than you expect. They belong in the distance; it is their domain.

Once there was a lot of sound in my grandmother's house, a lot of coming   13
and going, feasting and talk. The summers there were full of excitement and reunion. The Kiowas are a summer people; they abide the cold and keep to themselves, but when the season turns and the land becomes warm and vital they cannot hold still; an old love of going returns upon them. The aged visitors who came to my grandmother's house when I was a child were made of lean and leather, and they bore themselves upright. They wore great black hats and bright ample shirts that shook in the wind. They rubbed fat upon their hair and wound their braids with strips of colored cloth. Some of them painted their faces and carried the scars of old and cherished enmities. They were an old council of warlords, come to remind and be reminded of who they were. Their wives and daughters served them well. The women might indulge themselves; gossip was at once the mark and compensation of their servitude. They made loud and elaborate talk among themselves, full of jest and gesture, fright and false alarm. They went abroad in fringed and flowered shawls, bright beadwork and German silver. They were at home in the kitchen, and they prepared meals that were banquets.

There were frequent prayer meetings, and great nocturnal feasts. When   14
I was a child I played with my cousins outside, where the lamplight fell upon
the ground and the singing of the old people rose up around us and carried
away into the darkness. There were a lot of good things to eat, a lot of
laughter and surprise. And afterwards, when the quiet returned, I lay down
with my grandmother and could hear the frogs away by the river and feel
the motion of the air.

Now there is a funeral silence in the rooms, the endless wake of some   15
final word. The walls have closed in upon my grandmother's house. When
I returned to it in mourning, I saw for the first time in my life how small it
was. It was late at night, and there was a white moon, nearly full. I sat for a
long time on the stone steps by the kitchen door. From there I could see
out across the land; I could see the long row of trees by the creek, the low
light upon the rolling plains, and the stars of the Big Dipper. Once I looked
at the moon and caught sight of a strange thing. A cricket had perched upon
the handrail, only a few inches away from me. My line of vision was such
that the creature filled the moon like a fossil. It had gone there, I thought,
to live and die, for there, of all places, was its small definition made whole
and eternal. A warm wind rose up and purled like the longing within me.

The next morning I awoke at dawn and went out on the dirt road to   16
Rainy Mountain. It was already hot, and the grasshoppers began to fill the
air. Still, it was early in the morning, and the birds sang out of the shadows.
The long yellow grass on the mountain shone in the bright light, and a
scissortail hied above the land. There, where it ought to be, at the end of a
long and legendary way, was my grandmother's grave. Here and there on
the dark stones were ancestral names. Looking back once, I saw the mountain
and came away.

OPTIONS FOR READING LOGS: "THE LAST OF THE KIOWAS"

1. Use the double-entry journal technique to clarify the meaning of some
    of the powerful lines in "The Last of the Kiowas." Draw a vertical line
    down the middle of your journal page and, in the left-hand column,
    copy phrases or lines that you particularly like or are even puzzled by
    such as, "The Kiowas reckoned their stature by the distance they could
    see, and they were bent and blind in the wilderness." End your journal

entry with a brief statement about a significant discovery you made about the essay as a whole during this process.

2. Use your imagination to create some graphics—perhaps a picture of your version of what the area around Rainy Mountain looked like, or some other picture, either literal or symbolic. Another option would be to create a word picture of the place, using as many specific details or images as possible. Wrap up your journal entry by stating the central theme of "The Last of the Kiowas."

3. From your personal life, tell a parallel story that was triggered by reading "The Last of the Kiowas." Does the essay remind you of a particular place tied to your cultural roots? Jot down reminiscences that are similar to or different from Momaday's. Wrap up your journal entry by stating what you learned about your culture from the place you described.

OPTIONS FOR WRITING ASSIGNMENTS: "THE LAST OF THE KIOWAS"

1. Write a personal letter to N. Scott Momaday, giving him your own detailed, personal response to his essay, "The Last of the Kiowas." Use the traditional letter form, addressing Momaday directly. In your letter, express your reaction to some important aspect of his essay, such as his exploration of his grandmother's influence on him, the significance of certain places in the Kiowas' history, or the value of knowing one's culture for self-knowledge. You may choose to praise, criticize, or empathize with Momaday. Use whatever approach is most appropriate to express your reaction to the essay's theme of cultural knowledge.

2. Develop one of your journal entries on "The Last of the Kiowas" into a more polished piece of writing that explores its subject matter in greater range and depth, using an appropriate form—a poem, a fictional story, a personal narrative, or an essay—that examines a central idea. Whatever form your writing takes, be certain that it points in some way to a better understanding of the significance of one's culture and how it shapes one's daily life.

3. What cultural knowledge are we meant to gain from Momaday's piece? Would you like to talk with the author to ask him questions, hear his answers, and share your ideas and interpretations with him? Create a dialogue between you and Momaday. Your conversation might take the form of an argument between two opposing points of view or an open-ended exploration of the author's ideas about cultural identity.

4. If you were asked what "The Last of the Kiowas" means and how it teaches us to know or appreciate our cultural heritage, what would you say? Simply reading a text is often not enough to appreciate its full range of meaning. This requires rereading, rethinking, and discussing ideas with others before we can respond fully. Explain the meaning of "The Last of the Kiowas" in a well-developed essay. In an introductory paragraph, clearly voice your main idea in a thesis statement. In the following paragraphs, add supporting details that help clarify your main idea. In your commentary, use quotes from the essay and refer to specific passages to help clarify your ideas.

The Handsomest Drowned Man in the World: A Tale for Children

1984

GABRIEL GARCÍA MÁRQUEZ

 GABRIEL GARCÍA MÁRQUEZ, a major Colombian writer, has published many novels and short stories, often using fantasy and highly imaginative and bizarre situations and plots. In "The Handsomest Drowned Man in the World: A Tale for Children," Marquez writes about the dead body of an unknown sailor that strangely becomes the obsession of the villagers who discover it. The large, good-looking dead sailor soon becomes the focal point of the villagers' imaginations, which run wild as they create stories and qualities for the dead man. The dead sailor seems to serve as a catalyst, transforming and enriching the drab fishing village.

As you read the story, reflect on whether there is any truth to the many beliefs the inhabitants weave around the body. Is this too great a leap of faith? Are they fools for inventing the many ideas about the drowned sailor, or is the dead man indeed a mysterious agent that brings helpful changes to them and their barren cultural wasteland?

The first children who saw the dark and slinky bulge approaching 1
through the sea let themselves think it was an enemy ship. Then they
saw it had no flags or masts and they thought it was a whale. But
when it washed up on the beach, they removed the clumps of seaweed, the
jellyfish tentacles, and the remains of fish and flotsam, and only then did they
see that it was a drowned man.

They had been playing with him all afternoon, burying him in the sand 2
and digging him up again, when someone chanced to see them and spread
the alarm in the village. The men who carried him to the nearest house
noticed that he weighed more than any dead man they had ever known,
almost as much as a horse, and they said to each other that maybe he'd been
floating too long and the water had got into his bones. When they laid him
on the floor they said he'd been taller than all other men because there was

barely enough room for him in the house, but they thought that maybe the ability to keep on growing after death was part of the nature of certain drowned men. He had the smell of the sea about him and only his shape gave one to suppose that it was the corpse of a human being, because the skin was covered with a crust of mud and scales.

They did not even have to clean off his face to know that the dead man   3 was a stranger. The village was made up of only twenty-odd wooden houses that had stone courtyards with no flowers and which were spread about on the end of a desertlike cape. There was so little land that mothers always went about with the fear that the wind would carry off their children and the few dead that the years had caused among them had to be thrown off the cliffs. But the sea was calm and bountiful and all the men fit into seven boats. So when they found the drowned man they simply had to look at one another to see that they were all there.

That night they did not go out to work at sea. While the men went to   4 find out if anyone was missing in neighboring villages, the women stayed behind to care for the drowned man. They took the mud off with grass swabs, they removed the underwater stones entangled in his hair, and they scraped the crust off with tools used for scaling fish. As they were doing that they noticed that the vegetation on him came from faraway oceans and deep water and that his clothes were in tatters, as if he had sailed through labyrinths of coral. They noticed too that he bore his death with pride, for he did not have the lonely look of other drowned men who came out of the sea or that haggard, needy look of men who drowned in rivers. But only when they finished cleaning him off did they become aware of the kind of man he was and it left them breathless. Not only was he the tallest, strongest, most virile, and best built man they had ever seen, but even though they were looking at him there was no room for him in their imagination.

They could not find a bed in the village large enough to lay him on nor was   5 there a table solid enough to use for his wake. The tallest men's holiday pants would not fit him, nor the fattest ones' Sunday shirts, nor the shoes of the one with the biggest feet. Fascinated by his huge size and his beauty, the women then decided to make him some pants from a large piece of sail and a shirt from some bridal Brabant linen so that he could continue through his death with dignity. As they sewed, sitting in a circle and gazing at the corpse between stitches, it seemed to them that the wind had never been so steady nor the sea so restless as on that night and they supposed that the change had something to do with the dead man. They thought that if that magnificent man had lived in the village, his house would have had the widest doors, and highest ceiling, and the strongest floor; his bedstead would have been made from a midship frame held together by iron bolts, and his wife would have been the happiest woman. They thought that he would have had so much authority that he could have drawn fish out of the sea simply by calling their names and that he would have put so much work into his land that springs would have burst forth from among the rocks so that he would have been able to plant flowers on the cliffs. They secretly compared him to their own men, thinking that for all their lives theirs were incapable of doing what he could do in one night, and they ended up dismissing them deep in their hearts as the weakest, meanest, and most useless creatures on earth. They were wandering through that maze of fantasy when the oldest woman, who as the oldest had looked upon the drowned man with more compassion than passion, sighed:

"He has the face of someone called Esteban."   6

It was true. Most of them had only to take another look at him to see   7
that he could not have any other name. The more stubborn among them, who were the youngest, still lived for a few hours with the illusion that when they put his clothes on and he lay among the flowers in patent leather shoes his name might be Lautaro. But it was a vain illusion. There had not been enough canvas, the poorly cut and worse sewn pants were too tight, and the hidden strength of his heart popped the buttons on his shirt. After midnight the whistling of the wind died down and the sea fell into its Wednesday drowsiness. The silence put an end to any last doubts: he was Esteban. The women who had dressed him, who had combed his hair, had cut his nails and shaved him were unable to hold back a shudder of pity when they had to resign themselves to his being dragged along the ground. It was then that they understood how unhappy he must have been with that huge body since it bothered him even after death. They could see him in life, condemned to going through doors sideways cracking his head on crossbeams, remaining on his feet during visits, not knowing what to do with his soft pink, sealion hands while the lady of the house looked for her most resistant chair and begged him, frightened to death, sit here, Esteban, please, and he, leaning against the wall, smiling, don't bother, ma'am, I'm fine where I am, his heels raw and his back roasted from having done the same thing so many times whenever he paid a visit, don't bother, ma'am, I'm fine where I am to avoid the embarrassment of breaking up the chair, and never knowing perhaps that the one who said don't go, Esteban, at least wait till the coffee's ready, were the ones who later on would whisper the big boob finally left, how nice, the handsome fool has gone. That was what the women were thinking beside the body a little before dawn. Later, when they covered his face with a handkerchief so that the light would not bother him, he looked so forever dead, so defenseless, so much like their men that the first furrows of tears opened in their hearts. It was one of the younger ones who began the weeping. The others, coming to, went from sighs to wails, and the more they sobbed

the more they felt like weeping, because the drowned man was becoming all the more Esteban for them, and so they wept so much, for he was the most destitute, most peaceful, and most obliging man on earth, poor Esteban. So when the men returned with the news that the drowned man was not from the neighboring villages either, the women felt an opening of jubilation in the midst of their tears.

"Praise the Lord," they sighed, "he's ours!"   8

The men thought the fuss was only womanish frivolity. Fatigued because   9
of the difficult nighttime inquiries, all they wanted was to get rid of the bother of the newcomer once and for all before the sun grew strong on that arid, windless day. They improvised a litter with the remains of foremasts and gaffs, tying it together with rigging so that it would bear the weight of the body until they reached the cliffs. They wanted to tie the anchor from a cargo ship to him so that he would sink easily into the deepest waves, where the fish are blind and divers die of nostalgia, and bad currents would not bring him back to shore, as had happened with other bodies. But the more they hurried, the more the women thought of ways to waste time. They walked about like startled hens, pecking with the sea charms on their breasts, some interfering on one side to put a scapular of the good wind on the drowned man, some on the other side to put a wrist compass on him, and after a great deal of *get away from there, woman, stay out of the way, look, you almost made me fall on top of the dead man,* the men began to feel mistrust in their livers and started grumbling about why so many main-altar decorations for a stranger, because no matter how many nails and holy-water jars he had on him, the sharks would chew him all the same, but the women kept on piling on their junk relics, running back and forth, stumbling, while they released in sighs what they did not in tears, so that the men finally exploded with *since when has there ever been such a fuss over a drifting corpse, a drowned nobody, a piece of cold Wednesday meat.* One of the women, mortified by so much lack of care, then removed the handkerchief from the dead man's face and the men were left breathless too.

He was Esteban. It was not necessary to repeat it for them to recognize   10
him. If they had been told Sir Walter Raleigh, even they might have been impressed with his gringo accent, the macaw on his shoulder, his cannibal-killing blunderbuss, but there could be only one Esteban in the world and there he was, stretched out like a sperm whale, shoeless, wearing the pants of an undersized child, and with those stony nails that had to be cut with a knife. They had only to take the handkerchief off his face to see that he was ashamed, that it was not his fault that he was so big or so heavy or so handsome, and if he had known that this was going to happen, he would have looked for a more discreet place to drown in; seriously, I even would

have tied the anchor off a galleon around my neck and staggered off a cliff like someone who doesn't like things in order not to be upsetting people now with this Wednesday dead body, as you people say, in order not to be bothering anyone with this filthy piece of cold meat that doesn't have anything to do with me. There was so much truth in his manner that even the most mistrustful men, the ones who felt the bitterness of endless nights at sea fearing that their women would tire of dreaming about them and begin to dream of drowned men, even they and others who were harder still shuddered in the marrow of their bones at Esteban's sincerity.

That was how they came to hold the most splendid funeral they could conceive of for an abandoned drowned man. Some women who had gone to get flowers in the neighboring villages returned with other women who could not believe what they had been told, and those women went back for more flowers when they saw the dead man, and they brought more and more until there were so many flowers and so many people that it was hard to walk about. At the final moment it pained them to return him to the waters as an orphan and they chose a father and mother from among the best people, and aunts and uncles and cousins, so that through him all the inhabitants of the village became kinsmen. Some sailors who heard the weeping from a distance went off course, and people heard of one who had himself tied to the mainmast, remembering ancient fables about sirens. While they fought for the privilege of carrying him on their shoulders along the steep escarpment by the cliffs, men and women became aware for the first time of the desolation of their streets, the dryness of their courtyards, the narrowness of their dreams as they faced the splendor and beauty of their drowned man. They let him go without an anchor so that he could come back if he wished and whenever he wished, and they all held their breath for the fraction of centuries the body took to fall into the abyss. They did not need to look to one another to realize that they were no longer all present, that they would never be. But they also knew that everything would be different from then on, that their houses would have wider doors, higher ceilings, and stronger floors so that Esteban's memory could go everywhere without bumping into beams and so that no one in the future would dare whisper the big boob finally died, too bad, the handsome fool has finally died, because they were going to paint their house fronts gay colors to make Esteban's memory eternal and they were going to break their backs digging for springs among the stones and planting flowers on the cliffs so that in future years at dawn the passengers on great liners would awaken, suffocated by the smell of gardens on the high seas, and the captain would have to come down from the bridge in his dress uniform, with his astrolabe, his pole star, and his row of war medals and, pointing to the promontory of roses on the horizon, he would say in fourteen languages, look there, where the wind is so peaceful now that it's gone to

11

sleep beneath the beds, over there, where the sun's so bright that the sunflowers don't know which way to turn, yes, over there, that's Esteban's village.

◈ ◈ ◈

OPTIONS FOR READING LOGS: "THE HANDSOMEST DROWNED MAN IN THE WORLD: A TALE FOR CHILDREN"

1. Use the double-entry journal technique to comment on powerful or unclear passages in "The Handsomest Drowned Man in the World: A Tale for Children." Draw a vertical line down the middle of your journal page, creating two columns; in the left column, copy single sentences or passages that you particularly like or that you feel are somehow important, for example, " 'He has the face of someone called Esteban,' " or "They also knew that everything would be different from then on." In the right column, jot down word associations and comments, including those from your personal experience as well as from your reading. End your journal entry by selecting one of the sentences or passages and explaining why it held such power or meaning for you.

2. Drawing on your own life, tell a parallel story that you recalled while reading "The Handsomest Drowned Man in the World: A Tale for Children." Do the actions of the people in the village remind you of how people behave in your own life and culture? Jot down things you find similar or different. Wrap up your journal entry by stating what your experience taught you about yourself.

3. Use your imagination to create a picture of your version of the central meaning of "The Handsomest Drowned Man in the World: A Tale for Children." Your picture can be both literal and symbolic. After you complete your drawing, use words or phrases to label any portion of your picture, just as you would a diagram. Finally, wrap up your journal entry by writing a paragraph that explains the story, using as many specific details or images as possible. State the central theme of the story in your last sentence.

OPTIONS FOR WRITING ASSIGNMENTS: "THE HANDSOMEST DROWNED MAN IN THE WORLD: A TALE FOR CHILDREN"

1. Develop one of your reading logs for "The Handsomest Drowned Man in the World: A Tale for Children" into a more polished piece of writing

that explores in greater range and depth an important insight or idea you have discovered while working in your reading log. Use an appropriate form (a poem, a fictional story, a personal narrative, or an essay that examines a central idea) to express your idea.

2. Write a letter to the author of "The Handsomest Drowned Man in the World: A Tale for Children" or to the villagers in the story, describing your reaction to the story. For example, you could praise or criticize the author for portraying his characters as he did, or you might criticize the villagers for their overabundant imaginations.

3. At the end of "The Handsomest Drowned Man in the World: A Tale for Children," the village culture has been radically transformed. Instead of being a nameless, dreary little village in the middle of nowhere, the narrator says, it will now be recognized by sea captains and praised for its beautiful gardens. Have you ever seen a neighborhood or a group of people change in some dramatic way, either positively or negatively? Write a formal essay of five or more paragraphs about this change. Use a thesis statement in your introductory paragraph to make a generalization about what exactly changed. In your supporting paragraphs, use descriptive personal anecdotes to illustrate your thesis statement, developing each anecdote fully.

4. Write an interpretation of the "The Handsomest Drowned Man in the World: A Tale for Children" in order to explain the author's main point or idea. In a formal essay of five or more paragraphs, focus your attention on any parts of the story that caused you to have genuine questions, such as "Why did they decide to call him Esteban?" or "Are the villagers merely fools who believe their own imaginations and not the hard facts?" In your essay, you may want to quote from the story and refer to specific passages to clarify and support your central argument.

Lost Sister

1983

CATHY SONG

 CATHY SONG is a contemporary Asian-American poet. In her poem "Lost Sister," Song explores both the pull of the ancient Chinese culture of her ethnic roots and the influence of the modern American culture she currently inhabits. Though the poem's narrator realizes the restricted lifestyle that women once experienced in China, she nonetheless acknowledges the importance of her culture: "You find you need China."

Are we inevitably pulled back to our older cultural roots, or are they something that also must grow and change through time? How necessary to you are your own ethnic roots? Does your cultural or ethnic identity play a significant part in your daily life? Did your parents encourage you to leave your cultural past behind, or did they actively encourage you to learn more about it? As you read the poem, think about your own feelings about your cultural inheritance and its role in your life.

1

In China, 1
even the peasants
named their first daughters
Jade—
the stone that in the far fields 5
could moisten the dry season,
could make men move mountains
for the healing green of the inner hills
glistening like slices of winter melon.

And the daughters were grateful: 10
They never left home.
To move freely was a luxury

stolen from them at birth.
Instead, they gathered patience,
learning to walk in shoes   15
the size of teacups,
without breaking—
the arc of their movements
as dormant as the rooted willow,
as redundant as the farmyard hens.   20
But they traveled far
in surviving,
learning to stretch the family rice,
to quiet the demons,
the noisy stomachs.   25

2

There is a sister
across the ocean,
who relinquished her name,
diluting jade green
with the blue of the Pacific.   30
Rising with a tide of locusts,
she swarmed with others
to inundate another shore.
In America,
there are many roads   35
and women can stride along with men.

But in another wilderness,
the possibilities,
the loneliness,
can strangulate like jungle vines.   40
The meager provisions and sentiments
of once belonging—
fermented roots, Mah-Jong tiles and firecrackers—set but
a flimsy household
in a forest of nightless cities.   45
A giant snake rattles above,
spewing black clouds into your kitchen.
Dough-faced landlords
slip in and out of your keyholes,

making claims you don't understand,   50
tapping into your communication systems
of laundry lines and restaurant chains.

You find you need China:
your one fragile identification,
a jade link   55
handcuffed to your wrist.
You remember your mother
who walked for centuries,
footless—
and like her,   60
you have left no footprints,
but only because
there is an ocean in between,
the unremitting space of your rebellion.

OPTIONS FOR READING LOGS: "LOST SISTER"

1. Use the double-entry journal technique to comment on powerful lines
    or passages in "Lost Sister." Draw a vertical line down the middle of
    your journal page, and use the left column to copy lines or passages that
    you judge particularly important, such as "dormant as the farmyard
    hens." In the right column, enter word associations and comments, being
    sure to include those from your personal experience as well as from your
    reading. End your journal entry by selecting one line or phrase and
    explaining why it held such power or meaning for you.
2. Did reading "Lost Sister" remind you of some story from your own
    life—some event or a particular time period, perhaps? Have you ever
    experienced confusion or ambivalent feelings about your cultural roots?
    When people move to a place dominated by another culture, is it necessary
    for them to preserve their former values and beliefs? End your journal
    entry by stating the theme of "Lost Sister."
3. Write a poem that explores your own cultural background or ethnic
    roots. Start with a reflection on some aspect of your culture in earlier
    times, as Song does when she mentions women who learned "to walk
    in shoes the size of teacups." Halfway through your poem, explore the

impact that aspect of your cultural background has on you in the present. End your journal entry by stating the theme of your poem.

OPTIONS FOR WRITING ASSIGNMENTS: "LOST SISTER"

1. Write a letter to the narrator in "Lost Sister." Address the person directly and inform her about your reaction to the poem. Use the letter to express your own point of view. You may choose to comment on the advantages or disadvantages of being influenced by one's cultural past or to inquire further about what specific parts of the poem mean if they are unclear to you. Take whatever approach is most appropriate to express your honest reaction to the poem.

2. Develop one of your reading logs for "Lost Sister" into a more polished piece of writing that explores a moment of personal insight or development in greater range and depth, using an appropriate form (a poem, a fictional story, a personal narrative, or an essay that examines a central idea).

3. Write a formal essay of five or more paragraphs that explains the meaning of "Lost Sister." In an introductory paragraph, clearly state the poem's main idea. In your supporting paragraphs, focus on any parts of the poem that you have questions about, such as "What is the significance of jade in the first stanza?" or "What is the meaning of 'Dough-faced land-lords'?" In your essay, you will need to quote from the poem and refer to specific lines and passages to clarify and support your central argument.

4. Compare and contrast what Cathy Song has discovered about her cultural background in "Lost Sister" and what some other author or character discovered in another text in Chapter Three. For example, you might compare this work with Hernández's "Para Teresa" or Bambara's "The Lesson." In what ways do the two readings reach similar conclusions? In what ways do they differ? Begin with two lists. Then develop them into an outline and use transitional expressions that signal similarities or differences as you write your essay.

Battling Illegitimacy: Some Words Against the Darkness

1970

GREG SARRIS

 GREG SARRIS is a writer and a faculty member at the University of California at Los Angeles. He was born in California in 1947, of mixed Filipino and Pomo-Miwok California Native American ancestry. His essay, "Battling Illegitimacy: Some Words Against the Darkness," explores his multiple ethnic backgrounds and the difficulties of growing up in a world deeply prejudiced against minority groups.

Have you ever searched your own family's past and made important discoveries that helped you to understand yourself better? Have you ever asked your relatives or family friends about your own ancestors and what they were like? What surprising discoveries have you made? As you read this essay of self-discovery and self-definition, think of what such a search of your own family history could reveal that would help you better understand who you are.

I have heard that someone said to American Indian writer Louise Erdrich, "You don't look Indian." It was at a reading she gave, or perhaps when she received an award of some kind for her writing. Undoubtedly, whoever said this noted Erdrich's very white skin, her green eyes and her red hair. She retorted, "Gee, you don't look rude."   1

You don't look Indian.   2

How often I too have heard that. But unlike Erdrich, I never returned   3
the insult, or challenged my interlocutors.[1] Not with words anyway. I arranged the facts of my life to fit others' conceptions of what it is to be Indian. I used others' words, others' definitions. That way, if I didn't look Indian, I might still be Indian.

---

1. interlocuters: persons who question; interrogators

Well, I don't know if I am Indian, I said, or if I am, how much. I   4
was adopted. I know my mother was white—Jewish, German, Irish. I was
illegitimate. Father unknown. It was back in the fifties when having a baby
without being married was shameful. My mother uttered something on the
delivery table about the father being Spanish. Mexican maybe. Anyway, I was
given up and adopted, which is how I got a name. For awhile things went
well. Then they didn't. I found myself with other families, mostly on small
ranches where I milked cows and worked with horses. I met a lot of Indians—
Pomo Indians—and was taken in by one of the families. I learned bits and
pieces of two Pomo languages. So if you ask, I call myself Pomo. But I don't
know . . . My mother isn't around to ask. After she had me, she needed
blood. The hospital gave her the wrong type and it killed her.

The story always went something like that. It is true, all of it, but arranged   5
so that people might see how I fit. The last lines—about my mother—awe
people and cause them to forget, or to be momentarily distracted, from their
original concern about my not looking Indian. And I am illegitimate. That
explains any crossing of borders, anything beyond the confines of definition.
That is how I fit.

Last year I found my father. Well, I found out his name—Emilio. My   6
mother's younger brother, my uncle, whom I met recently, remembered
taking notes from his sister to a "big Hawaiian type" on the football field.
"I would go after school while the team was practicing," my uncle said. "The
dude was big, dark. They called him Meatloaf. I think his name though was
Emilio. Try Emilio."

To have a name, even a nickname, seemed unfathomable.[2] To be thirty-   7
six years old and for the first time to have a lead about a father somehow
frightened me. You imagine all your life; you find ways to account for that
which is missing, you tell stories, and now all that is leveled by a name.

In Laguna Beach I contacted the high school librarian and made arrange-   8
ments to look through old yearbooks. It was just after a conference there in
Southern California, where I had finished delivering a paper on American
Indian education. I found my mother immediately, and while I was staring
for the first time at an adult picture of my mother, a friend who was with
me scanned other yearbooks for an Emilio. Already we knew by looking at
the rows and rows of white faces, there wouldn't be too many Emilios. I was
still gazing at the picture of my mother when my friend jumped. "Look,"
she said. She was tilting the book, pointing to a name. But already, even as

2. unfathomable: not able to be comprehended or understood

I looked, a dark face caught my attention, and it was a face I saw myself in. Without a doubt. Darker, yes. But me nonetheless.

I interviewed several of my mother's and father's classmates. It was my   9
mother's friends who verified what I suspected. Emilio Hilario was my father. They also told me that he had died, that I missed him by about five years.

I had to find out from others what he couldn't tell me. I wanted to know   10
about his life. Did he have a family? What was his ethnicity? Luckily I obtained the names of several relatives, including a half-brother and a grandfather. People were quick about that, much more so than about the ethnicity question. They often circumvented the question by telling stories about my father's athletic prowess and about how popular he was. A few, however, were more candid. His father, my grandfather, is Filipino. "A short Filipino man," they said. "Your father got his height from his mother. She was fairer." Some people said my grandmother was Spanish, others said she was Mexican or Indian. Even within the family, there is discrepancy about her ethnicity. Her mother was definitely Indian, however. Coast Miwok from Tomales Bay just north of San Francisco, and just south of Santa Rosa, where I grew up. Her name was Rienette.

During the time my grandmother was growing up, probably when her   11
mother—Rienette—was growing up too, even until quite recently, when it became popular to be Indian, Indians in California sometimes claimed they were Spanish. And for good reason. The prejudice against Indians was intolerable, and often only remnants of tribes, or even families, remained to face the hatred and discrimination. My grandmother spoke Spanish. Her sister, Juanita, married a Mexican and her children's children are proud *Chicanos* living in East Los Angeles. Rienette's first husband, my grandmother and her sister's father, was probably part Mexican or Portuguese—I'm not sure.

The story is far from complete. But how much Indian I am by blood is   12
not the question whose answer concerns me now. Oh, I qualify for certain grants, and that is important. But knowing about my blood heritage will not change my complexion any more than it will my experience.

In school I was called the white beaner. This was not because some of   13
my friends happened to be Mexican, but because the white population had little sense of the local Indians. Anyone with dark hair and skin was thought to be Mexican. A counselor once called me in and asked if my family knew I went around with Mexicans. "Yes," I said. "They're used to it." At the time, I was staying with an Indian family—the McKays—and Mrs. McKay was a mother to me. But I said nothing more then. I never informed the counselor that most of my friends, the people she was referring to, were Indian—Pomo Indian. Kashaya Pomo Indian. Sulfur Bank Pomo Indian. Coyote Valley Pomo Indian. Yokaya Pomo Indian. Point Arena Pomo Indian.

Bodega Bay Miwok Indian. Tomales Bay Miwok Indian. And never mind that names such as Smith and Pinola are not Spanish (or Mexican) names.

As I think back, I said nothing more to the counselor not because I   14
didn't want to cause trouble (I did plenty of that), but because, like most other kids, I never really knew a way to tamper with how the authorities— counselors, teachers, social workers, police—categorized us. We talked about our ethnicity amongst ourselves, often speculating who was more or less this or that. So many of us are mixed with other groups—white, Mexican, Spanish, Portuguese, Filipino. I know of an Indian family who is half Mexican and they identify themselves as Mexicans. In another family of the same admixture just the opposite is true. Yet for most of the larger white community, we were Mexican, or something.

And here I am with blue eyes and fair skin. If I was a white beaner, I   15
was, more generally, a kid from the wrong side of the tracks. Hood. Greaser. Low Brow. Santa Rosa was a much smaller town then, the lines more clearly drawn between the haves and the have-nots, the non-colored and the colored. Suburban sprawl was just beginning; there was still the old downtown with its stone library and old Roman-columned courthouse. On the fringes of town lived the poorer folk. The civil rights movement had not yet engendered the ethnic pride typical of the late sixties and early seventies.

I remember the two guys who taught me to box, Manual and Robert.   16
They said they were Portuguese, Robert part Indian. People whispered that they were black. I didn't care. They picked me out, taught me to box. That was when I was fourteen. By the time I was sixteen, I beat heads everywhere and every time I could. I looked for fights and felt free somehow in the fight. I say I looked for fights, but really, as I think about it, fights seemed to find me. People said things, they didn't like me, they invaded my space. I had reason. So I fought. And afterwards I was somebody. Manny said I had a chip on my shoulder, which is an asset for a good fighter. "Hate in your eyes, brother," he told me. "You got hate in your eyes."

I heard a lot of "Indian" stories too. We used to call them old-time   17
stories, those about Coyote and the creation. Then there were the spook stories about spook men and women and evil doings. I knew of a spook man, an old guy who would be sitting on his family's front porch one minute and then five minutes later, just as you were driving uptown, there he'd be sitting on the old courthouse steps. The woman whose son I spent so much time with was an Indian doctor. She healed the sick with songs and prayer; she sucked pains from people's bodies. These are the things my professors and colleagues wanted to hear about.

I was different here too. I read books, which had something to do with   18
my getting into college. But when I started reading seriously—about the

middle of my junior year in high school—I used what I read to explain the world; I never engaged my experience to inform what I was reading. Again, I was editing my experience, and, not so ironically, I found meaning that way. And, not so ironically, the more I read the more I became separated from the world of my friends and what I had lived. So in college when I found people interested in my Indian experience as it related to issues of ecology, personal empowerment, and other worldviews, I complied and told them what I "knew" of these things. In essence I shaped what I knew to fit the books and read the books to shape what I knew. The woman who was a mother to me came off as Castaneda's Don Juan. Think of the "separate reality" of her dream world, never mind what I remember about her—the long hours in the apple cannery, her tired face, her clothes smelling of rotten apples.

Now, as I sort through things, I am beginning to understand why I hated   19
myself and those people at the university; how by sculpting my experience to their interests, I denied so much of my life, including the anger and self-hatred that seeps up from such denial. I wanted to strike back, beat the hell out of them; I imagined them angering me in some way I could recognize—maybe an insult, a push or shove—so that I could hurt them. Other times I just wanted them to be somewhere, perhaps outside the classroom, on a street, in a bar, where they came suddenly upon me and saw me fighting, pummelling somebody. Anger is like a cork in water. Push it down, push it down, and still it keeps coming to the surface.

Describing her life experience in a short autobiographical piece entitled   20
"The Autobiography of a Confluence," Paula Gunn Allen says, "Fences would have been hard to place without leaving something out . . . Essentially, my life, like my work, is a journey-in-between, a road." Poet Wendy Rose writes about how she went to the Highland Games in Fresno to search for her Scottish roots: "It may have looked funny to all those Scots to see an Indian [Rose] looking for a booth with her clan's name on it." She adds: "The colonizer and the colonized meet in my blood. It is so much more complex than just white and Indian. I will pray about this, too." These American Indian writers, just as so many other ethnic minority American writers, are attempting to mediate the cultural variables that constitute their experience as Americans. They are attempting to redefine their experience based on the experience itself and not in terms of others' notions of that experience.

During the late sixties and early seventies, an odd reversal of affairs took   21
place. Where some Indian people once denied, or at least kept quiet their Indian heritage, they suddenly began denying that part which is white, Span-

ish, or whatever. The point here is that in the name of ethnic pride we begin
to make illegitimate so much of what we are, and have been, about. We deny
aspects of our history and experience that could enrich any understanding
of what it means to be an American Indian in time, in history, and not just
as some relic from a prelapserian past, as the dominant culture so often likes
to see us. We in fact become oppressor-like; we internalize the oppression
we have felt, and, ironically, using others' definitions, or even those created
by ourselves, decide who is Indian and who is not. We perpetuate illegitimacy
in our ranks.

But the danger isn't just for ourselves here. Ultimately, by accepting or   22
creating certain definitions by which we judge our own experiences, we allow
others a definition by which we can be judged by them. Criteria that render
certain kinds of experience illegitimate enable people to escape the broader,
human issues in life as it is lived. They allow the phonies a way to dress up,
showing how they are Indian, and they cheat the rest of us of a true and
fully human and historical cultural identity. What we need are words—stories,
poems, histories, biographies—that qualify and challenge given definitions,
that allow all of us as students and teachers, Indians and non-Indians, the
opportunity to examine our own framing devices in order that we might be
able to see and consider the possibility of seeing beyond those frames. We
need to make visible the heretofore illegitimate so that we might consider
human experience in the broadest sense possible.

My father was a local hero, they say. He excelled in all sports, was voted   23
junior class president, and served as president of the local Hi-Y. He was
charming, outgoing, women loved him. But there was the other side, the
black-out drinking and violence. Like a Jeckyl and Hyde, people told me.
He would turn on a dime, get nasty and mean. He'd rip into people. Kick
ass. You could see it coming in his eyes.

When my grandfather brought his family from East Los Angeles to   24
Laguna Beach, there was only one other minority family in town—a black
family. Grandpa worked as a cook at Victor Hugo's, a glamorous waterfront
restaurant. He settled his family in a small house in "the canyon," where the
black family and season migrant families lived at the time, and where Grandpa
still lives today. While my father was exalted locally as an athlete, he was
constantly reminded of his color and class. Behind his back, people referred
to him as a "nigger." To his face, the fathers of girls he dated told him: "Go
away. We aren't hiring any gardeners."

I don't need to probe far here to get the picture. Illegitimacy in any   25
form cuts a wide swath. Those of us affected by it react in a number of ways.
Our histories, if they are presented and examined honestly, tell the stories.

For my father and me it was, among other things, violence. Unable to tell his story, unable to fill in those chasms between his acceptance and rejection by the world around him, my father fought, each blow a strike against the vast and imposing darkness. He became a professional boxer; in the Navy he was undefeated, and after he sparred with Floyd Patterson. He died at 52, three weeks before his fifty-third birthday, just five years before his first son would find his picture in a yearbook. He died of a massive heart attack, precipitated by years of chronic alcoholism.

Now sometimes I wonder at my being Filipino, for I am as much Filipino   26
by one definition, that is by blood, as I am anything by that same definition. Grandpa came from a small village on the island of Panay in the South Central Philippines. He tells me I have second cousins who have never worn shoes and speak only the Bisian dialect of that island. Yet, if I am Filipino, I am a Filipino separated from my culture and to backtrack, or go back, to that culture, I must carry my life with me, as it has been lived—in Santa Rosa with Pomo Indians and all others, and in the various cities and universities where I have lived and worked.

"You have quite a legacy in that man," a friend of my father's said to   27
me. "He was one hell of a guy."

Yes, I thought to myself, a legacy. Fitting in by not fitting in. Repression.   28
Violence. Walls of oppressive darkness. The urge now, the struggle, the very need to talk about the spaces, to word the darkness.

OPTIONS FOR READING LOGS: "BATTLING ILLEGITIMACY: SOME WORDS AGAINST THE DARKNESS"

1. Using the double-entry journal technique, draw a vertical line down the middle of your journal page to create two columns. In the left column, keep a running list of "what" or "why" questions that occur to you as you are reading "Battling Illegitimacy." Aim for three to five questions for which you genuinely want an answer, such as "Why did reading separate the narrator from the world of his friends?" or "What does he mean by 'the very need to talk about the spaces, to word the darkness'?" When you are finished with your list of questions, go back to the top of the right column and answer your questions as completely as you can. End your journal entry with a significant discovery you made about the essay.

2. Tell a parallel story from your own personal life that was triggered by "Battling Illegitimacy." Does the essay remind you of some particular event or time in your life when you were searching for your past or felt ill at ease in the dominant culture? Jot down things that were similar to or different from what went on in Sarris's essay. End your journal entry by stating the theme of "Battling Illegitimacy."

3. Examine your personal reaction to "Battling Illegitimacy" by completing one of the following statements:

   A. "I was confused by _____."
   B. "I was struck by _____."
   C. "I was surprised by _____."

   Refer to particular incidents described in the essay and explain your reactions. For example, "I was confused by Sarris's statement that he 'hated himself and those people at the university.' " Develop your journal entry by adding detailed explanations from your own experiences as well as from the essay. Wrap up your journal entry with a statement of the essay's main point or theme.

OPTIONS FOR WRITING ASSIGNMENTS: "BATTLING ILLEGITIMACY: SOME WORDS AGAINST THE DARKNESS"

1. Develop one of your reading logs for "Battling Illegitimacy" into a more polished piece of writing that explores a moment of personal insight or development in greater range and depth, using an appropriate form such as a poem, a fictional story, a personal narrative, or an essay that examines a central idea.

2. Create a conversation between you and the author of "Battling Illegitimacy" about the discovery of oneself through ethnic and cultural awareness. Your conversation might take the form of a question-and-answer interview, an argument between two opposing points of view, or a freewheeling exploration of his ideas and their implications.

3. We often rely on the advice of others in selecting essays to read, and we are influenced by their evaluations. Write a critical review of "Battling Illegitimacy," making a clear recommendation as to the value of the essay as an exploration of how the narrator sees himself. Your evaluation can be positive, negative, or an interesting mixture of both. Once you are clear about what sort of evaluation or judgment you want to make, express it clearly as a thesis statement in your opening paragraph. As you

work through your essay, come up with several good reasons, each with supporting evidence from the essay, that makes your judgment convincing.

4. Write a formal essay of five or more paragraphs explaining the theme of the value of ethnic knowledge and its importance in "Battling Illegitimacy." Your introductory paragraph should contain a thesis statement that makes your main idea clear. In your supporting paragraphs, focus your attention on what you perceive as the most important parts of Sarris's essay, the key points he is making. For example, he makes the point that as he was growing up, he often expressed his anger through fighting and violence; however, as he matured, the anger never left him but it became internalized into an intellectual anger. You may find it necessary to quote from the text and refer to specific passages to clarify and support your central argument.

Societal Knowledge: What Do Others Think?

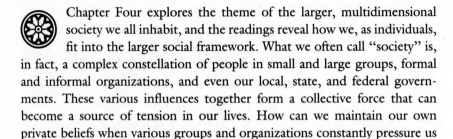

Chapter Four explores the theme of the larger, multidimensional society we all inhabit, and the readings reveal how we, as individuals, fit into the larger social framework. What we often call "society" is, in fact, a complex constellation of people in small and large groups, formal and informal organizations, and even our local, state, and federal governments. These various influences together form a collective force that can become a source of tension in our lives. How can we maintain our own private beliefs when various groups and organizations constantly pressure us to compromise or even surrender our own values and to accept theirs?

Exploring how the subtle and not-so-subtle influences of our society affect us, nonetheless, can be quite rewarding. Doing so can challenge us to be more precise in defining who we are and what we believe. The ideas of the writers in Chapter Four help us to see ourselves in relation to the society of which we are an indissoluble part. For example, Janice Mirikitani recalls with great power American society's treatment of Japanese Americans during the Second World War, and her work celebrates the inner strength they gained from the experience. Martin Luther King, Jr., in his "Letter from Birmingham Jail" attacks the laws society itself once endorsed to keep African Americans legally separate from whites. T. S. Eliot's "The Love Song of J. Alfred Prufrock" explores the painful experience of personal alienation from people in a surrounding social group. These writers explore the boundaries of the individual and of society. They remind us that each of us forms a part of the social whole and, conversely, that society forms a part of each individual.

As you read the following selections, think about the many external social influences on your own life. Is conforming to society's definition of "who we are" a lesson each of us must learn? Or is our relationship to society a far more complex, dynamic condition—one in which our unique, individual self can face serious challenges? Think about whether you feel secure when your beliefs and values conform to those of a group, or whether you feel uneasy, perhaps even threatened with the loss of individuality. Whatever the case, each of the following readings examines the individual's relationship to society in its many manifestations and leads us to a clearer definition of who we are and what we value.

A & P

1961

JOHN UPDIKE

 JOHN UPDIKE, born in Pennsylvania in 1932, is one of America's most important contemporary writers. After attending Harvard, he worked for the *New Yorker* magazine. A prolific novelist, short story writer, and poet, he has featured the manners and values of the American middle-class as a major theme throughout his writing. "A & P" is from a collection of short stories entitled *Pigeon Feathers,* and in it Updike focuses on a small East coast community's definition of propriety. When three young women in bare feet and bathing suits enter the local grocery store, they confront an unwritten code of what is considered proper attire for such a public place. After witnessing the manager's treatment of the girls, Sammy—the story's narrator—reacts in a way that surprises even himself.

Have you ever witnessed an injustice against an individual or a group—no matter how small or seemingly insignificant—yet stood silently by? Do you recall a time when you decided to step in and voice your opinion after observing such an injustice? As you read this story, think about the power that peer and societal pressures exert on us when we face situations in which we must stand up for our beliefs.

In walks these three girls in nothing but bathing suits. I'm in the third checkout slot, with my back to the door, so I don't see them until they're over by the bread. The one that caught my eye first was the one in the plaid green two-piece. She was a chunky kid, with a good tan and a sweet broad soft-looking can with those two crescents of white just under it, where the sun never seems to hit, at the top of the backs of her legs. I stood there with my hand on a box of HiHo crackers trying to remember if I rang it up or not. I ring it up again and the customer starts giving me hell. She's one of these cash-register-watchers, a witch about fifty with rouge on her cheekbones and no eyebrows, and I know it made her day to trip me up. She'd been watching cash registers for fifty years and probably never seen a mistake before.

By the time I got her feathers smoothed and her goodies into a bag—she 2
gives me a little snort in passing, if she'd been born at the right time they
would have burned her over in Salem—by the time I get her on her way the
girls had circled around the bread and were coming back, without a pushcart,
back my way along the counters, in the aisle between the checkouts and the
Special bins. They didn't even have shoes on. There was this chunky one,
with the two-piece—it was bright green and the seams on the bra were still
sharp and her belly was still pretty pale so I guessed she just got it (the
suit)—there was this one, with one of those chubby berry-faces, the lips all
bunched together under her nose, this one, and a tall one, with black hair
that hadn't quite frizzed right, and one of these sunburns right across under
the eyes, and a chin that was too long—you know, the kind of girl other girls
think is very "striking" and "attractive" but never quite makes it, as they
very well know, which is why they like her so much—and then the third one,
that wasn't quite so tall. She was the queen. She kind of led them, the other
two peeking around and making their shoulders round. She didn't look
around, not this queen, she just walked straight on slowly, on these long
white prima-donna legs. She came down a little hard on her heels, as if she
didn't walk in her bare feet that much, putting down her heels and then
letting the weight move along to her toes as if she was testing the floor with
every step, putting a little deliberate extra action into it. You never know for
sure how girls' minds work (do you really think it's a mind in there or just
a little buzz like a bee in a glass jar?) but you got the idea she had talked the
other two into coming in here with her, and now she was showing them
how to do it, walk slow and hold yourself straight.

She had on a kind of dirty pink—beige maybe, I don't know—bathing 3
suit with a little nubble all over it and, what got me, the straps were down.
They were off her shoulders looped loose around the cool tops of her arms,
and I guess as a result the suit had slipped a little on her, so all around the
top of the cloth there was this shining rim. If it hadn't been there you
wouldn't have known there could have been anything whiter than those
shoulders. With the straps pushed off, there was nothing between the top of
the suit and the top of her head except just *her*, this clean bare plane of the
top of her chest down from the shoulder bones like a dented sheet of metal
tilted in the light. I mean, it was more than pretty.

She had sort of oaky hair that the sun and salt had bleached, done up 4
in a bun that was unraveling, and a kind of prim face. Walking into the
A & P with your straps down, I suppose it's the only kind of face you *can*
have. She held her head so high her neck, coming up out of those white
shoulders, looked kind of stretched, but I didn't mind. The longer her neck
was, the more of her there was.

She must have felt in the corner of her eye me and over my shoulder   5
Stokesie in the second slot watching, but she didn't tip. Not this queen. She
kept her eyes moving across the racks, and stopped, and turned so slow it
made my stomach rub the inside of my apron, and buzzed to the other two,
who kind of huddled against her for relief, and then they all three of them
went up the cat-and-dog-food-breakfast-cereal-macaroni-rice-raisins-season-
ings-spreads-spaghetti-soft-drinks-crackers-and-cookies aisle. From the third
slot I look straight up this aisle to the meat counter, and I watched them all
the way. The fat one with the tan sort of fumbled with the cookies, but on
second thought she put the package back. The sheep pushing their carts
down the aisle—the girls were walking against the usual traffic (not that we
have one-way signs or anything)—were pretty hilarious. You could see them,
when Queenie's white shoulders dawned on them, kind of jerk, or hop, or
hiccup, but their eyes snapped back to their own baskets and on they pushed.
I bet you could set off dynamite in an A & P and the people would by and
large keep reaching and checking oatmeal off their lists and muttering "Let
me see, there was a third thing, began with A, asparagus, no, ah, yes, apple-
sauce!" or whatever it is they do mutter. But there was no doubt, this jiggled
them. A few houseslaves in pin curlers even looked around after pushing their
carts past to make sure what they had seen was correct.

You know, it's one thing to have a girl in a bathing suit down on the   6
beach, where what with the glare nobody can look at each other much anyway,
and another thing in the cool of the A & P, under the fluorescent lights,
against all those stacked packages, with her feet paddling along naked over
our checkerboard green-and-cream rubber-tile floor.

"Oh Daddy," Stokesie said beside me. "I feel so faint."   7

"Darling," I said. "Hold me tight." Stokesie's married with two babies   8
chalked up on his fuselage already, but as far as I can tell that's the only
difference. He's twenty-two, and I was nineteen this April.

"Is it done?" he asks, the responsible married man finding his voice. I   9
forgot to say he thinks he's going to be manager some sunny day, maybe in
1990 when it's called the Great Alexandrov and Petrooshki Tea Company
or something.

What he meant was, our town is five miles from a beach, with a big   10
summer colony out on the Point, but we're right in the middle of town, and
the women generally put on a shirt or shorts or something before they get
out of the car into the street. And anyway these are usually women with six
children and varicose veins mapping their legs and nobody, including them,
could care less. As I say, we're right in the middle of town, and if you stand
at our front doors you can see two banks and the Congregational church
and the newspaper store and three real-estate offices and about twenty-seven

old freeloaders tearing up Central Street because the sewer broke again. It's not as if we're on the Cape, we're north of Boston and there's people in this town haven't seen the ocean for twenty years.

The girls had reached the meat counter and were asking McMahon something. He pointed, they pointed, and they shuffled out of sight behind a pyramid of Diet Delight peaches. All that was left for us to see was old McMahon patting his mouth and looking after them sizing up their joints. Poor kids, I began to feel sorry for them, they couldn't help it.   11

Now here comes the sad part of the story, at least my family says it's sad, but I don't think it's so sad myself. The store's pretty empty, it being Thursday afternoon, so there was nothing much to do except lean on the register and wait for the girls to show up again. The whole store was like a pinball machine and I didn't know which tunnel they'd come out of. After a while they come around out of the far aisle, around the light bulbs, records at discount of the Caribbean Six or Tony Martin Sings or some such gunk you wonder they waste the wax on, six-packs of candy bars, and plastic toys done up in cellophane that fall apart when a kid looks at them anyway. Around they come, Queenie still leading the way, and holding a little gray jar in her hands. Slots Three through Seven are unmanned and I could see her wondering between Stokes and me, but Stokesie with his usual luck draws an old party in baggy gray pants who stumbles up with four giant cans of pineapple juice (what do these bums *do* with all that pineapple juice? I've often asked myself). So the girls come to me. Queenie puts down the jar and I take it into my fingers icy cold. Kingfish Fancy Herring Snacks in Pure Sour Cream: 49¢. Now her hands are empty, not a ring or a bracelet, bare as God made them, and I wonder where the money's coming from. Still with that prim look she lifts a folded dollar bill out of the hollow at the center of her nubbled pink top. The jar went heavy in my hand. Really, I thought that was so cute.   12

Then everybody's luck begins to run out. Lengel comes in from haggling with a truck full of cabbages on the lot and is about to scuttle into that door marked MANAGER behind which he hides all day when the girls touch his eye. Lengel's pretty dreary, teaches Sunday school and the rest, but he doesn't miss that much. He comes over and says, "Girls, this isn't the beach."   13

Queenie blushes, though maybe it's just a brush of sunburn I was noticing   14
for the first time, now that she was so close. "My mother asked me to pick up a jar of herring snacks." Her voice kind of startled me, the way voices do when you see the people first, coming out so flat and dumb yet kind of tony, too, the way it ticked over "pick up" and "snacks." All of a sudden I slid right down her voice into the living room. Her father and the other men

were standing around in ice-cream coats and bow ties and the women were in sandals picking up herring snacks on toothpicks off a big glass plate and they were all holding drinks the color of water with olives and sprigs of mint in them. When my parents have somebody over they get lemonade and if it's a real racy affair Schlitz in tall glasses with "They'll Do It Every Time" cartoons stenciled on.

"That's all right," Lengel said. "But this isn't the beach." His repeating   15
this struck me as funny, as if it had just occurred to him, and he had been thinking all these years the A & P was a great big dune and he was the head lifeguard. He didn't like my smiling—as I say he doesn't miss much—but he concentrates on giving the girls that sad Sunday-school-superintendent stare.

Queenie's blush is no sunburn now, and the plump one in plaid, that I   16
liked better from the back—a really sweet can—pipes up. "We weren't doing any shopping. We just came in for the one thing."

"That makes no difference," Lengel tells her, and I could see from the   17
way his eyes went that he hadn't noticed she was wearing a two-piece before. "We want you decently dressed when you come in here."

"We *are* decent," Queenie says suddenly, her lower lip pushing, getting   18
sore now that she remembers her place, a place from which the crowd that runs the A & P must look pretty crummy. Fancy Herring Snacks flashed in her very blue eyes.

"Girls, I don't want to argue with you. After this come in here with your   19
shoulders covered. It's our policy." He turns his back. That's policy for you. Policy is what the kingpins want. What the others want is juvenile delinquency.

All this while, the customers had been showing up with their carts but,   20
you know, sheep, seeing a scene, they had all bunched up on Stokesie, who shook open a paper bag as gently as peeling a peach, not wanting to miss a word. I could feel in the silence everybody getting nervous, most of all Lengel, who asks me, "Sammy, have you rung up their purchase?"

I thought and said "No" but it wasn't about that I was thinking. I go   21
through the punches, 4, 9, GROC. TOT—it's more complicated than you think, and after you do it often enough, it begins to make a little song, that you hear words to, in my case "Hello (*bing*) there, you (*gung*) hap-py pee-pul (*splat*)!"—the *splat* being the drawer flying out. I uncrease the bill, tenderly as you may imagine, it just having come from between the two smoothest scoops of vanilla I had ever known were there, and pass a half and a penny into her narrow pink palm, and nestle the herrings in a bag and twist its neck and hand it over, all the time thinking.

The girls, and who'd blame them, are in a hurry to get out, so I say "I   22
quit" to Lengel quick enough for them to hear, hoping they'll stop and watch me, their unsuspected hero. They keep right on going, into the electric

eye; the door flies open and they flicker across the lot to their car. Queenie and Plaid and Big Tall Goony Goony (not that as raw material she was so bad), leaving me with Lengel and a kink in his eyebrow.

"Did you say something, Sammy?"   23

"I said I quit."   24

"I thought you did."   25

"You didn't have to embarrass them."   26

"It was they who were embarrassing us."   27

I started to say something that came out "Fiddle-de-doo." It's a saying   28
of my grandmother's, and I know she would have been pleased.

"I don't think you know what you're saying," Lengel said.   29

"I know you don't," I said. "But I do." I pull the bow at the back of   30
my apron and start shrugging it off my shoulders. A couple customers that
had been heading for my slot begin to knock against each other, like scared
pigs in a chute.

Lengel sighs and begins to look very patient and old and gray. He's   31
been a friend of my parents for years. "Sammy, you don't want to do
this to your mom and dad," he tells me. It's true, I don't. But it seems
to me that once you begin a gesture it's fatal not to go through with
it. I fold the apron, "Sammy" stitched in red on the pocket, and put it
on the counter, and drop the bow tie on top of it. The bow tie is theirs,
if you've ever wondered. "You'll feel this for the rest of your life," Lengel
says, and I know that's true, too, but remembering how he made the
pretty girl blush makes me so scrunchy inside I punch the No Sale tab
and the machine whirs "pee-pul" and the drawer splats out. One advantage
to this scene taking place in summer, I can follow this up with a clean
exit, there's no fumbling around getting your coat and galoshes. I just
saunter into the electric eye in my white shirt that my mother ironed the
night before, and the door heaves itself open, and outside the sunshine
is skating around on the asphalt.

I look around for my girls, but they're gone, of course. There wasn't   32
anybody but some young married screaming with her children about some
candy they didn't get by the door of a powder-blue Falcon station wagon.
Looking back in the big windows, over the bags of peat moss and aluminum
lawn furniture stacked on the pavement, I could see Lengel in my place in
the slot, checking the sheep through. His face was dark gray and his back
stiff, as if he'd just had an injection of iron, and my stomach kind of fell as
I felt how hard the world was going to be to me hereafter.

OPTIONS FOR READING LOGS: "A & P"

1. Use the double-entry journal technique by asking "what" or "why" questions to explore the theme of societal knowledge in "A & P." Draw a vertical line down the middle of your journal page to create two columns. In the left column, keep a running list of three to five questions that occur to you as you are reading, such as, "Why is Sammy so irritated at his first customer?" After your list is complete, write the answers to your questions in the right column. Remember that interpretation requires you to take educated guesses and that you should make your answers as complete as possible. Finally, demonstrate that you have a basic understanding of the text by jotting down the main idea of the story.

2. Copy what you think is the most powerful line or passage in "A & P." Try to focus on an aspect of the story that challenges your beliefs about an individual's place in society. Using anecdotes and examples from your own personal experience, explain fully why that particular passage held such power or meaning for you.

3. Discover meaning in "A & P" by freewriting or jotting down your own personal reflections on one of the following:

    a. Your beliefs and values in connection with the story.
    b. Your doubts, expectations, and moral insights that surfaced while you were reading.

    End your journal entry by stating the theme of the story.

OPTIONS FOR WRITING ASSIGNMENTS: "A & P"

1. Expand and develop one of your reading logs for "A & P" into a more polished piece of writing that explores its subject matter in greater range and depth. Write a formal essay of five or more paragraphs based on the theme of societal pressure. End your introductory paragraph with a thesis statement that reveals an important discovery you made about conformity. Remember that even small discoveries can be significant. Consider arranging your paper in a cause-and-effect order, and add anecdotes and specific details in the body of the essay. By the end of your essay, you should have convinced your reader of the significance of your self-discovery.

2. In "A & P," Sammy, the narrator, is critical of people's reactions toward the girls who are shopping in their bathing suits. Yet he is also part of

the whole small-town mentality, as his initial response toward the girls shows. Interview someone from a small town. Then write an essay based on what you learned from the interview. How did growing up in a small town shape his or her character? Before your interview, make a list of appropriate questions. In your essay you might want to include biographical information that clarifies the influences shaping the person's attitudes.

3. Write a letter to either John Updike, the author of the story, or to one of the characters in "A & P." Address the person directly, using the letter to express your own point of view. For example, you might write to Sammy, praising or criticizing his decision to quit or empathizing with him. Use whatever tone—harsh or sympathetic—that is most appropriate to express your reaction to the story.

4. We are often influenced by other people's evaluations of novels or movies. Write a critical review of "A & P," giving your recommendation of whether or not a friend should read this story. Give your views on whether it challenges us to make personal discoveries about our place in society as a whole. Your evaluation of Sammy's action can be positive, negative, or some mixture of the two. Write a thesis statement that states your overall judgment as to the value of "A & P." Once you are clear about the sort of evaluation you want to make, support it with several good reasons, each with evidence from the story, that will make your judgment convincing.

We, the Dangerous

1978

JANICE MIRIKITANI

 JANICE MIRIKITANI is a contemporary poet, prose writer, teacher, and community activist who often addresses the issue of racism in America. In particular, she writes about her own background and shows how racism affected thousands of Japanese Americans who were imprisoned during the Second World War in internment camps, such as Manzanar, located in the dry deserts of California, Arizona, and Colorado. Because the U.S. government feared they might engage in espionage for the Japanese, these American citizens of Japanese ancestry were forcibly relocated in isolated detention camps away from the West coast of the United States and were forced to remain there until the end of the war. Not only did they lose their rights as citizens, as guaranteed by the U.S. Constitution, but many also lost their homes and property. The U.S. government recently offered formal apologies and a small financial compensation to these people who were treated so shamefully.

As you read this poem, think about other instances in which cultural or ethnic groups of people have been subjected to discrimination and oppression. Why did those experiences happen? Were they inevitable or could they have been avoided? What have we learned from such experiences?

I swore   1
it would not devour me
I swore
it would not humble me
I swore   5
it would not break me.

  And they commanded we dwell in the desert
  Our children be spawn of barbed wire and barracks

We, closer to the earth,

233

squat, short thighed,   10
knowing the dust better.

    And they would have us make the garden
    Rake the grass to soothe their feet

We, akin to the jungle,
plotting with the snake,   15
tails shedding in civilized America.

    And they would have us skin their fish
    deft hands like blades / sliding back flesh / bloodless

We, who awake in the river
Ocean's child   20
Whale eater.

    And they would have us strange scented women,
    Round shouldered / strong and yellow / like the moon
    to pull the thread to the cloth
    to loosen their backs massaged in myth   25

We, who fill the secret bed,
the sweat shops
the laundries.

    And they would dress us in napalm,
    Skin shred to clothe the earth,   30
    Bodies filling pock marked fields.
    Dead fish bloating our harbors.

We, the dangerous,
Dwelling in the ocean.
Akin to the jungle.   35
Close to the earth.

    Hiroshima
    Vietnam
    Tule Lake[1]

And yet we were not devoured.   40
And yet we were not humbled
And yet we are not broken.

1. Tule Lake: site of a World War II internment camp in the United States where people of Japanese ancestry
were imprisoned

OPTIONS FOR READING LOGS: "WE, THE DANGEROUS"

1. Discover meaning in "We, the Dangerous" by using the double-entry journal technique. Draw the usual vertical line to divide your journal page into two columns. In the left column, keep a running list of three to five "what" or "why" questions, such as "What does 'it' refer to in the first 6 lines?" When you have no additional questions about the poem, begin filling in your answers, as completely as you can, in the right column of your journal page. Trying to make meaning out of a text requires taking some risks, so don't be afraid to guess at an answer. To demonstrate that you have reached a basic understanding of "We, the Dangerous," end your journal entry by jotting down its main idea.

2. Paraphrase "We, the Dangerous" by writing down its meaning in your own words. Work your way through the poem, explaining it line by line or stanza by stanza. Complete your journal entry by stating the poem's theme.

3. Tell a personal story of discrimination you experienced because of your appearance, your beliefs, your background, or even your abilities. The sharp edge of discrimination—whether based on race or on some other characteristic—always hurts because discrimination alienates us from the larger society. In what ways is your own experience similar to or different from the experience Mirikitani describes? End your journal entry by stating what you discovered in "We, the Dangerous."

OPTIONS FOR WRITING ASSIGNMENTS: "WE, THE DANGEROUS"

1. How does "We, the Dangerous" help us to gain knowledge about society and what others think? Explain the meaning of "We, the Dangerous" in a formal essay of five or more paragraphs. Reread and think about the poem fully before you begin your essay. In an introductory paragraph state the poem's main idea clearly, using a thesis statement. In your supporting paragraphs focus your attention on parts of the poem about which you have questions and on words or phrases that help clarify the main idea. In your commentary, you will need to quote from the poem and refer to specific passages to back up your ideas.

2. Did you identify with or empathize with the narrator's feelings in "We, the Dangerous"? Write a letter to the narrator of the poem. Address the narrator directly, conveying your reaction to the message of the poem,

especially as it pertains to the theme of societal knowledge and the relationship of the individual to the more powerful pressures of a group.

3. What do you think of "We, the Dangerous" as a poem about societal prejudices or societal knowledge? Would you recommend it to a friend? Write a critical review that makes a clear recommendation as to the value of "We, the Dangerous" as a poem of discovery about injustice and oppression. Your evaluation might be positive, negative, or a mixture of the two, but your judgment should be stated as a thesis statement in your introductory paragraph. Each of the following paragraphs should be complete with supporting evidence that makes your judgment convincing.

4. If you were asked what "We, the Dangerous" means and how it relates to knowing the truth about our society and how we are shaped, what would you say? Simply reading a text is often not enough to appreciate its range of meanings fully. Write a formal essay of five or more paragraphs explaining the meaning of societal knowledge in "We, the Dangerous." Why does the author include the references to "Hiroshima/Vietnam/Tule Lake"? Who is the "they" referred to throughout the poem? In your introductory paragraph, express your main idea in a clear thesis statement. For instance, in " 'We, the Dangerous' Miritikani explores both the historical oppression and the hidden power of Asian-Americans." In your supporting paragraphs explore any parts of the poem that you have questions about or that clarify your main idea. In your commentary you will need to quote from the poem and refer to specific words or passages to prove your thesis statement.

Black Men and Public Space

1986

BRENT STAPLES

 BRENT STAPLES, who was born in 1951 in Chester, Pennsylvania, is the author of the memoir *Parallel Time: Growing Up in Black and White.* He earned his undergraduate degree at Widener University and a Ph.D. in psychology from the University of Chicago. After working at the *Chicago Sun-Times* and several Chicago periodicals, he joined the *New York Times* in 1985, where he is now an editorial writer. This essay describes his own experience of "being ever the suspect" in urban America.

Do you think racial stereotypes exert a strong influence on our feelings and subsequent reactions? Have you ever reacted first and later felt embarrassed by your reaction to someone from a different racial or ethnic group?

My first victim was a woman—white, well dressed, probably in her early twenties. I came upon her late one evening on a deserted street in Hyde Park, a relatively affluent neighborhood in an otherwise mean, impoverished section of Chicago. As I swung onto the avenue behind her, there seemed to be a discreet, uninflammatory distance between us. Not so. She cast back a worried glance. To her, the youngish black man—a broad six feet two inches with a beard and billowing hair, both hands shoved into the pockets of a bulky military jacket—seemed menacingly close. After a few more quick glimpses, she picked up her pace and was soon running in earnest. Within seconds she disappeared into a cross street.

That was more than a decade ago. I was twenty-two years old, a graduate student newly arrived at the University of Chicago. It was in the echo of that terrified woman's footfalls that I first began to know the unwieldy inheritance I'd come into—the ability to alter public space in ugly ways. It was clear that she thought herself the quarry of a mugger, a rapist, or worse. Suffering a bout of insomnia, however, I was stalking sleep, not defenseless wayfarers. As a softy who is scarcely able to take a knife to a raw chicken—let alone hold one to a person's throat—I was surprised, embarrassed, and dismayed all at once. Her flight made me feel like an accomplice in tyranny. It also made it clear that I was indistinguishable from the muggers who occasionally seeped into the area from the surrounding ghetto. That first encounter, and those that followed, signified that a vast, unnerving gulf lay between nighttime pedestrians—particularly women—and me. And I soon gathered that being perceived as dangerous is a hazard in itself. I only needed to turn a corner into a dicey situation, or crowd some frightened, armed person in a foyer somewhere, or make an errant move after being pulled over by a policeman. Where fear and weapons meet—and they often do in urban America—there is always the possibility of death.

In that first year, my first away from my hometown, I was to become   3
thoroughly familiar with the language of fear. At dark, shadowy intersections, I could cross in front of a car stopped at a traffic light and elicit the *thunk, thunk, thunk, thunk* of the driver—black, white, male, or female—hammering down the door locks. On less traveled streets after dark, I grew accustomed to but never comfortable with people crossing to the other side of the street rather than pass me. Then there were the standard unpleasantries with policemen, doormen, bouncers, cabdrivers, and others whose business it is to screen out troublesome individuals *before* there is any nastiness.

I moved to New York nearly two years ago and I have remained an avid   4
night walker. In central Manhattan, the near-constant crowd cover minimizes tense one-on-one street encounters. Elsewhere—in SoHo, for example, where sidewalks are narrow and tightly spaced buildings shut out the sky—things can get very taut[1] indeed.

After dark, on the warrenlike streets of Brooklyn where I live, I often see   5
women who fear the worst from me. They seem to have set their faces on neutral, and with their purse straps strung across their chests bandolier-style, they forge ahead as though bracing themselves against being tackled. I understand, of course, that the danger they perceive is not a hallucination. Women are particularly vulnerable to street violence, and young black males are drastically overrepresented among the perpetrators of that violence. Yet these truths are no solace[2] against the kind of alienation[3] that comes of being ever the suspect, a fearsome entity with whom pedestrians avoid making eye contact.

It is not altogether clear to me how I reached the ripe old age of twenty-   6
two without being conscious of the lethality[4] nighttime pedestrians attributed to me. Perhaps it was because in Chester, Pennsylvania, the small, angry

---

1. taut: tightly drawn; tense; not slack   2. solace: a source of consolation or relief   3. alienation: the act of turning away the affection of; making indifferent or hostile   4. lethality: of or causing death

industrial town where I came of age in the 1960s, I was scarcely noticeable against a backdrop of gang warfare, street knifings, and murders. I grew up one of the good boys, had perhaps a half-dozen fistfights. In retrospect, my shyness of combat has clear sources.

As a boy, I saw countless tough guys locked away; I have since buried   7
several, too. They were babies, really—a teenage cousin, a brother of twenty-two, a childhood friend in his mid-twenties—all gone down in episodes of bravado played out in the streets. I came to doubt the virtues of intimidation early on. I chose, perhaps unconsciously, to remain a shadow—timid, but a survivor.

The fearsomeness mistakenly attributed to me in public places often has   8
a perilous flavor. The most frightening of these confusions occurred in the late 1970s and early 1980s, when I worked as a journalist in Chicago. One day, rushing into the office of a magazine I was writing for with a deadline story in hand, I was mistaken for a burglar. The office manager called security and, with an ad hoc posse, pursued me through the labyrinthine[5] halls, nearly to my editor's door. I had no way of proving who I was. I could only move briskly toward the company of someone who knew me.

Another time I was on assignment for a local paper and killing time   9
before an interview. I entered a jewelry store on the city's affluent Near North Side. The proprietor excused herself and returned with an enormous red Doberman pinscher straining at the end of a leash. She stood, the dog extended toward me, silent to my questions, her eyes bulging nearly out of her head. I took a cursory look around, nodded, and bade her good night.

Relatively speaking, however, I never fared as badly as another black   10
male journalist. He went to nearby Waukegan, Illinois, a couple of summers ago to work on a story about a murderer who was born there. Mistaking the reporter for the killer, police officers hauled him from his car at gunpoint and but for his press credentials would probably have tried to book him. Such episodes are not uncommon. Black men trade tales like this all the time.

Over the years, I learned to smother the rage I felt at so often being   11
taken for a criminal. Not to do so would surely have led to madness. I now take precautions to make myself less threatening. I move about with care, particularly late in the evening. I give a wide berth to nervous people on subway platforms during the wee hours, particularly when I have exchanged business clothes for jeans. If I happen to be entering a building behind some people who appear skittish, I may walk by, letting them clear the lobby before

5. labrynthine: complicated; tortuous

I return, so as not to seem to be following them. I have been calm and extremely congenial on those rare occasions when I've been pulled over by the police.

And on late-evening constitutionals[6] I employ what has proved to be an   12 excellent tension-reducing measure: I whistle melodies from Beethoven and Vivaldi and the more popular classical composers. Even steely New Yorkers hunching toward nighttime destinations seem to relax, and occasionally they even join in the tune. Virtually everybody seems to sense that a mugger wouldn't be warbling bright, sunny selections from Vivaldi's *Four Seasons*. It is my equivalent of the cowbell that hikers wear when they know they are in bear country.

6. constitutionals: walks taken regularly for health

OPTIONS FOR READING LOGS: "BLACK MEN AND PUBLIC SPACE"

1. Use the double-entry journal technique to discover meaning in "Black Men and Public Space." Draw a vertical line down the middle of your journal page, creating a double column. Use the left column to keep a running list of "what" or "why" questions that occur to you as you are reading. Try to come up with three to five questions, such as "Why did the narrator feel responsible for making himself 'less threatening'?" After you finish your list, move to the top of the right column and answer your questions as completely as you can. Show that you have a basic understanding of the text by ending your journal entry with a statement of the main idea of the essay.
2. From your personal life, tell a parallel story that was triggered by your reading of "Black Men and Public Space." Does the essay remind you of an experience of either being treated or treating another person in a way that was based on ignorance or prejudices? Explain how your view of the world changed after this experience.
3. Examine your personal reaction to "Black Men and Public Space" by completing one of the following statements:

    A. "I was confused by _____."
    B. "I was struck by _____."
    C. "I was surprised by _____."

Develop your journal entry by adding detailed explanations, both from your own experiences and from events in the essay. Finish your entry with a statement of the central idea of the essay.

OPTIONS FOR WRITING ASSIGNMENTS: "BLACK MEN AND PUBLIC SPACE"

1. Expand and develop one of your reading logs for "Black Men and Public Space" into a more polished piece of writing that explores its subject matter in greater range and depth. Begin with a thesis statement that reveals an important discovery you made about the world around you. Arrange your story in a clear chronological order, adding enough specific details to make the event come alive for your reader. By the end of your essay, you should have convinced your reader of the significance of your discovery.

2. How can an awareness of Staples's feelings in "Black Men and Public Space" make us better members of our society and the world in which we live? What limitations do we set for ourselves, and how do those boundaries affect our vision of what we can do to make the world a better place? Write a fully developed essay on this topic. Make sure that your thesis statement is clearly defined and that your supporting paragraphs stay focused on your thesis.

3. Write a well-developed essay explaining the meaning of "Black Men and Public Space." Focus on ideas that you had genuine questions about, such as, "Why does Staples feel he has to compromise his own values and his integrity by altering his own behavior rather than educating others about how they should be responding to him?" Begin with a thesis statement that makes an arguable point about the central theme of the essay. Brainstorm or prewrite to come up with reasons to support your thesis statement. In your essay, you may need to quote from "Black Men and Public Space," referring to specific words and passages to clarify and support your argument.

4. In "Black Men and Public Space," Staples gives a first-hand account of how he has been stereotyped. Think about other ways in which people are stereotyped, for example, as being too intelligent, athletic, thin, poor, and so on. In what ways have you been stereotyped? Write an essay examining how a particular stereotype falsifies qualities that are good and true in your nature. Begin with a thesis statement that declares how being stereotyped has affected you. Follow with supporting paragraphs that prove your statement.

The Two

1982

GLORIA NAYLOR

 GLORIA NAYLOR, an African-American novelist, was born in New York City. She attended Brooklyn College and earned her M.A. degree from Yale University. In this chapter from her novel *The Women of Brewster Place* she explores the relationship of two women, Lorraine and Theresa, and their neighbors in an apartment house on Brewster Place. The two women are lesbians trying to live a normal life, but society with its norms and values presents many challenges. The social tensions between Lorraine and Theresa and their neighbors threaten their own private relationship and even their sense of identity.

Have you ever had a serious conflict or misunderstanding with people living nearby? As you read "The Two," consider the subtle pressures society often imposes on our private lives. Why do close neighbors often want to know everything about the personal lives of others in their neighborhood? How sacred are our private lives?

At first they seemed like such nice girls. No one could remember exactly when they had moved into Brewster. It was earlier in the year before Ben was killed—of course, it had to be before Ben's death. But no one remembered if it was in the winter or spring of that year that the two had come. People often came and went on Brewster Place like a restless night's dream, moving in and out in the dark to avoid eviction notices or neighborhood bulletins about the dilapidated condition of their furnishings. So it wasn't until the two were clocked leaving in the mornings and returning in the evenings at regular intervals that it was quietly absorbed that they now claimed Brewster as home. And Brewster waited, cautiously prepared to claim them, because you never knew about young women, and obviously single at that. But when no wild music or drunken friends careened[1]

1. careened: to move rapidly in an uncontrolled manner

out of the corner building on weekends, and especially, when no slightly eager husbands were encouraged to linger around that first-floor apartment and run errands for them, a suspended sigh of relief floated around the two when they dumped their garbage, did their shopping, and headed for the morning bus.

The women of Brewster had readily accepted the lighter, skinny one. There wasn't much threat in her timid mincing walk and the slightly protruding teeth she seemed so eager to show everyone in her bell-like good mornings and evenings. Breaths were held a little longer in the direction of the short dark one—too pretty, and too much behind. And she insisted on wearing those thin Qiana dresses that the summer breeze molded against the maddening rhythm of the twenty pounds of rounded flesh that she swung steadily down the street. Through slitted eyes, the women watched their men watching her pass, knowing the bastards were praying for a wind. But since she seemed oblivious[2] to whether these supplications[3] went answered, their sighs settled around her shoulders too. Nice girls.

And so no one even cared to remember exactly when they had moved into Brewster Place, until the rumor started. It had first spread through the block like a sour odor that's only faintly perceptible and easily ignored until it starts growing in strength from the dozen mouths it had been lying in, among clammy gums and scum-coated teeth. And then it was everywhere— lining the mouths and whitening the lips of everyone as they wrinkled up their noses at its pervading smell, unable to pinpoint the source or time of its initial arrival. Sophie could—she had been there.

It wasn't that the rumor had actually begun with Sophie. A rumor needs no true parent. It only needs a willing carrier, and it found one in Sophie. She had been there—on one of those August evenings when the sun's absence is a mockery because the heat leaves the air so heavy it presses the naked skin down on your body, to the point that a sheet becomes unbearable and sleep impossible. So most of Brewster was outside that night when the two had come in together, probably from one of those air-conditioned movies downtown, and had greeted the ones who were loitering around their building. And they had started up the steps when the skinny one tripped over a child's ball and the darker one had grabbed her by the arm and around the waist to break her fall. "Careful, don't wanna lose you now." And the two of them had laughed into each other's eyes and went into the building.

The smell had begun there. It outlined the image of the stumbling woman and the one who had broken her fall. Sophie and a few other women sniffed at the spot and then, perplexed, silently looked at each other. Where

2. oblivious: unaware   3. supplications: beggings

had they seen that before? They had often laughed and touched each other—held each other in joy or its dark twin—but where had they seen *that* before? It came to them as the scent drifted down the steps and entered their nostrils on the way to their inner mouths. They had seen that—done that—with their men. That shared moment of invisible communion reserved for two and hidden from the rest of the world behind laughter or tears or a touch. In the days before babies, miscarriages, and other broken dreams, after stolen caresses in barn stalls and cotton houses, after intimate walks from church and secret kisses with boys who were now long forgotten or permanently fixed in their lives—that was where. They could almost feel the odor moving about in their mouths, and they slowly knitted themselves together and let it out into the air like a yellow mist that began to cling to the bricks on Brewster.

So it got around that the two in 312 were *that* way. And they had seemed like such nice girls. Their regular exits and entrances to the block were viewed with a jaundiced[4] eye. The quiet that rested around their door on the weekends hinted of all sorts of secret rituals, and their friendly indifference to the men on the street was an insult to the women as a brazen flaunting of unnatural ways. 6

Since Sophie's apartment windows faced theirs from across the air shaft, she became the official watchman for the block, and her opinions were deferred to whenever the two came up in conversation. Sophie took her position seriously and was constantly alert for any telltale signs that might creep out around their drawn shades, across from which she kept a religious vigil. An entire week of drawn shades was evidence enough to send her flying around with reports that as soon as it got dark they pulled their shades down and put on the lights. Heads nodded in knowing unison—a definite sign. If doubt was voiced with a "But I pull my shades down at night too," a whispered "Yeah, but you're not *that* way" was argument enough to win them over. 7

Sophie watched the lighter one dumping their garbage, and she went outside and opened the lid. Her eyes darted over the crushed tin cans, vegetable peelings, and empty chocolate chip cookie boxes. What do they do with all them chocolate chip cookies? It was surely a sign, but it would take some time to figure that one out. She saw Ben go into their apartment, and she waited and blocked his path as he came out, carrying his toolbox. 8

"What ya see?" She grabbed his arm and whispered wetly in his face. 9

Ben stared at her squinted eyes and drooping lips and shook his head slowly. "Uh, uh, uh, it was terrible." 10

---

4. jaundiced: prejudiced; envious; jealous

"Yeah?" She moved in a little closer.   11

"Worst busted faucet I seen in my whole life." He shook her hand off   12
his arm and left her standing in the middle of the block.

"You old sop bucket," she muttered, as she went back up on her stoop.   13
A broken faucet, huh? Why did they need to use so much water?

Sophie had plenty to report that day. Ben had said it was terrible in there.   14
No, she didn't know exactly what he had seen, but you can imagine—and
they did. Confronted with the difference that had been thrust into their
predictable world, they reached into their imaginations and, using an ancient
pattern, weaved themselves a reason for its existence. Out of necessity they
stitched all of their secret fears and lingering childhood nightmares into this
existence, because even though it was deceptive enough to try and look as
they looked, talk as they talked, and do as they did, it had to have some
hidden stain to invalidate it—it was impossible for them both to be right. So
they leaned back, supported by the sheer weight of their numbers and comforted by the woven barrier that kept them protected from the yellow mist
that enshrouded the two as they came and went on Brewster Place.

Lorraine was the first to notice the change in the people on Brewster   15
Place. She was a shy but naturally friendly woman who got up early, and had
read the morning paper and done fifty sit-ups before it was time to leave for
work. She came out of her apartment eager to start her day by greeting any
of her neighbors who were outside. But she noticed that some of the people
who had spoken to her before made a point of having something else to do
with their eyes when she passed, although she could almost feel them staring
at her back as she moved on. The ones who still spoke only did so after an
uncomfortable pause, in which they seemed to be peering through her before
they begrudged her a good morning or evening. She wondered if it was all
in her mind and she thought about mentioning it to Theresa, but she didn't
want to be accused of being too sensitive again. And how would Tee even
notice anything like that anyway? She had a lousy attitude and hardly ever
spoke to people. She stayed in that bed until the last moment and rushed
out of the house fogged-up and grumpy, and she was used to being stared
at—by men at least—because of her body.

Lorraine thought about these things as she came up the block from work,   16
carrying a large paper bag. The group of women on her stoop parted silently
and let her pass.

"Good evening," she said, as she climbed the steps.   17

Sophie was standing on the top step and tried to peek into the bag. "You   18
been shopping, huh? What ya buy?" It was almost an accusation.

"Groceries." Lorraine shielded the top of the bag from view and squeezed   19
past her with a confused frown. She saw Sophie throw a knowing glance to
the others at the bottom of the stoop. What was wrong with this old woman?
Was she crazy or something?

Lorraine went into her apartment. Theresa was sitting by the window,   20
reading a copy of *Mademoiselle*. She glanced up from her magazine. "Did
you get my chocolate chip cookies?"

"Why good evening to you, too, Tee. And how was my day? Just wonder-   21
ful." She sat the bag down on the couch. "The little Baxter boy brought in
a puppy for show-and-tell, and the damn thing pissed all over the floor and
then proceeded to chew the heel off my shoe, but, yes, I managed to hobble
to the store and bring you your chocolate chip cookies."

Oh, Jesus, Theresa thought, she's got a bug up her ass tonight.   22

"Well, you should speak to Mrs. Baxter. She ought to train her kid better   23
than that." She didn't wait for Lorraine to stop laughing before she tried to
stretch her good mood. "Here, I'll put those things away. Want me to make
dinner so you can rest? I only worked half a day, and the most tragic thing
that went down was a broken fingernail and that got caught in my typewriter."

Lorraine followed Theresa into the kitchen. "No, I'm not really tired,   24
and fair's fair, you cooked last night. I didn't mean to tick off like that; it's
just that . . . well, Tee, have you noticed that people aren't as nice as they
used to be?"

Theresa stiffened. Oh, God, here she goes again. "What people, Lorraine?   25
Nice in what way?"

"Well, the people in this building and on the street. No one hardly speaks   26
anymore. I mean, I'll come in and say good evening—and just silence. It
wasn't like that when we first moved in. I don't know, it just makes you
wonder; that's all. What are they thinking?"

"I personally don't give a shit what they're thinking. And their good   27
evenings don't put any bread on my table."

"Yeah, but you didn't see the way that woman looked at me out there.   28
They must feel something or know something. They probably—"

"They, they, they!" Theresa exploded. "You know, I'm not starting up   29
with this again, Lorraine. Who in the hell are they? And where in the hell
are we? Living in some dump of a building in this God-forsaken part of town
around a bunch of ignorant niggers with the cotton still under their fingernails
because of you and your theys. They knew something in Linden Hills, so I
gave up an apartment for you that I'd been in for the last four years. And
then they knew in Park Heights, and you made me so miserable there we
had to leave. Now these mysterious theys are on Brewster Place. Well, look
out that window, kid. There's a big wall down that block, and this is the end

of the line for me. I'm not moving anymore, so if that's what you're working yourself up to—save it!"

When Theresa became angry she was like a lump of smoldering coal, and her fierce bursts of temper always unsettled Lorraine.

"You see, that's why I didn't want to mention it." Lorraine began to pull at her fingers nervously. "You're always flying up and jumping to conclusions—no one said anything about moving. And I didn't know your life has been so miserable since you met me. I'm sorry about that," she finished tearfully.

Theresa looked at Lorraine, standing in the kitchen door like a wilted leaf, and she wanted to throw something at her. Why didn't she ever fight back? The very softness that had first attracted her to Lorraine was now a frequent cause for irritation. Smoked honey. That's what Lorraine had reminded her of, sitting in her office clutching that application. Dry autumn days in Georgia woods, thick bloated smoke under a beehive, and the first glimpse of amber honey just faintly darkened about the edges by the burning twigs. She had flowed just that heavily into Theresa's mind and had stuck there with a persistent sweetness.

But Theresa hadn't known then that this softness filled Lorraine up to the very middle and that she would bend at the slightest pressure, would be constantly seeking to surround herself with the comfort of everyone's good-will, and would shrivel up at the least touch of disapproval. It was becoming a drain to be continually called upon for this nurturing and support that she just didn't understand. She had supplied it at first out of love for Lorraine, hoping that she would harden eventually, even as honey does when exposed to the cold. Theresa was growing tired of being clung to—of being the one who was leaned on. She didn't want a child—she wanted someone who could stand toe to toe with her and be willing to slug it out at times. If they practiced that way with each other, then they could turn back to back and beat the hell out of the world for trying to invade their territory. But she had found no such sparring partner in Lorraine, and the strain of fighting alone was beginning to show on her.

"Well, if it was that miserable, I would have been gone a long time ago," she said, watching her words refresh Lorraine like a gentle shower.

"I guess you think I'm some sort of a sick paranoid, but I can't afford to have people calling my job or writing letters to my principal. You know I've already lost a position like that in Detroit. And teaching is my whole life, Tee."

"I know," she sighed, not really knowing at all. There was no danger of that ever happening on Brewster Place. Lorraine taught too far from this neighborhood for anyone here to recognize her in that school. No, it wasn't her job she feared losing this time, but their approval. She wanted to stand out there and chat and trade makeup secrets and cake recipes. She wanted to be secretary of their block association and be asked to mind their kids while they ran to the store. And none of that was going to happen if they couldn't even bring themselves to accept her good evenings.

Theresa silently finished unpacking the groceries. "Why did you buy cottage cheese? Who eats that stuff?" 37

"Well, I thought we should go on a diet." 38

"If *we* go on a diet, then you'll disappear. You've got nothing to lose but your hair." 39

"Oh, I don't know. I thought that we might want to try and reduce our hips or something." Lorraine shrugged playfully. 40

"No, thank you. We are very happy with our hips the way they are," Theresa said, as she shoved the cottage cheese to the back of the refrigerator. "And even when I lose weight, it never comes off there. My chest and arms just get smaller, and I start looking like a bottle of salad dressing." 41

The two women laughed, and Theresa sat down to watch Lorraine fix dinner. "You know, this behind has always been my downfall. When I was coming up in Georgia with my grandmother, the boys used to promise me penny candy if I would let them pat my behind. And I used to love those jawbreakers—you know, the kind that lasted all day and kept changing colors in your mouth. So I was glad to oblige them, because in one afternoon I could collect a whole week's worth of jawbreakers." 42

"Really. That's funny to you? Having some boy feeling all over you." 43

Theresa sucked her teeth. "We were only kids, Lorraine. You know, you remind me of my grandmother. That was one straight-laced old lady. She had a fit when my brother told her what I was doing. She called me into the smokehouse and told me in this real scary whisper that I could get pregnant from letting little boys pat my butt and that I'd end up like my cousin Willa. But Willa and I had been thick as fleas, and she had already given me a step-by-step summary of how she'd gotten into her predicament. But I sneaked around to her house that night just to double-check her story, since that old lady had seemed so earnest. 'Willa, are you sure?' I whispered through her bedroom window. 'I'm tellin' ya, Tee,' she said. 'Just keep both feet on the ground and you home free.' Much later I learned that advice wasn't too biologically sound, but it worked in Georgia because those country boys didn't have much imagination." 44

Theresa's laughter bounced off of Lorraine's silent, rigid back and died in her throat. She angrily tore open a pack of the chocolate chip cookies. "Yeah," she said, staring at Lorraine's back and biting down hard into the cookie, "it wasn't until I came up north to college that I found out there's 45 a whole lot of things that a dude with a little imagination can do to you even with both feet on the ground. You see, Willa forgot to tell me not to bend over or squat or—"

"Must you!" Lorraine turned around from the stove with her teeth 46
clenched tightly together.

"Must I what, Lorraine? Must I talk about things that are as much a 47
part of life as eating or breathing or growing old? Why are you always so uptight about sex or men?"

"I'm not uptight about anything. I just think it's disgusting when you 48
go on and on about—"

"There's nothing disgusting about it, Lorraine. You've never been with 49
a man, but I've been with quite a few—some better than others. There were a couple who I still hope to this day will die a slow, painful death, but then there were some who were good to me—in and out of bed."

"If they were so great, then why are you with me?" Lorraine's lips were 50
trembling.

"Because—" Theresa looked steadily into her eyes and then down at the 51
cookie she was twirling on the table. "Because," she continued slowly, "you can take a chocolate chip cookie and put holes in it and attach it to your ears and call it an earring, or hang it around your neck on a silver chain and pretend it's a necklace—but it's still a cookie. See—you can toss it in the air and call it a Frisbee or even a flying saucer, if the mood hits you, and it's still just a cookie. Send it spinning on a table—like this—until it's a wonderful blur of amber and brown light that you can imagine to be a topaz or rusted gold or old crystal, but the law of gravity has got to come into play, sometime, and it's got to come to rest—sometime. Then all the spinning and pretending and hoopla is over with. And you know what you got?"

"A chocolate chip cookie," Lorraine said. 52

"Uh-huh." Theresa put the cookie in her mouth and winked. "A les- 53
bian." She got up from the table. "Call me when dinner's ready, I'm going back to read." She stopped at the kitchen door. "Now, why are you putting gravy on that chicken, Lorraine? You know it's fattening."

◼︎   ◼︎   ◼︎

OPTIONS FOR READING LOGS: "THE TWO"

1. Use the double-entry journal technique by asking several "what" or "why" questions to discover meaning in "The Two." Divide your journal page into two vertical columns. In the left column, keep a running list

of questions that occur to you as you are reading. Aim for three to five questions, such as, "What kind of neighborhood is Brewster Place?" Finish your list of questions, and then answer them as completely as you can in the right column. Taking risks is an important part of critical thinking, so allow yourself to "go out on a limb" with your guesses. To demonstrate your basic understanding of "The Two," end your journal entry by jotting down its main idea.

2. Examine your personal reaction to "The Two" by completing this statement:

> "I was struck by _____ ."

You might say, for example, "I was struck by how quickly the other women in the building sensed that their two new neighbors were different." End your journal entry with a detailed explanation of your statement.

3. Drawing on your own life, tell a parallel story that was triggered by reading "The Two." Does the couple's experience remind you of a difficult time when your personal values were in conflict with those of your immediate social situation? Jot down things that were similar to or different from those in Naylor's story. End your journal entry by stating the theme of "The Two."

OPTIONS FOR WRITING ASSIGNMENTS: "THE TWO"

1. Expand and develop one of your reading logs for "The Two" into a more polished piece of writing that explores its subject matter in greater range and depth. Begin with a thesis statement that reveals an important discovery you made about a time your values conflicted with those of the people around you. Arrange your story in a clear chronological order, adding enough specific details to make the event come alive for your reader. By the end of your essay, you should have convinced your reader of the significance of your self-discovery.

2. Write a letter to Lorraine and Theresa's neighbors, telling them what you think of their treatment of the lesbian couple. Address them directly, describing your reaction to the attitudes they displayed in the story. Use the letter to express your own point of view. You may choose to criticize, question, or inquire. Use the approach most appropriate to express your reaction.

3. Toward the end of "The Two," Theresa and Lorraine discuss society's lack of acceptance of their lifestyle and the identities they have found within themselves. How do the two women's attitudes differ? Does one seem to have a better grasp of the conflicts and issues their sexual identity creates in our society? What is the point of the discussion of the chocolate chip cookie and the law of gravity? Write a formal essay of five or more paragraphs contrasting Lorraine's and Theresa's sense of themselves, of their relationship with their neighbors, and of their overall place in society. Begin by preparing a list for each character for comparisons and contrasts. Then develop the lists into an outline and use transitional expressions that signal similarities or differences.

4. What did you think of "The Two" as a story about the conflict between an individual's personal identity and values and those of the society at large? Does the story shed light on these issues? Would you recommend this story to a friend? Write a formal essay of five or more paragraphs evaluating "The Two" as a story of the individual in conflict with society. End your introductory paragraph with a thesis statement that makes a clear judgment of the story's worth. Your evaluation can be positive, negative, or some interesting mixture of positive and negative. Once you are sure of the evaluation or judgment you want to make, use your supporting paragraphs to give the reasons for your judgment and to offer evidence from the story that will make your judgment convincing.

Dulce et Decorum Est

1920

WILFRED OWEN

 WILFRED OWEN, an English poet, was born in 1893. He was killed in World War I at the age of twenty-five. During his service in the war, he saw a good deal of action and wrote numerous poems based on these first-hand experiences and observations. His poem "Dulce et Decorum Est" is perhaps his best known poem and is, in fact, one of the most famous war poems in the English language. The quote in Latin "Dulce et decorum est / Pro patria mori" is from a poem by Horace, a Roman poet; the quote is customarily translated as "It is sweet and proper to die for your country."

Have you ever been told one thing by the media, society, or someone you greatly respect, only to discover later that it simply is not true? In our society we are often told by others what to believe and value; however, sometimes we may learn from experience that we do not know the whole story or that we have been foolish to believe the words of others without really considering the consequences.

Bent double, like old beggars under sacks,   1
Knock-kneed, coughing like hags, we cursed through sludge,
Till on the haunting flares we turned our backs
And towards our distant rest began to trudge.
Men marched asleep. Many had lost their boots   5
But limped on, blood-shod. All went lame; all blind;
Drunk with fatigue; deaf even to the hoots
Of tired, outstripped Five-Nines that dropped behind.

Gas! Gas! Quick, boys!—An ecstasy of fumbling,
Fitting the clumsy helmets just in time;   10
But someone still was yelling out and stumbling
And flound'ring like a man in fire or lime . . .
Dim, through the misty panes and thick green light,
As under a green sea, I saw him drowning.

In all my dreams, before my helpless sight,   15
He plunges at me, guttering, choking, drowning.

If in some smothering dreams you too could pace
Behind the wagon that we flung him in,
And watch the white eyes writhing in his face,
His hanging face, like a devil's sick of sin;   20
If you could hear, at every jolt, the blood
Come gargling from the froth-corrupted lungs,
Obscene as cancer, bitter as the cud
Of vile, incurable sores on innocent tongues,—
My friend, you would not tell with such high zest   25
To children ardent for some desperate glory,
The old Lie: *Dulce et decorum est*
Pro patria mori.

OPTIONS FOR READING LOGS: "DULCE ET DECORUM EST"

1. Use the double-entry journal technique to clarify the meaning of some of the imagery and powerful lines in "Dulce et Decorum Est." End your journal entry with a brief statement about a significant discovery you made about the poem as a whole during this process. ("I discovered that . . . .")

2. Use your imagination to create some graphics or draw a picture that best represents what you see in the poem "Dulce et Decorum Est." Your picture can be literal or symbolic. An option would be to create a word picture of the poem, using as many specific details or images as possible. Wrap up your journal entry by stating the central theme of the poem.

3. What is the message of Owen's poem? What does he mean when he says, "The old Lie"? Does the theme of the poem cause you to reflect on a conflict you have had with the values and attitudes of others or with a powerful social institution? End your entry by clarifying what you learned from reading the poem.

OPTIONS FOR WRITING ASSIGNMENTS: "DULCE ET DECORUM EST"

1. Develop one of your reading logs for "Dulce et Decorum Est" into a more polished piece of writing that explores a conflict between an individual and a social institution (such as a school, church, or government) in greater range and depth, using an appropriate form (a poem, a fictional story, a personal narrative, or an essay that examines a central idea).

2. What do you think a decorated war hero would have to say to Wilfred Owen? Create a conversation between the poet and a real or imaginary war hero. In your dialogue, remain neutral, allowing both sides to express their points of view thoroughly and fairly.

3. Write a personal letter to Wilfred Owen, the author of "Dulce et Decorum Est." Use the letter form, addressing him directly about your reaction to his poem. Use the letter to express your own reaction to the poem's theme. You may choose to praise, criticize, empathize, console, or inquire. Use whatever approach is most appropriate.

4. If you were asked what "Dulce et Decorum Est" means and how it teaches us to understand better the relationship of the individual and the social institutions that guide and shape him or her, what would you say? Simply reading a text is often not enough to appreciate its range of meaning fully. We often need to reread, think about, discuss, and write about a poem before we fully appreciate its meaning. Explain the meaning of "Dulce et Decorum Est" in a well-developed essay. Are we to assume that all wars are based on "lies" or that the pain and hideous suffering in a war cannot justify fighting one? What do you think? In an introductory paragraph, clearly state the poem's main idea. In your supporting paragraphs, focus your attention on those parts of the poem that you have questions about and that help clarify your main idea. In your commentary you will need to quote from the poem and refer to specific passages to help clear up any difficulties in understanding.

Letter from Birmingham Jail

1963

MARTIN LUTHER KING, JR.

 MARTIN LUTHER KING was the most important leader of the civil rights struggle in the 1960s. He won the Nobel Peace Prize in 1964. He is perhaps best known for his brilliant and moving speeches, the most famous of which was his "I Have a Dream" speech delivered at the Lincoln Memorial in Washington, D.C. In "Letter from Birmingham Jail" King is responding to a published statement by eight fellow clergymen from Alabama who criticized his advocacy of nonviolent protest as a means of battling racist laws and attitudes. Evidently they thought he had gone too far in his protests against social injustice, and King felt the need to explain his point of view and his reasons for becoming more politically active in the civil rights movement.

As you read King's letter, consider your own relationship to the society in which you live. What would you do if you encountered unjust laws that discriminate against you? What should be done if local or city government does not listen to the people it represents? Does King provide any answers to those who feel society is treating them unfairly?

April 16, 1963

MY DEAR FELLOW CLERGYMEN:[1]

While confined here in the Birmingham city jail, I came across your recent statement calling my present activities "unwise and untimely." Seldom do I pause to answer criticism of my work and ideas. If I sought to answer all the criticisms that cross my desk, my secretaries would

---

1. This response to a published statement by eight fellow clergymen from Alabama (Bishop C. C. J. Carpenter, Bishop Joseph A. Durick, Rabbi Hilton L. Grafman, Bishop Paul Hardin, Bishop Holan B. Harmon, the Reverend George M. Murray, the Reverend Edward V. Ramage, and the Reverend Earl Stallings) was composed under somewhat constricting circumstances. Begun on the margins of the newspaper in which the statement appeared while I was in jail, the letter was continued on scraps of writing paper supplied by a friendly Negro trusty, and concluded on a pad my attorneys were eventually permitted to leave me. Although the text remains in substance unaltered, I have indulged in the author's prerogative of polishing it for publication. [King's note]

have little time for anything other than such correspondence in the course of the day, and I would have no time for constructive work. But since I feel that you are men of genuine good will and that your criticisms are sincerely set forth, I want to try to answer your statement in what I hope will be patient and reasonable terms.

I think I should indicate why I am here in Birmingham, since you have been influenced by the view which argues against "outsiders coming in." I have the honor of serving as president of the Southern Christian Leadership Conference, an organization operating in every southern state, with headquarters in Atlanta, Georgia. We have some eighty-five affiliated organizations across the South, and one of them is the Alabama Christian Movement for Human Rights. Frequently we share staff, educational, and financial resources with our affiliates. Several months ago the affiliate here in Birmingham asked us to be on call to engage in a nonviolent direct-action program if such were deemed necessary. We readily consented, and when the hour came we lived up to our promise. So I, along with several members of my staff, am here because I was invited here. I am here because I have organizational ties here.

But more basically, I am in Birmingham because injustice is here. Just as the prophets of the eighth century B.C. left their villages and carried their "thus saith the Lord" far beyond the boundaries of their home towns, and just as the Apostle Paul left his village of Tarsus and carried the gospel of Jesus Christ to the far corners of the Greco-Roman world, so am I compelled to carry the gospel of freedom beyond my own home town. Like Paul, I must constantly respond to the Macedonian call for aid.

Moreover, I am cognizant[2] of the interrelatedness of all communities and states. I cannot sit idly by in Atlanta and not be concerned about what happens in Birmingham. Injustice anywhere is a threat to justice everywhere. We are caught in an inescapable network of mutuality, tied in a single garment of destiny. Whatever affects one directly, affects all indirectly. Never again can we afford to live with the narrow, provincial, "outside agitator" idea. Anyone who lives inside the United States can never be considered an outsider anywhere within its bounds.

You deplore the demonstrations taking place in Birmingham. But your statement, I am sorry to say, fails to express a similar concern for the conditions that brought about the demonstrations. I am sure that none of you would want to rest content with the superficial kind of social analysis that deals merely with effects and does not grapple with underlying causes. It is unfortunate that demonstrations are taking place in Birmingham, but it is even more

2. cognizant: aware

unfortunate that the city's white power structure left the Negro community with no alternative.

In any nonviolent campaign there are four basic steps: collection of the 7 facts to determine whether injustices exist; negotiation; self-purification; and direct action. We have gone through all these steps in Birmingham. There can be no gainsaying[3] the fact that racial injustice engulfs this community. Birmingham is probably the most thoroughly segregated city in the United States. Its ugly record of brutality is widely known. Negroes have experienced grossly unjust treatment in the courts. There have been more unsolved bombings of Negro homes and churches in Birmingham than in any other city in the nation. These are the hard brutal facts of the case. On the basis of these conditions, Negro leaders sought to negotiate with the city fathers. But the latter consistently refused to engage in good-faith negotiation.

Then, last September, came the opportunity to talk with leaders of Birmingham's economic community. In the course of the negotiations, certain promises were made by the merchants—for example, to remove the stores' humiliating racial signs. On the basis of these promises, the Reverend Fred Shuttlesworth and the leaders of the Alabama Christian Movement for Human Rights agreed to a moratorium on all demonstrations. As the weeks and months went by, we realized that we were the victims of a broken promise. A few signs, briefly removed, returned; the others remained.

As in so many past experiences, our hopes had been blasted, and the 9 shadow of deep disappointment settled upon us. We had no alternative except to prepare for direct action, whereby we would present our very bodies as a means of laying our case before the conscience of the local and the national community. Mindful of the difficulties involved, we decided to undertake a process of self-purification. We began a series of workshops on nonviolence, and we repeatedly asked ourselves: "Are you able to accept blows without retaliating?" "Are you able to endure the ordeal of jail?" We decided to schedule our direct-action program for the Easter season, realizing that except for Christmas, this is the main shopping period of the year. Knowing that a strong economic-withdrawal program would be the by-product of direct action, we felt that this would be the best time to bring pressure to bear on the merchants for the needed change.

Then it occurred to us that Birmingham's mayoral election was coming 10 up in March, and we speedily decided to postpone action until after election day. When we discovered that the Commissioner of Public Safety, Eugene "Bull" Connor, had piled up enough votes to be in the run-off, we decided

---

3. gainsaying: denying; disputing; contradicting

again to postpone action until the day after the run-off so that the demonstrations could not be used to cloud the issues. Like many others, we waited to see Mr. Connor defeated, and to this end we endured postponement after postponement. Having aided in this community need, we felt that our direct-action program could be delayed no longer.

You may well ask, "Why direct action? Why sit-ins, marches, and so   11
forth? Isn't negotiation a better path?" You are quite right in calling for negotiation. Indeed, this is the very purpose of direct action. Non-violent direct action seeks to create such a crisis and foster such a tension that a community which has constantly refused to negotiate is forced to confront the issue. It seeks so to dramatize the issue that it can no longer be ignored. My citing the creation of tension as part of the work of the nonviolent resister may sound rather shocking. But I must confess that I am not afraid of the word "tension." I have earnestly opposed violent tension, but there is a type of constructive, nonviolent tension which is necessary for growth. Just as Socrates felt that it was necessary to create a tension in the mind so that individuals could rise from the bondage of myths and half truths to the unfettered realm of creative analysis and objective appraisal, so must we see the need for nonviolent gadflies[4] to create the kind of tension in society that will help men rise from the dark depths of prejudice and racism to the majestic heights of understanding and brotherhood.

The purpose of our direct-action program is to create a situation so crisis-   12
packed that it will inevitably open the door to negotiation. I therefore concur with you in your call for negotiation. Too long has our beloved Southland been bogged down in a tragic effort to live in monologue rather than dialogue.

One of the basic points in your statement is that the action that I and   13
my associates have taken in Birmingham is untimely. Some have asked: "Why didn't you give the new city administration time to act?" The only answer that I can give to this query is that the new Birmingham administration must be prodded about as much as the outgoing one, before it will act. We are sadly mistaken if we feel that the election of Albert Boutwell as mayor will bring the millennium[5] to Birmingham. While Mr. Boutwell is a much more gentle person than Mr. Connor, they are both segregationists, dedicated to maintenance of the status quo. I have hoped that Mr. Boutwell will be reasonable enough to see the futility of massive resistance to desegregation. But he will not see this without pressure from devotees of civil rights. My friends, I must say to you that we have not made a single gain in civil rights without determined legal and nonviolent pressure. Lamentably,[6] it is an

---

4. gadflies: persons who persistently annoy or stir up others   5. millenium: a period of 1,000 years
6. lamentably: regrettably

historical fact that privileged groups seldom give up their privileges voluntarily. Individuals may see the moral light and voluntarily give up their unjust posture; but, as Reinhold Niebuhr has reminded us, groups tend to be more immoral than individuals.

We know through painful experience that freedom is never voluntarily given by the oppressor; it must be demanded by the oppressed. Frankly, I have yet to engage in a direct-action campaign that was "well timed" in the view of those who have not suffered unduly from the disease of segregation. For years now I have heard the word "Wait!" It rings in the ear of every Negro with piercing familiarity. This "Wait" has almost always meant "Never." We must come to see, with one of our distinguished jurists, that "justice too long delayed is justice denied." 14

We have waited for more than 340 years for our constitutional and God-given rights. The nations of Asia and Africa are moving with jet-like speed toward gaining political independence, but we still creep at horse-and-buggy pace toward gaining a cup of coffee at a lunch counter. Perhaps it is easy for those who have never felt the stinging darts of segregation to say, "Wait." But when you have seen vicious mobs lynch your mothers and fathers at will and drown your sisters and brothers at whim; when you have seen hate-filled policemen curse, kick, and even kill your black brothers and sisters; when you see the vast majority of your twenty million Negro brothers smothering in an airtight cage of poverty in the midst of an affluent society; when you suddenly find your tongue twisted and your speech stammering as you seek to explain to your six-year-old daughter why she can't go to the public amusement park that has just been advertised on television, and see tears welling up in her eyes when she is told that Funtown is closed to colored children, and see ominous[7] clouds of inferiority beginning to form in her little mental sky, and see her beginning to distort her personality by developing an unconscious bitterness toward white people; when you have to concoct[8] an answer for a five-year-old son who is asking, "Daddy, why do white people treat colored people so mean?"; when you take a cross-country drive and find it necessary to sleep night after night in the uncomfortable corners of your automobile because no motel will accept you; when you are humiliated day in and day out by nagging signs reading "white" and "colored"; when your first name becomes "nigger," your middle name becomes "boy" (however old you are) and your last name becomes "John," and your wife and mother are never given the respected title "Mrs."; when you are harried by day and haunted by night by the fact that you are a Negro, living constantly at tiptoe stance, never quite knowing what to expect next, and are plagued 15

---

7. ominous: threatening   8. concoct: to prepare or make by combining ingredients

with inner fears and outer resentments; when you are forever fighting a degenerating sense of "nobodiness"—then you will understand why we find it difficult to wait. There comes a time when the cup of endurance runs over, and men are no longer willing to be plunged into the abyss of despair. I hope, sirs, you can understand our legitimate and unavoidable impatience.

You express a great deal of anxiety over our willingness to break laws. **16** This is certainly a legitimate concern. Since we so diligently urge people to obey the Supreme Court's decision of 1954 outlawing segregation in the public schools, at first glance it may seem rather paradoxical[9] for us consciously to break laws. One may well ask: "How can you advocate breaking some laws and obeying others?" The answer lies in the fact that there are two types of laws: just and unjust. I would be the first to advocate obeying just laws. One has not only a legal but a moral responsibility to obey just laws. Conversely, one has a moral responsibility to disobey unjust laws. I would agree with St. Augustine that "an unjust law is no law at all."

Now, what is the difference between the two? How does one determine **17** whether a law is just or unjust? A just law is a man-made code that squares with the moral law or the law of God. An unjust law is a code that is out of harmony with the moral law. To put it in the terms of St. Thomas Aquinas: An unjust law is a human law that is not rooted in eternal law and natural law. Any law that uplifts human personality is just. Any law that degrades human personality is unjust. All segregation statutes are unjust because segregation distorts the soul and damages the personality. It gives the segregator a false sense of superiority and the segregated a false sense of inferiority. Segregation, to use the terminology of the Jewish philosopher Martin Buber, substitutes an "I-it" relationship for an "I-thou" relationship and ends up relegating persons to the status of things. Hence segregation is not only politically, economically, and sociologically unsound, it is morally wrong and sinful. Paul Tillich has said that sin is separation. Is not segregation an existential expression of man's tragic separation, his awful estrangement, his terrible sinfulness? Thus it is that I can urge men to obey the 1954 decision of the Supreme Court, for it is morally right; and I can urge them to disobey segregation ordinances, for they are morally wrong.

Let us consider a more concrete example of just and unjust laws. An **18** unjust law is a code that a numerical or power majority group compels a minority group to obey but does not make binding on itself. This is *difference* made legal. By the same token, a just law is a code that a majority compels a minority to follow and that it is willing to follow itself. This is *sameness* made legal.

---

9. paradoxical: the state of being a seeming contradiction or absurd statement that expresses a possible truth

Let me give another explanation. A law is unjust if it is inflicted on a   19
minority that, as a result of being denied the right to vote, had no part in
enacting or devising the law. Who can say that the legislature of Alabama which
set up that state's segregation laws was democratically elected? Throughout
Alabama all sorts of devious methods are used to prevent Negroes from
becoming registered voters, and there are some counties in which, even
though Negroes constitute a majority of the population, not a single Negro
is registered. Can any law enacted under such circumstances be considered
democratically structured?

Sometimes a law is just on its face and unjust in its application. For   20
instance, I have been arrested on a charge of parading without a permit.
Now, there is nothing wrong in having an ordinance which requires a permit
for a parade. But such an ordinance becomes unjust when it is used to
maintain segregation and to deny citizens the First Amendment privilege of
peaceful assembly and protest.

I hope you are able to see the distinction I am trying to point out.   21
In no sense do I advocate evading or defying the law, as would the rabid
segregationist. That would lead to anarchy. One who breaks an unjust law
must do so openly, lovingly, and with a willingness to accept the penalty. I
submit that an individual who breaks a law that conscience tells him is unjust,
and who willingly accepts the penalty of imprisonment in order to arouse
the conscience of the community over its injustice, is in reality expressing
the highest respect for law.

Of course, there is nothing new about this kind of civil disobedience. It   22
was evidenced sublimely in the refusal of Shadrach, Meshach, and Abednego
to obey the laws of Nebuchadnezzar, on the ground that a higher moral law
was at stake. It was practiced superbly by the early Christians, who were
willing to face hungry lions and the excruciating pain of chopping blocks
rather than submit to certain unjust laws of the Roman Empire. To a degree,
academic freedom is a reality today because Socrates practiced civil disobedience. In our own nation, the Boston Tea Party represented a massive act of
civil disobedience.

We should never forget that everything Adolf Hitler did in Germany was   23
"legal" and everything the Hungarian freedom fighters did in Hungary was
"illegal." It was "illegal" to aid and comfort a Jew in Hitler's Germany. Even
so, I am sure that, had I lived in Germany at the time, I would have aided
and comforted my Jewish brothers. If today I lived in a Communist country
where certain principles dear to the Christian faith are suppressed, I would
openly advocate disobeying that country's antireligious laws.

I must make two honest confessions to you, my Christian and Jewish   24
brothers. First, I must confess that over the past few years I have been gravely

disappointed with the white moderate. I have almost reached the regrettable conclusion that the Negro's great stumbling block in his stride toward freedom is not the White Citizen's Counciler or the Ku Klux Klanner, but the white moderate, who is more devoted to "order" than to justice; who prefers a negative peace which is the absence of tension to a positive peace which is the presence of justice; who constantly says, "I agree with you in the goal you seek, but I cannot agree with your methods of direct action"; who paternalistically[10] believes he can set the timetable for another man's freedom; who lives by a mythical concept of time and who constantly advises the Negro to wait for a "more convenient season." Shallow understanding from people of good will is more frustrating than absolute misunderstanding from people of ill will. Lukewarm acceptance is much more bewildering than outright rejection.

I had hoped that the white moderate would understand that law and 25 order exist for the purpose of establishing justice and that when they fail in this purpose they become the dangerously structured dams that block the flow of social progress. I had hoped that the white moderate would understand that the present tension in the South is a necessary phase of the transition from an obnoxious negative peace, in which the Negro passively accepted his unjust plight, to a substantive and positive peace, in which all men will respect the dignity and worth of human personality. Actually, we who engage in nonviolent direct action are not the creators of tension. We merely bring to the surface the hidden tension that is already alive. We bring it out in the open, where it can be seen and dealt with. Like a boil that can never be cured so long as it is covered up but must be opened with all its ugliness to the natural medicines of air and light, injustice must be exposed, with all the tension its exposure creates, to the light of human conscience and the air of national opinion, before it can be cured.

In your statement you assert that our actions, even though peaceful, 26 must be condemned because they precipitate violence. But is this a logical assertion? Isn't this like condemning a robbed man because his possession of money precipitated the evil act of robbery? Isn't this like condemning Socrates because his unswerving commitment to truth and his philosophical inquiries precipitated the act by the misguided populace in which they made him drink hemlock? Isn't this like condemning Jesus because his unique God-consciousness and never-ceasing devotion to God's will precipitated the evil act of crucifixion? We must come to see that, as the federal courts have consistently affirmed, it is wrong to urge an individual to cease his efforts to gain his basic constitutional rights because the quest may precipitate violence. Society must protect the robbed and punish the robber.

---

10. paternalistically: managing or governing individuals in the manner of a father dealing with his children

I had also hoped that the white moderate would reject the myth concern-   27
ing time in relation to the struggle for freedom. I have just received a letter
from a white brother in Texas. He writes: "All Christians know that the
colored people will receive equal rights eventually, but it is possible that you
are in too great a religious hurry. It has taken Christianity almost two thousand
years to accomplish what it has. The teachings of Christ take time to come
to earth." Such an attitude stems from a tragic misconception of time, from
the strangely irrational notion that there is something in the very flow of
time that will inevitably cure all ills. Actually, time itself is neutral; it can be
used either destructively or constructively. More and more I feel that the
people of ill will have used time much more effectively than have the people
of good will. We will have to repent in this generation not merely for the
hateful words and actions of the bad people, but for the appalling silence of
the good people. Human progress never rolls in on wheels of inevitability;
it comes through the tireless efforts of men willing to be co-workers with
God, and without this hard work, time itself becomes an ally of the forces
of social stagnation. We must use time creatively, in the knowledge that the
time is always ripe to do right. Now is the time to make real the promise of
democracy and transform our pending national elegy into a creative psalm
of brotherhood. Now is the time to lift our national policy from the quicksand
of racial injustice to the solid rock of human dignity.

You speak of our activity in Birmingham as extreme. At first I was rather   28
disappointed that fellow clergymen would see my nonviolent efforts as those
of an extremist. I began thinking about the fact that I stand in the middle
of two opposing forces in the Negro community. One is a force of compla-
cency, made up in part of Negroes who, as a result of long years of oppression,
are so drained of self-respect and a sense of "somebodiness" that they have
adjusted to segregation; and in part of a few middle-class Negroes who,
because of a degree of academic and economic security and because in some
ways they profit by segregation, have become insensitive to the problems of
the masses. The other force is one of bitterness and hatred, and it comes
perilously close to advocating violence. It is expressed in the various black
nationalist groups that are springing up across the nation, the largest and
best known being Elijah Muhammad's Muslim movement. Nourished by the
Negro's frustration over the continued existence of racial discrimination, this
movement is made up of people who have lost faith in America, who have
absolutely repudiated[11] Christianity, and who have concluded that the white
man is an incorrigible[12] "devil."

I have tried to stand between these two forces, saying that we need   29
emulate neither the "do-nothingism" of the complacent nor the hatred and

---

11. repudiated: to reject   12. incorrigible: bad beyond reform

despair of the black nationalist. For there is the more excellent way of love
and nonviolent protest. I am grateful to God that, through the influence of
the Negro church, the way of nonviolence became an integral part of our
struggle.

If this philosophy had not emerged, by now many streets of the South   30
would, I am convinced, be flowing with blood. And I am further convinced
that if our white brothers dismiss as "rabble-rousers" and "outside agitators"
those of us who employ nonviolent direct action, and if they refuse to support
our nonviolent efforts, millions of Negroes will, out of frustration and despair,
seek solace and security in black nationalist ideologies—a development that
would inevitably lead to a frightening racial nightmare.

Oppressed people cannot remain oppressed forever. The yearning for   31
freedom eventually manifests itself, and that is what has happened to the
American Negro. Something within has reminded him of his birthright of
freedom, and something without has reminded him that it can be gained.
Consciously or unconsciously, he has been caught up by the *Zeitgeist*,[13] and
with his black brothers of Africa and his brown and yellow brothers of Asia,
South America, and the Caribbean, the United States Negro is moving with
a sense of great urgency toward the promised land of racial justice. If one
recognizes this vital urge that has engulfed the Negro community, one should
readily understand why public demonstrations are taking place. The Negro
has many pent-up resentments and latent frustrations, and he must release
them. So let him march; let him make prayer pilgrimages to the city hall; let
him go on freedom rides—and try to understand why he must do so. If his
repressed emotions are not released in nonviolent ways, they will seek expression through violence; this is not a threat but a fact of history. So I have not
said to my people, "Get rid of your discontent." Rather, I have tried to say
that this normal and healthy discontent can be channeled into the creative
outlet of nonviolent direct action. And now this approach is being termed
extremist.

But though I was initially disappointed at being categorized as an extrem-   32
ist, as I continued to think about the matter I gradually gained a measure of
satisfaction from the label. Was not Jesus an extremist for love: "Love your
enemies, bless them that curse you, do good to them that hate you, and pray
for them which despitefully use you, and persecute you." Was not Amos an
extremist for justice: "Let justice roll down like waters and righteousness like
an ever-flowing stream." Was not Paul an extremist for the Christian gospel:
"I bear in my body the marks of the Lord Jesus." Was not Martin Luther
an extremist: "Here I stand; I cannot do otherwise, so help me God." And

13. Zeitgeist: intellectual, moral, and cultural spirit of the times (German)

John Bunyan: "I will stay in jail to the end of my days before I make a butchery of my conscience." And Abraham Lincoln: "This nation cannot survive half slave and half free." And Thomas Jefferson: "We hold these truths to be self-evident, that all men are created equal. . . ." So the question is not whether we will be extremists, but what kind of extremists we will be. Will we be extremists for hate or for love? Will we be extremists for the preservation of injustice or for the extension of justice? In that dramatic scene on Calvary's hill three men were crucified. We must never forget that all three were crucified for the same crime—the crime of extremism. Two were extremists for immorality, and thus fell below their environment. The other, Jesus Christ, was an extremist for love, truth, and goodness, and thereby rose above his environment. Perhaps the South, the nation, and the world are in dire need of creative extremists.

33 I had hoped that the white moderate would see this need. Perhaps I was too optimistic; perhaps I expected too much. I suppose I should have realized that few members of the oppressor race can understand the deep groans and passionate yearnings of the oppressed race, and still fewer have the vision to see that injustice must be rooted out by strong, persistent, and determined action. I am thankful, however, that some of our white brothers in the South have grasped the meaning of this social revolution and committed themselves to it. They are still all too few in quantity, but they are big in quality. Some—such as Ralph McGill, Lillian Smith, Harry Golden, James McBride Dabbs, Ann Braden, and Sarah Patton Boyle—have written about our struggle in eloquent and prophetic[14] terms. Others have marched with us down nameless streets of the South. They have languished in filthy, roach-infested jails, suffering the abuse and brutality of policemen who view them as "dirty nigger-lovers." Unlike so many of their moderate brothers and sisters, they have recognized the urgency of the moment and sensed the need for powerful "action" antidotes to combat the disease of segregation.

34 Let me take note of my other major disappointment. I have been so greatly disappointed with the white church and its leadership. Of course, there are some notable exceptions. I am not unmindful of the fact that each of you has taken some significant stands on this issue. I commend you, Reverend Stallings, for your Christian stand on this past Sunday, in welcoming Negroes to your worship service on a non-segregated basis. I commend the Catholic leaders of this state for integrating Spring Hill College several years ago.

35 But despite these notable exceptions, I must honestly reiterate that I have been disappointed with the church. I do not say this as one of those

14. prophetic: of or pertaining to a prophet

negative critics who can always find something wrong with the church. I say this as a minister of the gospel, who loves the church; who was nurtured in its bosom; who has been sustained by its spiritual blessings and who will remain true to it as long as the cord of life shall lengthen.

When I was suddenly catapulted into the leadership of the bus protest in Montgomery, Alabama, a few years ago, I felt we would be supported by the white church. I felt that the white ministers, priests, and rabbis of the South would be among our strongest allies. Instead, some have been outright opponents, refusing to understand the freedom movement and misrepresenting its leaders; all too many others have been more cautious than courageous and have remained silent behind the anesthetizing[15] security of stained-glass windows.   36

In spite of my shattered dreams, I came to Birmingham with the hope that the white religious leadership of this community would see the justice of our cause and, with deep moral concern, would serve as the channel through which our just grievances could reach the power structure. I had hoped that each of you would understand. But again I have been disappointed. . . .   37

There was a time when the church was very powerful—in the time when the early Christians rejoiced at being deemed worthy to suffer for what they believed. In those days the church was not merely a thermometer that recorded the ideas and principles of popular opinion; it was a thermostat that transformed the mores of society. Whenever the early Christians entered a town, the people in power became disturbed and immediately sought to convict the Christians for being "disturbers of the peace" and "outside agitators." But the Christians pressed on, in the conviction that they were "a colony of heaven," called to obey God rather than man. Small in number, they were big in commitment. They were too God intoxicated to be "astronomically intimidated." By their effort and example they brought an end to such ancient evils as infanticide and gladiatorial contests.   38

Things are different now. So often the contemporary church is a weak, ineffectual voice with an uncertain sound. So often it is an arch-defender of the status quo. Far from being disturbed by the presence of the church, the power structure of the average community is consoled by the church's silent—and often even vocal—sanction of things as they are.   39

But the judgment of God is upon the church as never before. If today's church does not recapture the sacrificial spirit of the early church, it will lose its authenticity, forfeit the loyalty of millions, and be dismissed as an irrelevant social club with no meaning for the twentieth century. Every day I meet   40

---

15. anesthetizing: to render physically insensible

young people whose disappointment with the church has turned into outright disgust.

Perhaps I have once again been too optimistic. Is organized religion too   41
inextricably bound to the status quo to save our nation and the world? Perhaps I must turn my faith to the inner spiritual church, the church within the church, as the true *ekklesia*[16] and the hope of the world. But again I am thankful to God that some noble souls from the ranks of organized religion have broken loose from the paralyzing chains of conformity and joined us as active partners in the struggle for freedom. They have left their secure congregations and walked the streets of Albany, Georgia, with us. They have gone down the highways of the South on torturous rides for freedom. Yes, they have gone to jail with us. Some have been dismissed from their churches, have lost the support of their bishops and fellow ministers. But they have acted in the faith that right defeated is stronger than evil triumphant. Their witness has been the spiritual salt that has preserved the true meaning of the gospel in these troubled times. They have carved a tunnel of hope through the dark mountain of disappointment.

I hope the church as a whole will meet the challenge of this decisive   42
hour. But even if the church does not come to the aid of justice, I have no despair about the future. I have no fear about the outcome of our struggle in Birmingham, even if our motives are at present misunderstood. We will reach the goal of freedom in Birmingham and all over the nation, because the goal of America is freedom. Abused and scorned though we may be, our destiny is tied up with America's destiny. Before the pilgrims landed at Plymouth, we were here. Before the pen of Jefferson etched the majestic words of the Declaration of Independence across the pages of history, we were here. For more than two centuries our forebears labored in this country without wages; they made cotton king; they built the homes of their masters while suffering gross injustice and shameful humiliation—and yet out of a bottomless vitality they continued to thrive and develop. If the inexpressible cruelties of slavery could not stop us, the opposition we now face will surely fail. We will win our freedom because the sacred heritage of our nation and the eternal will of God are embodied in our echoing demands.

Before closing I feel impelled to mention one other point in your state-   43
ment that has troubled me profoundly. You warmly commended the Birmingham police force for keeping "order" and "preventing violence." I doubt that you would have so warmly commended the police force if you had seen its dogs sinking their teeth into unarmed, nonviolent Negroes. I doubt that you would so quickly commend the policemen if you were to

16. *ekklesia:* the spirit of the church (Greek)

observe their ugly and inhumane treatment of Negroes here in the city jail; if you were to watch them push and curse old Negro women and young Negro girls; if you were to see them slap and kick old Negro men and young boys; if you were to observe them, as they did on two occasions, refuse to give us food because we wanted to sing our grace together. I cannot join you in your praise of the Birmingham police department.

It is true that the police have exercised a degree of discipline in handling   44
the demonstrators. In this sense they have conducted themselves rather "non-violently" in public. But for what purpose? To preserve the evil system of segregation. Over the past few years I have consistently preached that nonviolence demands that the means we use must be as pure as the ends we seek. I have tried to make clear that it is wrong to use immoral means to attain moral ends. But now I must affirm that it is just as wrong, or perhaps even more so, to use moral means to preserve immoral ends. Perhaps Mr. Connor and his policemen have been rather nonviolent in public, as was Chief Pritchett in Albany, Georgia, but they have used the moral means of nonviolence to maintain the immoral end of racial injustice. As T. S. Eliot has said, "The last temptation is the greatest treason: To do the right deed for the wrong reason."

I wish you had commended the Negro sit-inners and demonstrators of   45
Birmingham for their sublime courage, their willingness to suffer, and their amazing discipline in the midst of great provocation. One day the South will recognize its real heroes. They will be the James Merediths, with the noble sense of purpose that enables them to face jeering and hostile mobs, and with the agonizing loneliness that characterizes the life of the pioneer. They will be old, oppressed, battered Negro women, symbolized in a seventy-two-year-old woman in Montgomery, Alabama, who rose up with a sense of dignity and with her people decided not to ride segregated buses, and who responded with ungrammatical profundity to one who inquired about her weariness: "My feets is tired, but my soul is at rest." They will be the young high school and college students, the young ministers of the gospel and a host of their elders, courageously and nonviolently sitting in at lunch counters and willingly going to jail for conscience' sake. One day the South will know that when these disinherited children of God sat down at lunch counters, they were in reality standing up for what is best in the American dream and for the most sacred values in our Judaeo-Christian heritage, thereby bringing our nation back to those great wells of democracy which were dug deep by the founding fathers in their formulation of the Constitution and the Declaration of Independence.

Never before have I written so long a letter. I'm afraid it is much too   46
long to take your precious time. I can assure you that it would have been

much shorter if I had been writing from a comfortable desk, but what else can one do when he is alone in a narrow jail cell, other than write long letters, think long thoughts, and pray long prayers?

If I have said anything in this letter that overstates the truth and indicates   47
an unreasonable impatience, I beg you to forgive me. If I have said anything that understates the truth and indicates my having a patience that allows me to settle for anything less than brotherhood, I beg God to forgive me.

I hope this letter finds you strong in the faith. I also hope that circum-   48
stances will soon make it possible for me to meet each of you, not as an integrationist or a civil rights leader but as a fellow clergyman and a Christian brother. Let us all hope that the dark clouds of racial prejudice will soon pass away and the deep fog of misunderstanding will be lifted from our fear-drenched communities, and in some not too distant tomorrow the radiant stars of love and brotherhood will shine over our great nation with all their scintillating[17] beauty.

> Yours in the cause of
> Peace and Brotherhood,
> MARTIN LUTHER KING, JR.

17. scintillating: to be animated or witty; sparkle

OPTIONS FOR READING LOGS: "LETTER FROM BIRMINGHAM JAIL"

1. Your immediate personal reaction to an essay can often begin a process that will lead you to an important insight. Complete the following statement by referring to a particular idea of King's in his "Letter from Birmingham Jail":

    "I was surprised by ＿＿＿＿＿＿＿＿ ."

    Freewrite to fill up at least three-fourths of a journal page. End your journal entry with a fresh new discovery you made about the text.

2. Use the double-entry journal technique to comment on powerful lines or passages in "Letter from Birmingham Jail." Draw a vertical line down the middle of your journal page to create two columns. In the left column, copy lines or passages that you particularly like or that you feel are important, for example, "Why does King say, 'there are two types of laws, just and unjust'?" In the right column, jot down word associations

and comments, being sure to include those from your personal experience as well as those from your reading. End your journal entry by selecting one of the lines or phrases and explaining why it held such power or meaning for you.

3. Does King's letter remind you of some recent event you observed or a particular time in your life? Briefly explore some of the connections you can make between that event or time period and the issues with which King is dealing in "Letter from Birmingham Jail." Jot down things that were similar to or different from the feelings and events King describes in "Letter from Birmingham Jail." End your journal entry by stating the central theme of this letter.

OPTIONS FOR WRITING ASSIGNMENTS: "LETTER FROM BIRMINGHAM JAIL"

1. Create an extended conversation between you and Martin Luther King, Jr. about his views in "Letter from Birmingham Jail." For example, what do you think about his statement, "One who breaks an unjust law must do so openly, lovingly, and with a willingness to accept the penalty." Your conversation might take the form of a question-and-answer interview, an argument representing two opposing points of view, or a freewheeling exploration of King's ideas and their implications.

2. Write a letter replying to King's "Letter from Birmingham Jail." Address King directly, giving your reaction to his letter. You may choose to praise, criticize, empathize, console, or inquire. Use any approach that is appropriate to express your reaction to the letter's exploration of social injustice and the need for an oppressed people to force such an unjust society to change, even if it means breaking the law.

3. In "Letter from Birmingham Jail" King explains why he has chosen the path of nonviolent protests against racist and unjust laws, urging his followers to break unjust laws peaceably, to be arrested willingly, and to go to jail as a protest. What causes does King give for this protest? In your opinion, what are the most important reasons he gives to justify doing what he advocates? Why is he no longer willing to wait for society to change its unjust laws? Be sure your thesis statement expresses your main point about the causes of King's discontent. Use that statement as the basis of a formal essay of five or more paragraphs.

4. If you were asked what "Letter from Birmingham Jail" means and what it teaches us about the rights of the individual in society, what would you say? Simply reading the letter once may not let you appreciate its

range of meaning fully. We often need to reread and write about a such a complex text before we fully appreciate its meaning. Explain the meaning of King's letter in a formal essay of five or more paragraphs. In your introductory paragraph, clearly state King's main idea. In your supporting paragraphs, focus your attention on any ideas in the letter that cause you to have questions and that help you clarify your main idea. In your commentary you will need to quote from the letter and to refer to specific passages to present your points clearly.

Sunday in the Park

1985

BEL KAUFMAN

 BEL KAUFMAN is a writer who was born in Germany but grew up in New York, where she graduated from Hunter College and Columbia University. She later taught high school and university classes. Her best-known novel is *Up the Down Staircase,* later made into a feature film. "Sunday in the Park" is a story about an issue that is an important concern in our increasingly violent society. In the story Kaufman challenges our notions of manners and proper behavior, forcing us to consider what we would do in a similar situation.

If you encountered a situation that threatened or challenged your codes of proper behavior, would you defend your honor and "stand up and fight"? Or would you feel it was more appropriate to turn away from your aggressor to avoid a confrontation?

It was still warm in the late-afternoon sun, and the city noises came 1 muffled through the trees in the park. She put her book down on the bench, removed her sunglasses, and sighed contentedly. Morton was reading the *Times Magazine* section, one arm flung around her shoulder; their three-year-old son, Larry, was playing in the sandbox: A faint breeze fanned her hair softly against her check. It was five-thirty of a Sunday afternoon, and the small playground, tucked away in a corner of the park was all but deserted. The swings and seesaws stood motionless and abandoned, the slides were empty, and only in the sandbox two little boys squatted diligently side by side. *How good this is,* she thought, and almost smiled at her sense of well-being. They must go out in the sun more often; Morton was so city-pale, cooped up all week inside the gray factorylike university. She squeezed his arm affectionately and glanced at Larry, delighting in the pointed little face frowning in concentration over the tunnel he was digging. The other boy suddenly stood up and with a quick, deliberate swing of his chubby arm threw a spadeful of sand at Larry. It just missed his head. Larry continued digging; the boy remained standing, shovel raised, stolid and impassive.

"No, no, little boy." She shook her finger at him, her eyes searching for   2
the child's mother or nurse. "We mustn't throw sand. It may get in someone's
eyes and hurt. We must play nicely in the nice sandbox." The boy looked at
her in unblinking expectancy. He was about Larry's age but perhaps ten
pounds heavier, a husky little boy with none of Larry's quickness and sensitiv-
ity in his face. Where was his mother? The only other people left in the
playground were two women and a little girl on roller skates leaving now
through the gate, and a man on a bench a few feet away. He was a big man,
and he seemed to be taking up the whole bench as he held the Sunday comics
close to his face. She supposed he was the child's father. He did not look up
from his comics, but spat once deftly out of the corner of his mouth. She
turned her eyes away.

At that moment, as swiftly as before, the fat little boy threw another   3
spadeful of sand at Larry. This time some of it landed on his hair and forehead.
Larry looked up at his mother, his mouth tentative; her expression would
tell him whether to cry or not.

Her first instinct was to rush to her son, brush the sand out of his hair,   4
and punish the other child, but she controlled it. She always said that she
wanted Larry to learn to fight his own battles.

"Don't *do* that, little boy," she said sharply, leaning forward on the   5
bench. "You mustn't throw sand!"

The man on the bench moved his mouth as if to spit again, but instead   6
he spoke. He did not look at her, but at the boy only.

"You go right ahead, Joe," he said loudly. "Throw all you want. This   7
here is a *public* sandbox."

She felt a sudden weakness in her knees as she glanced at Morton. He   8
had become aware of what was happening. He put his *Times* down carefully
on his lap and turned his fine, lean face toward the man, smiling the shy,
apologetic smile he might have offered a student in pointing out an error in
his thinking. When he spoke to the man, it was with his usual reasonableness.

"You're quite right," he said pleasantly, "but just because this is a public   9
place. . . ."

The man lowered his funnies and looked at Morton. He looked at him   10
from head to foot, slowly and deliberately. "Yeah?" His insolent voice was
edged with menace. "My kid's got just as good right here as yours, and if
he feels like throwing sand, he'll throw it, and if you don't like it, you can
take your kid the hell out of here."

The children were listening, their eyes and mouths wide open, their   11
spades forgotten in small fists. She noticed the muscle in Morton's jaw tighten.
He was rarely angry; he seldom lost his temper. She was suffused with a

tenderness for her husband and an impotent rage against the man for involving him in a situation so alien and so distasteful to him.

"Now, just a minute," Morton said courteously, "you must realize . . ."   12

"Aw, shut up," said the man.   13

Her heart began to pound. Morton half rose; the *Times* slid to the   14
ground. Slowly the other man stood up. He took a couple of steps toward Morton, then stopped. He flexed his great arms, waiting. She pressed her trembling knees together. Would there be violence, fighting? How dreadful, how incredible. . . . She must do something, stop them, call for help. She wanted to put her hand on her husband's sleeve, to pull him down, but for some reason she didn't.

Morton adjusted his glasses. He was very pale. "This is ridiculous," he   15
said unevenly. "I must ask you . . ."

"Oh, yeah?" said the man. He stood with his legs spread apart, rocking   16
a little, looking at Morton with utter scorn. "You and who else?"

For a moment the two men looked at each other nakedly. Then Morton   17
turned his back on the man and said quietly, "Come on, let's get out of here." He walked awkwardly, almost limping with self-consciousness, to the sandbox. He stooped and lifted Larry and his shovel out.

At once Larry came to life, his face lost its rapt expression and he began   18
to kick and cry. "I don't *want* to go home, I want to play better, I don't *want* any supper, I don't *like* supper. . . ." It became a chant as they walked, pulling their child between them, his feet dragging on the ground. In order to get to the exit gate they had to pass the bench where the man sat sprawling again. She was careful not to look at him. With all the dignity she could summon, she pulled Larry's sandy, perspiring little hand, while Morton pulled the other. Slowly and with head high she walked with her husband and child out of the playground.

Her first feeling was one of relief that a fight had been avoided, that no one   19
was hurt. Yet beneath it there was a layer of something else, something heavy and inescapable. She sensed that it was more than just an unpleasant incident, more than defeat of reason by force. She felt dimly it had something to do with her and Morton, something acutely personal, familiar, and important.

Suddenly Morton spoke. "It wouldn't have proved anything."   20

"What?" she asked.   21

"A fight. It wouldn't have proved anything beyond the fact that he's   22
bigger than I am."

"Of course," she said.   23

"The only possible outcome," he continued reasonably, "would have   24
been—what? My glasses broken, perhaps a tooth or two replaced, a couple of days' work missed—and for what? For justice? For truth?"

"Of course," she repeated. She quickened her step. She wanted only to   25
get home and to busy herself with her familiar tasks; perhaps then the feeling,
glued like heavy plaster on her heart, would be gone. *Of all the stupid,*
despicable bullies, she thought, pulling harder on Larry's hand. The child was
still crying. Always before she had felt a tender pity for his defenseless little
body, the frail arms, the narrow shoulders with sharp, winglike shoulder
blades, the thin and unsure legs, but now her mouth tightened in resentment.

"Stop crying," she said sharply. "I'm ashamed of you!" She felt as if all   26
three of them were tracking mud along the street. The child cried louder.

If there had been an issue involved, she thought, *if there had been something*   27
to fight for. . . . But what else could he possibly have done? Allow himself to be
beaten? Attempt to educate the man? Call a policeman? "Officer, there's a
man in the park who won't stop his child from throwing sand on mine. . . ."
The whole thing was as silly as that, and not worth thinking about.

"Can't you keep him quiet, for Pete's sake?" Morton asked irritably.   28

"What do you suppose I've been trying to do?" she said.   29

Larry pulled back, dragging his feet.   30

"If you can't discipline this child, I will," Morton snapped, making a   31
move toward the boy.

But her voice stopped him. She was shocked to hear it, thin and cold   32
and penetrating with contempt. "Indeed?" she heard herself say. "You and
who else?"

◈   ◈   ◈

OPTIONS FOR READING LOGS: "SUNDAY IN THE PARK"

1. Use the double-entry journal technique to discover meaning in "Sunday
    in the Park." Separate your journal page into two columns by drawing
    a vertical line down the page. In the left column, keep a running list of
    three to five "what" or "why" questions that occur to you as you are
    reading, such as, "Why does Larry's mother decide against intervening
    at the first hint of violence between her husband and the father of the
    boy who threw the sand?" When you finish your list, use the right column
    to answer your questions as completely as you can. Then demonstrate
    your understanding of the text by jotting down the main idea of the
    story.

2. Copy the most powerful line or passage in "Sunday in the Park," such
    as, "Beneath it there was a layer of something else." Then, drawing on

your personal experience, use anecdotes and examples to explain fully why that particular passage held such power or meaning for you.

3. Create some graphics, such as a cartoon or caricature of one of the characters described in "Sunday in the Park." Describe your graphic, using as many specific details as possible. End your journal entry by stating the main idea the author was trying to communicate in "Sunday in the Park."

OPTIONS FOR WRITING ASSIGNMENTS: "SUNDAY IN THE PARK"

1. Does the situation in "Sunday in the Park" remind you of an experience that happened to you when you "turned the other cheek" and walked away from a confrontation? Compose a narrative essay that focuses on that event. Throughout your essay, concentrate on using vivid details and descriptions to help make that situation come alive for your reader.

2. In "Sunday in the Park," Larry's mother reacts harshly to her husband's decision to walk away from the explosive situation. In five or more paragraphs, write a formal essay either defending her feelings of contempt toward her husband or criticizing her for not standing behind her husband's actions. Make sure that you have a thesis statement declaring your position and that you support it in each paragraph with convincing arguments to back up your position.

3. At the end of "Sunday in the Park," you should have developed a particular attitude toward Morton, whether favorable or unfavorable. Write a formal essay of five or more paragraphs explaining how you formed your attitude. Come up with a thesis statement that expresses your point of view. You may want to use anecdotes from your own personal experience for support.

4. Write a formal essay of five or more paragraphs explaining the societal knowledge gained by the mother in "Sunday in the Park." Focus on parts of the story that caused you to have genuine questions, such as, "Why does Larry's mother wonder if there is anything really at stake?" In a thesis statement at the end of your introductory paragraph, clearly present what you believe the mother is thinking when she wonders if the whole thing is "not worth thinking about." In the remaining paragraphs you will need to quote from the story and refer to specific passages to clarify and support your thesis statement.

The World Is Too Much with Us

1807

WILLIAM WORDSWORTH

 WILLIAM WORDSWORTH was born in England's Lake District in 1770. Together with Samuel Taylor Coleridge, he published *Lyrical Ballads,* an important book that introduced Romanticism to English poetry. Wordsworth
later held the honor of being poet laureate of England and is remembered
especially for his poems of nature. In "The World Is Too Much with Us,"
he laments humankind's loss of communion with nature.

*As you read this poem, consider whether any of your individual actions
contribute to the make-up of our business-oriented society. Have you
ever contemplated escaping from our world of "getting and spending"?
What are the alternatives to the workaday society to which we belong?*

The world is too much with us; late and soon, 1
 Getting and spending, we lay waste our powers;
 Little we see in Nature that is ours;
We have given our hearts away, a sordid boon!
This Sea that bares her bosom to the moon, 5
The winds that will be howling at all hours,
And are up-gathered now like sleeping flowers,
For this, for everything, we are out of tune;
It moves us not.—Great God! I'd rather be
A Pagan suckled in a creed outworn; 10
So might I, standing on this pleasant lea,
Have glimpses that would make me less forlorn;
Have sight of Proteus[1] rising from the sea;
Or hear old Triton[2] blow his wreathèd horn.

1. Proteus: ancient Greek sea god 2. Triton: a sea god in a Greek myth

OPTIONS FOR READING LOGS: "THE WORLD IS TOO MUCH WITH US"

1. Use the double-entry journal technique to comment on powerful lines or passages in "The World Is Too Much with Us." Draw a vertical line down the middle of your journal page to create two columns. In the left column, copy lines or passages that you particularly like or that you feel are somehow important—for example, "For this, for everything, we are out of tune." In the right column, jot down word associations and comments, including those from your personal experience as well as from your reading. End your journal entry by selecting one line or phrase and explaining why it held such power or meaning for you.

2. Examine any apparent contradictions you see in "The World Is Too Much with Us." For example, isn't financial progress a positive step toward a more civilized society? Use freewriting to examine your personal response to any ideas that seem on the surface to be contradictory. Try beginning with a question and writing a few lines of response. Then, if this process raises new questions, write responses to them also. Without worrying about form, allow a free flow of ideas so you will end up with some new discoveries about the price of progress.

3. Create an original poem that explores your own societal identity. Start your poem with the following lines, and fill in the missing words.

    The world is _____

    _____ ,

    we _____ ;

    Little we see in _____ that

    is ours. . . .

    Then, continuing to follow the pattern of "The World Is Too Much with Us," add lines that characterize the condition of our current situation. Your poem should end, as Wordsworth's does, with six lines telling what you would "rather be."

OPTIONS FOR WRITING ASSIGNMENTS: "THE WORLD IS TOO MUCH WITH US"

1. "The World Is Too Much with Us" could be seen as having some of the characteristics of a prophecy. The images are vivid and clear, yet they are also mythical and mysterious, containing a hidden or symbolic meaning. Have you ever had a strange prophecy or a puzzling vision of the future? Recreate the prophecy as a story or poem, using concrete

details, vivid imagery, and, if possible, an outcry: "Great God!" Explore the value of the prophecy in defining your societal values. What do you feel the vision is trying to tell you about who you are? What can you learn about yourself from analyzing the vision? Does it help you make any generalizations about your place in society or the world you live in?

2. Does "The World Is Too Much with Us" remind you of a personal experience that is somehow connected to your social identity? Compose a narrative or descriptive essay that focuses on a similar experience from your life. Write a thesis statement that points out the significance of that experience in your life. Throughout your essay, concentrate on using vivid details and descriptions to help recreate your memory. As an example, you might remember how you made a discovery about the importance of staying in touch with your natural environment, even though you did not know its full significance at the time. Your thesis statement might be worded like this: "Little did I know what effect my views about environment would have on society as a whole."

3. In "The World Is Too Much with Us," the narrator reveals strong feelings of dismay about humankind's being out of touch with the natural world. Is he advocating a return to a simpler way of life? What are your feelings about the narrator's dismay? Would you call his position overly romantic or idealistic, or would you say he has every right to protest?

4. Write a well-developed essay explaining the meaning of "The World Is Too Much with Us." Focus your attention on parts of the poem that you have genuine questions about, such as, "Does the narrator display feelings of complete hopelessness about the condition of humankind, or is there still hope?" You should begin your essay with an arguable thesis statement, such as, "In 'The World Is Too Much with Us', the narrator is merely cautioning us that we should not lose sight of beauty and power inherent in the natural world." Clarify and support your central argument with quotes from the poem and references to specific passages.

From

The Myth of Sisyphus

1955

ALBERT CAMUS

 ALBERT CAMUS was a French author and existential philosopher, certainly one of the most important writers and thinkers of the twentieth century. He won the Nobel Prize for Literature in 1957.

Although one of his common themes was the absurdity of life, he encouraged people to respond to that absurdity with courage, not despair. Many people want to blame a parent, an employer, a spouse, society, government—all are suitable candidates—for their own personal failures. However, like Sisyphus, Camus would conclude that we are each responsible for our own fate and have no one except ourselves to blame for our own misery. Accepting responsibility for one's own happiness, even in an absurd world, is a necessary first step: "It makes of fate a human matter, which must be settled among men."

As you read this essay, think about the number of people in today's world who are caught up in the endless struggle of staying busy and working endlessly with no reward except money. Have you, like Sisyphus, ever felt caught up in "futile and hopeless labor"? Have you ever blamed others for your own limitations and failures?

The gods had condemned Sisyphus to ceaselessly rolling a rock to the top of a mountain, whence the stone would fall back of its own weight. They had thought with some reason that there is no more dreadful punishment than futile and hopeless labor. 1

If one believes Homer, Sisyphus was the wisest and most prudent of mortals. According to another tradition, however, he was disposed to practice the profession of highwayman. I see no contradiction in this. Opinions differ as to the reasons why he became the futile laborer of the underworld. To begin with, he is accused of a certain levity[1] in regard to the gods. He stole 2

---

1. levity: a lack of appropriate seriousness or earnestness

their secrets. Aegina, the daughter of Aesopus, was carried off by Jupiter. The father was shocked by that disappearance and complained to Sisyphus. He, who knew of the abduction, offered to tell about it on condition that Aesopus would give water to the citadel of Corinth. To the celestial thunderbolts he preferred the benediction[2] of water. He was punished for this in the underworld. Homer tells us also that Sisyphus had put Death in chains. Pluto could not endure the sight of his deserted, silent empire. He dispatched the god of War, who liberated Death from the hands of her conqueror.

It is said also that Sisyphus, being near to death, rashly wanted to test   3 his wife's love. He ordered her to cast his unburied body into the middle of the public square. Sisyphus woke up in the underworld. And there, annoyed by an obedience so contrary to human love, he obtained from Pluto permission to return to earth in order to chastise his wife. But when he had seen again the face of this world, enjoyed water and sun, warm stones and the sea, he no longer wanted to go back to the infernal darkness. Recalls, signs of anger, warnings were of no avail. Many years more he lived facing the curve of the gulf, the sparkling sea, and the smiles of earth. A decree of the gods was necessary. Mercury came and seized the impudent man by the collar and, snatching him from his joys, led him forcibly back to the underworld, where his rock was ready for him.

You have already grasped that Sisyphus is the absurd hero. He *is*, as much   4 through his passions as through his torture. His scorn of the gods, his hatred of death, and his passion for life won him that unspeakable penalty in which the whole being is exerted toward accomplishing nothing. This is the price that must be paid for the passions of this earth. Nothing is told us about Sisyphus in the underworld. Myths are made for the imagination to breathe life into them. As for this myth, one sees merely the whole effort of a body straining to raise the huge stone, to roll it and push it up a slope a hundred times over; one sees the face screwed up, the cheek tight against the stone, the shoulder bracing the claycovered mass, the foot wedging it, the fresh start with arms outstretched, the wholly human security of two earth-clotted hands. At the very end of this long effort measured by skyless space and time without depth, the purpose is achieved. Then Sisyphus watches the stone rush down in a few moments toward that lower world whence he will have to push it up again toward the summit. He goes back down to the plain.

It is during that return, that pause, that Sisyphus interests me. A face   5 that toils so close to stones is already stone itself! I see that man going back down with a heavy yet measured step toward the torment of which he will never know the end. That hour like a breathing-space which returns as surely

2. benediction: an utterance of good wishes

as his suffering, that is the hour of consciousness. At each of those moments when he leaves the heights and gradually sinks toward the lairs of the gods, he is superior to his fate. He is stronger than his rock.

If this myth is tragic, that is because its hero is conscious. Where would his torture be, indeed, if at every step the hope of succeeding upheld him? The workman of today works every day in his life at the same tasks, and this fate is no less absurd. But it is tragic only at the rare moments when it becomes conscious. Sisyphus, proletarian of the gods, powerless and rebellious, knows the whole extent of his wretched condition: it is what he thinks of during his descent. The lucidity[3] that was to constitute his torture at the same time crowns his victory. There is no fate that cannot be surmounted by scorn.   6

If the descent is thus sometimes performed in sorrow, it can also take place in joy. This word is not too much. Again I fancy Sisyphus returning toward his rock, and the sorrow was in the beginning. When the images of earth cling too tightly to memory, when the call of happiness becomes too insistent, it happens that melancholy rises in man's heart: this is the rock's victory, this is the rock itself. The boundless grief is too heavy to bear. These are our nights of Gethsemane.[4] But crushing truths perish from being acknowledged. Thus, Oedipus at the outset obeys fate without knowing it. But from the moment he knows, his tragedy begins. Yet at the same moment, blind and desperate, he realizes that the only bond linking him to the world is the cool hand of a girl. Then a tremendous remark rings out: "Despite so many ordeals, my advanced age and the nobility of my soul make me conclude that all is well." Sophocles' Oedipus, like Dostoevsky's Kirilov, thus gives the recipe for the absurd victory. Ancient wisdom confirms modern heroism.   7

One does not discover the absurd without being tempted to write a manual of happiness. "What! by such narrow ways—?" There is but one world, however. Happiness and the absurd are two sons of the same earth. They are inseparable. It would be a mistake to say that happiness necessarily springs from the absurd discovery. It happens as well that the feeling of the absurd springs from happiness. "I conclude that all is well," says Oedipus, and that remark is sacred. It echoes in the wild and limited universe of man. It teaches that all is not, has not been, exhausted. It drives out of this world a god who had come into it with dissatisfaction and a preference for futile sufferings. It makes of fate a human matter, which must be settled among men.   8

All Sisyphus' silent joy is contained therein. His fate belongs to him. His rock is his thing. Likewise, the absurd man, when he contemplates his torment,   9

---

3. lucidity: easily understood; intelligible   4. Gethsemane: garden that was the scene of the agony and betrayal of Jesus Christ

silences all the idols. In the universe suddenly restored to its silence, the myriad wondering little voices of the earth rise up. Unconscious, secret calls, invitations from all the faces, they are the necessary reverse and price of victory. There is no sun without shadow, and it is essential to know the night. The absurd man says yes and his effort will henceforth be unceasing. If there is a personal fate, there is no higher destiny, or at least there is but one which he concludes is inevitable and despicable. For the rest, he knows himself to be the master of his days. At that subtle moment when man glances backward over his life, Sisyphus returning toward his rock, in that slight pivoting he contemplates that series of unrelated actions which becomes his fate, created by him, combined under his memory's eye and soon sealed by his death. Thus, convinced of the wholly human origin of all that is human, a blind man eager to see who knows that the night has no end, he is still on the go. The rock is still rolling.

I leave Sisyphus at the foot of the mountain! One always finds one's   10
burden again. But Sisyphus teaches the higher fidelity[5] that negates the gods and raises rocks. He too concludes that all is well. This universe henceforth without a master seems to him neither sterile nor futile. Each atom of that stone, each mineral flake of that night-filled mountain, in itself forms a world. The struggle itself toward the heights is enough to fill a man's heart. One must imagine Sisyphus happy.

5. fidelity: strict observance of promises and duties

OPTIONS FOR READING LOGS: FROM *THE MYTH OF SISYPHUS*

1. Use the double-entry journal technique, asking three to five "what" or "why" questions that will help you discover meaning in this excerpt from *The Myth of Sisyphus*. Draw a vertical line down the middle of your journal page to create two columns, and in the left column, enter the questions that occur to you as you are reading, such as "Why does Camus call the story of Sisyphus a 'myth'?" or "What is the source of Sisyphus's happiness?" When you finish your list, answer your questions as completely as you can in the right column. To demonstrate your understanding of this essay, end your journal entry by jotting down its main idea.
2. Tell a parallel story, based on your own life, that you recalled while reading this excerpt from *The Myth of Sisyphus*. Does the essay remind

you of a job or some other experience that felt like "futile and hopeless labor"? Explain the struggles involved in your experience and tell how you responded to the tedium.

3. Examine your personal reaction to "From *The Myth of Sisyphus*" by completing one of the following statements:

    A. "I was confused by _____ ."
    B. "I was struck by _____ ."
    C. "I was surprised by _____ ."

    Develop your journal entry by adding detailed explanations from your own experiences as well as from events in the essay. End your journal entry by stating the central idea of the essay.

OPTIONS FOR WRITING ASSIGNMENTS: FROM *THE MYTH OF SISYPHUS*

1. Expand and develop one of your reading logs for "From *The Myth of Sisyphus*" into a more polished piece of writing that explores its subject matter in greater range and depth. Begin with a thesis statement that reveals an important discovery you made about your social identity and its price, even though the discovery may not have been an earth-shaking event. Arrange your story in a clear chronological order, adding enough specific details to make the event come alive for your reader. By the end of your essay, you should have convinced your reader of the significance of your self-discovery.

2. Why does Camus think that Sisyphus is an appropriate symbol of humankind's struggle? Why does he say that "the struggle itself toward the heights is enough to fill a man's heart"? Write a formal essay of five or more paragraphs showing that absurdity can lead to happiness rather than despair. Explain the logic of *The Myth of Sisyphus* to someone who has not yet read it. Come up with a thesis that states the essay's main idea and goes on to explain the reasons Camus gives for arriving at his conclusions.

3. Write a formal essay of five or more paragraphs arguing for or against Camus's ideas in *The Myth of Sisyphus*. Focus on ideas that raised genuine questions for you, such as "Why is Sisyphus 'stronger than his rock'?" End your introductory paragraph with a thesis statement that makes an arguable point about the central theme of the essay. Brainstorm or prewrite to develop support for your thesis statement. In the body of your

essay, you will need to quote from the essay and refer to specific words and passages to clarify and support your argument.

4. In *The Myth of Sisyphus*, Camus points out the absurdity of the human condition. Interview a friend or a family member about whether his or her job includes performing repetitive tasks. Ask the person to share with you the thoughts and feelings that make those tasks easier. Before the interview, spend some time drawing up three to five questions that might open up the conversation. Then write an essay of five or more paragraphs showing how that person's attitude toward work affects his or her attitude toward life in general. In your essay you might want to include biographical information that shows how your friend or family member's experiences fit into society's definition of struggle and happiness.

Swaddling Clothes

1966

YUKIO MISHIMA
TRANSLATED BY IVAN MORRIS

 YUKIO MISHIMA is one of the best-known Japanese writers. He wrote many short stories and novels before his death in 1970. In "Swaddling Clothes," Mishima explores the feelings of a young woman struggling to understand a shocking experience: a new nurse for her baby unexpectedly gives birth in her home, and the infant is callously wrapped in newspapers due to its illegitimate state. This upsetting event forces the young woman to examine her own social conscience and morality.

Have you some memory of a defining event that suddenly made you aware of social differences? As you read "Swaddling Clothes," reflect on the knowledge the young woman acquires about herself and the society in which she lives. What is her husband's attitude to the experience? Reflect on what the woman finally begins to understand about the society she inhabits and its attitudes toward those who are less fortunate.

He was always busy, Toshiko's husband. Even tonight he had to dash off to an appointment, leaving her to go home alone by taxi. But what else could a woman expect when she married an actor—an attractive one? No doubt she had been foolish to hope that he would spend the evening with her. And yet he must have known how she dreaded going back to their house, unhomely with its Western-style furniture and with the bloodstains still showing on the floor.

Toshiko had been oversensitive since girlhood: that was her nature. As the result of constant worrying she never put on weight, and now, an adult woman, she looked more like a transparent picture than a creature of flesh and blood. Her delicacy of spirit was evident to her most casual acquaintance.

Earlier that evening, when she had joined her husband at a night club, she had been shocked to find him entertaining friends with an account of "the incident." Sitting there in his American-style suit, puffing at a cigarette, he had seemed to her almost a stranger.

"It's a fantastic story," he was saying, gesturing flamboyantly[1] as if in an attempt to outweigh the attractions of the dance band. "Here this new nurse for our baby arrives from the employment agency, and the very first thing I notice about her is her stomach. It's enormous—as if she had a pillow stuck under her kimono! No wonder, I thought, for I soon saw that she could eat more than the rest of us put together. She polished off the contents of our rice bin like that. . . ." He snapped his fingers. " 'Gastric dilation'—that's how she explained her girth and her appetite. Well, the day before yesterday we heard groans and moans coming from the nursery. We rushed in and found her squatting on the floor, holding her stomach in her two hands, and moaning like a cow. Next to her our baby lay in his cot, scared out of his wits and crying at the top of his lungs. A pretty scene, I can tell you!"   4

"So the cat was out of the bag?" suggested one of their friends, a film actor like Toshiko's husband.   5

"Indeed it was! And it gave me the shock of my life. You see, I'd completely swallowed that story about 'gastric dilation.' Well, I didn't waste any time. I rescued our good rug from the floor and spread a blanket for her to lie on. The whole time the girl was yelling like a stuck pig. By the time the doctor from the maternity clinic arrived, the baby had already been born. But our sitting room was a pretty shambles!"   6

"Oh, that I'm sure of!" said another of their friends, and the whole company burst into laughter.   7

Toshiko was dumbfounded to hear her husband discussing the horrifying happening as though it were no more than an amusing incident which they chanced to have witnessed. She shut her eyes for a moment and all at once she saw the newborn baby lying before her: on the parquet[2] floor the infant lay, and his frail body was wrapped in bloodstained newspapers.   8

Toshiko was sure that the doctor had done the whole thing out of spite. As if to emphasize his scorn for this mother who had given birth to a bastard under such sordid conditions, he had told his assistant to wrap the baby in some loose newspapers, rather than proper swaddling. This callous treatment of the newborn child had offended Toshiko. Overcoming her disgust at the entire scene, she had fetched a brand-new piece of flannel from her cupboard and, having swaddled the baby in it, had lain him carefully in an armchair.   9

This all had taken place in the evening after her husband had left the house. Toshiko had told him nothing of it, fearing that he would think her   10

1. flamboyantly: extravagantly   2. parquet: pattern composed of short strips or blocks of wood, often used for wood floors

oversoft, oversentimental; yet the scene had engraved itself deeply in her mind. Tonight she sat silently thinking back on it, while the jazz orchestra brayed and her husband chatted cheerfully with his friends. She knew that she would never forget the sight of the baby, wrapped in stained newspapers and lying on the floor—it was a scene fit for a butchershop. Toshiko, whose own life had been spent in solid comfort, poignantly felt the wretchedness of the illegitimate baby.

I am the only person to have witnessed its shame, the thought occurred   11
to her. The mother never saw the child lying there in its newspaper wrappings, and the baby itself of course didn't know. I alone shall have to preserve that terrible scene in my memory. When the baby grows up and wants to find out about his birth, there will be no one to tell him, so long as I preserve silence. How strange that I should have this feeling of guilt! After all, it was I who took him up from the floor, swathed him properly in flannel, and laid him down to sleep in the armchair.

They left the night club and Toshiko stepped into the taxi that her   12
husband had called for her. "Take this lady to Ushigom" he told the driver and shut the door from the outside. Toshiko gazed through the window at her husband's smiling face and noticed his strong, white teeth. Then she leaned back in the seat, oppressed by the knowledge that their life together was in some way too easy, too painless. It would have been difficult for her to put her thoughts into words. Through the rear window of the taxi she took a last look at her husband. He was striding along the street toward his Nash car, and soon the back of his rather garish tweed coat had blended with the figures of the passers-by.

The taxi drove off, passed down a street dotted with bars and then by a   13
theatre, in front of which the throngs of people jostled each other on the pavement. Although the performance had only just ended, the lights had already been turned out and in the half dark outside it was depressingly obvious that the cherry blossoms decorating the front of the theatre were merely scraps of white paper.

Even if that baby should grow up in ignorance of the secret of his birth,   14
he can never become a respectable citizen, reflected Toshiko, pursuing the same train of thought. Those soiled newspaper swaddling clothes will be the symbol of his entire life. But why should I keep worrying about him so much? Is it because I feel uneasy about the future of my own child? Say twenty years from now, when our boy will have grown up into a fine, carefully educated young man, one day by a quirk of fate he meets that other boy, who then will also have turned twenty. And say that the other boy, who has been sinned against, savagely stabs him with a knife. . . .

It was a warm, overcast April night, but thoughts of the future made   15
Toshiko feel cold and miserable. She shivered on the back seat of the car.

No, when the time comes I shall take my son's place, she told herself   16
suddenly. Twenty years from now I shall be forty-three. I shall go to that
young man and tell him straight out about everything—about his newspaper
swaddling clothes, and about how I went and wrapped him in flannel.

The taxi ran along the dark wide road that was bordered by the park and   17
by the Imperial Palace moat. In the distance, Toshiko noticed the pinpricks of
light which came from the blocks of tall office buildings.

Twenty years from now that wretched child will be in utter misery. He   18
will be living a desolate, hopeless, poverty-stricken existence—a lonely rat.
What else could happen to a baby who has had such a birth? He'll be
wandering through the streets by himself, cursing his father, loathing his
mother.

No doubt Toshiko derived a certain satisfaction from her somber   19
thoughts: she tortured herself with them without cease. The taxi approached
Hanzomon and drove past the compound of the British Embassy. At that
point the famous rows of cherry trees were spread out before Toshiko in all
their purity. On the spur of the moment she decided to go and view the
blossoms by herself in the dark night. It was a strange decision for a timid
and unadventurous young woman, but then she was in a strange state of
mind and she dreaded the return home. That evening all sorts of unsettling
fancies had burst open in her mind.

She crossed the wide street—a slim, solitary figure in the darkness. As a   20
rule when she walked in the traffic Toshiko used to cling fearfully to her
companion, but tonight she darted alone between the cars and a moment
later had reached the long narrow park that borders the Palace moat. Chidori-
gafuchi, it is called—the Abyss of the Thousand Birds.

Tonight the whole park had become a grove of blossoming cherry trees.   21
Under the calm cloudy sky the blossoms formed a mass of solid whiteness.
The paper lanterns that hung from wires between the trees had been put
out; in their place electric light bulbs, red, yellow, and green, shone dully
beneath the blossoms. It was well past ten o'clock and most of the flower-
viewers had gone home. As the occasional passers-by strolled through the
park, they would automatically kick aside the empty bottles or crush the
waste paper beneath their feet.

Newspapers, thought Toshiko, her mind going back once again to those   22
happenings. Bloodstained newspapers. If a man were ever to hear of that
piteous birth and know that it was he who had lain there, it would ruin his
entire life. To think that I, a perfect stranger, should from now on have to
keep such a secret—the secret of a man's whole existence. . . .

Lost in these thoughts, Toshiko walked on through the park. Most of   23
the people still remaining there were quiet couples; no one paid her any
attention. She noticed two people sitting on a stone bench beside the moat,

not looking at the blossoms, but gazing silently at the water. Pitch black it was, and swathed in heavy shadows. Beyond the moat the somber forest of the Imperial Palace blocked her view. The trees reached up, to form a solid dark mass against the night sky. Toshiko walked slowly along the path beneath the blossoms hanging heavily overhead.

On a stone bench, slightly apart from the others, she noticed a pale object— 24 not, as she had at first imagined, a pile of cherry blossoms, nor a garment forgotten by one of the visitors to the park. Only when she came closer did she see that it was a human form lying on the bench. Was it, she wondered, one of those miserable drunks often to be seen sleeping in public places? Obviously not, for the body had been systematically covered with newspapers, and it was the whiteness of those papers that had attracted Toshiko's attention. Standing by the bench, she gazed down at the sleeping figure.

It was a man in a brown jersey who lay there, curled up on layers of 25 newspapers, other newspapers covering him. No doubt this had become his normal night residence now that spring had arrived. Toshiko gazed down at the man's dirty, unkempt hair, which in places had become hopelessly matted. As she observed the sleeping figure wrapped in its newspapers, she was inevitably reminded of the baby who had lain on the floor in its wretched swaddling clothes. The shoulder of the man's jersey rose and fell in the darkness in time with his heavy breathing.

It seemed to Toshiko that all her fears and premonitions[3] had suddenly 26 taken concrete form. In the darkness the man's pale forehead stood out, and it was a young forehead, though carved with the wrinkles of long poverty and hardship. His khaki trousers had been slightly pulled up; on his sockless feet he wore a pair of battered gym shoes. She could not see his face and suddenly had an overmastering desire to get one glimpse of it.

She walked to the head of the bench and looked down. The man's head 27 was half buried in his arms, but Toshiko could see that he was surprisingly young. She noticed the thick eyebrows and the fine bridge of his nose. His slightly open mouth was alive with youth.

But Toshiko had approached too close. In the silent night the newspaper 28 bedding rustled, and abruptly the man opened his eyes. Seeing the young woman standing directly beside him, he raised himself with a jerk, and his eyes lit up. A second later a powerful hand reached out and seized Toshiko by her slender wrist.

She did not feel in the least afraid and made no effort to free herself. In 29 a flash the thought had struck her. Ah, so the twenty years have already gone by! The forest of the Imperial Palace was pitch dark and utterly silent.

3. premonition: a feeling of anticipation or of anxiety over a future event

OPTIONS FOR READING LOGS: "SWADDLING CLOTHES"

1. Use clustering to draw a concept (idea) map that explores the meaning of "Swaddling Clothes." Recalling vivid details and experiences from the story, draw balloons, clusters, flowcharts, visual symbols, outlines, or diagrams to examine the relationship of one idea to another. When you have created your concept map, examine it closely and write a brief entry that explains your graphic depiction. Conclude with a statement of the central theme of the story.

2. Examine your personal reaction to "Swaddling Clothes" by contrasting the reactions that the wife and the husband have to the unexpected birth. How do their responses reflect different social values and attitudes? List their differences, showing the chief characteristics of each difference and the actions that reveal them. End your journal entry by explaining what you believe is the theme of the story.

3. Search your memory of your own life for some similar story. Does the young woman's struggle with her conscience remind you of a time when you had to consider the situation of someone less fortunate than you? Also consider your reaction when someone asks you for money on the street. Are you repelled or sympathetic? End your journal entry by stating the theme of "Swaddling Clothes."

OPTIONS FOR WRITING ASSIGNMENTS: "SWADDLING CLOTHES"

1. Develop one of your reading logs for "Swaddling Clothes" into a more polished piece of writing that explores in greater range and depth a moment of personal insight or development. Use an appropriate form, such as a poem, a fictional story, a personal narrative, or an essay, to examine your central idea.

2. Explore your own reaction to people—the homeless, panhandlers, or illegal aliens—who exist on the fringes or even outside of our society. Write a narrative or descriptive essay exploring some contact you have had with such an individual or group. What specific personal insight or insights did you gain from the experience? Does your experience in any way resemble that of the young woman in "Swaddling Clothes," who searches her conscience to clarify what she believes is right? Throughout your essay, present your main point clearly in a thesis statement in your first paragraph. Concentrate on using vivid details, dialogue, and descriptions to help recreate the event for your reader.

3. Write a letter to the young wife in "Swaddling Clothes," telling her what the story has taught you about society and its treatment of its less fortunate members. Address her directly, giving your own values and beliefs and telling her how they relate to the story. Use the letter to express your own point of view. You may choose to praise, criticize, or inquire, taking the approach that is most appropriate for expressing your reaction to the story.

4. Write a formal essay of five or more paragraphs explaining the point that Yukio Mishima wants to make clear in his story "Swaddling Clothes." Focus your attention on parts of the story that you have genuine questions about, such as "Why do the husband and wife have such different reactions to the unexpected birth? What is it about the experience that causes the wife to become concerned with the future of the illegitimate child? What draws her so close to the young homeless man on the park bench? Why does she 'not feel in the least afraid and made no effort to free herself' when he grabs her wrist?" In a thesis statement in your introductory paragraph, clearly state what you believe the wife learns. You will need to quote from the story and refer to specific passages in your essay's supporting paragraphs to clarify and present evidence for your central idea.

The Love Song of J. Alfred Prufrock

1917

T. S. ELIOT

 T. S. ELIOT is a twentieth-century poet who moved from America to England early in his career and later became a British citizen. In his poem "The Love Song of J. Alfred Prufrock" he creates an outwardly sophisticated narrator who speaks to us of his inability to have meaningful relationships with those in his social environment. As readers of the poem, we seem to be overhearing Prufrock's thoughts as he encounters, remembers, or overhears people in his world of tea parties and other social encounters. Although Prufrock appears very much a part of his society on the surface, in many ways he discloses that he is not at all happy or comfortable with his role in it.

Have you ever experienced the frustrating inability to communicate or relate purposefully to those around you? Were there obvious reasons for the problem or were the causes unclear in your mind? As you read the poem, recall your own problematic relationships with others in a group in which you were a member.

S'io credesse che mia risposta fosse
A persona che mai tornasse al mondo,
Questa fiamma staria senza piu scosse.
Ma perciocché giammai di questo fondo
Non torno vivo alcun, s'i'odo il vero,
Senza tema d'infamia ti rispondo.[1]

Let us go then, you and I,   1
When the evening is spread out against the sky

---

1. *S'io credesse . . . rispondo:* From Dante's *Inferno.* The speaker is Guido da Montefeltro, one of the False Counselors, who is punished by being enveloped in an eternal flame. When Dante asks Guido to tell his life story, the spirit replies: "If I thought that my answer were to one who might ever return to the world, this flame would shake no more; but since from this depth none ever returned alive, if what I hear is true, I answer you without fear of infamy."

Like a patient etherized upon a table;
Let us go, through certain half-deserted streets,
The muttering retreats   5
Of restless nights in one-night cheap hotels
And sawdust restaurants with oyster-shells:
Streets that follow like a tedious argument
Of insidious intent
To lead you to an overwhelming question . . .   10
Oh, do not ask, "What is it?"
Let us go and make our visit.

In the room the women come and go
Talking of Michelangelo.[2]

The yellow fog that rubs its back upon the window-panes,   15
The yellow smoke that rubs its muzzle on the window-panes
Licked its tongue into the corners of the evening,
Lingered upon the pools that stand in drains,
Let fall upon its back the soot that falls from chimneys,
Slipped by the terrace, made a sudden leap,   20
And seeing that it was a soft October night,
Curled once about the house, and fell asleep.

And indeed there will be time
For the yellow smoke that slides along the street,
Rubbing its back upon the window-panes;   25
There will be time, there will be time
To prepare a face to meet the faces that you meet;
There will be time to murder and create,

And time for all the works and days of hands
That lift and drop a question on your plate;   30
Time for you and time for me,
And time yet for a hundred indecisions,
And for a hundred visions and revisions,
Before the taking of a toast and tea.

In the room the women come and go   35
Talking of Michelangelo.

And indeed there will be time
To wonder, "Do I dare?" and, "Do I dare?"

2. Michelangelo: Italian artist, architect, and poet (1475–1564)

Time to turn back and descend the stair,
With a bald spot in the middle of my hair—   40
(They will say: "How his hair is growing thin!")
My morning coat, my collar mounting firmly to the chin,
My necktie rich and modest, but asserted by a simple pin—
(They will say: "But how his arms and legs are thin!")
Do I dare   45
Disturb the universe?
In a minute there is time
For decisions and revisions which a minute will reverse.

    For I have known them all already, known them all—
Have known the evenings, mornings, afternoons,   50
I have measured out my life with coffee spoons;
I know the voices dying with a dying fall
Beneath the music from a farther room.
    So how should I presume?

    And I have known the eyes already, known them all—   55
The eyes that fix you in a formulated phrase,
And when I am formulated, sprawling on a pin,
When I am pinned and wriggling on the wall,
Then how should I begin
To spit out all the butt-ends of my days and ways?   60
    And how should I presume?

    And I have known the arms already, known them all—
Arms that are braceleted and white and bare
(But in the lamplight, downed with light brown hair!)
Is it perfume from a dress   65
That makes me so digress?
Arms that lie along a table, or wrap about a shawl.
    And should I then presume?
    And how should I begin?

  . . . . .

Shall I say, I have gone at dusk through narrow streets   70
And watched the smoke that rises from the pipes
Of lonely men in shirt-sleeves, leaning out of windows? . . .

    I should have been a pair of ragged claws
Scuttling across the floors of silent seas.

  . . . . .

And the afternoon, the evening, sleeps so peacefully!   75
Smoothed by long fingers,
Asleep . . . tired . . . or it malingers,[3]
Stretched on the floor, here beside you and me.
Should I, after tea and cakes and ices,
Have the strength to force the moment to its crisis?   80
But though I have wept and fasted, wept and prayed,
Though I have seen my head (grown slightly bald) brought in upon a platter,
I am no prophet[4]—and here's no great matter;
I have seen the moment of my greatness flicker,
And I have seen the eternal Footman hold my coat, and snicker,   85
And in short, I was afraid.

   And would it have been worth it, after all,
After the cups, the marmalade, the tea,
Among the porcelain, among some talk of you and me,
Would it have been worth while,   90
To have bitten off the matter with a smile,
To have squeezed the universe into a ball
To roll it toward some overwhelming question,
To say: "I am Lazarus,[5] come from the dead,
Come back to tell you all, I shall tell you all"—   95
If one, settling a pillow by her head,
   Should say: "That is not what I meant at all.
   That is not it, at all."

   And would it have been worth it, after all,
Would it have been worth while,   100
After the sunsets and the dooryards and the sprinkled streets,
After the novels, after the teacups, after the skirts that trail along the floor—
And this, and so much more?—
It is impossible to say just what I mean!
But as if a magic lantern threw the nerves in patterns on a screen: 105
Would it have been worth while
If one, settling a pillow or throwing off a shawl,
And turning toward the window, should say:
   "That is not it at all,
   That is not what I meant, at all."   110

. . . . .

3. malingers: to pretend illness   4. prophet: a person who speaks for God or a deity   5. Lazarus: man
raised from the dead by Jesus

No! I am not Prince Hamlet,[6] nor was meant to be;
Am an attendant lord, one that will do
To swell a progress, start a scene or two,
Advise the prince; no doubt, an easy tool,
Deferential,[7] glad to be of use,   115
Politic, cautious, and meticulous;
Full of high sentence, but a bit obtuse;[8]
At times, indeed, almost ridiculous—
Almost, at times, the Fool.

  I grow old . . . I grow old . . .   120
I shall wear the bottoms of my trousers rolled.

  Shall I part my hair behind? Do I dare to eat a peach?
I shall wear white flannel trousers, and walk upon the beach.
I have heard the mermaids singing, each to each.

  I do not think that they will sing to me.   125

  I have seen them riding seaward on the waves
Combing the white hair of the waves blown back
When the wind blows the water white and black.

  We have lingered in the chambers of the sea
By sea-girls wreathed with seaweed red and brown   130
Till human voices wake us, and we drown.

OPTIONS FOR READING LOGS: "THE LOVE SONG OF J. ALFRED PRUFROCK"

1. Jot down questions to clarify the meaning of some of the powerful lines
    in "The Love Song of J. Alfred Prufrock," for example, "Where do you
    think Prufrock is taking us when he says, 'Let us go and make our visit'?"
    Another question might be, "Why does he mention mermaids in the last
    sections of the poem?" End your journal entry with a brief entry about
    a significant discovery you made about the poem as a whole during this
    questioning process. Complete the following sentence: "I discovered
    that _____ ."

6. Hamlet: the hero of a tragedy by Shakespeare   7. deferential: respectful   8. obtuse: not quick or
alert in perception, feeling, or intellect; insensible; dull

2. Use your imagination to draw a picture that best represents what you see in a specific part of the poem "The Love Song of J. Alfred Prufrock." What part of "Prufrock" best represents the heart of the poem for you? Would it be a tea party, a mysterious seascape, or dimly lighted city streets? Your picture can be literal or symbolic. Wrap up your journal entry by stating the central theme of the poem.

3. Tell a personal story that you recalled while reading "The Love Song of J. Alfred Prufrock." Does the poem cause you to reflect on a social situation you have been in? In what ways is your own experience similar to or different from that which Prufrock describes? What do you feel is the message of Eliot's poem? End your journal entry by clarifying what you learned from reading "The Love Song of J. Alfred Prufrock."

OPTIONS FOR WRITING ASSIGNMENTS: "THE LOVE SONG OF J. ALFRED PRUFROCK"

1. Try a creative writing response to "The Love Song of J. Alfred Prufrock" by writing an original poem of your own. If you have trouble getting started, you might begin by writing the first line of Eliot's poem, "Let us go then, you and I." Build on that line and explore a remembered social gathering or ceremony in which you participated, such as a class meeting, a birthday party, or a wedding. Take the reader with you as a companion in your mind, sharing your innermost thoughts and feelings. Describe the settings and people you encounter and let your poem grow in any way you wish. You can use rhymes if you wish, but you can also use free verse, or a combination of the two, as Eliot does. After you have written your poem, briefly explain why "The Love Song of J. Alfred Prufrock" triggered this creative response from you.

2. Can you recall a phase in your life when you, like Prufrock, felt socially alienated or ill at ease among others of a particular group? How long did this distinctive phase in your life last? Was it several months or even longer? Explore this specific period in your life when your relationship with a group was dissatisfying, for example, a time when you inwardly rebelled against your family, your school, or some larger component of society. Consider the beginning, middle, and end of that phase. How did it start? In what ways did others influence you? Why did the phase end?

3. Create an extended conversation between you and Prufrock, the troubled, even alienated, narrator of "The Love Song of J. Alfred Prufrock." Your conversation might take the form of a question-and-answer interview

in which you offer him help in establishing better, more substantial relationships with others in his social world. Also, see if you can gain some insight into your own identity through the process of creating a dialogue. What perceptions of yourself and your relationship with society have grown sharper because you have read and thought about "The Love Song of J. Alfred Prufrock"?

4. If you were asked what "The Love Song of J. Alfred Prufrock" means and what it teaches you about your relationship to society, what would you say? To fully appreciate its range of meaning, you may need to reread, think about, discuss, and write about this poem. Explain the meaning of "The Love Song of J. Alfred Prufrock" in a formal essay of five or more paragraphs. In your introductory paragraph, clearly state the poem's main idea in your thesis statement. Use your supporting paragraphs to focus attention on parts of the poem that you have questions about and that help you clarify your main idea. In your commentary you will need to quote from the poem and refer to specific passages to help your reader understand your ideas.

From

Civilization and Its Discontents

1930

SIGMUND FREUD

 SIGMUND FREUD, considered by many to be the founder of modern psychology, spent his career exploring the deep origins of human behavior, which he often attributed to powerful, primary forces such as sex and survival instincts. He believed people are generally unaware of the full influence of these psychic forces, and his term for them was *the subconscious*. According to Freud, our subconscious mind constantly directs our thoughts and actions without our awareness of its enormous power.

In Civilization and Its Discontents, *Freud uses his psychological theories about human behavior to explore not only the reasons individuals desire to join together in social groups but also the reasons these same individuals find that living in such groups is often very frustrating and threatening. As you read through the following passages excerpted from different portions of the last chapter of* Civilization and Its Discontents, *see if you agree or disagree with his theories. Does he help you to understand your own experiences or clarify how you feel about living in your society? To what extent do you agree that deeper, subconscious forces shape our conscious lives?*

How has it happened that so many people have come to take up this strange attitude of hostility to civilization? I believe that the basis of it was a deep and long-standing dissatisfaction with the then existing state of civilization and that on that basis a condemnation of it was built up, occasioned by certain specific historical events. 1

· · ·

It is time for us to turn our attention to the nature of this civilization of whose value as a means to happiness doubts have been thrown. 2

300

. . .

The first stage is easy. We recognize as cultural all activities and resources   3
which are useful to men for making the earth serviceable to them, for protecting them against the violence of the forces of nature, and so on. As regards
this side of civilization, there can be scarcely any doubt. If we go back far
enough, we find that the first acts of civilization were the use of tools, the
gaining of control over fire and the construction of dwellings. Among these,
the control over fire stands out as a quite extraordinary and unexampled
achievement, while the others opened up paths which man has followed ever
since, and the stimulus to which is easily guessed. With every tool man is
perfecting his own organs, whether motor or sensory, or is removing the
limits to their functioning. Motor power places gigantic forces at his disposal,
which, like his muscles, he can employ in any direction; thanks to ships and
aircraft neither water nor air can hinder his movements; by means of spectacles
he corrects defects in the lens of his own eye; by means of the telescope he
sees into the far distance; and by means of the microscope he overcomes the
limits of visibility set by the structure of his retina. In the photographic camera
he has created an instrument which retains the fleeting visual impressions,
just as a gramophone disc retains the equally fleeting auditory ones; both are
at bottom materializations of the power he possesses of recollection, his
memory. With the help of the telephone he can hear at distances which would
be respected as unattainable even in a fairy tale. Writing was in its origin the
voice of an absent person; and the dwelling-house was a substitute for the
mother's womb, the first lodging, for which in all likelihood man still longs,
and in which he was safe and felt at ease.

. . .

The last, but certainly not the least important, of the characteristic features   4
of civilization remains to be assessed: the manner in which the relationships
of men to one another, their social relationships, are regulated—relationships
which affect a person as a neighbor, as a source of help, as another person's
sexual object, as a member of a family and of a State. Here it is especially
difficult to keep clear of particular ideal demands and to see what is civilized
in general. Perhaps we may begin by explaining that the element of civilization
enters on the scene with the first attempt to regulate these social relationships.
If the attempt were not made, the relationships would be subject to the
arbitrary will of the individual: that is to say, the physically stronger man
would decide them in the sense of his own interests and instinctual impulses.
Nothing would be changed in this if this stronger man should in his turn

meet someone even stronger than he. Human life in common is only made possible when a majority comes together which is stronger than any separate individual and which remains united against all separate individuals. The power of this community is then set up as 'right' in opposition to the power of the individual, which is condemned as 'brute force.' This replacement of the power of the individual by the power of a community constitutes the decisive step of civilization. The essence of it lies in the fact that the members of the community restrict themselves in their possibilities of satisfaction, whereas the individual knew no such restrictions. The first requisite of civilization, therefore, is that of justice—that is, the assurance that a law once made will not be broken in favor of an individual. This implies nothing as to the ethical value of such a law. The further course of cultural development seems to tend towards making the law no longer an expression of the will of a small community—a caste[1] or a stratum[2] of the population or a racial group—which, in its turn, behaves like a violent individual towards other, and perhaps more numerous, collections of people. The final outcome should be a rule of law to which all—except those who are not capable of entering a community—have contributed by a sacrifice of their instincts, and which leaves no one—again with the same exception—at the mercy of brute force.

The liberty of the individual is no gift of civilization. It was greatest   5
before there was any civilization, though then, it is true, it had for the most part no value, since the individual was scarcely in a position to defend it. The development of civilization imposes restrictions on it, and justice demands that no one shall escape those restrictions. What makes itself felt in a human community as a desire for freedom may be their revolt against some existing injustice, and so may prove favorable to a further development of civilization; it may remain compatible with civilization. But it may also spring from the remains of their original personality, which is still untamed by civilization and may thus become the basis in them of hostility to civilization. The urge for freedom, therefore, is directed against particular forms and demands of civilization or against civilization altogether. It does not seem as though any influence could induce a man to change his nature into a termite's. No doubt he will always defend his claim to individual liberty against the will of the group. A good part of the struggles of mankind center round the single task of finding an expedient[3] accommodation—one, that is, that will bring happiness—between this claim of the individual and the cultural claims of

---

1. caste: a social group limited to persons of the same hereditary rank   2. stratum: a level or grade of a people or population, especially with reference to social position and education   3. expedient: fit or suitable for the purpose

the group; and one of the problems that touches the fate of humanity is whether such an accommodation can be reached by means of some particular form of civilization or whether this conflict is irreconcilable.

By allowing common feeling to be our guide in deciding what features [6] of human life are to be regarded as civilized, we have obtained a clear impression of the general picture of civilization; but it is true that so far we have discovered nothing that is not universally known. At the same time we have been careful not to fall in with the prejudice that civilization is synonymous with perfecting, that it is the road to perfection preordained for men. But now a point of view presents itself which may lead in a different direction. The development of civilization appears to us as a peculiar process which mankind undergoes, and in which several things strike us as familiar. We may characterize this process with reference to the changes which it brings about in the familiar instinctual dispositions of human beings, to satisfy which is, after all, the economic task of our lives. A few of these instincts are used up in such a manner that something appears in their place which, in an individual, we describe as a character-trait. The most remarkable example of such a process is found in the anal erotism of young human beings. Their original interest in the excretory[4] function, its organs and products, is changed in the course of their growth into a group of traits which are familiar to us as parsimony,[5] a sense of order and cleanliness—qualities which, though valuable and welcome in themselves, may be intensified till they become markedly dominant and produce what is called the anal character. How this happens we do not know, but there is no doubt about the correctness of the finding. Now we have seen that order and cleanliness are important requirements of civilization, although their vital necessity is not very apparent, any more than their suitability as sources of enjoyment. At this point we cannot fail to be struck by the similarity between the process of civilization and the libidinal[6] development of the individual. Other instincts [besides anal erotism] are induced to displace the conditions for their satisfaction, to lead them into other paths. In most cases this process coincides with that of the *sublimation*[7] (of instinctual aims) with which we are familiar, but in some it can be differentiated from it. Sublimation of instinct is an especially conspicuous feature of cultural development; it is what makes it possible for higher psychical activities, scientific, artistic or ideological, to play such an important part in civilized life. If one were to yield to a first impression, one would say that sublimation

---

4. excretory: pertaining to human or other animal waste   5. parsimony: extreme or excessive economy or frugality; stinginess   6. libidinal: the state of sexual instinct or drive   7. sublimation: the diversion of sexual or other biological energy from its immediate goal to a more acceptable social or moral use

is a vicissitude[8] which has been forced upon the instincts entirely by civilization. But it would be wiser to reflect upon this a little longer.

. . .

The element of truth behind all this, which people are so ready to disavow,[9] is that men are not gentle creatures who want to be loved, and who at the most can defend themselves if they are attacked; they are, on the contrary, creatures among whose instinctual endowments is to be reckoned a powerful share of aggressiveness. As a result, their neighbor is for them not only a potential helper or sexual object, but also someone who tempts them to satisfy their aggressiveness on him, to exploit his capacity for work without compensation, to use him sexually without his consent, to seize his possessions, to humiliate him, to cause him pain, to torture and to kill him. *Homo homini lupus.*[10] Who, in the face of all his experience of life and of history, will have the courage to dispute this assertion? As a rule this cruel aggressiveness waits for some provocation or puts itself at the service of some other purpose, whose goal might also have been reached by milder measures. In circumstances that are favorable to it, when the mental counter-forces which ordinarily inhibit it are out of action, it also manifests itself spontaneously and reveals man as a savage beast to whom consideration towards his own kind is something alien. Anyone who calls to mind the atrocities committed during the racial migrations or the invasions of the Huns, or by the people known as Mongols under Jenghiz Khan and Tamerlane, or at the capture of Jerusalem by the pious Crusaders, or even, indeed, the horrors of the recent World War—anyone who calls these things to mind will have to bow humbly before the truth of this view.

The existence of this inclination to aggression, which we can detect in ourselves and justly assume to be present in others, is the factor which disturbs our relations with our neighbor and which forces civilization into such a high expenditure [of energy]. In consequence of this primary mutual hostility of human beings, civilized society is perpetually threatened with disintegration. The interest of work in common would not hold it together; instinctual passions are stronger than reasonable interests. Civilization has to use its utmost efforts in order to set limits to man's aggressive instincts and to hold the manifestations of them in check by psychical reaction-formations. Hence, therefore, the use of methods intended to incite people into identifications and aim-inhibited relationships of love, hence the restriction upon sexual life,

7

8

---

8. vicissitude: change or variation   9. disavow: to disclaim knowledge of   10. *homo homini lupus:* man is a wolf to man

and hence too the ideal's commandment to love one's neighbor as oneself—a commandment which is really justified by the fact that nothing else runs so strongly counter to the original nature of man. In spite of every effort, these endeavors of civilization have not so far achieved very much. It hopes to prevent the crudest excesses of brutal violence by itself assuming the right to use violence against criminals, but the law is not able to lay hold of the more cautious and refined manifestations of human aggressiveness. The time comes when each one of us has to give up as illusions the expectations which, in his youth, he pinned upon his fellowmen, and when he may learn how much difficulty and pain has been added to his life by their ill-will. At the same time, it would be unfair to reproach civilization with trying to eliminate strife and competition from human activity. These things are undoubtedly indispensable. But opposition is not necessarily enmity;[11] it is merely misused and made an *occasion* for enmity.

. . .

If civilization imposes such great sacrifices not only on man's sexuality   9 but on his aggressivity, we can understand better why it is hard for him to be happy in that civilization. In fact, primitive man was better off in knowing no restrictions of instinct. To counterbalance this, his prospects of enjoying this happiness for any length of time were very slender. Civilized man has exchanged a portion of his possibilities of happiness for a portion of security. We must not forget, however, that in the primal family only the head of it enjoyed this instinctual freedom; the rest lived in slavish suppression. In that primal period of civilization, the contrast between a minority who enjoyed the advantages of civilization and a majority who were robbed of those advantages was, therefore, carried to extremes. As regards the primitive peoples who exist to-day, careful researches have shown that their instinctual life is by no means to be envied for its freedom. It is subject to restrictions of a different kind but perhaps of greater severity than those attaching to modern civilized man.

When we justly find fault with the present state of our civilization for so   10 inadequately fulfilling our demands for a plan of life that shall make us happy, and for allowing the existence of so much suffering which could probably be avoided—when, with unsparing criticism, we try to uncover the roots of its imperfection, we are undoubtedly exercising a proper right and are not showing ourselves enemies of civilization. We may expect gradually to carry through such alterations in our civilization as will better satisfy our needs

11. enmity: a feeling or condition of hostility

and will escape our criticisms. But perhaps we may also familiarize ourselves with the idea that there are difficulties attaching to the nature of civilization which will not yield to any attempt at reform. Over and above the tasks of restricting the instincts, which we are prepared for, there forces itself on our notice the danger of a state of things which might be termed 'the psychological poverty of groups.'

. . .

What means does civilization employ in order to inhibit the aggressiveness 11 which opposes it, to make it harmless, to get rid of it, perhaps? We have already become acquainted with a few of these methods, but not yet with the one that appears to be the most important. This we can study in the history of the development of the individual. What happens in him to render his desire for aggression innocuous?[12] Something very remarkable, which we should never have guessed and which is nevertheless quite obvious. His aggressiveness is introjected, internalized; it is, in point of fact, sent back to where it came from—that is, it is directed towards his own ego. There it is taken over by a portion of the ego, which sets itself over against the rest of the ego[13] as super-ego,[14] and which now, in the form of 'conscience,' is ready to put into action against the ego the same harsh aggressiveness that the ego would have liked to satisfy upon other, extraneous[15] individuals. The tension between the harsh super-ego and the ego that is subjected to it, is called by us the sense of guilt; it expresses itself as a need for punishment. Civilization, therefore, obtains mastery over the individual's dangerous desire for aggression by weakening and disarming it and by setting up an agency within him to watch over it, like a garrison in a conquered city.

. . .

For a wide variety of reasons, it is very far from my intention to express 12 an opinion upon the value of human civilization. I have endeavored to guard myself against the enthusiastic prejudice which holds that our civilization is the most precious thing that we possess or could acquire and that its path will necessarily lead to heights of unimagined perfection. I can at least listen without indignation to the critic who is of the opinion that when one surveys the aims of cultural endeavor and the means it employs, one is bound to come to the conclusion that the whole effort is not worth the trouble, and

12. innocuous: not harmful or injurious   13. ego: the rational, conscious part of the human personality
14. superego: the part of the personality represented by the conscience   15. extraneous: irrelevant

that the outcome of it can only be a state of affairs which the individual will be unable to tolerate. My impartiality is made all the easier to me by my knowing very little about all these things. One thing only do I know for certain and that is that man's judgments of value follow directly his wishes for happiness—that, accordingly, they are an attempt to support his illusions with arguments. I should find it very understandable if someone were to point out the obligatory nature of the course of human civilization and were to say for instance, that the tendencies to a restriction of sexual life or to the institution of a humanitarian ideal at the expense of natural selection were developmental trends which cannot be averted or turned aside and to which it is best for us to yield as though they were necessities of nature. I know, too, the objection that can be made against this, to the effect that in the history of mankind, trends such as these, which were considered unsurmountable, have often been thrown aside and replaced by other trends. Thus I have not the courage to rise up before my fellowmen as a prophet, and I bow to their reproach that I can offer them no consolation: for at bottom that is what they are all demanding—the wildest revolutionaries no less passionately than the most virtuous believers.

The fateful question for the human species seems to me to be whether and to what extent their cultural development will succeed in mastering the disturbance of their communal life by the human instinct of aggression and self-destruction. It may be that in this respect precisely the present time deserves a special interest. Men have gained control over the forces of nature to such an extent that with their help they would have no difficulty in exterminating one another to the last man. They know this, and hence comes a large part of their current unrest, their unhappiness and their mood of anxiety.

OPTIONS FOR READING LOGS: FROM *CIVILIZATION AND ITS DISCONTENTS*

1. Does anything in this excerpt from Freud's *Civilization and Its Discontents* remind you of your own experience as an individual living in a group? Can you trace any of your own frustrations to the explanations Freud provides? Freewrite on an event that focuses on a remembered person, place, or event. Try to make connections between your personal experience and some of Freud's ideas that stand out in this reading.

Concentrate on using vivid details and descriptions to enhance the discovery process.

2. Use clustering to draw a concept (idea) map that explores the meaning of this excerpt from *Civilization and Its Discontents*. Recall vivid details, examples, and ideas in Freud's writing and try brainstorming by creating balloons, clusters, flowcharts, visual symbols, word lists, outlines, or diagrams. Once you have done this, examine their relationships to one another, and draw lines or use arrows to create your concept map. End your journal entry by explaining what you have done and stating the central theme of "From *Civilization and Its Discontents.*"

3. Use the double-entry journal technique to clarify the meaning of some of the memorable statements in this excerpt from *Civilization and Its Discontents*. Draw a vertical line down the middle of your journal page; in the left column, copy phrases or sentences you particularly like or find puzzling, such as "Men have gained control over the forces of nature to such an extent that with their help they would have no difficulty in exterminating one another to the last man." Use the right column to jot down possible interpretations, personal memories, or explanatory comments. End your journal entry with a brief comment about a significant discovery you made about Freud's ideas as a whole during this process.

OPTIONS FOR WRITING ASSIGNMENTS: FROM *CIVILIZATION AND ITS DISCONTENTS*

1. Develop one of your reading logs for this excerpt from *Civilization and Its Discontents* into a more polished piece of writing that explores an insight about your society and its influence, using an appropriate form, such as a poem, a fictional story, a personal narrative, or an essay that examines a central idea.

2. What knowledge about our relationship with society are we meant to gain from this excerpt from *Civilization and Its Discontents*? Would you like to talk with Freud, the father of modern psychology, to ask him questions, hear his answers, and give him your ideas and interpretations of human nature? Create a conversation between you and Freud about the ideas expressed in this excerpt from *Civilization and Its Discontents*. You can structure your conversation as a question-and-answer interview, an argument between two opposing points of view, or a freewheeling exploration of the author's ideas and their implications for understanding the individual's relationship to society.

3. We often rely on the advice of others in selecting essays to read, and we are influenced by their evaluations. Write a critical review of this excerpt from *Civilization and Its Discontents,* assessing the value of Freud's essay as an exploration of how the individual fits into society. Your evaluation can be positive, negative, or an interesting mixture of both. Once you know what sort of evaluation or judgment you want to make, state it clearly in a thesis statement in your opening paragraph. As you work through your essay, come up with several good reasons, each with supporting evidence from the essay, that makes your judgment convincing.

4. Write a formal essay of five or more paragraphs explaining Freud's theme of the individual and his or her relationship to society. Be sure your introductory paragraph contains a thesis statement that clearly states your main idea. In your supporting paragraphs, focus on important parts of Freud's essay that you have genuine questions about, such as, "Does civilization really protect us from what Freud calls 'brute force'? Is Freud right when he says that civilization imposes restrictions on human liberty? Isn't it supposed to protect liberty?" In your essay, you will need to quote from the text and refer to specific passages to clarify and support your central argument.

Disturbing Knowledge: What Do I Think?

The readings in Chapter Five explore the remarkable viewpoints of writers who have looked the world squarely in the face and proceeded to tell the truth, each in his or her own unique way. The truths these writers have perceived, however, may not be popular, easy to accept, or immediately apparent. In fact, their intention is not to make the search for truth a simple one, but rather, to make some truth known to us. Understanding their complex, sometimes disturbing, view of the world can sometimes be extremely challenging, but only by considering a full spectrum of ideas will we ever be able to answer the question, "What do I think?"

Ultimately, the message of these writers will alter, in subtle but infinitely significant ways, our commonplace perceptions of the world around us. Dino Buzzati's "The Falling Girl," for instance, causes us to confront humankind's increasing indifference toward others. Other selections, like Barbara Grizzuti Harrison's "Growing Up Apocalyptic" and the excerpt from Niccolo Machiavelli's "The Qualities of the Prince" challenge readers to revisit and reassess deeply held beliefs about religion and politics.

Of course, writers who are uncompromising in their message, refusing to modify or make palatable the way they view the world, could be called subversive, even dangerous. They do not want to leave their readers satisfied or complacent about how things are. They may even want—as the theologian, Paul Tillich, has said—to shake like an earthquake the very foundations of our individual and collective assumptions about life. Reading the works of these writers will most certainly challenge our own private beliefs and values. Theirs is an unrelenting search for the truth—don't be surprised if their message echoes in your mind for a long time.

The Falling Girl

1982

DINO BUZZATI
TRANSLATED BY LAWRENCE
VENUTI

 Italian author DINO BUZZATI was born in 1906 and died in 1972. He is known for his unusual fiction and plays. His most famous novel, *The Tartar Steppe*, focuses on the pain and solitude of life and how it is tempered by Christianity. Published after Buzzati's death, "The Falling Girl" is a strange story of a young woman named Marta who falls all night from the top of a tall skyscraper. Marta's long fall takes her past the apartments, parties, workplaces, and lives of many people. During the course of her fall, she undergoes some curious changes, in both attitude and appearance, that point to meanings and interpretations lying far below the surface of the story.

Have you ever wondered about how quickly life goes by? Have you ever felt that your whole life, like that of the young woman falling from the building, can pass by all too quickly, even before you have a chance to learn all that you hoped to learn or to achieve all the goals you have set for yourself? As you read this strange story, think of your own goals and your feelings about where you are on the path toward attaining them.

Marta was nineteen. She looked out over the roof of the skyscraper, and seeing the city below shining in the dusk, she was overcome with dizziness. 1

The skyscraper was silver, supreme and fortunate in that most beautiful 2 and pure evening, as here and there the wind stirred a few fine filaments of cloud against an absolutely incredible blue background. It was in fact the hour when the city is seized by inspiration and whoever is not blind is swept away by it. From that airy height the girl saw the streets and the masses of buildings writhing in the long spasm of sunset; and at the point where the white of the houses ended, the blue of the sea began. Seen from above, the sea looked as if it were rising. And since the veils of the night were advancing from the east, the city became a sweet abyss[1] burning with pulsating lights. Within it were powerful men, and women who were even more powerful, furs and violins, cars glossy as onyx,[2] the neon signs of nightclubs, the entrance halls of darkened mansions, fountains, diamonds, old silent gardens, parties, desires, affairs, and, above all, that consuming sorcery of the evening which provokes dreams of greatness and glory.

Seeing these things, Marta hopelessly leaned out over the railing and let   3
herself go. She felt as if she were hovering in the air, but she was falling. Given the extraordinary height of the skyscraper, the streets and squares down at the bottom were very far away. Who knows how long it would take her to get there. Yet the girl was falling.

At that hour the terraces and balconies of the top floors were filled   4
with rich and elegant people who were having cocktails and making silly conversation. They were scattered in crowds, and their talk muffled the music. Marta passed before them and several people looked out to watch her.

Flights of that kind (mostly by girls, in fact) were not rare in the skyscraper   5
and they constituted an interesting diversion for the tenants; this was also the reason why the price of those apartments was very high.

The sun had not yet completely set and it did its best to illuminate Marta's   6
simple clothing. She wore a modest, inexpensive spring dress bought off the rack. Yet the lyrical light of the sunset exalted it somewhat, making it chic.[3]

From the millionaires' balconies, gallant hands were stretched out toward   7
her, offering flowers and cocktails. "Miss, would you like a drink? . . . Gentle butterfly, why not stop a minute with us?"

She laughed, hovering, happy (but meanwhile she was falling): "No,   8
thanks, friends. I can't. I'm in a hurry."

"Where are you headed?" they ask her.   9

"Ah, don't make me say," Marta answered, waving her hands in a friendly   10
good-bye.

A young man, tall, dark, very distinguished, extended an arm to snatch   11
her. She liked him. And yet Marta quickly defended herself: "How dare you, sir?" and she had time to give him a little tap on the nose.

The beautiful people, then, were interested in her and that filled her with   12
satisfaction. She felt fascinating, stylish. On the flower-filled terraces, amid the bustle of waiters in white and the bursts of exotic songs, there was talk for a few minutes, perhaps less, of the young woman who was passing by

1. abyss: a deep, immeasurable space, gulf, or cavity   2. onyx: a translucent variety of quartz having straight parallel bands of different colors   3. chic: attractive and fashionable

(from top to bottom, on a vertical course). Some thought her pretty, others thought her so-so, everyone found her interesting.

"You have your entire life before you," they told her, "why are you in such a hurry? You still have time to rush around and busy yourself. Stop with us for a little while, it's only a modest little party among friends, really, you'll have a good time." 13

She made an attempt to answer but the force of gravity had already quickly carried her to the floor below, then two, three, four floors below; in fact, exactly as you gaily rush around when you are just nineteen years old. 14

Of course, the distance that separated her from the bottom, that is, from street level, was immense. It is true that she began falling just a little while ago, but the street always seemed very far away. 15

In the meantime, however, the sun had plunged into the sea; one could see it disappear, transformed into a shimmering reddish mushroom. As a result, it no longer emitted its vivifying[4] rays to light up the girl's dress and make her a seductive comet. It was a good thing that the windows and terraces of the skyscraper were almost all illuminated and the bright reflections completely gilded her as she gradually passed by. 16

Now Marta no longer saw just groups of carefree people inside the apartments; at times there were even some businesses where the employees, in black or blue aprons, were sitting at desks in long rows. Several of them were young people as old as or older than she, and weary of the day by now, every once in a while they raised their eyes from their duties and from typewriters. In this way they too saw her, and a few ran to the windows. "Where are you going? Why so fast? Who are you?" they shouted to her. One could divine something akin to envy in their words. 17

"They're waiting for me down there," she answered. "I can't stop. Forgive me." And again she laughed, wavering on her headlong fall, but it wasn't like her previous laughter anymore. The night had craftily fallen and Marta started to feel cold. 18

Meanwhile, looking downward, she saw a bright halo of lights at the entrance of a building. Here long black cars were stopping (from the great distance they looked as small as ants), and men and women were getting out, anxious to go inside. She seemed to make out the sparkling of jewels in that swarm. Above the entrance flags were flying. 19

They were obviously giving a large party, exactly the kind that Marta dreamed of ever since she was a child. Heaven help her if she missed it. Down 20

4. vivifying: to give life; animate

there opportunity was waiting for her, fate, romance, the true inauguration of her life. Would she arrive in time?

She spitefully noticed that another girl was falling about thirty meters 21 above her. She was decidedly prettier than Marta and she wore a rather classy evening gown. For some unknown reason she came down much faster than Marta, so that in a few moments she passed by her and disappeared below, even though Marta was calling her. Without doubt she would get to the party before Marta; perhaps she had a plan all worked out to supplant her.

Then she realized that they weren't alone. Along the sides of the sky- 22 scraper many other young women were plunging downward, their faces taut with the excitement of the flight, their hands cheerfully waving as if to say: look at us, here we are, entertain us, is not the world ours?

It was a contest, then. And she only had a shabby little dress while those 23 other girls were dressed smartly like high-fashion models and some even wrapped luxurious mink stoles tightly around their bare shoulders. So self-assured when she began the leap, Marta now felt a tremor growing inside her; perhaps it was just the cold; but it may have been fear too, the fear of having made an error without remedy.

It seemed to be late at night now. The windows were darkened one after 24 another, the echoes of music became more rare, the offices were empty, young men no longer leaned out from the windowsills extending their hands. What time was it? At the entrance to the building down below—which in the meantime had grown larger, and one could now distinguish all the architectural details—the lights were still burning, but the bustle of cars had stopped. Every now and then, in fact, small groups of people came out of the main floor wearily drawing away. Then the lights of the entrance were also turned off.

Marta felt her heart tightening. Alas, she wouldn't reach the ball in time. 25 Glancing upwards, she saw the pinnacle[5] of the skyscraper in all its cruel power. It was almost completely dark. On the top floors a few windows here and there were still lit. And above the top the first glimmer of dawn was spreading.

In a dining recess on the twenty-eighth floor a man about forty years 26 old was having his morning coffee and reading his newspaper while his wife tidied up the room. A clock on the sideboard indicated 8:45. A shadow suddenly passed before the window.

"Alberto!" the wife shouted. "Did you see that? A woman passed by." 27

"Who was it?" he said without raising his eyes from the newspaper. 28

"An old woman," the wife answered. "A decrepit[6] old woman. She 29 looked frightened."

---

5. pinnacle: the highest or culminating point   6. decrepit: weakened by old age

"It's always like that," the man muttered. "At these low floors only 30
falling old women pass by. You can see beautiful girls from the hundred-and-
fiftieth floor up. Those apartments don't cost so much for nothing."

"At least down here there's the advantage," observed the wife, "that 31
you can hear the thud when they touch the ground."

"This time not even that," he said, shaking his head, after he stood 32
listening for a few minutes. Then he had another sip of coffee.

◙   ◙   ◙

OPTIONS FOR READING LOGS: "THE FALLING GIRL"

1. Your immediate, personal reaction to a story can often begin a process
   that will lead you to an important insight. You might try the question-
   journal method, whereby you begin with a question and freewrite for a
   while. As an example, you might ask, "Why are 'flights of that kind' taken
   'mostly by girls'?" Write a few sentences in response to that question. This,
   in turn, will lead to other questions and to further freewriting. After you
   freewrite for about a page, allow this open-ended question-and-answer
   format to help you make a generalization about the story's message.

2. Use clustering to draw a concept (idea) map that explores the meaning
   of "The Falling Girl." Recall vivid details and experiences from Buzzati's
   short story, such as the girl's early enthusiasm during her fall; her concern
   about her modest, inexpensive spring dress, bought off the rack; the
   young man who tries to save her; or the couple near the bottom of the
   building. Draw balloons, clusters, flowcharts, visual symbols, outlines,
   or diagrams to represent the complex relationships in the story. When
   you have created your concept map, review the connections and conclude
   with a statement of the central theme of "The Falling Girl."

3. Examine your personal reaction to "The Falling Girl" by contrasting the
   nineteen-year-old woman who leaps from the building with the "decrepit
   old woman" she becomes near the bottom of her fall. What does the
   contrast tell us about the meaning of the story? What causes this change?
   What does this change in the main character reveal to the reader?

OPTIONS FOR WRITING ASSIGNMENTS: "THE FALLING GIRL"

1. A possible interpretation of Buzzati's "The Falling Girl" is that Marta's
   fall represents a gradual disillusionment. She starts out with great self-

confidence and a wonderful sense of adventure in a shining city that "provokes dreams of greatness and glory," like the magical sunset described in the second paragraph. She goes on to aim her fall at a large party, "a bright halo of lights at the entrance of a building." However, before she can reach that place, she senses that she has made an "error without remedy." Write a personal narrative essay that explores an experience in which you took on more than you should have and, thus, were disappointed by the outcome. What specific personal insight or insights did you gain as a result of this experience? Throughout your essay, focus on the idea you express in your thesis statement and concentrate on using vivid details, dialogue, and descriptions to help recreate the event for your reader.

2. What do you think about all of the observers in the story, the ones who notice Marta as she passes by so quickly? Consider the people at the fancy parties, the ones still working late at night, the older couple near the ground floor. How do their attitudes toward the falling woman differ? Where does each live or work in the huge skyscraper, in relation to the others? Why do the apartments differ in cost? Explore the observers' various situations, attitudes, and reactions to Marta in order to help explain the meaning of the story.

3. Toward the end of "The Falling Girl," Marta discovers that she is not alone in her long fall. Another "decidedly prettier" woman falls past her as if racing with her to reach the street-level party. Marta becomes aware that there are "many other young women . . . plunging downward, their faces taut with the excitement of the flight, their hands cheerfully waving as if to say: look at us, here we are, entertain us, is not the world ours?" What statement does the story make about these women? Why are only women involved? Are they all going to be disappointed, as the main character is in the end? Is the author being critical of them or not? Is everything for them "just a contest"? Write a formal essay of five or more paragraphs about this story's message about these women and what they want in life. End your introductory paragraph with a thesis statement that contains a generalization about the women in the "The Falling Girl." In the remaining paragraphs, bring in vivid details and other evidence that support your main point.

4. We often rely on the advice of others in selecting things to read and evaluating their worth. What did you think of the short story, "The Falling Girl"? Even though it is a bizarre, even disturbing, story, would you recommend it to a friend? Write a critical review that assesses the value of "The Falling Girl." In your introductory paragraph, state your judgment clearly in your thesis statement. Your evaluation might be

positive, negative, or some interesting mixture of positive and negative. After you decide what sort of evaluation or judgment you want to make, use your supporting paragraphs to show good reasons for that judgment, offering specific evidence from the story to make your judgment convincing.

I heard a Fly buzz—when I died—

1862

EMILY DICKINSON

 EMILY DICKINSON, one of the most important nineteenth-century American poets, was born in 1830 and died in 1886. Although she wrote many poems, only a handful were published during her lifetime, mainly because of her great fear that she would be misunderstood by the public. The daughter of a strict, authoritarian father, she was shy and reclusive, never seeking publicity and rarely leaving her family's house. In "I heard a Fly buzz—when I died—," Dickinson describes the consciousness of one who is facing death. Her exploration of this inevitable moment takes the form of a curious, surprising event, in which the anticipated dignity and revelation of one's final moments of life are oddly undercut by an unwelcome, distracting fly. Her poem seems, in a totally unexpected way, to challenge the high seriousness and piety of such a profound moment.

Have you ever wondered what happens in your brain at the moment of death? Do you believe in near-death or after-death experiences? Have you ever had an important belief—one you had been taught to respect—suddenly become ordinary or even laughable? As you read Dickinson's poem, reflect on a time when one of your own beliefs or values was tested in a profound and startling way.

I heard a Fly buzz—when I died— 1
The Stillness in the Room
Was like the Stillness in the Air—
Between the Heaves of Storm—

The Eyes around—had wrung them dry— 5
And Breaths were gathering firm
For that last Onset—when the King
Be witnessed—in the Room—

I willed my Keepsakes—Signed away
What portion of me be   10
Assignable—and then it was
There interposed a Fly—

With Blue—uncertain stumbling Buzz—
Between the light—and me—
And then the Windows failed—and then   15
I could not see to see—

❖ ❖ ❖

OPTIONS FOR READING LOGS: "I HEARD A FLY BUZZ—WHEN I DIED—"

1. Use the double-entry journal technique to discover meaning in "I heard
    a Fly buzz—when I died—." Draw a vertical line down the middle of
    your journal page, creating two columns. In the left column, list three
    to five "what" or "why" questions that occur to you as you are reading.
    Aim for questions that are puzzling, yet answerable, such as, "What are
    the 'heaves of storm'?" Then, when your list is finished, answer your
    questions as completely as you can in the right column. Remember that
    interpretation will require you to take educated guesses. Demonstrate a
    basic understanding of the story by ending your journal entry with an
    explanation of the main idea of Dickinson's poem.
2. Examine your personal reaction to "I heard a Fly buzz—when I died—"
    by completing the following statement:

    "I was struck by _____ ."

    Complete your journal entry with a detailed explanation of your state-
    ment, including commentary based on personal experience.
3. Create an original poem in response to the text. You might want to begin
    by substituting your own words for some in the poem. Keep working
    on the draft of your poem until none of Emily Dickinson's phrasing
    remains. When you complete your poem, write an explanation of why
    you think "I heard a Fly buzz—when I died—" triggered this specific
    creative response from you. End your journal entry by stating the theme
    of the original poem as well as the theme of your own poem.

OPTIONS FOR WRITING ASSIGNMENTS: "I HEARD A FLY BUZZ—WHEN I DIED—"

1. Develop one of your reading logs for "I heard a Fly buzz—when I died—" into a more polished piece of writing that explores an insight about the poem and its theme. Use an appropriate form—a poem, a fictional story, a personal narrative, or an essay that examines a central idea.

2. Write a letter to Emily Dickinson about her poem, "I heard a Fly buzz—when I died—." Using the letter form, address Dickinson personally, giving her your reaction to the poem and its treatment of the moment of death. Raise honest questions, speculate about meaning in the more difficult portions of the poem, and praise or criticize her treatment of the theme.

3. What are we meant to learn by reading this curious poem? Create a dialogue, an intellectual descussion, in which you talk with Emily Dickinson, the author of "I heard a Fly buzz—when I died—." Try for a more formal, academic tone as you ask her questions, get answers, and give her your ideas and interpretations. Does she believe in an afterlife, or is she mocking those who do? Is the poem spoken by a dead person? If so, does that imply that there is life after death? Was "the King" ever "witnessed"? What is the role of the fly? Try to create a natural flow in the discussion between you and Emily Dickinson. You might shape it in the form of a question-and-answer interview, an argument representing two opposing points of view, or a freewheeling exploration of the author's ideas about the meaning of the poem.

4. If you were asked what "I heard a Fly buzz—when I died—" means, and what it teaches us about death and the afterlife, what would you say? One simple reading of a poem is often not enough to give us an appreciation of its full range of meaning. Interpretation often requires rereading, thinking, discussing, and writing. To expand your understanding of this poem, work your way through it one stanza at a time, paying attention to individual words and their meaning. Then write an essay of five or more paragraphs commenting on what you found. In the introductory paragraph, clearly state the poem's central idea. In your supporting paragraphs, focus your attention on each of the four stanzas in chronological order. Look closely at the words, images, tone, and ideas. In your commentary you may need to quote from the poem and refer to specific passages to help your reader understand your viewpoint.

Growing Up Apocalyptic

1978

BARBARA GRIZZUTI HARRISON

 BARBARA GRIZZUTI HARRISON is a fiction and nonfiction writer from New York. The following essay is a personal narrative of her thirteen-year experience with a religious group and her eventual departure from it. In "Growing Up Apocalyptic," Harrison explores the complex attractions and the inevitable limitations of living within a fundamentalist religious group, looking with gripping honesty at the price self-surrender exacts from the individual. Throughout this essay, Harrison reminds us of the dangers of accepting easy answers to the problems of a complex world.

Do you know anyone who joined a group that limited or controlled his or her personal growth and view of the world? If not, have you ever read about someone who had that experience? In what ways did the individual's life change due to membership in the group? Were there both positive and negative developments in the person's life? As you read Harrison's essay, reflect on your own attitudes and values.

"The trouble with you," Anna said, in a voice in which compassion, disgust, and reproach fought for equal time, "is that you can't remember what it was like to be young. And even if you could remember—well, when you were my age, you were in that crazy Jehovah's Witness religion, and you probably didn't even play spin the bottle." 1

Anna, my prepubescent[1] eleven-year-old, feels sorry for me because I did not have "a normal childhood." It has never occurred to her to question whether her childhood is "normal" . . . which is to say, she is happy. She cannot conceive of a life in which one is not free to move around, explore, argue, flirt with ideas and dismiss them, form passionate alliances and friendships according to no imperative but one's own nature and volition;[2] she 2

---

1. prepubescent: the state just preceding sexual maturation   2. volition: the act of willing, choosing, or resolving

regards love as unconditional, she expects nurturance as her birthright. It fills her with terror and pity that anyone—especially her mother—could have grown up any differently—could have grown up in a religion where love was conditional upon rigid adherence to dogma[3] and established practice . . . where approval had to be bought from authoritarian sources . . . where people did not fight openly and love fiercely and forgive generously and make decisions of their own and mistakes of their own and have adventures of their own.

"Poor Mommy," she says. To have spent one's childhood in love with/   3
tyrannized by a vengeful Jehovah is not Anna's idea of a good time—nor is it her idea of goodness. As, in her considered opinion, my having been a proselytizing[4] Jehovah's Witness for thirteen years was about as good a preparation for real life as spending a commensurate[5] amount of time in a Skinner box on the North Pole, she makes allowances for me. And so, when Anna came home recently from a boy-girl party to tell me that she had kissed a boy ("interesting," she pronounced the experiment), and I had heard my mouth ask that atavistic[6] mother-question, "And what else did you do?" Anna was inclined to be charitable with me: "Oh, for goodness' sake, what do you think we did, screw? The trouble with you is . . ." And then she explained to me about spin the bottle.

I do worry about Anna. She is, as I once explained drunkenly to someone   4
who thought that she might be the better for a little vigorous repression, a teleological[7] child. She is concerned with final causes, with ends and purposes and means; she would like to see evidence of design and order in the world; and all her adventures are means to that end. That, combined with her love for the music, color, poetry, ritual, and drama of religion, might, I think, if she were at all inclined to bow her back to authority—and if she didn't have my childhood as an example of the perils thereof—have made her ripe for conversion to an apocalyptic,[8] messianic[9] sect.

That fear may be evidence of my special paranoia, but it is not an entirely   5
frivolous conjecture.[10] Ardent preadolescent girls whose temperament tends toward the ecstatic are peculiarly prone to conversion to fancy religions.

I know. My mother and I became Jehovah's Witnesses in 1944, when I   6
was nine years old. I grew up drenched in the dark blood-poetry of a fierce

---

3. dogma: specific doctrine authoritatively put forth by a church   4. proselytizing: to convert or attempt to convert religious beliefs   5. commensurate: having the same measure   6. atavistic: the reappearance in an individual of some remote ancestor that has been absent in intervening generations   7. teleological: the doctrine that final causes exist   8. apocalyptic: of or like revelations of the ultimate divine purpose
9. messianic: of or like an expected deliverer or savior   10. conjecture: the formation or expression of an opinion without sufficient evidence for proof

messianic sect. Shortly after my conversion, I got my first period. We used to sing this hymn: "Here is He who comes from Eden / all His raiment stained with blood." My raiments were stained with blood, too. But the blood of the Son of Man was purifying, redemptive, cleansing, sacrificial. Mine was filthy—proof of my having inherited the curse placed upon the seductress Eve. I used to "read" my used Kotexes compulsively, as if the secret of life—or a harbinger[11] of death—were to be found in that dull, mysterious effluence.[12]

My brother, at the time of our conversion, was four. After a few years of listlessly following my mother and me around in our door-to-door and street-corner proselytizing, he allied himself with my father, who had been driven to noisy, militant atheism by the presence of two female religious fanatics in his hitherto patriarchal household. When your wife and daughter are in love with God, it's hard to compete—particularly since God is good enough not to require messy sex as proof or expression of love. As a child, I observed that it was not extraordinary for women who became Jehovah's Witnesses to remove themselves from their husband's bed as a first step to getting closer to God. For women whose experience had taught them that all human relationships were treacherous and capricious and frighteningly volatile, an escape from the confusions of the world into the certainties of a fundamentalist religion provided the illusion of safety and of rest. It is not too simple to say that the reason many unhappily married and sexually embittered women fell in love with Jehovah was that they didn't have to go to bed with Him.

Apocalyptic religions are, by their nature, antierotic.[13] Jehovah's Witnesses believe that the world—or, as they would have it, "this evil system under Satan the Devil"—will end in our lifetime. After the slaughter Jehovah has arranged for his enemies at Armageddon, say the Witnesses, this quintessentially[14] masculine God—vengeful in battle, benevolent to survivors—will turn the earth into an Edenic paradise for true believers. I grew up under the umbrella of the slogan, "Millions Now Living Will Never Die," convinced that 1914 marked "the beginning of the times of the end." So firmly did Jehovah's Witnesses believe this to be true that there were those who, in 1944, refused to get their teeth filled, postponing all care of their bodies until God saw to their regeneration in His New World, which was just around the corner.

7

8

---

11. harbinger: one that announces the approach of someone or something   12. effluence: the action or process of flowing out   13. antierotic: opposed to sexual love   14. quintessentially: having the most perfect embodiment of something

Some corner.   9

Despite the fact that their hopes were not immediately rewarded, Jeho-   10
vah's Witnesses have persevered with increasing fervor and conviction, and
their attitude toward the world remains the same: Because all their longing
is for the future, they are bound to hate the present—the material, the sexual,
the flesh. It's impossible, of course, truly to savor and enjoy the present, or
to bend one's energies to shape and mold the world into the form of goodness,
if you are only waiting for it to be smashed by God. There is a kind of ruthless
glee in the way in which Jehovah's Witnesses point to earthquakes, race riots,
heroin addiction, the failure of the United Nations, divorce, famine, and
liberalized abortion laws as proof of the nearest Armageddon.

The world will end, according to the Witnesses, in a great shaking and   11
rending and tearing of unbelieving flesh, with unsanctified babies swimming
in blood—torrents of blood. They await God's Big Bang—the final orgasmic
burst of violence, after which all things will come together in a cosmic orgasm
of joy. In the meantime, they have disgust and contempt for the world; and
freedom and spontaneity, even playfulness, in sex are explicitly frowned upon.

When I was ten, it would have been more than my life was worth to   12
acknowledge, as Anna does so casually, that I knew what *screwing* was. (Ignorance, however, delivered me from that grave error.) Once, having read
somewhere that Hitler had a mistress, I asked my mother what a mistress
was. (I had an inkling that it was some kind of sinister superhousekeeper,
like Judith Anderson in *Rebecca*.) I knew from my mother's silence, and from
her cold, hard, and frightened face, that the question was somehow a grievous
offense. I knew that I had done something terribly wrong, but as usual, I
didn't know what. The fact was that I never knew how to buy God's—or my
mother's—approval. There were sins I consciously and knowingly committed.
That was bad, but it was bearable. I could always pray to God to forgive me,
say, for reading the Bible for its "dirty parts" (to prefer the Song of Solomon
to all the begats of Genesis was proof absolute of the sinfulness of my nature).
But the offenses that made me most cringingly guilty were those I had
committed unconsciously; as an imperfect human being descended from the
wretched Eve, I was bound—so I had been taught—to offend Jehovah seventy-seven times a day without my even knowing what I was doing wrong.

I knew that good Christians didn't commit "unnatural acts"; but I didn't   13
know what "unnatural acts" were. I knew that an increase in the number of
rapes was one of the signs heralding the end of the world, but I didn't know
what rape was. Consequently, I spent a lot of time praying that I was not
committing unnatural acts or rape.

My ignorance of all things sexual was so profound that it frequently led   14
to comedies of error. Nothing I've ever read has inclined me to believe that

Jehovah has a sense of humor, and I must say that I consider it a strike against Him that He wouldn't find this story funny: One night shortly after my conversion, a visiting elder of the congregation, as he was avuncularly[15] tucking me in bed, asked me if I were guilty of performing evil practices with my hands under the covers at night. I was puzzled. He was persistent. Finally, I thought I understood. And I burst into wild tears of self-recrimination: What I did under the covers at night was bite my cuticles—a practice which, in fact, did afford me a kind of sensual pleasure. I didn't learn about masturbation—which the Witnesses call "idolatry" because "the masturbator's affection is diverted away from the Creator and is bestowed upon a coveted object . . . his genitals"—until much later. So, having confessed to a sin that I didn't even know existed, I was advised of the necessity of keeping one's body pure from sin; cold baths were recommended. I couldn't see the connection between cold baths and my cuticles, but no one ever questioned the imperatives of an elder. So I subjected my impure body, in midwinter, to so many icy baths that I began to look like a bleached prune. My mother thought I was demented. But I couldn't tell her that I'd been biting my cuticles, because to have incurred God's wrath—and to see the beady eye of the elder steadfastly upon me at every religious meeting I went to—was torment enough. There was no way to win.

One never questioned the imperatives of an elder. I learned as a very small   15
child that it was my primary duty in life to "make nice." When I was little, I was required to respond to inquiries about my health in this manner: "Fine and dandy, just like sugar candy, thank you." And to curtsy. If that sounds like something from a Shirley Temple movie, it's because it is. Having been brought up to be the Italian working-class Shirley Temple from Bensonhurst, it was not terribly difficult for me to learn to "make nice" for God and the elders. Behaving well was relatively easy. The passionate desire to win approval guaranteed my conforming. But behaving well never made me feel good. I always felt as if I were a bad person.

I ask myself why it was that my brother was not hounded by the obsessive   16
guilt and the desperate desire for approval that informed all my actions. Partly, I suppose, luck, and an accident of temperament, but also because of the peculiarly guilt-inspiring double message girls received. Girls were taught that it was their nature to be spiritual, but paradoxically that they were more prone to absolute depravity than were boys.

In my religion, everything beautiful and noble and spiritual and good   17
was represented by a woman; and everything evil and depraved and monstrous was represented by a woman. I learned that "God's organization," the "bride

15. avuncularly: pertaining to or characteristic of an uncle

of Christ," or His 144,000 heavenly co-rulers were represented by a "chaste virgin." I also learned that "Babylon the Great," or "false religion," was "the mother of the abominations or the 'disgusting things of the earth.' . . . She likes to get drunk on human blood. . . . Babylon the Great is . . . pictured as a woman, an international harlot."

Young girls were thought not to have the "urges" boys had. They were not only caretakers of their own sleepy sexuality but protectors of boys' vital male animal impulses as well. They were thus doubly responsible, and, if they fell, doubly damned. Girls were taught that, simply by existing, they were provoking male sexuality . . . which it was their job then to subdue.   18

To be female, I learned, was to be Temptation; nothing short of death—the transformation of your atoms into a lilac bush—could change that. (I used to dream deliciously of dying, of being as inert—and as unaccountable—as the dust I came from.) Inasmuch as males naturally "wanted it" more, when a female "wanted it" she was doubly depraved, unnatural as well as sinful. She was the receptacle for male lust, "the weaker vessel." If the vessel, created by God for the use of males, presumed to have desires of its own, it was perforce consigned to the consuming fires of God's wrath. If then, a woman were to fall from grace, her fall would be mighty indeed—and her willful nature would lead her into that awful abyss where she would be deprived of the redemptive love of God and the validating love of man. Whereas, were a man to fall, he would be merely stumbling over his own feet of clay.   19

(Can this be accident? My brother, when he was young, was always falling over his own feet. I, on the other hand, to this day sweat with terror at the prospect of going down escalators or long flights of stairs. I cannot fly; I am afraid of the fall.)   20

I spent my childhood walking a religious tightrope, maintaining a difficult dizzying balance. I was, for example, expected to perform well at school, so that glory would accrue to Jehovah and "His organization." But I was also made continually aware of the perils of falling prey to "the wisdom of this world which is foolishness to God." I had constantly to defend myself against the danger of trusting my own judgment. To question or to criticize God's "earthly representatives" was a sure sign of "demonic influence"; to express doubt openly was to risk being treated like a spiritual leper. I was always an honor student at school; but this was hardly an occasion for unqualified joy. I felt, rather, as if I were courting spiritual disaster: While I was congratulated for having "given a witness" by virtue of my academic excellence, I was, in the next breath, warned against the danger of supposing that my intelligence could function independently of God's. The effect of all this was to convince me that my intelligence was like some kind of tricky, predatory animal, which, if it were not kept firmly reined, would surely spring on and destroy me.   21

"Vanity, thy name is woman." I learned very early what happened to   22
women with "independent spirits" who opposed the will and imperatives of
male elders. They were disfellowshipped (excommunicated) and thrown into
"outer darkness." Held up as an example of such perfidious conduct was
Maria Frances Russell, the wife of Charles Taze Russell, charismatic founder
of the sect.

Russell charged his wife with "the same malady which has smitted oth-   23
ers—*ambition*." Complaining of a "female conspiracy" against the Lord's
organization, he wrote: "The result was a considerable stirring up of slander
and misrepresentation, for of course it would not suit (her) purposes to tell
the plain unvarnished truth, that Sister Russell was ambitious. . . . When
she desired to come back, I totally refused, except upon a promise that she
should make reasonable acknowledgment of the wrong course she had been
pursuing." Ambition in a woman was, by implication, so reprehensible as to
exact from Jehovah the punishment of death.

(What the Witnesses appeared less eager to publicize about the Russells'   24
spiritual-cum-marital problems is that in April 1906, Mrs. Russell, having
filed suit for legal separation, told a jury that her husband had once remarked
to a young orphan woman the Russells had reared: "I am like a jellyfish. I
float around here and there. I touch this one and that one, and if she responds
I take her to me, and if not I float on to others." Mrs. Russell was unable
to prove her charge.)

I remember a line in *A Nun's Story:* "Dear God," the disaffected Belgian   25
nun anguished, "forgive me. I will never be able to love a Nazi." I, conversely,
prayed tormentedly for many years, "Dear God, forgive me, I am not able
to hate what you hate. I love the world." As a Witness I was taught that
"friendship with the world" was "spiritual adultery." The world was crawling
with Satan's agents. But Satan's agents—evolutionists, "false religionists,"
and all those who opposed, or were indifferent to, "Jehovah's message"—
often seemed like perfectly nice, decent, indeed lovable people to me. (They
were certainly interesting.) As I went from door to door, ostensibly to help
the Lord divide the "goats" from the "sheep," I found that I was more and
more listening to *their* lives; and I became increasingly more tentative about
telling them that I had *The* Truth. As I grew older, I found it more and more
difficult to eschew their company. I entertained fantasies, at one time or
another, about a handsome, ascetic[16] Jesuit priest I had met in my preaching
work and about Albert Schweitzer, J. D. Salinger, E. B. White, and Frank
Sinatra; in fact, I was committing "spiritual adultery" all over the place. And
then, when I was fifteen, I fell in love with an "unbeliever."

16. ascetic: a person who practices self-denial for religious reasons

If I felt—before having met and loved Arnold Horowitz, English 31,   26
New Utrecht High School—that life was a tightrope, I felt afterward that
my life was perpetually being lived on a high wire, with no safety net to catch
me. I was obliged, by every tenet of my faith, to despise him: to be "yoked
with an unbeliever," an atheist and an intellectual . . . the pain was exquisite.

He was the essential person, the person who taught me how to love,   27
and how to doubt. Arnold became interested in me because I was smart; he
loved me because he thought I was good. He nourished me. He nurtured
me. He paid me the irresistible compliment of totally comprehending me.
He hated my religion. He railed against the sect that would rather see babies
die than permit them to have blood transfusions, which were regarded as
unscriptural; he had boundless contempt for my overseers, who would not
permit me to go to college—the "Devil's playground," which would fill my
head with wicked, ungodly nonsense; he protested mightily, with the rage
that springs from genuine compassion, against a religion that could tolerate
segregation and apartheid, sneer at martyred revolutionaries, dismiss social
reform and material charity as "irrelevant," a religion that—waiting for God
to cure all human ills—would act by default to maintain the status quo, while
regarding human pain and struggle without pity and without generosity. He
loathed the world view that had been imposed on me, a black-and-white
view that allowed no complexities, no moral dilemmas, that disdained meta-
physical or philosophical or psychological inquiry; he loathed the bloated
simplicities that held me in thrall. But he loved *me*. I had never before felt
loved unconditionally.

This was a measure of his love: Jehovah's Witnesses are not permitted   28
to salute the flag. Arnold came, unbidden, to sit with me at every school
assembly, to hold my hand, while everyone else stood at rigid salute. We
were very visible; and I was very comforted. And this was during the McCarthy
era. Arnold had a great deal to lose, and he risked it all for me. Nobody had
ever risked anything for me before. How could I believe that he was wicked?

We drank malteds on his porch and read T. S. Eliot and listened to   29
Mozart. We walked for hours, talking of God and goodness and happiness
and death. We met surreptitiously.[17] (My mother so feared and hated the
man who was leading me into apostasy[18] that she once threw a loaf of Arnold
bread out the window; his very name was loathsome to her.) Arnold treated
me with infinite tenderness; he was the least alarming man I had ever known.
His fierce concentration on me, his solicitous care uncoupled with sexual

17. surreptitiously: acting in a stealthy way   18. apostasy: renunciation or abandonment of one's religious
faith

aggression, was the gentlest—and most thrilling—love I had ever known. He made me feel what I had never felt before—valuable, and good.

It was very hard. All my dreams centered around Arnold, who was becoming more important, certainly more real to me, than God. All my dreams were blood-colored. I would fantasize about Arnold's being converted and surviving Armageddon and living forever with me in the New World. Or I would fantasize about my dying with Arnold, in fire and flames, at Armageddon. I would try to make bargains with God—my life for his. When I confessed my terrors to the men in charge of my spiritual welfare—when I said that I knew I could not rejoice in the destruction of the "wicked" at Armageddon—I was told that I was presuming to be "more compassionate than Jehovah," the deadliest sin against the holy spirit. I was reminded that, being a woman and therefore weak and sentimental, I would have to go against my sinful nature and listen to their superior wisdom, which consisted of my never seeing Arnold again. I was also reminded of the perils of being over-smart: If I hadn't been such a good student, none of this would have happened to me.

I felt as if I were leading a double life, as indeed I was. I viewed the world as beautifully various, as a blemished but mysteriously wonderful place, as savable by humans, who were neither good nor bad but imperfectly wise; but I *acted* as if the world were fit for nothing but destruction, as if all human efforts to purchase happiness and goodness were doomed to failure and deserving of contempt, as if all people could be categorized as "sheep" or "goats" and herded into their appropriate destinies by a judgmental Jehovah, the all-seeing Father who knew better than His children what was good for them.

As I had when I was a little girl, I "made nice" as best I could. I maintained the appearance of "goodness," that is, of religiosity, although it violated my truest feelings. When I left high school, I went into the full-time preaching work. I spent a minimum of five hours a day ringing doorbells and conducting home Bible studies. I went to three religious meetings a week. I prayed that my outward conformity would lead to inner peace. I met Arnold very occasionally, when my need to see him overcame my elders' imperatives and my own devastating fears. He was always accessible to me. Our meetings partook equally of misery and of joy. I tried, by my busyness, to lock all my doubts into an attic of my mind.

And for a while, and in a way, it "took." I derived sustenance from communal surges of revivalist fervor at religious conventions and from the conviction that I was united, in a common cause, with a tiny minority of persecuted and comradely brothers and sisters whose approval became both my safety net and the Iron Curtain that shut me off from the world. I felt that I had chosen Jehovah, and that my salvation, while not assured, was at least a possibility; perhaps He would choose me. I vowed finally never to see Arnold again, hoping, by this sacrifice, to gain God's approval for him as well as for me.

I began to understand that for anyone so obviously weak and irresponsible   34 as I, only a life of self-sacrifice and abnegation[19] could work. I wanted to be consumed by Jehovah, to be locked so closely into the strait-jacket of His embrace that I would be impervious to the devilish temptations my irritable, independent intelligence threw up in my path.

I wished to be eaten up alive; and my wish was granted. When I was   35 nineteen, I was accepted into Bethel, the headquarters organization of Jehovah's Witnesses, where I worked and lived, one of twelve young women among two hundred and fifty men, for three years. "Making nice" had paid off. Every minute of my waking life was accounted for; there was no leisure in which to cultivate vice or reflection. I called myself happy. I worked as a housekeeper for my brothers, making thirty beds a day, sweeping and vacuuming and waxing and washing fifteen rooms a day (in addition to proselytizing in my "free time"); I daily washed the bathtub thirty men had bathed in. In fact, the one demurral I made during those years was to ask—I found it so onerous—if perhaps the brothers, many of whom worked in the Witnesses' factory, could not clean out their own bathtub (thirty layers of grease is a lot of grease). I was told by the male overseer who supervised housekeepers that Jehovah had assigned me this "privilege." And I told myself I was lucky.

I felt myself to be even luckier—indeed, blessed—when, after two years   36 of this servant's work, one of Jehovah's middlemen, the president of the Watch Tower Bible and Tract Society, told me that he was assigning me to proofread Watch Tower publications. He accompanied this benediction with a warning: This new honor, I was told, was to be a test of my integrity— "Remember in all things to defer to the brothers; you will have to guard your spirit against pride and vanity. Satan will try now to tempt you as never before."

And defer I did. There were days when I felt literally as if my eternal   37 destiny hung upon a comma: If the brother with whom I worked decided a comma should go out where I wanted to put one in, I prayed to Jehovah to forgive me for that presumptuous comma. I was perfectly willing to deny the existence of a split infinitive if that would placate my brother. I denied and denied—commas, split infinitives, my sexuality, my intelligence, my femaleness, my yearning to be part of the world—until suddenly with a great

19. abnegation: to refuse or deny rights or comforts to oneself; to renounce

silent shifting and shuddering, and with more pain than I had ever experienced or expect to experience again, I broke. I woke up one morning, packed my bags, and walked out of that place. I was twenty-two; and I had to learn how to begin to live. It required a great deal of courage; I do not think I will ever be capable of that much courage again.

The full story of life in that institution and the ramifications of my decision   38
to leave it is too long to tell here; and it will take me the rest of my life to understand fully the ways in which everything I have ever done since has been colored and informed by the guilt that was my daily bread for so many dry years, by the desperate need for approval that allowed me to be swallowed up whole by a devouring religion, by the carefully fostered desire to "make nice" and to be "a good girl," by the conviction that I was nothing and nobody unless I served a cause superior to that of my own necessities.

Arnold, of course, foresaw the difficulty; when I left religion, he said,   39
"Now you will be just like the rest of us." With no guiding passion, he meant; uncertain, he meant, and often muddled and confused, and always struggling. And he wept.

OPTIONS FOR READING LOGS: "GROWING UP APOCALYPTIC"

1. Use the double-entry journal technique to discover meaning in "Growing Up Apocalyptic." Create two columns by drawing a vertical line down the middle of your journal page. Use the left column for a running list of three to five "what" or "why" questions that occur to you as you are reading. The best questions are puzzling yet answerable, such as, "Why does the author connect being female with fundamentalism?" When you finish your list, answer your questions as completely as you can in the right column. (Remember that such interpretation will require you to take educated guesses.) To demonstrate that you have reached a basic understanding of Harrison's essay, end your journal entry by explaining its central idea.

2. Draw a picture of your own version of the central meaning of "Growing Up Apocalyptic." For example, you might draw a stick figure of the writer in the center of the page, surrounded by symbols depicting the pressures and influences she experienced when she was a Jehovah's Witness. After you complete your drawing, describe it in writing, using as

many specific details as possible. End your journal entry by stating the central theme of Harrison's essay.

3. Pulling ideas from your own personal life or the life of someone you know, tell a parallel story that was triggered by reading and thinking about "Growing Up Apocalyptic." Does Harrison's essay remind you of something that happened in your life or the life of someone you know? Jot down characteristics or events that were similar to or different from those described in "Growing Up Apocalyptic." Wrap up your journal entry by stating what you learned from the experience.

OPTIONS FOR WRITING ASSIGNMENTS: "GROWING UP APOCALYPTIC"

1. Write a formal essay of five or more paragraphs that explores your involvement or someone else's with a group that in some way controls one's experience with the world and limits new ideas. For example, you might describe an experience with a tight group of friends who share common attitudes and values. Ideological groups or even families or neighborhood groups can also be very controlling. Whatever group you choose to write about, be sure to state your main idea clearly in a thesis statement in your first paragraph. Throughout your essay, concentrate on using vivid details and anecdotes to help recreate the influence this group had on your way of seeing the world and its range of possibilities.

2. If you could have a discussion with Barbara Grizzuti Harrison, the author of "Growing Up Apocalyptic," what would you say? Create a dialogue in which you ask Harrison questions, get answers, and give her your own ideas and interpretations of her experience in the religious group. Discuss with her in detail the various ideas she presents in "Growing Up Apocalyptic." Your conversation can take the form of a question-and-answer interview, an argument representing two opposing points of view, or a freewheeling exploration of Harrison's ideas and their implications for what you think and believe.

3. In "Growing Up Apocalyptic," Harrison's life was greatly affected by her long-term involvement with a group whose belief system dictated that its members were right in all issues and ideas and that everyone else was wrong. Interview someone who is or has been involved with such a group, and write an essay explaining what the group is, what it believes, and how it influences the lives of its members. Draw up a list of appropriate questions before your interview. Then come up with a clear thesis that makes an appropriate generalization about the group. Write a formal

essay of five or more paragraphs informing your readers about the group and its beliefs. In your conclusion, consider your own reactions to what you have learned, and evaluate the group and its influence on its members.

4. Write a formal essay of five or more paragraphs explaining what Barbara Grizzuti Harrison learns through her relationship with the religious group to which she devoted thirteen years of her life. End your introductory paragraph with a thesis statement that clearly presents the author's central idea. In your supporting paragraphs, focus on the parts of the essay that reveal why Harrison eventually left the group. What conflicts finally caused her to grow uneasy with her otherwise exemplary career with this religious group? Why did she leave so suddenly? In your essay, refer to specific passages to clarify and support your central argument.

Young Goodman Brown

1835

NATHANIEL HAWTHORNE

 NATHANIEL HAWTHORNE, one of the best known 19th-century American writers, was born in 1804 in Salem, Massachusetts. His family lived in New England for many generations, and in the late 17th century, one of his ancestors had been a judge in the famous Salem witchcraft trials. Raised in both Massachusetts and Maine, Hawthorne attended Maine's Bowdoin College, where he decided to become a writer. Later, he became acquainted with the philosophers Emerson and Thoreau, two of the leading thinkers and writers of his time, as well as with Herman Melville, the author of *Moby Dick*. As his career progressed, he changed from the short-story form to the novel, the best known of which is *The Scarlet Letter*, written in 1849.

In the opening of Hawthorne's short story "Young Goodman Brown," a young, happily married man sets out on a brief journey into the forest. At the end of the story, when he returns to his village the next morning, he is a changed man, and his fellow villagers see him as behaving very oddly. He says and does inexplicable things, and ceases to trust in or believe any of them, even his own wife. Many strange and ambiguous experiences appear to have happened to Goodman Brown in the woods, and their influence will remain with him for the rest of his life.

Have you ever lost faith in someone or something you once believed in? Have any people you thought you knew well suddenly become strange or distant to you because of a particular experience? Have you ever been forced to reconsider someone or something you thought you knew well? What is required for people to have faith in one another, and what can cause it to be lost?

Young Goodman Brown came forth at sunset into the street of Salem village; but put his head back, after crossing the threshold, to exchange a parting kiss with his young wife. And Faith, as the wife was aptly named, thrust her own pretty head into the street, letting the wind play with the pink ribbons of her cap while she called to Goodman Brown.

"Dearest heart," whispered she, softly and rather sadly, when her lips were close to his ear, "prithee[1] put off your journey until sunrise and sleep in your own bed to-night. A lone woman is troubled with such dreams and such thoughts that she's afeard of herself sometimes. Pray tarry[2] with me this night, dear husband, of all nights in the year."

"My love and my Faith," replied young Goodman Brown, "of all nights in the year, this one night must I tarry away from thee. My journey, as thou callest it, forth and back again, must needs be done 'twixt[3] now and sunrise. What, my sweet, pretty wife, dost thou doubt me already, and we but three months married?"

"Then God bless you!" said Faith, with the pink ribbons; "and may you find all well when you come back."

"Amen!" cried Goodman Brown. "Say thy prayers, dear Faith, and go to bed at dusk, and no harm will come to thee."

So they parted; and the young man pursued his way until, being about to turn the corner by the meeting house, he looked back and saw the head of Faith still peeping after him with a melancholy air, in spite of her pink ribbons.

"Poor little Faith!" thought he, for his heart smote him. "What a wretch am I to leave her on such an errand! She talks of dreams, too. Methought as she spoke there was trouble in her face, as if a dream had warned her what work is to be done to-night. But, no, no; 'twould kill her to think it. Well, she's a blessed angel on earth; and after this one night I'll cling to her skirts and follow her to heaven."

With this excellent resolve for the future, Goodman Brown felt himself justified in making more haste on his present evil purpose. He had taken a dreary road, darkened by all the gloomiest trees of the forest, which barely stood aside to let the narrow path creep through, and closed immediately behind. It was all as lonely as could be; and there is this peculiarity in such a solitude, that the traveller knows not who may be concealed by the innumerable trunks and the thick boughs overhead; so that with lonely footsteps he may yet be passing through an unseen multitude.

"There may be a devilish Indian behind every tree," said Goodman Brown to himself; and he glanced fearfully behind him as he added, "What if the devil himself should be at my very elbow!"

His head being turned back, he passed a crook of the road, and, looking forward again, beheld the figure of a man, in grave and decent attire, seated at the foot of an old tree. He arose at Goodman Brown's approach and walked onward side by side with him.

1. prithee: pray thee   2. tarry: to stay in a place   3. twixt: between

"You are late, Goodman Brown," said he. "The clock of the Old South   11
was striking as I came through Boston; and that is full fifteen minutes agone."

"Faith kept me back a while," replied the young man, with a tremor in   12
his voice, caused by the sudden appearance of his companion, though not
wholly unexpected.

It was now deep dusk in the forest, and deepest in that part of it where   13
these two were journeying. As nearly as could be discerned, the second
traveller was about fifty years old, apparently in the same rank of life as
Goodman Brown, and bearing a considerable resemblance to him, though
perhaps more in expression than features. Still they might have been taken
for father and son. And yet, though the elder person was as simply clad as
the younger, and as simple in manner too, he had an indescribable air of one
who knew the world, and who would not have felt abashed at the governor's
dinner table or in King William's court, were it possible that his affairs should
call him thither.[4] But the only thing about him that could be fixed upon as
remarkable was his staff, which bore the likeness of a great black snake, so
curiously wrought that it might almost be seen to twist and wriggle itself
like a living serpent. This, of course, must have been an ocular[5] deception,
assisted by the uncertain light.

"Come, Goodman Brown," cried his fellow-traveller, "this is a dull pace   14
for the beginning of a journey. Take my staff, if you are so soon weary."

"Friend," said the other, exchanging his slow pace for a full stop, "having   15
kept covenant[6] by meeting thee here, it is my purpose now to return whence
I came. I have scruples touching the matter thou wot'st of."

"Sayest thou so?" replied he of the serpent, smiling apart. "Let us walk   16
on, nevertheless, reasoning as we go; and if I convince thee not thou shalt
turn back. We are but a little way in the forest yet."

"Too far! too far!" exclaimed the goodman, unconsciously resuming his   17
walk. "My father never went into the woods on such an errand, nor his father
before him. We have been a race of honest men and good Christians since
the days of the martyrs; and shall I be the first of the name of Brown that
ever took this path and kept"—

"Such company, thou wouldst say," observed the elder person, interpret-   18
ing his pause. "Well said, Goodman Brown! I have been as well acquainted
with your family as with ever a one among the Puritans; and that's no trifle
to say. I helped your grandfather, the constable, when he lashed the Quaker
woman so smartly through the streets of Salem; and it was I that brought
your father a pitch-pine knot, kindled at my own hearth,[7] to set fire to an
Indian village, in King Philip's war. They were my good friends, both; and

---

4. thither: there   5. ocular: of the eyes   6. covenant: a formal agreement   7. hearth: home or fireside

many a pleasant walk have we had along this path, and returned merrily after midnight. I would fain be friends with you for their sake."

"If it be as thou sayest," replied Goodman Brown, "I marvel they never 19
spoke of these matters; or, verily,[8] I marvel not, seeing that the least rumor of the sort would have driven them from New England. We are a people of prayer, and good works to boot, and abide no such wickedness."

"Wickedness or not," said the traveller with the twisted staff, "I have a 20
very general acquaintance here in New England. The deacons of many a church have drunk the communion[9] wine with me; the selectmen of divers towns make me their chairman; and a majority of the Great and General Court are firm supporters of my interest. The governor and I, too—But these are state secrets."

"Can this be so?" cried Goodman Brown, with a stare of amazement at 21
his undisturbed companion. "Howbeit, I have nothing to do with the governor and council; they have their own ways, and are no rule for a simple husbandman like me. But, were I to go on with thee, how should I meet the eye of that good old man, our minister, at Salem village? O, his voice would make me tremble both Sabbath day and lecture day."

Thus far the elder traveller had listened with due gravity; but now burst 22
into a fit of irrepressible mirth, shaking himself so violently that his snakelike staff actually seemed to wriggle in sympathy.

"Ha! ha! ha!" shouted he again and again; then composing himself. 23
"Well, go on, Goodman Brown, go on; but, prithee, don't kill me with laughing."

"Well, then, to end the matter at once," said Goodman Brown, consider- 24
ably nettled, "there is my wife, Faith. It would break her dear little heart; and I'd rather break my own."

"Nay, if that be the case," answered the other, "e'en go thy ways, 25
Goodman Brown. I would not for twenty old women like the one hobbling before us that Faith should come to any harm."

As he spoke he pointed his staff at a female figure on the path, in whom 26
Goodman Brown recognized a very pious and exemplary[10] dame, who had taught him his catechism in youth, and was still his moral and spiritual adviser, jointly with the minister and Deacon Gookin.

"A marvel, truly, that Goody Cloyse should be so far in the wilderness 27
at nightfall," said he. "But with your leave, friend, I shall take a cut through the woods until we have left this Christian woman behind. Being a stranger to you, she might ask whom I was consorting with and whither I was going."

8. verily: in truth; indeed   9. communion: the religious rite of receiving the consecrated bread and wine
10. exemplary: worthy of imitation; commendable

"Be it so," said his fellow-traveller. "Betake you to the woods, and let   28
me keep the path."

Accordingly the young man turned aside, but took care to watch his   29
companion, who advanced softly along the road until he had come within a
staff's length of the old dame. She, meanwhile, was making the best of her
way, with singular speed for so aged a woman, and mumbling some indistinct
words—a prayer, doubtless—as she went. The traveller put forth his staff and
touched her withered neck with what seemed the serpent's tail.

"The devil!" screamed the pious old lady.   30

"Then Goody Cloyse knows her old friend?" observed the traveller,   31
confronting her and leaning on his writing stick.

"Ah, forsooth, and is it your worship indeed?" cried the good dame.   32
"Yea, truly is it, and in the very image of my old gossip, Goodman Brown,
the grandfather of the silly fellow that now is. But—would your worship
believe it?—my broomstick hath strangely disappeared, stolen, as I suspect,
by that unhanged witch, Goody Cory, and that, too, when I was all anointed[11]
with the juice of smallage, and cinquefoil, and wolf's bane—"

"Mingled with fine wheat and the fat of a new-born babe," said the   33
shape of old Goodman Brown.

"Ah, your worship knows the recipe," cried the old lady, cackling aloud.   34
"So, as I was saying, being all ready for the meeting, and no horse to ride
on, I made up my mind to foot it; for they tell me there is a nice young man
to be taken into communion tonight. But now your good worship will lend
me your arm, and we shall be there in a twinkling."

"That can hardly be," answered her friend. "I may not spare you my   35
arm, Goody Cloyse; but here is my staff, if you will."

So saying, he threw it down at her feet, where, perhaps, it assumed life,   36
being one of the rods which its owner had formerly lent to the Egyptian
magi. Of this fact, however, Goodman Brown could not take cognizance.[12]
He had cast up his eyes in astonishment, and, looking down again, beheld
neither Goody Cloyse nor the serpentine[13] staff, but his fellow-traveller alone,
who waited for him as calmly as if nothing had happened.

"That old woman taught me my catechism," said the young man; and   37
there was a world of meaning in this simple comment.

They continued to walk onward, while the elder traveller exhorted[14] his   38
companion to make good speed and persevere in the path, discoursing so
aptly that his arguments seemed rather to spring up in the bosom of his

---

11. anointed: to make sacred in a ceremony that includes the token applying of oil   12. cognizance:
awareness or realization   13. serpentine: characteristic of or resembling a serpent, as in form or movement   14. exhorted: to urge, advise, or caution earnestly

auditor than to be suggested by himself. As they went, he plucked a branch of maple to serve for a walking stick, and began to strip it of the twigs and little boughs, which were wet with evening dew. The moment his fingers touched them they became strangely withered and dried up as with a week's sunshine. Thus the pair proceeded, at a good free pace, until suddenly, in a gloomy hollow of the road, Goodman Brown sat himself down on the stump of a tree and refused to go any farther.

"Friend," said he, stubbornly, "my mind is made up. Not another step   39 will I budge on this errand. What if a wretched old woman do choose to go to the devil when I thought she was going to heaven: is that any reason why I should quit my dear Faith and go after her?"

"You will think better of this by and by," said his acquaintance, compos-   40 edly. "Sit here and rest yourself a while; and when you feel like moving again, there is my staff to help you along."

Without more words, he threw his companion the maple stick, and was   41 as speedily out of sight as if he had vanished into the deepening gloom. The young man sat a few moments by the roadside, applauding himself greatly, and thinking with how clear a conscience he should meet the minister in his morning walk, nor shrink from the eye of good old Deacon Gookin. And what calm sleep would be his that very night, which was to have been spent so wickedly, but so purely and sweetly now, in the arms of Faith! Amidst these pleasant and praiseworthy meditations, Goodman Brown heard the tramp of horses along the road, and deemed it advisable to conceal himself within the verge of the forest, conscious of the guilty purpose that had brought him thither, though now so happily turned from it.

On came the hoof tramps and the voices of the riders, two grave old   42 voices, conversing soberly as they drew near. These mingled sounds appeared to pass along the road, within a few yards of the young man's hiding-place; but, owing doubtless to the depth of the gloom at that particular spot, neither the travellers nor their steeds were visible. Though their figures brushed the small boughs by the wayside, it could not be seen that they intercepted, even for a moment, the faint gleam from the strip of bright sky athwart[15] which they must have passed. Goodman Brown alternately crouched and stood on tiptoe, pulling aside the branches and thrusting forth his head as far as he durst[16] without discerning so much as a shadow. It vexed[17] him the more, because he could have sworn, were such a thing possible, that he recognized the voices of the minister and Deacon Gookin, jogging along quietly, as they were wont to do, when bound to some ordination[18]

15. athwart: in opposition to   16. durst: dare   17. vexed: to irritate, annoy, provoke   18. ordination: the act or ceremony of conferring holy orders on someone

or ecclesiastical[19] council. While yet within hearing, one of the riders stopped to pluck a switch.

"Of the two, reverend sir," said the voice like the deacon's, "I had rather   43
miss an ordination dinner than to-night's meeting. They tell me that some of our community are to be here from Falmouth and beyond, and others from Connecticut and Rhode Island, besides several of the Indian powwows, who, after their fashion, know almost as much deviltry as the best of us. Moreover, there is a goodly young woman to be taken into communion."

"Mighty well, Deacon Gookin!" replied the solemn old tones of the   44
minister. "Spur up, or we shall be late. Nothing can be done, you know, until I get on the ground."

The hoofs clattered again; and the voices, talking so strangely in the   45
empty air, passed on through the forest, where no church had ever been gathered or solitary Christian prayed. Whither, then, could these holy men be journeying so deep into the heathen wilderness? Young Goodman Brown caught hold of a tree for support, being ready to sink down on the ground, faint and overburdened with the heavy sickness of his heart. He looked up to the sky, doubting whether there really was a heaven above him. Yet there was the blue arch, and the stars brightening in it.

"With heaven above and Faith below, I will yet stand firm against the   46
devil!" cried Goodman Brown.

While he still gazed upward into the deep arch of the firmament[20] and   47
had lifted his hands to pray, a cloud, though no wind was stirring, hurried across the zenith and hid the brightening stars. The blue sky was still visible, except directly overhead, where this black mass of cloud was sweeping swiftly northward. Aloft in the air, as if from the depths of the cloud, came a confused and doubtful sound of voices. Once the listener fancied that he could distinguish the accents of townspeople of his own, men and women, both pious and ungodly, many of whom he had met at the communion table, and had seen others rioting at the tavern. The next moment, so indistinct were the sounds, he doubted whether he had heard aught but the murmur of the old forest, whispering without a wind. Then came a stronger swell of those familiar tones, heard daily in the sunshine at Salem village, but never until now from a cloud of night. There was one voice, of a young woman, uttering lamentations, yet with an uncertain sorrow, and entreating for some favor, which, perhaps, it would grieve her to obtain; and all the unseen multitude, both saints and sinners, seemed to encourage her onward.

"Faith!" shouted Goodman Brown, in a voice of agony and desperation;   48
and the echoes of the forest mocked him, crying, "Faith! Faith!" as if bewildered wretches were seeking her all through the wilderness.

19. ecclesiastical: pertaining to the church or clergy   20. firmament: the arch or vault of heaven; the sky

The cry of grief, rage, and terror was yet piercing the night, when the   49
unhappy husband held his breath for a response. There was a scream, drowned
immediately in a louder murmur of voices, fading into far-off laughter, as
the dark cloud swept away, leaving the clear and silent sky above Goodman
Brown. But something fluttered lightly down through the air and caught on
the branch of a tree. The young man seized it, and beheld a pink ribbon.

"My Faith is gone!" cried he, after one stupefied moment. "There is no   50
good on earth; and sin is but a name. Come, devil; for to thee is this world
given."

And, maddened with despair, so that he laughed loud and long, did   51
Goodman Brown grasp his staff and set forth again, at such a rate that he
seemed to fly along the forest path rather than to walk or run. The road
grew wilder and drearier and more faintly traced, and vanished at length,
leaving him in the heart of the dark wilderness, still rushing onward with the
instinct that guides mortal man to evil. The whole forest was peopled with
frightful sounds—the creaking of the trees, the howling of wild beasts, and
the yell of Indians; while sometimes the wind tolled like a distant church
bell, and sometimes gave a broad roar around the traveller, as if all Nature
were laughing him to scorn. But he was himself the chief horror of the scene,
and shrank not from its other horrors.

"Ha! ha! ha!" roared Goodman Brown when the wind laughed at him.   52
"Let us hear which will laugh loudest. Think not to frighten me with your
deviltry. Come witch, come wizard, come Indian powwow, come devil himself, and here comes Goodman Brown. You may as well fear him as he fear
you."

In truth, all through the haunted forest there could be nothing more   53
frightful than the figure of Goodman Brown. On he flew among the black
pines, brandishing his staff with frenzied gestures, now giving vent to an
inspiration of horrid blasphemy, and now shouting forth such laughter as set
all the echoes of the forest laughing like demons around him. The fiend in
his own shape is less hideous than when he rages in the breast of man. Thus
sped the demoniac on his course, until, quivering among the trees, he saw
a red light before him, as when the felled trunks and branches of a clearing
have been set on fire, and throw up their lurid blaze against the sky, at the
hour of midnight. He paused, in a lull of the tempest that had driven him
onward, and heard the swell of what seemed a hymn, rolling solemnly from
a distance with the weight of many voices. He knew the tune; it was a familiar
one in the choir of the village meeting house. The verse died heavily away,
and was lengthened by a chorus, not of human voices, but of all the sounds
of the benighted[21] wilderness pealing[22] in awful harmony together. Goodman

---

21. benighted: overtaken by darkness or night   22. pealing: any loud sustained sound or series of sounds

Brown cried out; and his cry was lost to his own ear by its unison with the cry of the desert.

In the interval of silence he stole forward until the light glared full upon his eyes. At one extremity of an open space, hemmed[23] in by the dark wall of the forest, arose a rock, bearing some rude, natural resemblance either to an altar or a pulpit, and surrounded by four blazing pines, their tops aflame, their stems untouched, like candles at an evening meeting. The mass of foliage that had overgrown the summit of the rock was all on fire, blazing high into the night and fitfully illuminating the whole field. Each pendent[24] twig and leafy festoon[25] was in a blaze. As the red light arose and fell, a numerous congregation alternately shone forth, then disappeared in shadow, and again grew, as it were, out of the darkness, peopling the heart of the solitary woods at once.   54

"A grave and dark-clad company," quoth Goodman Brown.   55

In truth they were such. Among them, quivering to and fro between gloom and splendor, appeared faces that would be seen next day at the council board of the province, and others which, Sabbath after Sabbath, looked devoutly heavenward, and benignantly[26] over the crowded pews, from the holiest pulpits in the land. Some affirm that the lady of the governor was there. At least there were high dames well known to her, and wives of honored husbands, and widows, a great multitude, and ancient maidens, all of excellent repute, and fair young girls, who trembled lest their mothers should espy them. Either the sudden gleams of light flashing over the obscure field bedazzled Goodman Brown, or he recognized a score of the church members of Salem village famous for their especial sanctity. Good old Deacon Gookin had arrived, and waited at the skirts of that venerable[27] saint, his revered pastor. But, irreverently consorting with these grave, reputable, and pious people, these elders of the church, these chaste dames and dewy virgins, there were men of dissolute lives and women of spotted fame, wretches given over to all mean and filthy vice, and suspected even of horrid crimes. It was strange to see that the good shrank not from the wicked, nor were the sinners abashed by the saints. Scattered also among their palefaced enemies were the Indian priests, or powwows, who had often scared their native forest with more hideous incantations[28] than any known to English witchcraft.   56

"But where is Faith?" thought Goodman Brown; and, as hope came into his heart, he trembled.   57

Another verse of the hymn arose, a slow and mournful strain, such as the pious love, but joined to words which expressed all that our nature can   58

---

23. hemmed: to enclose or confine   24. pendent: hanging or suspended   25. festoon: a chain of foliage suspended in a curve between two points   26. benignantly: graciously, exerting a good influence   27. venerable: worthy of respect or reverence, as because of great age, high office, or noble character   28. incantations: the chanting or uttering of words purporting to have magical power

conceive of sin, and darkly hinted at far more. Unfathomable[29] to mere mortals is the lore of fiends. Verse after verse was sung; and still the chorus of the desert swelled between like the deepest tone of a mighty organ; and with the final peal of that dreadful anthem there came a sound, as if the roaring wind, the rushing streams, the howling beasts, and every other voice of the unconverted wilderness were mingling and according with the voice of guilty man in homage to the prince of all. The four blazing pines threw up a loftier flame, and obscurely discovered shapes and visages[30] of horror on the smoke wreaths above the impious assembly. At the same moment the fire on the rock shot redly forth and formed a glowing arch above its base, where now appeared a figure. With reverence be it spoken, the figure bore no slight similitude, both in garb and manner, to some grave divine of the New England churches.

"Bring forth the converts!" cried a voice that echoed through the field and rolled into the forest.   59

At the word, Goodman Brown stepped forth from the shadow of the trees and approached the congregation, with whom he felt a loathful brotherhood by the sympathy of all that was wicked in his heart. He could have well nigh sworn that the shape of his own dead father beckoned him to advance, looking downward from a smoke wreath, while a woman, with dim features of despair, threw out her hand to warn him back. Was it his mother? But he had no power to retreat one step, nor to resist, even in thought, when the minister and good old Deacon Gookin seized his arms and led him to the blazing rock. Thither came also the slender form of a veiled female, led between Goody Cloyse, that pious teacher of the catechism, and Martha Carrier, who had received the devil's promise to be queen of hell. A rampant hag was she. And there stood the proselytes[31] beneath the canopy of fire.   60

"Welcome, my children," said the dark figure, "to the communion of your race. Ye have found thus young your nature and your destiny. My children, look behind you!"   61

They turned; and flashing forth, as it were, in a sheet of flame, the fiend worshippers were seen; the smile of welcome gleamed darkly on every visage.   62

"There," resumed the sable[32] form, "are all whom ye have reverenced from youth. Ye deemed them holier than yourselves, and shrank from your own sin, contrasting it with their lives of righteousness and prayerful aspirations heavenward. Yet here are they all in my worshipping assembly. This night it shall be granted you to know their secret deeds; how hoary-bearded elders of the church have whispered wanton words to the young maids of their households; how many a woman, eager for widow's weeds, has given   63

---

29. unfathomable: being unable to penetrate to the truth   30. visages: faces   31. proselytes: converts; people who have changed from one religious belief or sect to another   32. sable: very dark

her husband a drink at bedtime and let him sleep his last sleep in her bosom; how beardless youths have made haste to inherit their father's wealth; and how fair damsels—blush not, sweet ones—have dug little graves in the garden, and bidden me, the sole guest, to an infant's funeral. By the sympathy of your human hearts for sin ye shall scent out all the places—whether in church, bed-chamber, street, field, or forest—where crime has been committed, and shall exult[33] to behold the whole earth one stain of guilt, one mighty blood spot. Far more than this. It shall be yours to penetrate, in every bosom, the deep mystery of sin, the fountain of all wicked arts, and which inexhaustibly supplies more evil impulses than human power—than my power at its utmost—can make manifest in deeds. And now, my children, look upon each other."

They did so; and, by the blaze of the hell-kindled torches, the wretched man beheld his Faith, and the wife her husband, trembling before that unhallowed altar.   64

"Lo, there ye stand, my children," said the figure, in a deep and solemn tone, almost sad with its despairing awfulness, as if his once angelic nature could yet mourn for our miserable race. "Depending upon one another's hearts, ye had still hoped that virtue were not all a dream. Now are ye undeceived. Evil is the nature of mankind. Evil must be your only happiness. Welcome again, my children, to the communion of your race."   65

"Welcome," repeated the fiend worshippers, in one cry of despair and triumph.   66

And there they stood, the only pair, as it seemed, who were yet hesitating on the verge of wickedness in this dark world. A basin was hollowed, naturally, in the rock. Did it contain water, reddened by the lurid[34] light? or was it blood? or, perchance, a liquid flame? Herein did the shape of evil dip his hand and prepare to lay the mark of baptism upon their foreheads, that they might be partakers of the mystery of sin, more conscious of the secret guilt of others, both in deed and thought, than they could now be of their own. The husband cast one look at his pale wife, and Faith at him. What polluted wretches would the next glance show them to each other, shuddering alike at what they disclosed and what they saw!   67

"Faith! Faith!" cried the husband, "look up to heaven, and resist the wicked one."   68

Whether Faith obeyed, he knew not. Hardly had he spoken when he found himself amid calm night and solitude, listening to a roar of the wind which died heavily away through the forest. He staggered against the rock, and felt it chill and damp; while a hanging twig, that had been all on fire, besprinkled his cheek with the coldest dew.   69

---

33. exult: to show or feel a lively or triumphant joy   34. lurid: gruesome; horrible; revolting

The next morning young Goodman Brown came slowly into the street 70 of Salem village, staring around him like a bewildered man. The good old minister was taking a walk along the graveyard to get an appetite for breakfast and meditate his sermon, and bestowed a blessing, as he passed, on Goodman Brown. He shrank from the venerable saint as if to avoid an anathema.[35] Old Deacon Gookin was at domestic worship, and the holy words of his prayer were heard through the open window. "What God doth the wizard pray to?" quoth Goodman Brown. Goody Cloyse, that excellent old Christian, stood in the early sunshine at her own lattice,[36] catechizing a little girl who had brought her a pint of morning's milk. Goodman Brown snatched away the child as from the grasp of the fiend himself. Turning the corner by the meeting-house, he spied the head of Faith, with the pink ribbons, gazing anxiously forth, and bursting into such joy at the sight of him that she skipped along the street and almost kissed her husband before the whole village. But Goodman Brown looked sternly and sadly into her face, and passed on without a greeting.

Had Goodman Brown fallen asleep in the forest and only dreamed a 71 wild dream of a witch meeting?

Be it so, if you will; but, alas! it was a dream of evil omen for young 72 Goodman Brown. A stern, a sad, a darkly meditative, a distrustful, if not a desperate, man did he become from the night of that fearful dream. On the Sabbath day, when the congregation were singing a holy psalm, he could not listen because an anthem of sin rushed loudly upon his ear and drowned all the blessed strain.[37] When the minister spoke from the pulpit, with power and fervid eloquence and with his hand on the open Bible, of the sacred truths of our religion, and of saintlike lives and triumphant deaths, and of future bliss or misery unutterable, then did Goodman Brown turn pale, dreading lest the roof should thunder down upon the gray blasphemer and his hearers. Often, awaking suddenly at midnight, he shrank from the bosom of Faith; and at morning or eventide, when the family knelt down at prayer, he scowled, and muttered to himself, and gazed sternly at his wife, and turned away. And when he had lived long, and was borne to his grave, a hoary[38] corpse, followed by Faith, an aged woman, and children and grandchildren, a goodly procession, besides neighbors not a few, they carved no hopeful verse upon his tombstone; for his dying hour was gloom.

---

35. anathema: a person or thing condemned to damnation　　36. lattice: a structure of crossed wooden or metal strips; a window, gate or the like consisting of such a structure　　37. strain: a melody; tune
38. hoary: gray or white with age

OPTIONS FOR READING LOGS: "YOUNG GOODMAN BROWN"

1. Use the double-entry journal technique (asking "what" or "why" questions in the left-hand side of your journal page) to discover meaning in "Young Goodman Brown." Draw a vertical line down the middle of your journal page to create two columns. In the left column, keep a running list of questions that occur to you as you are reading. Aim for three to five questions that are puzzling, yet answerable, such as, "Why did Goodman Brown choose to go into the woods?" or "Did he really see all of those people in the forest that night?" Proceed down the page, asking several more significant questions. When you are finished with your list of questions, go back to the top of your list and answer your questions as completely as you can in the right column. Attempt to answer your questions by taking educated guesses and looking for answers in the text and between the lines. (Remember that such an interpretation will require you to take risks and guesses.) Finally, to demonstrate that you have reached a basic understanding of the text, end your journal entry by jotting down the main idea of the story.

2. Examine your personal reaction to "Young Goodman Brown" by completing one of the following statements: "I was confused by . . ." or "I was struck by . . ." or "I was surprised by. . . ." For example, "I was struck by Goodman Brown's brave rejection of evil" or "I was confused by his harsh reaction to his wife and fellow townspeople at the end of the story." Develop your journal entry by adding detailed explanations from your own experiences as well as from the story. Refer to particular incidents in the story and explain your reactions. Finalize your journal entry with a statement of the theme of "Young Goodman Brown."

3. Tell a parallel story from your own personal life that was triggered by "Young Goodman Brown." Does the story remind you of a particular situation in your life in which you or someone you know lost faith in someone or something? Jot down things that were similar or different from Hawthorne's story. Wrap up your journal entry by stating what your experience taught you about yourself or others.

OPTIONS FOR WRITING ASSIGNMENTS: "YOUNG GOODMAN BROWN"

1. Toward the end of the story, Hawthorne writes, "Had Goodman Brown fallen asleep in the forest, and only dreamed a wild dream . . .?" Some-

times we dream of life-threatening or frightening experiences. Does "Young Goodman Brown" remind you of one of your own dreams? Does thinking about such a dream make you reassess your life and values? Recreate the dream as a story or a poem, using concrete details, vivid imagery, and, if possible, dialogue. Also, explore whatever explanations or reasons you can think of for the dream. What do you feel the dream is trying to tell you? End with a generalization about the purpose of your dream and how it helped you to make a discovery about yourself or some aspect of your life.

2. Review your journal entries to see if you can make any connections between "Young Goodman Brown" and any of the other readings in our textbook. Notice whether or not similarities or differences are evident between Hawthorne's story and one of the other stories, poems, or essays you have read. For example, in terms of theme, you might see marked similarities between the dream-like quality of the mysterious poem by Paz called "The Street" and "Young Goodman Brown." You might also see some thematic similarities between Ghita Orth's poem "What Almost Happened in Arizona" and Hawthorne's story. You could combine and expand your journal entries into a more polished piece of writing that explores its subject matter (for example, how well we really know those around us) in greater range and depth. A comparison–and–contrast essay might be an appropriate mode for this purpose. Begin with a list (two lists for comparison/contrast), develop it into an outline, and use transitional expressions that signal similarities or differences.

3. Write a letter to Goodman Brown as he is at the end of the story. Address him directly, explaining your reaction to what has happened to him in the woods that night. You may choose to empathize with his difficult situation, explain what has happened to him, praise him for his actions, or criticize his conclusions about his wife and fellow villagers.

4. Write a formal essay of five or more paragraphs explaining the meaning of Hawthorne's story, "Young Goodman Brown." Focus your attention on parts of the story that you have genuine questions about, such as, "What is it in him that makes him want to meet the Devil in the woods that night? Is what happens to him just a bad dream or an actual horrifying, genuinely evil event? Is he a fool at the end of the story or is he now in the possession of a very disturbing truth about the world in which he lives?" Begin with a thesis statement that makes an arguable point about the central meaning of the story. For example, you may wish to analyze the significance of the people he encounters in the woods that night, such as the Deacon Gookin and Goody

Cloyse; or you may want to assert that he is the victim of illusions. Brainstorm or prewrite to come up with reasons to support your interpretation. In your essay, you will need to quote from the story and refer to specific passages to clarify and support your central argument.

What Didn't Happen in Arizona

1983

GHITA ORTH

 GHITA ORTH is a contemporary American poet. In her poem "What Didn't Happen in Arizona," Orth narrates the story of a woman whose family briefly leaves her at a lonely intersection. Orth describes the woman's sudden fantasy of deserting her family by simply disappearing from their lives, portraying a strangely realistic image of what it might be like to change one's life instantly through one deliberate action.

As you read Orth's poem, think about why the woman would suddenly feel the urge to disappear from her husband and young daughter. Is there any evidence in the poem that hints at reasons for her hidden desire? Do you believe she is seriously considering disappearing? Would she have accepted if a stranger had offered her a ride? Has someone you know ever made a snap decision that shocked others and revealed a hidden, unanticipated side to his or her personality?

She stands at an exit ramp 1
of the Interstate on a flat
beige plain of brush and dust.

In no direction is there anything
except this band of asphalt 5
joining nothing to nothing.

Far in the background clouds
daubed by some power plant
drift without connection

to the sky. She is by herself 10
at this roadside by choice—
husband and daughter have driven

over the bridge that marks
the interchange, the one rise
generous enough to hide a car.   15

She will smoke a cigarette
while he will take a picture,
their daughter will still sleep

curled in the backseat burrow
of duffels and suitcases   20
with a Walkman playing.

She has no fear that he might
leave her here, rather that she
will vanish in the only place

she'd ever been so perfectly   25
alone that disappearing seems
as likely as it is impossible.

She stands and waits in that
vacant landscape for a blue
Ford truck with a smiling Navajo   30

at the wheel, waits for an R.V.
splashed with bumper stickers—
I LOVE RETIREMENT, *Disney World*—

waits for a station wagon or
a tour bus, or a van covered   35
entirely in psychedelic swirls.

She waits for the one who must
surely pass, and slow, and back up,
and scoop her quickly into the trunk

so that her husband will return   40
to the place she was and find
it emptied, will drive long

into the night while their daughter
sleeps, marveling at how she managed
to disappear there in a flat land   45

with no cars, no hiding places,
and only manufactured clouds.
Then their bronze Honda rises

into the frame of sky and scrub.
She sticks her thumb out. Her husband   50
laughs, waves, drives past, stops.

And she runs to get inside a space
so filled with what belongs to her
that she can hardly breathe.

◆ ◆ ◆

OPTIONS FOR READING LOGS: "WHAT DIDN'T HAPPEN IN ARIZONA"

1. Use the double-entry journal technique to clarify the meaning of some of the powerful lines in "What Didn't Happen in Arizona." Divide your journal page in two with a vertical line, and in the left column copy phrases or lines that you particularly like or find puzzling, such as, ". . . this band of asphalt / joining nothing to nothing," or "so filled with what belongs to her / that she can hardly breathe." In the right column, jot down possible interpretations, personal associations, or explanatory comments. End your journal entry with a brief entry about a significant discovery you made about the poem as a whole during this process: "I discovered that _____ ."

2. As a creative writing response to "What Didn't Happen in Arizona" write an original poem of your own. You may want to describe a time when you had a secret fantasy; a moment when you made a sudden, snap decision that surprised even you; or a time when someone else surprised you with an unanticipated action. If you wish, try using relatively short lines and three-line stanzas like the ones in Ghita Orth's poem. After you have written your poem, briefly explain why "What Didn't Happen in Arizona" triggered this creative response from you.

3. Tell a personal story that "What Didn't Happen in Arizona" helps you to recall. Start your thoughts flowing by considering the message of Orth's poem. Is it the woman's realization of her desire to flee her family? Is it a poem of the need for liberation from a marriage? Is it a disturbing poem of a selfish person's egocentric fantasy? How does the theme of the poem cause you to reflect on some experience of your own? End your entry by clarifying what you learned from reading "What Didn't Happen in Arizona."

OPTIONS FOR WRITING ASSIGNMENTS: "WHAT DIDN'T HAPPEN IN ARIZONA"

1. Develop one of your reading log entries on "What Didn't Happen in Arizona" into a more polished piece of writing that explores its subject matter in greater range and depth, using an appropriate form—a poem, a fictional story, a personal narrative, or an essay that examines a central idea.

2. Write a letter to the woman in "What Didn't Happen in Arizona." Address her directly and give your reaction to her desire to "vanish in the only place / she'd ever been so perfectly alone." Use the letter to express your own reaction to the woman and her hidden, unexpressed desire. You may choose to criticize her or to empathize with her need for freedom.

3. What personal knowledge are we meant to gain from this poem? If you could talk with Ghita Orth, the author of "What Didn't Happen in Arizona," to ask her questions and give her your ideas and interpretations, how do you think she would respond to them? Create a conversation between you and Orth. Your conversation might take the form of a question-and-answer interview, an argument representing two opposing points of view, or an open-ended discussion of the author's ideas about the role of fantasy as an escape from the realities of our lives.

4. Reading a poem once may not enable us to appreciate its full range of meaning. That often follows only when we reread, think about, discuss, and write about the poem. To deepen your understanding of the meaning of "What Didn't Happen in Arizona" and the way it challenges what we know and value, write a formal essay of five or more paragraphs. Is the woman's disturbing desire to escape from her family understandable, or do you find it shocking and unsettling, even as a fantasy? In an introductory paragraph, clearly state the poem's main idea. In your supporting paragraphs, focus your attention on the parts of the poem that caused you to have questions or that clarify your main idea. In your commentary you will need to quote from the poem and refer to specific passages that support your ideas.

From

The Qualities of the Prince

1513

NICCOLO MACHIAVELLI

 NICCOLO MACHIAVELLI, born in 1469, was a citizen of the Renaissance Italian city-state of Florence. He was not a political leader himself, but he was involved to a considerable extent in the turbulent politics of his city. In fact, he was once banished from Florence for eighteen years for political reasons. He wrote *The Qualities of the Prince* after being imprisoned by his political opposition. In this famous book, Machiavelli gives advice to a young prince, instructing him how to get power, stay in power, and be a successful leader. His advice is often surprising, even shocking, to those of us not familiar with the dangerous cloak-and-dagger world of Florentine politics; nonetheless, much of his advice is still very useful to modern politicians at every level of government. Many historians believe Machiavelli's view of ethics and politics has been widely misinterpreted, but *Machiavellian* has come to mean "manipulative and opportunistic." Machiavelli died in 1527, after a lifetime of believing that class divisions were inevitable in human society and, indeed, that such conflicts spurred by open and widespread debate could ultimately strengthen republics.

As you read the following excerpt from The Qualities of the Prince, *reflect on whether Machiavelli's advice is still valuable for a modern politician. What aspects of it apply to today's politics? Do you agree with him when he tells the prince, "Everyone sees what you seem to be, few perceive what you are," and "Ordinary people are always deceived by appearances"? Does Machiavelli provide any disturbing insights into politicians in our government today?*

Proceeding to the other qualities mentioned above, I say that every 1 prince must desire to be considered merciful and not cruel; neverthe- less, he must take care not to misuse this mercy. Cesare Borgia was considered cruel; nonetheless, his cruelty had brought order to Romagna, united it, restored it to peace and obedience. If we examine this carefully, we shall see that he was more merciful than the Florentine people, who, in order to avoid being considered cruel, allowed the destruction of Pistoia. Therefore, a prince must not worry about the reproach of cruelty when it is a matter of keeping his subjects united and loyal; for with a very few examples of cruelty he will be more compassionate than those who, out of excessive mercy, permit disorders to continue, from which arise murders and plundering; for these usually harm the community at large, while the executions that come from the prince harm one individual in particular. And the new prince, above all other princes, cannot escape the reputation of being called cruel, since new states are full of dangers. And Virgil, through Dido, states: "My difficult condition and the newness of my rule make me act in such a manner, and to set guards over my land on all sides."

Nevertheless, a prince must be cautious in believing and in acting, nor   2 should he be afraid of his own shadow; and he should proceed in such a manner, tempered by prudence and humanity, so that too much trust may not render him imprudent nor too much distrust render him intolerable.

From this arises an argument: whether it is better to be loved than to   3 be feared, or the contrary. I reply that one should like to be both one and the other; but since it is difficult to join them together, it is much safer to be feared than to be loved when one of the two must be lacking. For one can generally say this about men: that they are ungrateful, fickle, simulators and deceivers, avoiders of danger, greedy for gain; and while you work for their good they are completely yours, offering you their blood, their property, their lives, and their sons, as I said earlier, when danger is far away; but when it comes nearer to you they turn away. And that prince who bases his power entirely on their words, finding himself stripped of other preparations, comes to ruin; for friendships that are acquired by a price and not by greatness and nobility of character are purchased but are not owned, and at the proper moment they cannot be spent. And men are less hesitant about harming someone who makes himself loved than one who makes himself feared because love is held together by a chain of obligation which, since men are a sorry lot, is broken on every occasion in which their own self-interest is concerned; but fear is held together by a dread of punishment which will never abandon you.

A prince must nevertheless make himself feared in such a manner that   4 he will avoid hatred, even if he does not acquire love; since to be feared and not to be hated can very well be combined; and this will always be so when he keeps his hands off the property and the women of his citizens and his subjects. And if he must take someone's life, he should do so when there is proper justification and manifest cause; but, above all, he should avoid the property of others; for men forget more quickly the death of their father than the loss of their patrimony. Moreover, the reasons for seizing their property are never lacking; and he who begins to live by stealing always finds a reason for taking what belongs to others; on the contrary, reasons for taking a life are rarer and disappear sooner.

But when the prince is with his armies and has under his command a multitude of troops, then it is absolutely necessary that he not worry about being considered cruel; for without that reputation he will never keep an army united or prepared for any combat. Among the praiseworthy deeds of Hannibal is counted this: that, having a very large army, made up of all kinds of men, which he commanded in foreign lands, there never arose the slightest dissention, neither among themselves nor against their prince, both during his good and his bad fortune. This could not have arisen from anything other than his inhuman cruelty, which, along with his many other abilities, made him always respected and terrifying in the eyes of his soldiers; and without that, to attain the same effect, his other abilities would not have sufficed. And the writers of history, having considered this matter very little, on the one hand admire these deeds of his and on the other condemn the main cause of them.

And that it be true that his other abilities would not have been sufficient can be seen from the example of Scipio, a most extraordinary man not only in his time but in all recorded history, whose armies in Spain rebelled against him; this came about from nothing other than his excessive compassion, which gave to his soldiers more liberty than military discipline allowed. For this he was censured in the senate by Fabius Maximus, who called him the corruptor of the Roman militia. The Locrians, having been ruined by one of Scipio's officers, were not avenged by him, nor was the arrogance of that officer corrected, all because of his tolerant nature; so that someone in the senate who tried to apologize for him said that there were many men who knew how not to err better than they knew how to correct errors. Such a nature would have, in time, damaged Scipio's fame and glory if he had maintained it during the empire; but, living under the control of the senate, this harmful characteristic of his not only concealed itself but brought him fame.

I conclude, therefore, returning to the problem of being feared and loved, that since men love at their own pleasure and fear at the pleasure of the prince, a wise prince should build his foundation upon that which belongs to him, not upon that which belongs to others: he must strive only to avoid hatred, as has been said.

HOW A PRINCE SHOULD KEEP HIS WORD

How praiseworthy it is for a prince to keep his word and to live by   8
integrity and not by deceit everyone knows; nevertheless, one sees from the
experience of our times that the princes who have accomplished great deeds
are those who have cared little for keeping their promises and who have
known how to manipulate the minds of men by shrewdness; and in the end
they have surpassed those who laid their foundations upon honesty.

You must, therefore, know that there are two means of fighting: one   9
according to the laws, the other with force; the first way is proper to man,
the second to beasts; but because the first, in many cases, is not sufficient,
it becomes necessary to have recourse to the second. Therefore, a prince
must know how to use wisely the natures of the beast and the man. This
policy was taught to princes allegorically by the ancient writers, who described
how Achilles and many other ancient princes were given to Chiron the Centaur
to be raised and taught under his discipline. This can only mean that, having
a half-beast and half-man as a teacher, a prince must know how to employ
the nature of the one and the other; and the one without the other cannot
endure.

Since, then, a prince must know how to make good use of the nature   10
of the beast, he should choose from among the beasts the fox and the lion;
for the lion cannot defend itself from traps and the fox cannot protect itself
from wolves. It is therefore necessary to be a fox in order to recognize the
traps and a lion in order to frighten the wolves. Those who play only the
part of the lion do not understand matters. A wise ruler, therefore, cannot
and should not keep his word when such an observance of faith would be
to his disadvantage and when the reasons which made him promise are
removed. And if men were all good, this rule would not be good; but since
men are a sorry lot and will not keep their promises to you, you likewise
need not keep yours to them. A prince never lacks legitimate reasons to break
his promises. Of this one could cite an endless number of modern examples
to show how many pacts, how many promises have been made null and void
because of the infidelity of princes; and he who has known best how to use
the fox has come to a better end. But it is necessary to know how to disguise
this nature well and to be a great hypocrite and a liar: and men are so
simpleminded and so controlled by their present necessities that one who
deceives will always find another who will allow himself to be deceived.

I do not wish to remain silent about one of these recent instances.   11
Alexander VI did nothing else, he thought about nothing else, except to
deceive men, and he always found the occasion to do this. And there never
was a man who had more forcefulness in his oaths, who affirmed a thing

with more promises, and who honored his word less; nevertheless, his tricks always succeeded perfectly since he was well acquainted with this aspect of the world.

Therefore, it is not necessary for a prince to have all of the above-   12
mentioned qualities, but it is very necessary for him to appear to have them. Furthermore, I shall be so bold as to assert this: that having them and practicing them at all times is harmful; and appearing to have them is useful; for instance, to seem merciful, faithful, humane, forthright, religious, and to be so; but his mind should be disposed in such a way that should it become necessary not to be so, he will be able and know how to change to the contrary. And it is essential to understand this: that a prince, and especially a new prince, cannot observe all those things by which men are considered good, for in order to maintain the state he is often obliged to act against his promise, against charity, against humanity, and against religion. And therefore, it is necessary that he have a mind ready to turn itself according to the way the winds of Fortune and the changeability of affairs require him; and, as I said above, as long as it is possible, he should not stray from the good, but he should know how to enter into evil when necessity commands.

A prince, therefore, must be very careful never to let anything slip from   13
his lips which is not full of the five qualities mentioned above: he should appear, upon seeing and hearing him, to be all mercy, all faithfulness, all integrity, all kindness, all religion. And there is nothing more necessary than to seem to possess this last quality. And men in general judge more by their eyes than their hands; for everyone can see but few can feel. Everyone sees what you seem to be, few perceive what you are, and those few do not dare to contradict the opinion of the many who have the majesty of the state to defend them; and in the actions of all men, and especially of princes, where there is no impartial arbiter,[1] one must consider the final result. Let a prince therefore act to seize and to maintain the state; his methods will always be judged honorable and will be praised by all; for ordinary people are always deceived by appearances and by the outcome of a thing; and in the world there is nothing but ordinary people; and there is no room for the few, while the many have a place to lean on. A certain prince of the present day, whom I shall refrain from naming, preaches nothing but peace and faith, and to both one and the other he is entirely opposed; and both, if he had put them into practice, would have cost him many times over either his reputation or his state.

1. arbiter: judge

OPTIONS FOR READING LOGS: FROM *THE QUALITIES OF THE PRINCE*

1. Examine your personal reaction to this excerpt from *The Qualities of the Prince* by completing one of the following statements:

    A. "I was confused by _____."
    B. "I was struck by _____."
    C. "I was surprised by _____."

    Refer to a particular idea of Machiavelli's and explain your reactions to it. For example, "I was struck by his negative view of the common people," or "I was confused by his idea that being feared is better than being loved." Develop your journal entry by adding detailed explanations from your own experiences as well as from the story. Finish your journal entry with a clear statement of your opinion of Machiavelli's advice.

2. Copy what you think is the most powerful sentence or passage in this excerpt from *The Qualities of the Prince*. Using anecdotes and examples from your personal experience, explain fully why that particular passage held such power or meaning for you.

3. Tell a personal story that you recalled while reading this excerpt from *The Qualities of the Prince*. Does Machiavelli's advice to a young prince remind you of a recent event featuring a world figure, a particular politician, or some individual you know? Jot down characteristics that were similar to or different from those that Machiavelli describes. End your journal entry by stating the main theme of this selection.

OPTIONS FOR WRITING ASSIGNMENTS: FROM *THE QUALITIES OF THE PRINCE*

1. Expand and develop one of your reading logs into a more polished piece of writing that explores its subject matter in greater range and depth. Begin with a thesis statement that connects Machiavelli's *The Qualities of the Prince* to a first-hand experience you have had. Arrange your story in a clear, chronological order, adding enough specific details to make the event come alive for your reader. By the end of your essay, you should have convinced your reader of the relationship of some aspect of Machiavelli's *The Qualities of the Prince* to an experience in your own life.

2. Although Machiavelli wrote *The Prince* in 1513, the ideas expressed in it still seem very relevant today. Select some past or present notable

individual, leader, or politician and write a formal essay of five or more paragraphs, showing how that person demonstrates a keen awareness of the principles expressed in this excerpt. If necessary, locate some biographical and historical information to support your assertion that the person is a Machiavellian.

3. Write a letter either to Machiavelli or to the young prince to whom he is giving advice in this excerpt from *The Qualities of the Prince*. Address the person directly, using the letter to express your own point of view. You may praise or criticize the ideas in this excerpt or give your own advice on some of the same issues. Use whatever tone is most appropriate to express your reaction to the reading.

4. We often rely on other people's advice when we select material to read. Write a critical review of this excerpt from *The Qualities of the Prince*, clearly evaluating its content, especially in challenging us to arrive at a better understanding of the complex and ambiguous world of politics. Your evaluation of this selection can be positive, negative, or an interesting mixture of the two. For example, your evaluation may be that all aspiring politicians should read Machiavelli very carefully to understand how to be successful in politics. Or you may recommend that they should read him to learn how *not* to rule. Take some time to decide the sort of evaluation or judgment you want to make; then come up with several good reasons, each with supporting evidence from Machiavelli's *The Qualities of the Prince* that make your judgment convincing.

The Grass-Eaters

1985

KRISHNAN VARNA

 KRISHNAN VARNA is a writer who was born in Kerala, a southwestern state of India. "The Grass-Eaters" describes life in the slums of Calcutta, India's largest city. In this disturbing story, the narrator is a homeless man who finds shelter wherever he can: in a pipe, a freight wagon, the roof of an old building.

As you read the story, consider our responsibilities to the many people all over the world who find themselves without even the basic necessities of survival: shelter and food. Do we have an obligation to help house and feed the poor or the less fortunate worldwide? Or should we instead mind our own business and look to our own country's needs, or even our own family's?

For some time several years ago I was tutor to a spherical[1] boy (now a spherical youth). One day his ovoid[2] father, Ramaniklal Misrilal, asked me where I lived. I told him. 1

Misrilal looked exceedingly distressed. "A pipe, Ajit Babu? Did you say—a *pipe,* Ajit Babu?" 2

His cuboid[3] wife was near to tears. "A *pipe,* Ajit Babu? How can you live in a pipe?" 3

It was true: at that time I was living in a pipe with my wife, Swapna. It was long and three or four feet across. With a piece of sack cloth hung at either end, we had found it far more comfortable than any of our previous homes. 4

The first was a footpath of Chittaranjan Avenue. We had just arrived in Calcutta from East Bengal where Hindus and Muslims were killing one another. The footpath was so crowded with residents, refugees like us and locals, that if you got up at night to relieve yourself you could not be sure 5

---

1. spherical: having the form of a sphere; globular   2. ovoid: egg-shaped   3. cuboid: resembling a cube in form

of finding your place again. One cold morning I woke to find that the woman beside me was not Swapna at all but a bag of bones instead. And about fifty or sixty or seventy years old. I had one leg over her too. I paid bitterly for my mistake. The woman very nearly scratched out my eyes. Then came Swapna, fangs bared, claws out . . . I survived, but minus one ear. Next came the woman's husband, a hill of a man, whirling a tree over his head, roaring. That was my impression, anyway. I fled.

Later in the day Swapna and I moved into an abandoned-looking freight wagon at the railway terminus. A whole wagon to ourselves—a place with doors which could be opened and shut—we did nothing but open and shut them for a full hour—all the privacy a man and wife could want—no fear of waking up with a complete stranger in your arms . . . it was heaven. I felt I was God.   6

Then one night we woke to find that the world was running away from us: we had been coupled to a freight train. There was nothing for it but to wait for the train to stop. When it did, miles from Calcutta, we got off, took a passenger train back, and occupied another unwanted-looking wagon. That was not the only time we went to bed in Calcutta and woke up in another place. I found it an intensely thrilling experience, but not Swapna.   7

She wanted a a stationary home; she insisted on it. But she would not say why. If I persisted in questioning her, she snivelled. If I tried to persuade her to change her mind, pointing out all the advantages of living in a wagon—four walls, a roof and door absolutely free of charge, and complete freedom to make love day or night—she still snivelled. If I ignored her nagging, meals got delayed, the rice undercooked, the curry over-salted. In the end I gave in. We would move, I said, even if we had to occupy a house by force, but couldn't she tell me the reason, however irrelevant, why she did not like the wagon?   8

For the first time in weeks Swapna smiled, a very vague smile. Then, slowly, she drew the edge of her sari over her head, cast her eyes down, turned her face from me, and said in a tremulous, barely audible whisper that she (short pause) did (long pause) not want (very long pause) her (at jet speed) baby-to-be-born-in-a-running-train. And she buried her face in her hands. Our fourth child. One died of diphtheria back home (no longer our home) in Dacca; two, from fatigue, on our long trek on foot to Calcutta. Would the baby be a boy? I felt no doubt about it; it would be. Someone to look after us in our old age, to do our funeral rites when we died. I suddenly kissed Swapna, since her face was hidden in her hands, on her elbow, and was roundly chided. Kissing, she holds, is a western practice, unclean also, since it amounts to licking, and should be eschewed[4] by all good Hindus.   9

4. eschewed: to abstain or keep away from; shun; avoid

I lost no time in looking for a suitable place for her confinement. She   10
firmly rejected all my suggestions: the railway station platform (too many
residents); a little-used overbridge (she was not a kite to live so high above
the ground); a water tank that had fallen down and was empty (Did I think
that she was a frog?). I thought of suggesting the municipal primary school
where I was teaching at the time, but felt very reluctant. Not that the headmas-
ter would have objected if we had occupied one end of the back veranda: a
kindly man, father of eleven, all girls, he never disturbed the cat that regularly
kittened in his in-tray. My fear was: suppose Swapna came running into my
class, saying, "Hold the baby for a moment, will you? I'm going to the l-a-
t-r-i-n-e." Anyway, we set out to the school. On the way, near the Sealdah
railway station, we came upon a cement concrete pipe left over from long-
ago repairs to underground mains. Unbelievably, it was not occupied and,
with no prompting from me, she crept into it. That was how we came to
live in a pipe.

"It is not proper," said Misrilal, "not at all, for a school master to live   11
in a pipe." He sighed deeply. "Why don't you move into one of my buildings,
Ajit Babu?"

The house I might occupy, if I cared to, he explained, was in Entally,   12
not far from where the pipe lay; I should have no difficulty in locating it; it
was an old building and there were a number of old empty coal tar drums
on the roof; I could live on the roof if I stacked the drums in two rows and
put a tarpaulin over them.

We have lived on that roof ever since. It is not as bad as it sounds. The roof   13
is flat, not gabled, and it is made of cement concrete, not corrugated iron sheets.
The rent is far less than that of other tenants below us—Bijoy Babu, Akhanda
Chatterjee and Sagar Sen. We have far more light and ventilation than they. We
don't get nibbled by rats and mice and rodents as often as they do. And our
son, Prodeep, has far more room to play than the children below.

Prodeep is not with us now; he is in the Naxalite underground. We miss   14
him, terribly. But there is some compensation, small though it is. Had he
been with us, we would have had to wear clothes. Now, we don't. Not much,
that is. I make do with a loin cloth and Swapna with a piece slightly wider
to save our few threadbare clothes from further wear and tear. I can spare
little from my pension for new clothes. Swapna finds it very embarrassing to
be in my presence in broad daylight so meagerly clad and so contrives to
keep her back turned to me. Like a chimp in the sulks. I am fed up with
seeing her backside and tell her that she has nothing that I have not seen.
But she is adamant;[5] she will not turn around. After nightfall, however, she
relents: we are both nightblind.

---

5. adamant: utterly unyielding in attitude or opinion; inflexible

When we go out—to the communal lavatory, to pick up pieces of coal   15
from the railway track, to gather grass—we do wear clothes. Grass is our
staple food now: a mound of green grass boiled with green peppers and salt,
and a few ladles of very thin rice gruel. We took to eating it when the price
of rice started soaring. I had a good mind to do as Bijoy Babu below us is
believed to be doing. He has a theory that if you reduce your consumption
of food by five grams each day, you will not only not notice that you are
eating less but after some time you can do without any food at all. One day
I happened to notice that he was not very steady on his feet. That gave me
pause. He can get around, however badly he totters, because he has two legs;
but I have only one. I lost the other after a fall from the roof of a tram. In
Calcutta the trams are always crowded and if you can't get into a carriage
you may get up on its roof. The conductor will not stop you. If he tries to,
the passengers beat him up, set fire to the tram and any other vehicles parked
in the vicinity, loot nearby shops, break street lamps, take out a procession,
hold a protest meeting, denounce British imperialism, American neo-
colonialism, the central government, capitalism and socialism, and set off
crackers. I don't mind my handicap at all; I need wear only one sandal and
thereby save on footwear.

So, on the whole, our life together has been very eventful. The events,   16
of course, were not always pleasant. But, does it matter? We have survived
them. And now, we have no fears or anxieties. We have a home made of coal
tar drums. We eat two square meals of grass every day. We don't need to
wear clothes. We have a son to do our funeral rites when we die. We live
very quietly, content to look at the passing scene: a tram burning, a man
stabbing another man, a woman dropping her baby in a garbage bin.

OPTIONS FOR READING LOGS: "THE GRASS-EATERS"

1. We have mentioned before that writers often use images or symbols to
    represent an idea or concept and in doing so provide a deeper, more
    important message than the initially apparent one. This is certainly true
    for "The Grass-Eaters." Use the double-entry journal technique to ex-
    plore the meaning of some of the more powerful images or symbols in
    this selection. For example, a question in the left column might be, "Why
    are the characters described as being 'spherical,' 'ovoid,' and 'cuboid'?"
    Follow with several other significant questions. Then use the right column
    to explore possible answers to each of your questions. To demonstrate

that you have reached a basic understanding of the story, end your journal entry by jotting down the main idea of the story.

2. In a short story, an analysis of the main characters helps us to determine the story's central idea. Draw a vertical line down the middle of your journal page to create two columns. In the left column, keep a list of characters from the story. In the right column, jot down your opinions, observations, and comments about those characters. Complete your journal entry by discussing some interesting insights you gained in your analysis of one of the characters.

3. Examine your personal reaction to "The Grass-Eaters" by completing one of the following statements:

   A. "I was confused by _____ ."
   B. "I was struck by _____ ."
   C. "I was disturbed by _____ ."

Refer to particular incidents in the story and explain your reactions—for example, "I was struck more by what is not said during the husband-wife conversation than by what is actually said. Their conversation, which is punctuated by long pauses, tells a lot about their relationship." Finish your journal entry with a detailed explanation of your statement.

OPTIONS FOR WRITING ASSIGNMENTS: "THE GRASS-EATERS"

1. Review your journal entries to see if you can make any connections between this story and any of the earlier readings in this textbook. Notice whether similarities or differences are evident between "The Grass-Eaters" and one of the other stories, poems, or essays. You could combine and expand your journal entries into a more polished piece of writing that explores its subject matter (for example, societal expectations and conflicts) in greater range and depth. A comparison-and-contrast essay might be an appropriate mode for this purpose. Begin with a list (two lists for comparison and contrast), develop it into an outline, and use transitional expressions that signal similarities or differences.

2. Does "The Grass-Eaters" remind you of an event from your own life or an incident you read about or heard about on the news? Compose a narrative or descriptive essay focusing on that event. Write a thesis statement that points out the significance of that event in your life. Throughout your essay, concentrate on using vivid details and descriptions to help recreate your story. (As an example, you might recall reading about a

homeless family found living in an automobile.) Your thesis statement might be, "While many of us are safe and warm in our homes, others in our society are forced to find shelter wherever they can due to the chance circumstances of their lives."

3. How would you characterize Ajit Babu, the narrator of the story? Since little is explained about him, except that he and his wife were refugees from an area torn by religious warfare, the reader is left to make inferences about what he is like and what made him that way. In "The Grass-Eaters," Ajit Babu was probably influenced greatly by tradition and family as well as by life's circumstances. Interview a close friend or someone from your own extended family, and write a formal essay of five or more paragraphs showing what influenced this person's choice of a place to live. Prepare for your interview by drawing up a list of appropriate questions. In your essay you might want to include biographical information that clarifies the influences (either positive or negative) that have shaped this person's decision to settle in a certain place.

4. Write a formal essay of five or more paragraphs connecting the theme of disturbing knowledge with "The Grass-Eaters." End your introductory paragraph with a thesis statement that clearly expresses your central idea. Use your supporting paragraphs to focus attention on important parts of the story that raised genuine questions, such as, "Do people choose their life circumstances or does fate somehow step in?" In your supporting paragraphs, quote from the story and refer to specific passages that clarify and support your central argument.

Traveling Through the Dark

1962

WILLIAM STAFFORD

 WILLIAM STAFFORD, a foremost American poet, was born in Kansas in 1914 and received degrees from the University of Kansas and the State University of Iowa. Readers like the simple, direct language of his poems and sometimes compare him with Robert Frost in terms of theme and content. In "Traveling Through the Dark," Stafford writes about a commonplace experience in rural areas: a roadside discovery of an animal that has been hit by a passing car. In his detailed description of the wilderness scene, he also hints at the dark side of the human condition.

Have you had the experience of hitting an animal that was innocently crossing the road? Do you recall driving by a wounded or dead animal by the side of the road? How did you react? Did you find that you had to "think hard" about your actions?

Traveling through the dark I found a deer   1
dead on the edge of the Wilson River road.
It is usually best to roll them into the canyon:
that road is narrow; to swerve might make more dead.

By glow of the tail-light I stumbled back of the car   5
and stood by the heap, a doe, a recent killing;
she had stiffened already, almost cold.
I dragged her off; she was large in the belly.

My fingers touching her side brought me the reason—
her side was warm; her fawn lay there waiting,   10
alive, still, never to be born.
Beside that mountain road I hesitated.

The car aimed ahead its lowered parking lights;
under the hood purred the steady engine.

I stood in the glare of the warm exhaust turning red;   15
around our group I could hear the wilderness listen.

I thought hard for us all—my only swerving—
then pushed her over the edge into the river.

       ▣   ▣   ▣

OPTIONS FOR READING LOGS: "TRAVELING THROUGH THE DARK"

1. Discover meaning in "Traveling Through the Dark" by dividing your journal page into two vertical columns. In the left column, keep a running list of questions, such as, "Why does the narrator 'hesitate' by the side of the road?" Proceed down the page, asking two to four more significant questions. Then go back to the top of the right column and answer all the questions as completely as you can. Take some educated guesses and look for answers in the text and between the lines. Finally, to demonstrate that you have a basic understanding of this poem, end your journal entry by jotting down its main idea.

2. Students and critics of "Traveling Through the Dark" usually have strong emotional reactions to this poem. Some see it in a positive light; others see it quite negatively. Use the double-entry journal technique to clarify the meaning of some of the powerful both positive and negative images or symbols in the poem. Draw a vertical line down the middle of your journal page. Use the left column to list all of the positive images or symbols, and the right column to list all the negative images. End your journal entry with a brief interpretation of the poem.

3. Use stick figures or a simple line drawing to depict the scene on the mountain road in "Traveling Through the Dark." Include the narrator, the car, the deer, the wilderness, and the canyon. Add some close-up details, like the glowing exhaust. After you have completed your drawing, write a detailed description of the event as you imagined it, clearly stating the main idea of the poem.

OPTIONS FOR WRITING ASSIGNMENTS: "TRAVELING THROUGH THE DARK"

1. What knowledge are we meant to gain from "Traveling Through the Dark"? Would you call it disturbing knowledge? If you could talk with

William Stafford, the author of the poem, and ask him questions, hear his answers, and discuss your ideas with him, what would you say? How might he answer? Create a dialogue between you and Stafford about the ideas in "Traveling Through the Dark." Your conversation might take the form of a question-and-answer interview, an argument, or an open-ended discussion of the author's ideas and their implications in terms of how people might react when faced with a decision involving the fate of humankind as well as the fate of the deer.

2. Write a letter to the narrator of "Traveling Through the Dark." Address the narrator directly and freely express your own point of view. As an example, you may choose to empathize with the narrator in the poem, explaining why you understand what he went through. Use whatever tone that is most appropriate to express your reaction to the poem.

3. Review your journal entries to see if you can make any connections between this poem and any of the previous readings in this text. Notice any similarities or differences that are evident between "Traveling Through the Dark" and one of the other stories, poems, or essays. For example, even though the two poems are different in many ways, you might see significant connections between the themes of "Traveling Through the Dark" and William Wordsworth's "The World Is Too Much With Us." You could combine and expand one of your journal entries into a more polished piece of writing that explores in greater range and depth its subject matter (for example, humankind's place in the natural world). A comparison-and-contrast essay might be an appropriate mode for this purpose. Begin with a list (two lists for comparison and contrast), develop it into an outline, and use transitional expressions that signal similarities or differences.

4. In "Traveling Through the Dark," the author writes about a common event, yet he infuses it with a meditative, philosophical tone, especially at the end of the poem. Does this reveal anything about the author? Write a formal essay of five or more paragraphs explaining the meaning of "Traveling Through the Dark," focusing on genuine questions, such as, "What is the author trying to say about the human condition?" This is a complex issue, but take a stand and begin with a thesis statement that makes an arguable point about your particular interpretation of the poem. Brainstorm to come up with reasons for your interpretation, and review the poem for words or phrases that support your central argument. Then develop each paragraph in the body of your essay, using direct quotations from the poem to prove your various points.

The Death of the Moth

1948

VIRGINIA WOOLF

 VIRGINIA WOOLF, born in 1882, was a British novelist and essayist, and one of the most important writers of the twentieth century. Throughout her writing career, she fought with varying degrees of success against nervous exhaustion and madness. She lost that battle when she committed suicide, drowning herself in 1941.

Woolf had the capacity to find profound meaning and significance in commonplace events such as a moth's death. Some readers may find it unsettling to think that a writer may be hinting that death is the ultimate answer to life's struggle; others are amazed by the beauty and courage shown in that very struggle.

Have you had an opportunity to observe closely the activities of an insect—perhaps an ant, a bee, or a spider? Did you see any parallels or connections to human beings? Have you ever thought about what we can learn about human development by studying other forms of life?

Moths that fly by day are not properly to be called moths; they do not excite that pleasant sense of dark autumn nights and ivy-blossom which the commonest yellow-underwing asleep in the shadow of the curtain never fails to rouse in us. They are hybrid creatures, neither gay like butterflies nor somber like their own species. Nevertheless the present specimen, with his narrow hay-colored wings, fringed with a tassel of the same color, seemed to be content with life. It was a pleasant morning, mid-September, mild, benignant,[1] yet with a keener breath than that of the summer months. The plow was already scoring the field opposite the window, and where the share had been, the earth was pressed flat and gleamed with moisture. Such vigor came rolling in from the fields and the down beyond that it was difficult to keep the eyes strictly turned upon the

1. benignant: of kindly disposition

book. The rooks[2] too were keeping one of their annual festivities; soaring round the tree tops until it looked as if a vast net with thousands of black knots in it had been cast up into the air; which, after a few moments sank slowly down upon the trees until every twig seemed to have a knot at the end of it. Then, suddenly, the net would be thrown into the air again in a wider circle this time, with the utmost clamor and vociferation,[3] as though to be thrown into the air and settle slowly down upon the tree tops were a tremendously exciting experience.

The same energy which inspired the rooks, the plowmen, the horses, and even, it seemed, the lean bare-backed downs, sent the moth fluttering from side to side of his square of the window-pane. One could not help watching him. One was, indeed, conscious of a queer feeling of pity for him. The possibilities of pleasure seemed that morning so enormous and so various that to have only a moth's part in life, and a day moth's at that, appeared a hard fate, and his zest in enjoying his meager opportunities to the full, pathetic. He flew vigorously to one corner of his compartment, and, after waiting there a second, flew across to the other. What remained for him but to fly to a third corner and then to a fourth? That was all he could do, in spite of the size of the downs, the width of the sky, the far-off smoke of houses, and the romantic voice, now and then, of a steamer out at sea. What he could do he did. Watching him, it seemed as if a fiber, very thin but pure, of the enormous energy of the world had been thrust into his frail and diminutive body. As often as he crossed the pane, I could fancy that a thread of vital light became visible. He was little or nothing but life.

Yet, because he was so small, and so simple a form of the energy that was rolling in at the open window and driving its way through so many narrow and intricate corridors in my own brain and in those of other human beings, there was something marvelous as well as pathetic about him. It was as if someone had taken a tiny bead of pure life and decking it as lightly as possible with down and feathers, had set it dancing and zigzagging to show us the true nature of life. Thus displayed one could not get over the strangeness of it. One is apt to forget all about life, seeing it humped and bossed[4] and garnished and cumbered[5] so that it has to move with the greatest circumspection[6] and dignity. Again, the thought of all that life might have been had he been born in any other shape caused one to view his simple activities with a kind of pity.

---

2. rooks: crows   3. vociferation: speaking or crying out, noisily   4. bossed: to be ornamented with protuberances of metal, ivory, etc.   5. cumbered: to be hindered or hampered   6. circumspection: watchful and discrete observation or action; caution; prudence

After a time, tired by his dancing apparently, he settled on the window ledge in the sun, and, the queer spectacle being at an end, I forgot about him. Then, looking up, my eye was caught by him. He was trying to resume his dancing, but seemed either so stiff or so awkward that he could only flutter to the bottom of the window-pane; and when he tried to fly across it he failed. Being intent on other matters I watched these futile attempts for a time without thinking, unconsciously waiting for him to resume his flight, as one waits for a machine, that has stopped momentarily, to start again without considering the reason of its failure. After perhaps a seventh attempt he slipped from the wooden ledge and fell, fluttering his wings, onto his back on the window sill. The helplessness of his attitude roused me. It flashed upon me he was in difficulties; he could no longer raise himself; his legs struggled vainly. But, as I stretched out a pencil, meaning to help him to right himself, it came over me that the failure and awkwardness were the approach of death. I laid the pencil down again.

The legs agitated themselves once more. I looked as if for the enemy against which he struggled. I looked out of doors. What had happened there? Presumably it was midday, and work in the fields had stopped. Stillness and quiet had replaced the previous animation. The birds had taken themselves off to feed in the brooks. The horses stood still. Yet the power was there all the same, massed outside indifferent, impersonal, not attending to anything in particular. Somehow it was opposed to the little hay-colored moth. It was useless to try to do anything. One could only watch the extraordinary efforts made by those tiny legs against an oncoming doom which could, had it chosen, have submerged an entire city, not merely a city, but masses of human beings; nothing, I knew had any chance against death. Nevertheless after a pause of exhaustion the legs fluttered again. It was superb this last protest, and so frantic that he succeeded at last in righting himself. One's sympathies, of course, were all on the side of life. Also, when there was nobody to care or to know, this gigantic effort on the part of an insignificant little moth, against a power of such magnitude, to retain what no one else valued or desired to keep, moved one strangely. Again, somehow, one saw life, a pure bead. I lifted the pencil again, useless though I knew it to be. But even as I did so, the unmistakable tokens of death showed themselves. The body relaxed, and instantly grew stiff. The struggle was over. The insignificant little creature now knew death. As I looked at the dead moth, this minute wayside triumph of so great a force over so mean an antagonist filled me with wonder. Just as life had been strange a few minutes before, so death was now as strange. The moth having righted himself now lay most decently and uncomplainingly composed. O yes, he seemed to say, death is stronger than I am.

◧   ◧   ◧

OPTIONS FOR READING LOGS: "THE DEATH OF THE MOTH"

1. Did you ever have an experience similar to Woolf's in "The Death of the Moth"? Can you now reflect on that experience in light of her ideas about the moth's dance of death? Compose a narrative or descriptive essay focusing on one of your own observations of nature. Throughout your essay, concentrate on using vivid details and descriptions to help recreate what you observed. Include your personal thoughts about life and death.

2. Writers often use images or symbols in poems and stories to represent an idea or concept and to provide a deeper, more important value or interpretation than is at first apparent. Use the double-entry journal technique to clarify the meaning of some of the powerful images or symbols in Woolf's "The Death of the Moth." Draw a vertical line down the middle of your journal page and in the left column list all the images or symbols you can identify in the essay, such as the moth's courageous struggle against death. Use the right column to jot down possible interpretations, personal associations, or explanatory comments. End your journal entry with a brief statement about a significant discovery you made during this process—for example, "I discovered that all forms of life must eventually meet death."

3. Draw a picture to represent the scene on the windowsill in Woolf's "The Death of the Moth." Create a detailed graphic representation that clearly illustrates all the components of Woolf's story and the way they work together to form what happens. After you finish your picture, write a detailed description of the scene and clearly state the main point Woolf is making in "The Death of the Moth."

OPTIONS FOR WRITING ASSIGNMENTS: "THE DEATH OF THE MOTH"

1. In "The Death of the Moth" Woolf makes connections between insect and human life to explore the dynamics of humankind's struggle to

protest against death. What can we hope to learn about human development by comparing our own life and death with that of a moth?

2. What knowledge about the human condition are we meant to gain from "The Death of the Moth"? If you could talk with Woolf, asking her questions and sharing with her your ideas and interpretations, how do you think she would respond to them? Create that conversation between you and Woolf. Your dialogue can take the form of a question-and-answer interview, an argument between two opposing points of view, or an in-depth exploration of the writer's ideas and their implications.

3. Write a formal essay of five or more paragraphs that evolves from your own understanding of Woolf's "The Death of the Moth." Is human existence like the moth's struggle? Perhaps the answer to that question could serve as your thesis statement. Think about your own discovery of the inevitability of death, and include commentary that reveals your understanding. Refer frequently to Woolf's "The Death of the Moth" to make your points clear.

4. If you were asked about the meaning of "The Death of the Moth" and how it relates to our attitude toward the world around us, what would you say? Think about that question and then, in an essay of five or more paragraphs, explain "The Death of the Moth." Express your main idea in a clear thesis statement in your introductory paragraph. Use your supporting paragraphs to explore those parts of the text that you have questions about or that clarify your main idea. In your commentary you will need to quote from the essay and refer to specific passages to help clear up any difficulties in understanding.

Good Country People

1955

FLANNERY O'CONNOR

 Born in Savannah, Georgia, FLANNERY O'CONNOR attended Georgia State University and the University of Iowa. Diagnosed with lupus, a serious disease, O'Connor appeared to lead an uneventful life, as she once said, between the chicken pen and the kitchen. Appearances were deceiving, however, for she was an extremely serious writer. A devoted Catholic, O'Connor wrote unique, often bizarre short stories exploring what she saw as the truths of Christian revelation hidden in the lives of common, everyday people. Her stories are not simple assertions of simple truths: they often focus on the complexities of being human, and her assertions of divine revelation tend to be much more painful than joyous for her characters. The people that inhabit her stories, whether they are religious or skeptical, often undergo difficult experiences that leave them profoundly shaken and amazed at what they did not know about themselves. The following story, "Good Country People," about a college-educated atheist and a country Bible salesman, explores how both self-deception and the deception by others can blind people to painful truths about themselves.

As you read "Good Country People," think about your own experiences with either self-deception or the deception by others. What values does O'Connor seem to attack or support? Is there an obvious religious message in the story, or does it deliver some other message? What memorable events and details hold your attention?

Besides the neutral expression that she wore when she was alone, 1 Mrs. Freeman had two others, forward and reverse, that she used for all her human dealings. Her forward expression was steady and driving like the advance of a heavy truck. Her eyes never swerved to left or right but turned as the story turned as if they followed a yellow line down the center of it. She seldom used the other expression because it was not often necessary for her to retract a statement, but when she did, her face came to a complete stop, there was an almost imperceptible movement of her black eyes, during which they seemed to be receding, and then the observer would see that Mrs. Freeman, though she might stand there as real as several grain sacks thrown on top of each other, was no longer there in spirit. As for getting anything across to her when this was the case, Mrs. Hopewell had given it up. She might talk her head off. Mrs. Freeman could never be brought to admit herself wrong on any point. She would stand there and if she could be brought to say anything, it was something like, "Well, I wouldn't of said it was and I wouldn't of said it wasn't," or letting her gaze range over the top kitchen shelf where there was an assortment of dusty bottles, she might remark, "I see you ain't ate many of them figs you put up last summer."

They carried on their most important business in the kitchen at breakfast.   2
Every morning Mrs. Hopewell got up at seven o'clock and lit her gas heater and Joy's. Joy was her daughter, a large blonde girl who had an artificial leg. Mrs. Hopewell thought of her as a child though she was thirty-two years old and highly educated. Joy would get up while her mother was eating and lumber into the bathroom and slam the door, and before long, Mrs. Freeman would arrive at the back door. Joy would hear her mother call, "Come on in," and then they would talk for a while in low voices that were indistinguishable in the bathroom. By the time Joy came in, they had usually finished the weather report and were on one or the other of Mrs. Freeman's daughters, Glynese or Carramae, Joy called them Glycerin and Caramel. Glynese, a redhead, was eighteen and had many admirers; Carramae, a blonde, was only fifteen but already married and pregnant. She could not keep anything on her stomach. Every morning Mrs. Freeman told Mrs. Hopewell how many times she had vomited since the last report.

Mrs. Hopewell liked to tell people that Glynese and Carramae were two   3
of the finest girls she knew and that Mrs. Freeman was a *lady* and that she was never ashamed to take her anywhere or introduce her to anybody they might meet. Then she would tell how she had happened to hire the Freemans in the first place and how they were a godsend to her and how she had had them four years. The reason for her keeping them so long was that they were not trash. They were good country people. She had telephoned the man whose name they had given as a reference and he had told her that Mr. Freeman was a good farmer but that his wife was the nosiest woman ever to walk the earth. "She's got to be into everything," the man said. "If she don't get there before the dust settles, you can bet she's dead, that's all. She'll want to know all your business. I can stand him real good," he had said, "but me nor my wife neither could have stood that woman one more minute on this place." That had put Mrs. Hopewell off for a few days.

She had hired them in the end because there were no other applicants   4
but she had made up her mind beforehand exactly how she would handle
the woman. Since she was the type who had to be into everything, then,
Mrs. Hopewell decided, she would not only let her be into everything,
she would *see to it* that she was into everything—she would give her the
responsibility of everything, she would put her in charge. Mrs. Hopewell had
no bad qualities of her own but she was able to use other people's in such
a constructive way that she never felt the lack. She had hired the Freemans
and she had kept them four years.

Nothing is perfect. This was one of Mrs. Hopewell's favorite sayings.   5
Another was: that is life! And still another, the most important, was: well,
other people have their opinions too. She would make these statements,
usually at the table, in a tone of gentle insistence as if no one held them but
her, and the large hulking Joy, whose constant outrage had obliterated[1] every
expression from her face, would stare just a little to the side of her, her eyes
icy blue, with the look of someone who has achieved blindness by an act of
will and means to keep it.

When Mrs. Hopewell said to Mrs. Freeman that life was like that, Mrs.   6
Freeman would say, "I always said so myself." Nothing had been arrived at
by anyone that had not first been arrived at by her. She was quicker than Mr.
Freeman. When Mrs. Hopewell said to her after they had been on the place
a while, "You know, you're the wheel behind the wheel," and winked, Mrs.
Freeman had said, "I know it. I've always been quick. It's some that are
quicker than others."

"Everybody is different," Mrs. Hopewell said.   7

"Yes, most people is," Mrs. Freeman said.   8

"It takes all kinds to make the world."   9

"I always said it did myself."   10

The girl was used to this kind of dialogue for breakfast and more of it   11
for dinner; sometimes they had it for supper too. When they had no guest
they ate in the kitchen because that was easier. Mrs. Freeman always managed
to arrive at some point during the meal and to watch them finish it. She
would stand in the doorway if it were summer but in the winter she would
stand with one elbow on top of the refrigerator and look down on them, or
she would stand by the gas heater, lifting the back of her skirt slightly.
Occasionally she would stand against the wall and roll her head from side to
side. At no time was she in any hurry to leave. All this was very trying on
Mrs. Hopewell but she was a woman of great patience. She realized that
nothing is perfect and that in the Freemans she had good country people

---

1. obliterated: destroyed completely; wiped out

and that if, in this day and age, you get good country people, you had better hang onto them.

She had had plenty of experience with trash. Before the Freemans she   12
had averaged one tenant family a year. The wives of these farmers were not the kind you would want to be around you for very long. Mrs. Hopewell, who had divorced her husband long ago, needed someone to walk over the fields with her; and when Joy had to be impressed[2] for these services, her remarks were usually so ugly and her face so glum that Mrs. Hopewell would say, "If you can't come pleasantly, I don't want you at all," to which the girl, standing square and rigid-shouldered with her neck thrust slightly forward, would reply, "If you want me, here I am—LIKE I AM."

Mrs. Hopewell excused this attitude because of the leg (which had been   13
shot off in a hunting accident when Joy was ten). It was hard for Mrs. Hopewell to realize that her child was thirty-two now and that for more than twenty years she had had only one leg. She thought of her still as a child because it tore her heart to think instead of the poor stout girl in her thirties who had never danced a step or had any *normal* good times. Her name was really Joy but as soon as she was twenty-one and away from home, she had had it legally changed. Mrs. Hopewell was certain that she had thought and thought until she had hit upon the ugliest name in any language. Then she had gone and had the beautiful name, Joy, changed without telling her mother until after she had done it. Her legal name was Hulga.

When Mrs. Hopewell thought the name, Hulga, she thought of the   14
broad blank hull of a battleship. She would not use it. She continued to call her Joy to which the girl responded but in a purely mechanical way.

Hulga had learned to tolerate Mrs. Freeman who saved her from taking   15
walks with her mother. Even Glynese and Carramae were useful when they occupied attention that might otherwise have been directed at her. At first she had thought she could not stand Mrs. Freeman for she had found that it was not possible to be rude to her. Mrs. Freeman would take on strange resentments and for days together she would be sullen but the source of her displeasure was always obscure; a direct attack, a positive leer, blatant[3] ugliness to her face—these never touched her. And without warning one day, she began calling her Hulga.

She did not call her that in front of Mrs. Hopewell who would have   16
been incensed but when she and the girl happened to be out of the house together, she would say something and add the name Hulga to the end of it, and the big spectacled Joy-Hulga would scowl and redden as if her privacy had been intruded upon. She considered the name her

---

2. impressed: forced into service   3. blatant: offensively conspicuous; obvious

personal affair. She had arrived at it first purely on the basis of its ugly sound and then the full genius of its fitness had struck her. She had a vision of the name working like the ugly sweating Vulcan who stayed in the furnace and to whom, presumably, the goddess had to come when called. She saw it as the name of her highest creative act. One of her major triumphs was that her mother had not been able to turn her dust into Joy, but the greater one was that she had been able to turn it herself into Hulga. However, Mrs. Freeman's relish for using the name only irritated her. It was as if Mrs. Freeman's beady steel-pointed eyes had penetrated far enough behind her face to reach some secret fact. Something about her seemed to fascinate Mrs. Freeman and then one day Hulga realized that it was the artificial leg. Mrs. Freeman had a special fondness for the details of secret infections, hidden deformities, assaults upon children. Of diseases, she preferred the lingering or incurable. Hulga had heard Mrs. Hopewell give her the details of the hunting accident, how the leg had been literally blasted off, how she had never lost consciousness. Mrs. Freeman could listen to it any time as if it had happened an hour ago.

When Hulga stumped into the kitchen in the morning (she could walk   17 without making the awful noise but she made it—Mrs. Hopewell was certain—because it was ugly-sounding), she glanced at them and did not speak. Mrs. Hopewell would be in her red kimono with her hair tied around her head in rags. She would be sitting at the table, finishing her breakfast and Mrs. Freeman would be hanging by her elbow outward from the refrigerator, looking down at the table. Hulga always put her eggs on the stove to boil and then stood over them with her arms folded, and Mrs. Hopewell would look at her—a kind of indirect gaze divided between her and Mrs. Freeman—and would think that if she would only keep herself up a little, she wouldn't be so bad looking. There was nothing wrong with her face that a pleasant expression wouldn't help. Mrs. Hopewell said that people who looked on the bright side of things would be beautiful even if they were not.

Whenever she looked at Joy this way, she could not help but feel that it   18 would have been better if the child had not taken the Ph.D. It had certainly not brought her out any and now that she had it, there was no more excuse for her to go to school again. Mrs. Hopewell thought it was nice for girls to go to school to have a good time but Joy had "gone through." Anyhow, she would not have been strong enough to go again. The doctors had told Mrs. Hopewell that with the best of care, Joy might see forty-five. She had a weak heart. Joy had made it plain that if it had not been for this condition, she would be far from these red hills and good country people. She would be in a university lecturing to people who knew what she was talking about. And Mrs. Hopewell could very well picture her there, looking like a scarecrow and lecturing to more of the same. Here she went about all day in a six-year-old skirt and a yellow sweat shirt with a faded cowboy on a horse embossed on it. She thought this was funny; Mrs. Hopewell thought it was idiotic and showed simply that she was still a child. She was brilliant but she didn't have a grain of sense. It seemed to Mrs. Hopewell that every year she grew less like other people and more like herself—bloated, rude, and squint-eyed. And she said such strange things! To her own mother she had said—without warning, without excuse, standing up in the middle of a meal with her face purple and her mouth half full—"Woman! do you ever look inside? Do you ever look inside and see what you are *not*? God!" she had cried sinking down again and staring at her plate, "Malebranche was right: we are not our own light. We are not our own light!" Mrs. Hopewell had no idea to this day what brought that on. She had only made the remark, hoping Joy would take it in, that a smile never hurt anyone.

19   The girl had taken the Ph.D. in philosophy and this left Mrs. Hopewell at a complete loss. You could say, "My daughter is a nurse," or "My daughter is a schoolteacher," or even, "My daughter is a chemical engineer." You could not say, "My daughter is a philosopher." That was something that had ended with the Greeks and Romans. All day Joy sat on her neck in a deep chair, reading. Sometimes she went for walks but she didn't like dogs or cats or birds or flowers or nature or nice young men. She looked at nice young men as if she could smell their stupidity.

20   One day Mrs. Hopewell had picked up one of the books the girl had just put down and opening it at random, she read, "Science, on the other hand, has to assert its soberness and seriousness afresh and declare that it is concerned solely with what-is. Nothing—how can it be for science anything but a horror and a phantasm?[4] If science is right, then one thing stands firm: science wishes to know nothing of nothing. Such is after all the strictly scientific approach to Nothing. We know it by wishing to know nothing of Nothing." These words had been underlined with a blue pencil and they worked on Mrs. Hopewell like some evil incantation[5] in gibberish.[6] She shut the book quickly and went out of the room as if she were having a chill.

21   This morning when the girl came in, Mrs. Freeman was on Carramae. "She thrown up four times after supper," she said, "and was up twict in the night after three o'clock. Yesterday she didn't do nothing but ramble in the bureau drawer. All she did. Stand up there and see what she could run up on."

22   "She's got to eat," Mrs. Hopewell muttered, sipping her coffee, while she watched Joy's back at the stove. She was wondering what the child had

4. phantasm: a phantom   5. incantation: a recitation of charms or spells to produce a magical effect
6. gibberish: rapid, meaningless speech

said to the Bible salesman. She could not imagine what kind of a conversation she could possibly have had with him.

He was a tall gaunt hatless youth who had called yesterday to sell them   23
a Bible. He had appeared at the door, carrying a large black suitcase that weighted him so heavily on one side that he had to brace himself against the door facing. He seemed on the point of collapse but he said in a cheerful voice, "Good morning, Mrs. Cedars!" and set the suitcase down on the mat. He was not a bad-looking young man though he had on a bright blue suit and yellow socks that were not pulled up far enough. He had prominent face bones and a streak of sticky-looking brown hair falling across his forehead.

"I'm Mrs. Hopewell," she said.   24

"Oh!" he said, pretending to look puzzled but with his eyes sparkling,   25
"I saw it said 'The Cedars' on the mailbox so I thought you was Mrs. Cedars!" and he burst out in a pleasant laugh. He picked up the satchel and under cover of a pant, he fell forward into her hall. It was rather as if the suitcase had moved first, jerking him after it. "Mrs. Hopewell!" he said and grabbed her hand. "I hope you are well!" and he laughed again and then all at once his face sobered completely. He paused and gave her a straight earnest look and said, "Lady, I've come to speak of serious things."

"Well, come in," she muttered, none too pleased because her dinner   26
was almost ready. He came into the parlor and sat down on the edge of a straight chair and put the suitcase between his feet and glanced around the room as if he were sizing her up by it. Her silver gleamed on the two sideboards; she decided he had never been in a room as elegant as this.

"Mrs. Hopewell," he began, using her name in a way that sounded   27
almost intimate, "I know you believe in Chrustian service."

"Well yes," she murmured.   28

"I know," he said and paused, looking very wise with his head cocked   29
on one side, "that you're a good woman. Friends have told me."

Mrs. Hopewell never liked to be taken for a fool. "What are you selling?"   30
she asked.

"Bibles," the young man said and his eye raced around the room before   31
he added, "I see you have no family Bible in your parlor, I see that is the one lack you got!"

Mrs. Hopewell could not say, "My daughter is an atheist and won't let   32
me keep the Bible in the parlor." She said, stiffening slightly, "I keep my Bible by my bedside." This was not the truth. It was in the attic somewhere.

"Lady," he said, "the word of God ought to be in the parlor."   33

"Well, I think that's a matter of taste," she began. "I think . . ."   34

"Lady," he said, "for a Chrustian, the word of God ought to be in every   35
room in the house besides in his heart. I know you're a Chrustian because I can see it in every line of your face."

She stood up and said, "Well, young man, I don't want to buy a Bible   36
and I smell my dinner burning."

He didn't get up. He began to twist his hands and looking down at them,   37
he said softly. "Well lady, I'll tell you the truth—not many people want to buy
one nowadays and besides, I know I'm real simple. I don't know how to say a
thing but to say it. I'm just a country boy." He glanced up into her unfriendly
face. "People like you don't like to fool with country people like me!"

"Why!" she cried, "good country people are the salt of the earth! Besides,   38
we all have different ways of doing, it takes all kinds to make the world go
'round. That's life!"

"You said a mouthful," he said.   39

"Why, I think there aren't enough good people in the world!" she said,   40
stirred. "I think that's what's wrong with it!"

His face had brightened. "I didn't introduce myself," he said. "I'm   41
Manley Pointer from out in the country around Willohobie, not even from
a place, just from near a place."

"You wait a minute," she said. "I have to see about my dinner." She   42
went out to the kitchen and found Joy standing near the door where she
had been listening.

"Get rid of the salt of the earth," she said, "and let's eat."   43

Mrs. Hopewell gave her a pained look and turned the heat down under   44
the vegetables. "*I* can't be rude to anybody," she murmured and went back
into the parlor.

He had opened the suitcase and was sitting with a Bible on each knee.   45

"You might as well put those up," she told him. "I don't want one."   46

"I appreciate your honesty," he said. "You don't see any more real honest   47
people unless you go way out in the country."

"I know," she said, "real genuine folks!" Through the crack in the door   48
she heard a groan.

"I guess a lot of boys come telling you they're working their way through   49
college," he said, "but I'm not going to tell you that. Somehow," he said, "I
don't want to go to college. I want to devote my life to Christian service. See,"
he said, lowering his voice, "I got this heart condition. I may not live long.
When you know it's something wrong with you and you may not live long, well
then, lady . . ." He paused, with his mouth open, and stared at her.

He and Joy had the same condition! She knew that her eyes were filling   50
with tears but she collected herself quickly and murmured, "Won't you stay
for dinner? We'd love to have you!" and was sorry the instant she heard
herself say it.

"Yes mam," he said in an abashed[7] voice, "I would sher love to do that!"   51

---

7. abashed: embarrassed

Joy had given him one look on being introduced to him and then   52
throughout the meal had not glanced at him again. He had addressed several
remarks to her, which she had pretended not to hear. Mrs. Hopewell could
not understand deliberate rudeness, although she lived with it, and she felt
she had always to overflow with hospitality to make up for Joy's lack of
courtesy. She urged him to talk about himself and he did. He said he was
the seventh child of twelve and that his father had been crushed under a tree
when he himself was eight years old. He had been crushed very badly, in
fact, almost cut in two and was practically not recognizable. His mother had
got along the best she could by hard working and she had always seen that
her children went to Sunday School and that they read the Bible every
evening. He was now nineteen years old and he had been selling Bibles for
four months. In that time he had sold seventy-seven Bibles and had the
promise of two more sales. He wanted to become a missionary because he
thought that was the way you could do most for people. "He who losest his
life shall find it," he said simply and he was so sincere, so genuine and earnest
that Mrs. Hopewell would not for the world have smiled. He prevented his
peas from sliding onto the table by blocking them with a piece of bread
which he later cleaned his plate with. She could see Joy observing sidewise
how he handled his knife and fork and she saw too that every few minutes,
the boy would dart a keen appraising glance at the girl as if he were trying
to attract her attention.

After dinner Joy cleared the dishes off the table and disappeared and   53
Mrs. Hopewell was left to talk with him. He told her again about his childhood
and his father's accident and about various things that had happened to him.
Every five minutes or so she would stifle a yawn. He sat for two hours until
finally she told him she must go because she had an appointment in town.
He packed his Bibles and thanked her and prepared to leave, but in the
doorway he stopped and wrung her hand and said that not on any of his
trips had he met a lady as nice as her and he asked if he could come again.
She had said she would always be happy to see him.

Joy had been standing in the road, apparently looking at something in   54
the distance, when he came down the steps toward her, bent to the side with
his heavy valise. He stopped where she was standing and confronted her
directly. Mrs. Hopewell could not hear what he said but she trembled to
think what Joy would say to him. She could see that after a minute Joy said
something and that then the boy began to speak again, making an excited
gesture with his free hand. After a minute Joy said something else at which
the boy began to speak once more. Then to her amazement, Mrs. Hopewell
saw the two of them walk off together, toward the gate. Joy had walked all
the way to the gate with him and Mrs. Hopewell could not imagine what
they had said to each other, and she had not yet dared to ask.

Mrs. Freeman was insisting upon her attention. She had moved from   55
the refrigerator to the heater so that Mrs. Hopewell had to turn and face her
in order to seem to be listening. "Glynese gone out with Harvey Hill again
last night," she said. "She had this sty."

"Hill," Mrs. Hopewell said absently, "is the one who works in the   56
garage?"

"Nome, he's the one that goes to chiropracter school," Mrs. Freeman   57
said. "She had this sty. Been had it two days. So she says when he brought
her in the other night he says, 'Lemme get rid of that sty for you,' and she
says, 'How?' and he says, 'You just lay yourself down acrost the seat of that
car and I'll show you.' So she done it and he popped her neck. Kept on a-
popping it several times until she made him quit. This morning," Mrs.
Freeman said, "she ain't got no sty. She ain't got no traces of a sty."

"I never heard of that before," Mrs. Hopewell said.   58

"He ast her to marry him before the Ordinary," Mrs. Freeman went on,   59
"and she told him she wasn't going to be married in no *office*."

"Well, Glynese is a fine girl," Mrs. Hopewell said. "Glynese and Carramae   60
are both fine girls."

"Carramae said when her and Lyman was married Lyman said it sure   61
felt sacred to him. She said he said he wouldn't take five hundred dollars for
being married by a preacher."

"How much would he take?" the girl asked from the stove.   62

"He said he wouldn't take five hundred dollars," Mrs. Freeman repeated.   63

"Well we all have work to do," Mrs. Hopewell said.   64

"Lyman said it just felt more sacred to him," Mrs. Freeman said. "The   65
doctor wants Carramae to eat prunes. Says instead of medicine. Says them
cramps is coming from pressure. You know where I think it is?"

"She'll be better in a few weeks," Mrs. Hopewell said.   66

"In the tube," Mrs. Freeman said. "Else she wouldn't be as sick as   67
she is."

Hulga had cracked her two eggs into a saucer and was bringing them   68
to the table along with a cup of coffee that she had filled too full. She sat
down carefully and began to eat, meaning to keep Mrs. Freeman there by
questions if for any reason she showed an inclination to leave. She could
perceive her mother's eye on her. The first round-about question would be
about the Bible salesman and she did not wish to bring it on. "How did he
pop her neck?" she asked.

Mrs. Freeman went into a description of how he had popped her neck.   69
She said he owned a '55 Mercury but that Glynese said she would rather
marry a man with only a '36 Plymouth who would be married by a preacher.
The girl asked what if he had a '32 Plymouth and Mrs. Freeman said what
Glynese had said was a '36 Plymouth.

Mrs. Hopewell said there were not many girls with Glynese's common 70
sense. She said what she admired in those girls was their common sense. She
said that reminded her that they had had a nice visitor yesterday, a young
man selling Bibles. "Lord," she said, "he bored me to death but he was so
sincere and genuine I couldn't be rude to him. He was just good country
people, you know," she said, "—just the salt of the earth."

"I seen him walk up," Mrs. Freeman said, "and then later—I seen him 71
walk off," and Hulga could feel the slight shift in her voice, the slight
insinuation,[8] that he had not walked off alone, had he? Her face remained
expressionless but the color rose into her neck and she seemed to swallow it
down with the next spoonful of egg. Mrs. Freeman was looking at her as if
they had a secret together.

"Well, it takes all kinds of people to make the world go 'round," Mrs. 72
Hopewell said. "It's very good we aren't all alike."

"Some people are more alike than others," Mrs. Freeman said. 73

Hulga got up and stumped, with about twice the noise that was necessary, 74
into her room and locked the door. She was to meet the Bible salesman at
ten o'clock at the gate. She had thought about it half the night. She had
started thinking of it as a great joke and then she had begun to see profound
implications in it. She had lain in bed imagining dialogues for them that were
insane on the surface but that reached below to depths that no Bible salesman
would be aware of. Their conversation yesterday had been of this kind.

He had stopped in front of her and had simply stood there. His face was 75
bony and sweaty and bright, with a little pointed nose in the center of it,
and his look was different from what it had been at the dinner table. He was
gazing at her with open curiosity, with fascination, like a child watching a
new fantastic animal at the zoo, and he was breathing as if he had run a great
distance to reach her. His gaze seemed somehow familiar but she could not
think where she had been regarded with it before. For almost a minute he
didn't say anything. Then on what seemed an insuck of breath, he whispered,
"You ever ate a chicken that was two days old?"

The girl looked at him stonily. He might have just put this question up 76
for consideration at the meeting of a philosophical association. "Yes," she
presently replied as if she had considered it from all angles.

"It must have been mighty small!" he said triumphantly and shook all 77
over with little nervous giggles, getting very red in the face, and subsiding
finally into his gaze of complete admiration, while the girl's expression remained exactly the same.

"How old are you?" he asked softly. 78

_____

8. insinuation: an indirect suggestion or hint

She waited some time before she answered. Then in a flat voice she said, "Seventeen."   79

His smiles came in succession like waves breaking on the surface of a little lake. "I see you got a wooden leg," he said. "I think you're brave. I think you're real sweet."   80

The girl stood blank and solid and silent.   81

"Walk to the gate with me," he said. "You're a brave sweet little thing and I liked you the minute I seen you walk in the door."   82

Hulga began to move forward.   83

"What's your name?" he asked, smiling down on the top of her head.   84

"Hulga," she said.   85

"Hulga," he murmured, "Hulga. Hulga. I never heard of anybody name Hulga before. You're shy, aren't you, Hulga?" he asked.   86

She nodded, watching his large red hand on the handle of the giant valise.   87

"I like girls that wear glasses," he said. "I think a lot. I'm not like these people that a serious thought don't ever enter their heads. It's because I may die."   88

"I may die too," she said suddenly and looked up at him. His eyes were very small and brown, glittering feverishly.   89

"Listen," he said, "don't you think some people was meant to meet on account of what all they got in common and all? Like they both think serious thoughts and all?" He shifted the valise to his other hand so that the hand nearest her was free. He caught hold of her elbow and shook it a little. "I don't work on Saturday," he said. "I like to walk in the woods and see what Mother Nature is wearing. O'er the hills and far away. Pic-nics and things. Couldn't we go on a pic-nic tomorrow? Say yes, Hulga," he said and gave her a dying look as if he felt his insides about to drop out of him. He had even seemed to sway slightly toward her.   90

During the night she had imagined that she seduced him. She imagined that the two of them walked on the place until they came to the storage barn beyond the two back fields and there, she imagined, that things came to such a pass that she very easily seduced him and that then, of course, she had to reckon with his remorse. True genius can get an idea across even to an inferior mind. She imagined that she took his remorse in hand and changed it into a deeper understanding of life. She took all his shame away and turned it into something useful.   91

She set off for the gate at exactly ten o'clock, escaping without drawing Mrs. Hopewell's attention. She didn't take anything to eat, forgetting that food is usually taken on a picnic. She wore a pair of slacks and a dirty white shirt, and as an afterthought, she had put some Vapex on the collar of it   92 since she did not own any perfume. When she reached the gate no one was there.

She looked up and down the empty highway and had the furious feeling 93 that she had been tricked, that he had only meant to make her walk to the gate after the idea of him. Then suddenly he stood up, very tall, from behind a bush on the opposite embankment. Smiling, he lifted his hat which was new and wide-brimmed. He had not worn it yesterday and she wondered if he had bought it for the occasion. It was toast-colored with a red and white band around it and was slightly too large for him. He stepped from behind the bush still carrying the black valise. He had on the same suit and the same yellow socks sucked down in his shoes from walking. He crossed the highway and said, "I knew you'd come!"

The girl wondered acidly how he had known this. She pointed to the 94 valise and asked, "Why did you bring your Bibles?"

He took her elbow, smiling down on her as if he could not stop. "You 95 can never tell when you'll need the word of God, Hulga," he said. She had a moment in which she doubted that this was actually happening and then they began to climb the embankment. They went down into the pasture toward the woods. The boy walked lightly by her side, bouncing on his toes. The valise did not seem to be heavy today; he even swung it. They crossed half the pasture without saying anything and then, putting his hand easily on the small of her back, he asked softly, "Where does your wooden leg join on?"

She turned an ugly red and glared at him and for an instant the boy 96 looked abashed. "I didn't mean you no harm," he said. "I only meant you're so brave and all. I guess God takes care of you."

"No," she said, looking forward and walking fast, "I don't even believe 97 in God."

At this he stopped and whistled. "No!" he exclaimed as if he were too 98 astonished to say anything else.

She walked on and in a second he was bouncing at her side, fanning 99 with his hat. "That's very unusual for a girl," he remarked, watching her out of the corner of his eye. When they reached the edge of the wood, he put his hand on her back again and drew her against him without a word and kissed her heavily.

The kiss, which had more pressure than feeling behind it, produced that 100 extra surge of adrenaline in the girl that enables one to carry a packed trunk out of a burning house, but in her, the power went at once to the brain. Even before he released her, her mind, clear and detached and ironic anyway, was regarding him from a great distance, with amusement but with pity. She had never been kissed before and she was pleased to discover that it was an unexceptional experience and all a matter of the mind's control. Some people might enjoy drain water if they were told it was vodka. When the boy, looking expectant but uncertain, pushed her gently away, she turned and walked on, saying nothing as if such business, for her, were common enough.

He came along panting at her side, trying to help her when he saw a   101
root that she might trip over. He caught and held back the long swaying blades of thorn vine until she had passed beyond them. She led the way and he came breathing heavily behind her. Then they came out on a sunlit hillside, sloping softly into another one a little smaller. Beyond, they could see the rusted top of the old barn where the extra hay was stored.

The hill was sprinkled with small pink weeds. "Then you ain't saved?"   102
he asked suddenly, stopping.

The girl smiled. It was the first time she had smiled at him at all. "In   103
my economy," she said, "I'm saved and you are damned but I told you I didn't believe in God."

Nothing seemed to destroy the boy's look of admiration. He gazed at   104
her now as if the fantastic animal at the zoo had put its paw through the bars and given him a loving poke. She thought he looked as if he wanted to kiss her again and she walked on before he had the chance.

"Ain't there somewheres we can sit down sometime?" he murmured,   105
his voice softening toward the end of the sentence.

"In that barn," she said.   106

They made for it rapidly as if it might slide away like a train. It was a   107
large two-story barn, cool and dark inside. The boy pointed up the ladder that led into the loft and said, "It's too bad we can't go up there."

"Why can't we?" she asked.   108

"Yer leg," he said reverently.   109

The girl gave him a contemptuous look and putting both hands on the   110
ladder, she climbed it while he stood below, apparently awestruck. She pulled herself expertly through the opening and then looked down at him and said, "Well, come on if you're coming," and he began to climb the ladder, awkwardly bringing the suitcase with him.

"We won't need the Bible," she observed.   111

"You never can tell," he said, panting. After he had got into the loft, he   112
was a few seconds catching his breath. She had sat down in a pile of straw. A wide sheath of sunlight, filled with dust particles, slanted over her. She lay back against a bale, her face turned away, looking out the front opening of the barn where hay was thrown from a wagon into the loft. The two pink-speckled hillsides lay back against a dark ridge of woods. The sky was cloudless and cold blue. The boy dropped down by her side and put one arm under her and the other over her and began methodically kissing her face, making

little noises like a fish. He did not remove his hat but it was pushed far enough back not to interfere. When her glasses got in his way, he took them off of her and slipped them into his pocket.

The girl at first did not return any of the kisses but presently she began   113
to and after she had put several on his cheek, she reached his lips and remained there, kissing him again and again as if she were trying to draw all the breath out of him. His breath was clear and sweet like a child's and the kisses were sticky like a child's. He mumbled about loving her and about knowing when he first seen her that he loved her, but the mumbling was like the sleepy fretting of a child being put to sleep by his mother. Her mind, throughout this, never stopped or lost itself for a second to her feelings. "You ain't said you loved me none," he whispered finally, pulling back from her. "You got to say that."

She looked away from him off into the hollow sky and then down at a   114
black ridge and then down farther into what appeared to be two green swelling lakes. She didn't realize he had taken her glasses but this landscape could not seem exceptional to her for she seldom paid any close attention to her surroundings.

"You got to say it," he repeated. "You got to say you love me."   115

She was always careful how she committed herself. "In a sense," she   116
began, "if you use the word loosely, you might say that. But it's not a word I use. I don't have illusions. I'm one of those people who see *through* to nothing."

The boy was frowning. "You got to say it. I said it and you got to say   117
it," he said.

The girl looked at him almost tenderly. "You poor baby," she murmured.   118
"It's just as well you don't understand," and she pulled him by the neck, facedown, against her. "We are all damned," she said, "but some of us have taken off our blindfolds and see that there's nothing to see. It's a kind of salvation."

The boy's astonished eyes looked blankly through the ends of her hair.   119
"Okay," he almost whined, "but do you love me or don'tcher?"

"Yes," she said and added, "in a sense. But I must tell you something.   120
There mustn't be anything dishonest between us." She lifted his head and looked him in the eye. "I am thirty years old," she said. "I have a number of degrees."

The boy's look was irritated but dogged. "I don't care," he said. "I   121
don't care a thing about what all you done. I just want to know if you love me or don'tcher?" and he caught her to him and wildly planted her face with kisses until she said, "Yes, yes."

"Okay then," he said, letting her go. "Prove it."   122

She smiled, looking dreamily out on the shifty landscape. She had seduced   123
him without even making up her mind to try. "How?" she asked, feeling
that he should be delayed a little.

He leaned over and put his lips to her ear. "Show me where your wooden   124
leg joins on," he whispered.

The girl uttered a sharp little cry and her face instantly drained of color.   125
The obscenity of the suggestion was not what shocked her. As a child she
had sometimes been subject to feelings of shame but education had removed
the last traces of that as a good surgeon scrapes for cancer; she would no
more have felt it over what he was asking than she would have believed in
his Bible. But she was as sensitive about the artificial leg as a peacock about
his tail. No one ever touched it but her. She took care of it as someone else
would his soul, in private and almost with her own eyes turned away. "No,"
she said.

"I known it," he muttered, sitting up. "You're just playing me for a   126
sucker."

"Oh no no!" she cried. "It joins on at the knee. Only at the knee. Why   127
do you want to see it?"

The boy gave her a long penetrating look. "Because," he said, "it's what   128
makes you different. You ain't like anybody else."

She sat staring at him. There was nothing about her face or her round   129
freezing-blue eyes to indicate that this had moved her; but she felt as if her
heart had stopped and left her mind to pump her blood. She decided that
for the first time in her life she was face to face with real innocence. This
boy, with an instinct that came from beyond wisdom, had touched the truth
about her. When after a minute, she said in a hoarse high voice, "All right,"
it was like surrendering to him completely. It was like losing her own life
and finding it again, miraculously, in his.

Very gently he began to roll the slack leg up. The artificial limb, in a   130
white sock and brown flat shoe, was bound in a heavy material like canvas
and ended in an ugly jointure where it was attached to the stump. The boy's
face and his voice were entirely reverent as he uncovered it and said, "Now
show me how to take it off and on."

She took it off for him and put it back on again and then he took it off   131
himself, handling it as tenderly as if it were a real one. "See!" he said with
a delighted child's face. "Now I can do it myself!"

"Put it back on," she said. She was thinking that she would run away   132
with him and that every night he would take the leg off and every morning
put it back on again. "Put it back on," she said.

"Not yet," he murmured, setting it on its foot out of her reach. "Leave   133
it off for a while. You got me instead."

She gave a little cry of alarm but he pushed her down and began to kiss   134
her again. Without the leg she felt entirely dependent on him. Her brain
seemed to have stopped thinking altogether and to be about some other
function that it was not very good at. Different expressions raced back and
forth over her face. Every now and then the boy, his eyes like two steel spikes,
would glance behind him where the leg stood. Finally she pushed him off
and said, "Put it back on me now."

"Wait," he said. He leaned the other way and pulled the valise toward   135
him and opened it. It had a pale blue spotted lining and there were only two
Bibles in it. He took one of these out and opened the cover of it. It was
hollow and contained a pocket flask of whiskey, a pack of cards, and a small
blue box with printing on it. He laid these out in front of her one at a time
in an evenly-spaced row, like one presenting offerings at the shrine of a
goddess. He put the blue box in her hand. THIS PRODUCT TO BE USED
ONLY FOR THE PREVENTION OF DISEASE, she read, and dropped it.
The boy was unscrewing the top of the flask. He stopped and pointed, with
a smile, to the deck of cards. It was not an ordinary deck but one with an
obscene picture on the back of each card. "Take a swig," he said, offering
her the bottle first. He held it in front of her, but like one mesmerized,[9] she
did not move.

Her voice when she spoke had an almost pleading sound. "Aren't you,"   136
she murmured, "aren't you just good country people?"

The boy cocked his head. He looked as if he were just beginning to   137
understand that she might be trying to insult him. "Yeah," he said, curling
his lip slightly, "but it ain't held me back none. I'm as good as you any day
in the week."

"Give me my leg," she said.   138

He pushed it farther away with his foot. "Come on now, let's begin to   139
have us a good time," he said coaxingly. "We ain't got to know one another
good yet."

"Give me my leg!" she screamed and tried to lunge for it but he pushed   140
her down easily.

"What's the matter with you all of a sudden?" he asked, frowning as he   141
screwed the top on the flask and put it quickly back inside the Bible. "You
just a while ago said you didn't believe in nothing. I thought you was some
girl!"

9. mesmerized: hypnotized

Her face was almost purple. "You're a Christian!" she hissed. "You're a   142
fine Christian! You're just like them all—say one thing and do another. You're
a perfect Christian, you're . . ."

The boy's mouth was set angrily. "I hope you don't think," he said in   143
a lofty indignant tone, "that I believe in that crap! I may sell Bibles but I
know which end is up and I wasn't born yesterday and I know where I'm
going!"

"Give me my leg!" she screeched. He jumped up so quickly that she   144
barely saw him sweep the cards and the blue box into the Bible and throw
the Bible into his valise. She saw him grab the leg and then she saw it for an
instant slanted forlornly across the inside of the suitcase with a Bible at either
side of its opposite ends. He slammed the lid shut and snatched up the valise
and swung it down the hole and then stepped through himself.

When all of him had passed but his head, he turned and regarded her   145
with a look that no longer had any admiration in it. "I've gotten a lot of
interesting things," he said. "One time I got a woman's glass eye this way.
And you needn't to think you'll catch me because Pointer ain't really my
name. I use a different name at every house I call at and don't stay nowhere
long. And I'll tell you another thing, Hulga," he said, using the name as if
he didn't think much of it, "you ain't so smart. I been believing in nothing
ever since I was born!" and then the toast-colored hat disappeared down the
hole and the girl was left, sitting on the straw in the dusty sunlight. When
she turned her churning face toward the opening, she saw his blue figure
struggling successfully over the green speckled lake.

Mrs. Hopewell and Mrs. Freeman, who were in the back pasture, digging   146
up onions, saw him emerge a little later from the woods and head across the
meadow toward the highway. "Why, that looks like that nice dull young man
that tried to sell me a Bible yesterday," Mrs. Hopewell said, squinting. "He
must have been selling them to the Negroes back in there. He was so simple,"
she said, "but I guess the world would be better off if we were all that
simple."

Mrs. Freeman's gaze drove forward and just touched him before he   147
disappeared under the hill. Then she returned her attention to the evil-
smelling onion shoot she was lifting from the ground. "Some can't be that
simple," she said. "I know I never could."

OPTIONS FOR READING LOGS: "GOOD COUNTRY PEOPLE"

1. Explore the meaning of "Good Country People" through the double-entry journal technique. Divide your journal page into two vertical columns; in the left column, keep a running list of questions that occur to you as you are reading. Aim for three to five questions, such as, "What is the significance of the salesman's toast-colored hat?" When you finish your list of questions, answer them as completely as you can in the right column. Remember that taking risks is an important part of critical thinking, so allow yourself to guess at answers to some questions. To demonstrate that you have reached a basic understanding of the story, end your journal entry by jotting down the main idea of "Good Country People."

2. To explore two of the main characters in "Good Country People," draw a vertical line down the middle of your journal page, creating two columns. In the left column, keep a list of your observations about Hulga and her role in the story. In the right column, write your comments about the Bible salesman. Complete your journal entry by discussing some interesting insights you gained about these two characters. What exactly is it that draws these two characters together? How does each perceive the other?

3. From your own life, tell a parallel story you recalled while reading "Good Country People." Do the various actions and words of Hulga, her mother, or the Bible salesman remind you of someone you know? Jot down your memories of events that were similar to or different from those in "Good Country People." Wrap up your journal entry by stating what new knowledge Flannery O'Connor's story offers you about your own life experience.

OPTIONS FOR WRITING ASSIGNMENTS: "GOOD COUNTRY PEOPLE"

1. Write a letter to Hulga, addressing her directly and giving your reaction to her role in the story, her ideas, and what happens to her. You may want to praise or criticize her or offer her some advice. At some point in your letter, focus on the religious issues that the story raises, offering Hulga some knowledge from your own perspective.

2. What did you think of "Good Country People"? Would you recommend it to a friend? Write a critical review that makes a clear recommendation

that your friend should or should not read "Good Country People." In your introductory paragraph, state your recommendation clearly in your thesis statement. Your evaluation might be positive, negative, or some interesting mixture of the two. Once you are clear on what sort of evaluation or judgment you want to make, offer some good reasons in your supporting paragraphs, referring to the characters, their motivations, and the overall theme of the story to make your judgment convincing.

3. At the end of "Good Country People," Hulga undergoes a bizarre experience. What do you think is going through her mind as the Bible salesman runs away with her wooden leg? How might she explain this experience either to herself or to someone else? How do the dual themes of deception and religion fit into the story? In your prewriting, explore her attitude toward the Bible salesman. Do her feelings change in relation to him? At one point she regards him "from a great distance, with amusement but with pity." At yet another point she thinks, "This boy, with an instinct that came from beyond wisdom, had touched the truth about her." However, at the end when she says, "You're a Christian!" he replies, "I been believing in nothing ever since I was born!" Write a formal essay of five or more paragraphs that explores "Good Country People" as a story about Hulga's learning something new about herself and who she really is. Include a thesis statement at the end of your introductory paragraph, and, in your supporting paragraphs, examine specific parts of the story to support your thesis statement.

4. None of the characters in "Good Country People" are individuals of strong faith: Hulga is an avowed atheist; the Bible salesman apparently believes in nothing; Mrs. Hopewell does not appear to be particularly devout and Mrs. Freeman appears to be a confirmed gossip. Yet O'Connor is clearly a Christian author making a statement. Write a formal essay of five or more paragraphs explaining what you believe to be the main point O'Connor is making about religion and faith in "Good Country People." Clearly state your understanding of that point in a thesis statement in your introductory paragraph. In your essay's supporting paragraphs, you will need to quote from the story and refer to specific passages to clarify and support your central idea.

Ethics

1980

LINDA PASTAN

 LINDA PASTAN was born in New York in 1932. She graduated from Radcliffe College and received master's degrees from Simmons College and Brandeis University. In Pastan's poem, students in an ethics class encounter a hypothetical situation dealing with a question of values. "Which would you save?" the teacher asks in the poem, "a Rembrandt painting / or an old woman who hadn't many / years left anyhow?" Of course, the choice is not an easy one and, according to the narrator, the answer changes as a person develops and matures.

As you read and reread "Ethics," think about the people and objects you value most. Do you agree that our values change as we mature and grow older? If so, how do you account for this change?

In ethics class so many years ago   1
our teacher asked this question every fall:
if there were a fire in a museum
which would you save, a Rembrandt painting
or an old woman who hadn't many   5
years left anyhow? Restless on hard chairs
caring little for pictures or old age
we'd opt one year for life, the next for art
and always half-heartedly. Sometimes
the woman borrowed my grandmother's face   10
leaving her usual kitchen to wander
some drafty, half imagined museum.
One year, feeling clever, I replied
why not let the woman decide herself?
Linda, the teacher would report, eschews[1]   15

---

1. eschews: to abstain or keep away from

the burdens of responsibility.
This fall in a real museum I stand
before a real Rembrandt, old woman,
or nearly so, myself. The colors
within this frame are darker than autumn,   20
darker even than winter—the browns of earth,
though earth's most radiant elements burn
through the canvas. I know now that woman
and painting and season are almost one
and all beyond saving by children.   25

OPTIONS FOR READING LOGS: "ETHICS"

1. Use the double-entry journal technique (asking "what" or "why" questions) to discover meaning in "Ethics." Draw a vertical line down the middle of your journal page to create two columns. In the left column, keep a running list of three to five puzzling, yet answerable questions that occur to you as you are reading. For example, you might ask, "Why would it be so difficult to make a choice between an object (however priceless) and a human life?" Proceed down the page, asking several more significant questions. Then go back to the top of your list and answer the questions as completely as you can in the right column. If you are unsure of an answer, take an educated guess. Also look for answers in the poem, interpreting the lines and searching for meaning. Finally, to demonstrate that you have reached a basic understanding of the text, end your journal entry by stating the main idea of "Ethics."
2. Paraphrase the poem by writing its meaning in your own words. Work your way through "Ethics" line by line. Complete your journal entry by stating the theme of the poem.
3. Use your imagination to represent the central issue in the poem in a drawing. Your picture can be literal or symbolic, but you should use as many specific details as possible. Wrap up your journal entry by stating the central theme of "Ethics."

OPTIONS FOR WRITING ASSIGNMENTS: "ETHICS"

1. Write a creative writing response to "Ethics" by writing an original poem of your own. If you have trouble getting started, you might imitate the first few lines of the poem:

   In _____ class
   our teacher asked this question:
   if there were a _____ somewhere in the world
   which would you save, a _____
   or a _____ .

   Adding words that allow you to explore an important choice of your own, use these lines as your own first stanza. Allow your poem to develop in any way that pleases you as you follow your own private path, exploring your idea. You can use rhymes if you wish, but you can also use free verse, as Pastan does. After you have written your poem, briefly explain why "Ethics" triggered this creative response from you.

2. Create a conversation between you and the poet, Linda Pastan, about her poem. Your conversation might take the form of a question-and-answer interview to get at the meaning of "Ethics." For example, you could ask her to explain what she means by "I know now that woman / and painting and season are almost one." Question her on other matters in the poem.

3. We often rely on the advice of others in selecting poems to read, and we are also influenced by their evaluations. In five or more paragraphs, write a review of "Ethics," making a clear recommendation as to either the positive or negative value of the poem. Write your evaluation or judgment as a thesis statement. Then come up with several good reasons to make your judgment convincing, each with supporting evidence from the poem.

4. Write a formal essay of five or more paragraphs explaining the meaning of "Ethics." Focus your attention on parts of the poem that you have genuine questions about, such as, "Is it significant that 'children' cannot do the 'saving'? Does this imply that adults can?" Your essay should begin with an arguable thesis statement, which you develop further in the supporting paragraphs. You might need to quote from the poem and refer to specific passages to clarify and support your central argument.

Civil War in Corcyra

424 B.C.

THUCYDIDES

 Many scholars consider THUCYDIDES to be the greatest of the ancient historians. He was an Athenian citizen during the twenty-six-year war between
Sparta and Athens, the two most powerful Greek city-states, which were
located only about a hundred miles from each other. At one point Thucydides
was a general in the Athenian army, but he lost his command and was
banished in 424 B.C. because of his failure to win a battle against the Spartans.
He retired to write the complex history of the long, exhausting war that
kept Greek civilization in turmoil throughout much of his lifetime. His great
work, *History of the Peloponnesian War,* is an extraordinary record of the
tragic fate of the great city of Athens, to which the Western world owes
much of its knowledge of art, philosophy, and democratic government.

Thucydides' "Civil War in Corcyra," is an excerpt from his *History of
the Peloponnesian War.* This excerpt describes the vicious civil war that broke
out between the Corcyraean supporters of Athens and those of Sparta when
the Athenians were about to invade Corcyra. Thucydides describes these
disturbing events to expound on his increasingly dark view of "human
nature."

*As you read this selection, think of world events, especially the U.S.
Civil War and those in Ireland, Rwanda, the former Yugoslavia, and
other places where people seem to have lost all respect for one another.
Is the ancient world Thucydides describes like ours in any way? Do you
find more similarities or more differences?*

When the Corcyraeans realized that the Athenian fleet was ap- 1
proaching and that their enemies had gone, they brought the
Messenians, who had previously been outside the walls, into
the city and ordered the fleet which they had manned to sail round into the
Hyllaic harbour. While it was doing so, they seized upon all their enemies
whom they could find and put them to death. They then dealt with those

whom they had persuaded to go on board the ships, killing them as they landed. Next they went to the temple of Hera and persuaded about fifty of the suppliants[1] there to submit to a trial. They then condemned every one of them to death. Seeing what was happening, most of the other suppliants, who had refused to be tried, killed each other there in the temple; some hanged themselves on the trees, and others found various other means of committing suicide. During the seven days that Eurymedon stayed there with his sixty ships, the Corcyraeans continued to massacre those of their own citizens whom they considered to be their enemies. Their victims were accused of conspiring to overthrow the democracy, but in fact men were often killed on grounds of personal hatred or else by their debtors because of the money that they owed. There was death in every shape and form. And, as usually happens in such situations, people went to every extreme and beyond it. There were fathers who killed their sons; men were dragged from the temples or butchered on the very altars; some were actually walled up in the temple of Dionysus and died there.

So savage was the progress of this revolution, and it seemed all the more   2 so because it was one of the first which had broken out. Later, of course, practically the whole of the Hellenic world was convulsed, with rival parties in every state—democratic leaders trying to bring in the Athenians, and oligarchs[2] trying to bring in the Spartans. In peacetime there would have been no excuse and no desire for calling them in, but in time of war, when each party could always count upon an alliance which would do harm to its opponents and at the same time strengthen its own position, it became a natural thing for anyone who wanted a change of government to call in help from outside. In the various cities these revolutions were the cause of many calamities—as happens and always will happen while human nature is what it is, though there may be different degrees of savagery, and, as different circumstances arise, the general rules will admit of some variety. In times of peace and prosperity cities and individuals alike follow higher standards, because they are not forced into a situation where they have to do what they do not want to do. But war is a stern teacher; in depriving them of the power of easily satisfying their daily wants, it brings most people's minds down to the level of their actual circumstances.

So revolutions broke out in city after city, and in places where the revolu-   3 tions occurred late the knowledge of what had happened previously in other places caused still new extravagances of revolutionary zeal, expressed by an elaboration in the methods of seizing power and by unheard-of atrocities in

---

1. suppliants: persons who make an earnest and humble entreaty   2. oligarchs: one of the rulers in a form of government in which power is vested in a few persons or a dominant class

revenge. To fit in with the change of events, words, too, had to change their usual meanings. What used to be described as a thoughtless act of aggression was now regarded as the courage one would expect to find in a party member; to think of the future and wait was merely another way of saying one was a coward; any idea of moderation was just an attempt to disguise one's unmanly character; ability to understand a question from all sides meant that one was totally unfitted for action. Fanatical enthusiasm was the mark of a real man, and to plot against an enemy behind his back was perfectly legitimate self-defence. Anyone who held violent opinions could always be trusted, and anyone who objected to them became a suspect. To plot successfully was a sign of intelligence, but it was still cleverer to see that a plot was hatching. If one attempted to provide against having to do either, one was disrupting the unity of the party and acting out of fear of the opposition. In short, it was equally praise-worthy to get one's blow in first against someone who was going to do wrong, and to denounce someone who had no intention of doing any wrong at all. Family relations were a weaker tie than party membership, since party members were more ready to go to any extreme for any reason whatever. These parties were not formed to enjoy the benefits of the established laws, but to acquire power by overthrowing the existing regime; and the members of these parties felt confidence in each other not because of any fellowship in a religious communion, but because they were partners in crime. If an opponent made a reasonable speech, the party in power, so far from giving it a generous reception, took every precaution to see that it had no practical effect.

Revenge was more important than self-preservation. And if pacts of 4 mutual security were made, they were entered into by the two parties only in order to meet some temporary difficulty, and remained in force only so long as there was no other weapon available. When the chance came, the one who first seized it boldly, catching his enemy off his guard, enjoyed a revenge that was all the sweeter from having been taken, not openly, but because of a breach of faith. It was safer that way, it was considered, and at the same time a victory won by treachery gave one a title for superior intelligence. And indeed most people are more ready to call villainy cleverness than simple-mindedness honesty. They are proud of the first quality and ashamed of the second.

Love of power, operating through greed and through personal ambition, 5 was the cause of all these evils. To this must be added the violent fanaticism which came into play once the struggle had broken out. Leaders of parties in the cities had programmes which appeared admirable—on one side political equality for the masses, on the other the safe and sound government of the aristocracy—but in professing to serve the public interest they were seeking to win the prizes for themselves. In their struggles for ascendancy nothing was barred; terrible indeed were the actions to which they committed themselves, and in taking revenge they went farther still. Here they were deterred neither by the claims of justice nor by the interests of the state; their one standard was the pleasure of their own party at that particular moment, and so, either by means of condemning their enemies on an illegal vote or by violently usurping power over them, they were always ready to satisfy the hatreds of the hour. Thus neither side had any use for conscientious motives; more interest was shown in those who could produce attractive arguments to justify some disgraceful action. As for the citizens who held moderate views, they were destroyed by both the extreme parties, either for not taking part in the struggle or in envy at the possibility that they might survive.

As the result of these revolutions, there was a general deterioration of character throughout the Greek world. The simple way of looking at things, which is so much the mark of a noble nature, was regarded as a ridiculous quality and soon ceased to exist. Society had become divided into two ideologically hostile camps, and each side viewed the other with suspicion. As for ending this state of affairs, no guarantee could be given that would be trusted, no oath sworn that people would fear to break; everyone had come to the conclusion that it was hopeless to expect a permanent settlement and so, instead of being able to feel confident in others, they devoted their energies to providing against being injured themselves. As a rule those who were least remarkable for intelligence showed the greater powers of survival. Such people recognized their own deficiencies and the superior intelligence of their opponents; fearing that they might lose a debate or find themselves outmanoeuvred in intrigue by their quick-witted enemies, they boldly launched straight into action; while their opponents, over-confident in the belief that they would see what was happening in advance, and not thinking it necessary to seize by force what they could secure by policy, were the more easily destroyed because they were off their guard.

Certainly it was in Corcyra that there occurred the first examples of the breakdown of law and order. There was the revenge taken in their hour of triumph by those who had in the past been arrogantly oppressed instead of wisely governed; there were the wicked resolutions taken by those who, particularly under the pressure of misfortune, wished to escape from their usual poverty and coveted the property of their neighbours; there were the savage and pitiless actions into which men were carried not so much for the sake of gain as because they were swept away into an internecine[3] struggle by their ungovernable passions. Then, with the ordinary conventions of civi-

3. internecine: of or pertaining to conflict or struggle within a group

lized life thrown into confusion, human nature, always ready to offend even where laws exist, showed itself proudly in its true colors, as something incapable of controlling passion, insubordinate to the idea of justice, the enemy to anything superior to itself; for, if it had not been for the pernicious[4] power of envy, men would not so have exalted vengeance above innocence and profit above justice. Indeed, it is true that in these acts of revenge on others men take it upon themselves to begin the process of repealing those general laws of humanity which are there to give a hope of salvation to all who are in distress, instead of leaving those laws in existence, remembering that there may come a time when they, too, will be in danger and will need their protection.

So, . . . the people of Corcyra were the first to display in their city the   8 passions of civil war.

---

4. pernicious: subtly causing harm or ruin

OPTIONS FOR READING LOGS: "CIVIL WAR IN CORCYRA"

1. Use the double-entry journal technique to clarify thoughts and discover meaning in "Civil War in Corcyra." Create two columns by drawing a vertical line down the middle of your journal page. In the left column, keep a running list of "what" or "why" questions that occur to you as you are reading, such as, "How can a formerly unified group of people, all citizens of the same city, suddenly turn so viciously on one another?" Another question might be, "In what sense did 'words . . . change their usual meanings' during the civil war?" Proceed down the journal page, asking several more significant questions. When you finish, go to the top of the right column and answer your questions as completely as possible, taking educated guesses and looking for answers in the text and between the lines. (Remember that such interpretation requires you to take risks.) Finally, to demonstrate that you have reached a basic understanding of the text, end your journal entry with a significant discovery you made about Thucydides' view of human nature.

2. From your own knowledge of world or local events tell some parallel story that was triggered by reading "Civil War in Corcyra." Does Thucydides'

account remind you of some historical event, particular time period, or current conflict, such as those in Bosnia, Haiti, or Ireland? Jot down characteristics that resemble or differ from those described in "Civil War in Corcyra." End your journal entry by stating the main point of this reading selection.

3. Use the double-entry journal technique to clarify the meaning of some of the memorable statements in "Civil War in Corcyra." After drawing a vertical line down the middle of your journal page, copy into the left column the phrases or sentences that you particularly like or find puzzling. One example might be "Revenge was more important than self-preservation"; another is "Fanatical enthusiasm was the mark of a real man." In the right column, note your possible interpretations, personal associations, or explanatory comments. End your journal entry with a brief entry about a significant discovery you made about Thucydides' ideas during this process.

OPTIONS FOR WRITING ASSIGNMENTS: "CIVIL WAR IN CORCYRA"

1. Develop one of your reading logs for "Civil War in Corcyra" into a more polished piece of writing that explores in greater range and depth a moment of personal insight or development. Use an appropriate form, (a poem, a fictional story, a personal narrative, or an essay) that examines a central idea to present your ideas.

2. Create a conversation between you and Thucydides about human nature. Do you agree with him about the fragility of civilized behavior and our capacity for violence and deceit? Your conversation might take the form of a question-and-answer interview, an argument representing two opposing points of view, or an in-depth exploration of his ideas and their implications for our world today.

3. In five or more paragraphs, write a review of "Civil War in Corcyra," clearly evaluating it as an exploration of human behavior. Your evaluation can be positive, negative, or an interesting mixture of both. State your evaluation or judgment clearly in a thesis statement at the end of your opening paragraph. For example, your thesis statement might be as follows: "Thucydides' disturbing criticism of the breakdown of law and order in Corcyra is relevant to understanding the collapse of discipline in our high schools today." As you work through your essay, give several good reasons, each with supporting evidence from Thucydides, that make your judgment convincing.

4. Write a formal essay of five or more paragraphs explaining Thucydides' explanation for the total collapse of Corcyra. End your introductory paragraph with a thesis statement that makes your central idea clear. In your remaining paragraphs, focus on important aspects of Thucydides' commentary, such as love of power, fanaticism, and a general deterioration of character that support your main idea. In your essay, you will need to quote from the text and to refer to specific passages to clarify and support your central argument.

Glossary of Terms

Analysis   The method of explaining or clarifying a story, poem, or essay, by breaking it into its logical parts or divisions and showing how they work together to form a coherent whole.

Anecdote   A brief story used in a larger piece of writing to make a point.

Argument   A type of discourse used to prove a point or to persuade.

Audience   The intended readership for a literary work or a piece of writing.

Brainstorming   The use of free association to explore ideas and to discover what one thinks about a topic.

Caricature   A representation, usually pictorial, in which a subject's distinct features are exaggerated for comic or grotesque effect.

Cause/Effect   A type of exposition used to show why something occurred (causes) and also to show what will happen (effects) as a result of preceding events.

Central Idea   The chief purpose or significance of a poem, story, or essay.

Chronological Order   Ideas arranged according to the time when they occurred.

Commentary   A series of comments, explanations, annotations, or interpretations.

Clustering   A prewriting technique that allows a writer to use free association for ideas by jotting down words at random, circling related ideas, and connecting them with lines to establish relationships.

Comparison/Contrast   A type of exposition that suggests similarities and differences between two or more things.

Concept (idea) Map: A graphic representation of ideas whereby words or phrases are placed in interconnected bubbles (clusters), linked accordingly to establish relationships. See "clustering."

Conclusion   A final sentence or a paragraph that brings closure to a piece of writing; it often restates the thesis statement or summarizes the main points of an essay.

Critical Review   An evaluation of a story, poem, or essay that points out its strengths and weaknesses, usually taking a stand on its merits.

Descriptive Essay   An essay that chiefly uses detailed sensory description, using sight, hearing, touch, smell, and taste to make its point.

Diagram   A drawing or schematic plan designed to explain how something works.

Dialogue   The actual words used by two or more people in conversation with one another.

Double-Entry Journal   A two-columned journal containing questions in the left column and answers or commentary in the right.

Educated Guess   A guess based on prior knowledge and reasoning.

Evaluation   A type of discourse that judges the value of something positively, negatively, or degrees of both.

Evidence   Information used to prove or disprove a point.

Fictional Story   A product of the imagination, with made-up characters and events.

Formal Essay   An essay generally written with an academic purpose in mind. It begins with an introductory paragraph that includes a thesis statement, and all of its supporting paragraphs contribute to its central idea or purpose. It usually ends with a concluding paragraph that restates the thesis or summarizes the main points of the essay.

Freewriting   Writing rapidly and without any concern for correctness to get one's ideas on paper.

Generalization   A broad statement or principle that holds a universal truth.

Graphics   A simple or elaborate pictoral representation of ideas or symbols in a story, poem, or essay.

Image   A description or representation of a person, place, or thing, often through comparison with something else that is more familiar; a picture drawn with words.

Implications   Ideas involved that are suggested or are expressed indirectly without stating them.

Interpretation   The meaning assigned by a reader or critics to a poem, story, essay, or any other creative work.

Introductory Paragraph   A paragraph used to get the reader's attention at the beginning of an essay. It often contains the thesis statement in a formal essay.

License   Permission, freedom, or authorization to do something.

Listing   A prewriting device whereby a writer jots down ideas or words in columns.

Literal Meaning   The primary or surface meaning of a word or experience.

Meaning   The end purpose or significance of a story, poem, or essay.

Monologue   The spoken words of a single person generally talking to him- or herself.

Narrative Essay   An essay that primarily tells a story in chronological order to make its point.

Parallel Story   A story from a reader's own life that is triggered by a story, poem, or essay.

Personal Reaction   A personal, spontaneous response or "gut reaction" to a story, poem, or essay.

Personal Reflection   A response to a story, poem, or essay based on one's beliefs, values, doubts, and expectations.

Point of View   The vantage point from which an author writes, for example, first-person point of view or third-person point of view.

Prewrite   Informal, associative writing done to get ideas down on paper in order to see what a writer has to say about a topic.

Reading Log   A journal consisting of regular entries that focus on a reader's thoughts, ideas, and questions while reading.

Recurring Dream   A dream that occurs repeatedly.

Reminiscences   Recollections or memories of past experiences.

Review   An evaluation that recommends or criticizes a short story, poem, or essay.

Sarcasm   The use of remarks that are bitter in tone.

CREDITS *(continued from the copyright page)*

"Family Album" by Siv Cedering from *The Georgia Review,* Vol XXXII, Number 2, Summer 1978:336–338. Copyright © 1978, 1989 by Siv Cedering. Reprinted by permission of the author.

"Homage to My Hips" by Lucille Clifton. Reprinted by permission of Curtis Brown Ltd. Copyright © 1980 by *University of Massachusetts Press.* First appeared in **two-headed woman** published by *University of Massachusetts Press.*

"The Hand" from *The Collected Stories of Colette* translated by Matthew Ward. Translation copyright © 1957, 1966, 1983 by Farrar, Straus & Giroux, Inc. Reprinted by permission of Farrar, Straus & Giroux, Inc.

"I heard a Fly buzz when I die" by Emily Dickinson. Reprinted by permission of the publishers and the Trustees of Amherst College from *The Poems of Emily Dickinson,* Thomas H. Johnson, ed., Cambridge, Mass.: The Belknap Press of Harvard University Press, Copyright © 1951, 1955, 1979, 1983 by the President and Fellows of Harvard College.

"On Going Home" from *Slouching Towards Bethlehem* by Joan Didion. Copyright © 1967, 1968 by Joan Didion. Reprinted by permission of Farrar, Straus and Giroux, Inc.

"The Brown Wasps" by Leon Eiseley. Reprinted with the permission of Scribner, an imprint of Simon & Schuster, Inc. from *The Night Country* by Loren Eiseley. Copyright © 1971 by Loren Eiseley.

"The Love Song of J. Alfred Prufrock" from *Collected Poems 1909–1962* by T.S. Eliot. Copyright © 1936 by Harcourt Brace Jovanovich, Inc. 1964, 1963 by T.S. Eliot. Reprinted by permission of the publisher.

Reprinted from *Civilization and Its Discontents* by Sigmund Freud, translated from the German by James Strachey, with the permission of W.W. Norton & Company, Inc. Copyright © 1961 by James Strachey, renewed 1989 by Alix Strachey.

"Birches" by Robert Frost from *The Poetry of Robert Frost* edited by Edward Connery Lathem. Henry Holt and Company, publisher.

"Growing Up Apocalyptic" from *Off Center* by Barbara Grizzuti Harrison. Copyright © 1980 by Barbara Grizzuti Harrison. Reprinted by permission of Georges Borchardt, Inc.

"Those Winter Sundays" by Robert Hayden. Reprinted from *Angle of Ascent: New and Selected Poems* by Robert Hayden, with the permission of Liveright Publishing Corporation. Copyright © 1966 by Robert Hayden.

"The Stolen Party" by Liliana Heker from *Other Fires: Short Fiction by Latin American Women* by Alberto Manguel. Copyright © 1982 by Liliana Heker. Translation copyright © 1986 by Alberto Manguel. Reprinted by permission of Crown Publishers, Inc.

"Para Teresa" by Ines Hernandez from *Con Razon Corazon.* M&A Editions, San Antonio, Texas (1987, Second Edition). Copyright © 1987 by Ines Hernandez. Reprinted by permission of the author. Ines Hernandez-Avila is a poet, scholar, and an Associate Professor of Native American Studies at the University of California at Davis where she teaches courses on Native American literature and Native American women. She is Chicana and Nez Perce.

"Theme for English B" from *Collected Poems* by Langston Hughes. Copyright © 1994 by the Estate of Langston Hughes. Reprinted by permission of Alfred A. Knopf, Inc.

"A Family Supper" by Kazuo Ishiguro. Copyright © by Kazuo Ishiguro. Reprinted by permission of International Creative Management.

"Love, Your Only Mother" from *Comfort* by David Michael Kaplan. Copyright © 1987 by David Michael Kaplan. Reprinted by permission of Brandt & Brandt Literary Agents, Inc.

"Sunday in the Park" by Bel Kaufman as printed in The Available Press/PEN Short

Index